A LONG GOODBYE TO BISMARC

D1757368

CHANGING WELFARE STATES

Advanced welfare states seem remarkably stable at first glance. Although most member states of the European Union (EU) have undertaken comprehensive welfare reform, especially since the 1990s, much comparative welfare state analysis portrays a 'frozen welfare landscape'. Social spending is stable. However, if we interpret the welfare state as more than aggregate social spending and look at long-term trends, we can see profound transformations across several policy areas, ranging from labor market policy and regulation, industrial relations, social protection, social services like child care and education, pensions, and long-term care. This series is about trajectories of change. Have there been path-breaking welfare innovations or simply attempts at political reconsolidation? What new policies have been added, and with what consequences for competitiveness, employment, income equality and poverty, gender relations, human capital formation, and fiscal sustainability? What is the role of the European Union in shaping national welfare state reform? Are advanced welfare states moving in a similar or even convergent direction, or are they embarking on ever more divergent trajectories of change? These issues raise fundamental questions about the politics of reform. If policy-makers *do* engage in major reforms (despite the numerous institutional, political and policy obstacles), what factors enable them to do so? While the overriding objective of the series is to trace trajectories of contemporary welfare state reform, the editors also invite the submission of manuscripts which focus on theorizing institutional change in the social policy arena.

EDITORS OF THE SERIES

Gøsta Esping-Andersen, University of Pompeu Fabra, Barcelona, Spain
Anton Hemerijck, VU University Amsterdam, the Netherlands
Kees van Kersbergen, VU University Amsterdam, the Netherlands
Kimberly Morgan, George Washington University, Washington, USA
Romke van der Veen, Erasmus University, Rotterdam, the Netherlands
Jelle Visser, University of Amsterdam, the Netherlands

A Long Goodbye to Bismarck?

**The Politics of Welfare Reforms
in Continental Europe**

Bruno Palier (ed.)

AMSTERDAM UNIVERSITY PRESS

Cover illustration: Sir John Tenniel 'Dropping the Pilot' in *Punch* March 29, 1890, pp. 150-51

Note on the cover illustration, by Stephan Leibfried:
'Dropping the Pilot' is a political cartoon published in the British satirical magazine *Punch* on March 29, 1890, a week after Kaiser Wilhelm II dismissed Bismarck. This iconic cartoon by Sir John Tenniel (1820-1914) shows a uniformed and capriciously crowned Kaiser (1869-1941) watching contentedly from the guard rail of the royal yacht, as Bismarck – *de facto* captain of the German ship of state – disembarks in his civilian clothes. Founder of the German Empire in 1871, Bismarck (1815-1898) not only built the first unified German state, but was also the architect of the world's first modern welfare state.

Cover design: Jaak Crasborn BNO, Valkenburg a/d Geul
Layout: V3-Services, Baarn

ISBN   978 90 8964 234 9
e-ISBN   978 90 4851 245 4
NUR   754

Table of Contents

Acknowledgments

As shown in this book, the Conservative corporatist road to welfare reforms was long and difficult. The journey to the completion of this book was also long and consisted of many phases. It started in Paris in December 2005, where the team of authors first met, before going to Harvard in 2006, where our first drafts were intensely discussed, and then back to Paris in 2007 and 2008, where chapters were harmonized. For me, it also passed via Berlin, Chicago and other conference locations in 2008, where the results were tested, and finally Stockholm in 2009, where final editing and writing was undertaken. The journey was long but much less difficult than the 'Bismarckian' welfare trajectory itself, thanks to the considerable and generous support we received from various institutions, and thanks to interested colleagues and their inspirational ideas.

Many institutions provided us with both financial and organizational help: the French Ministry of Social Affairs (DREES-MIRE), Sciences po (Direction scientifique, Cevipof and Centre d'Études Européennes), the EU-funded Networks of Excellence CONNEX and RECWOWE, the Friedrich Ebert Stifftung, the Fondation Jean Jaurès and the Harvard Center for European Studies.

In the various phases of our project, we benefited enormously from the remarks and input of many scholars, whose feedback always had constructive consequences for the following stage of our project. I wish to thank Giuliano Bonoli, Daniel Clegg, Patrick Hassenteufel, Nathalie Morel and Philippe Pochet for their contribution to other parts of the project, and their constant contribution to this one; Fritz Scharpf and Jochen Clasen, who were present in Paris 2005; and Peter Hall, Pepper Culpepper, Mary Daly, Peter Gourevitch, Torben Iversen, Jane Jenson, John Myles, Jonas Pontusson, George Ross, Bo Rothstein, John Stephens, Rosemary Taylor and Jonathan Zeitlin who gave us a wonderful (if challenging) time in Harvard. Too many other people have suffered and commented upon my good old 'Bismarck power point' to all be mentioned here, but I would like to specifically show appreciation to the students who attended the doctoral seminar I taught with Kathleen Thelen in 2007, and of course to Kathleen herself, and to Karen Anderson, for their suggestions.

Besides the institutional support and the interesting comments by colleagues, I must acknowledge how much I have been inspired for this work by the important ideas formulated in their own work by Jean Leca, Pierre Muller, Yves Surel, Peter Hall, Gøsta Esping-Andersen, Giuliano Bonoli, Maurizio Ferrera, Paul Pierson and Kathleen Thelen.

This journey was a collective one, and I wish to thank all the authors of this volume for their efficiency and friendship, the 'Paris team' (Nathalie Morel, Daniel Clegg and Alfio Cerami, later complemented by Marie-Pierre Hamel and Louise Hervier) with whom it has always been fun and stimulating to work; Daniel Clegg and Silja Häusermann for their careful reading of my pieces; Marek Naczyk and Nadia Hilliard for their meticulous make up of the manuscript and Anton Hemerijck for his enthusiastic support as a publisher.

Finally, I wish to give my warmest thanks to my family, which has been growing as this project advanced. They have always been understanding and supportive. Love and gratitude to Nathalie, Lucas, Garance, Solveig and Mia, who are as much delighted as relieved that this journey eventually came to an end.

BRUNO PALIER

Prologue: What does it Mean to Break with Bismarck?

Gøsta Esping-Andersen

The task of an editor is to take one step back and digest the core message that emerges from the various contributions to the volume. The prologue writer should, I suppose, do the same but with the proviso that he, or she, will then take one great leap forward and interpret all the material in a new light. I shall try my best, but please do not expect an earthshattering eureka. My task has unquestionably been eased by the admirable efforts to make the chapters in this volume as homogenous and comparable as possible. I can think of few edited volumes that manage so successfully to furnish the reader with rich detail and holism all at once. And not least, these contributions to our never-ending concern with the welfare state provide interesting reading, indeed.

The core question is straightforward: is the Bismarckian or, if you wish, the Conservative, or Continental welfare model being undone? Where is it heading? The answers I have managed to distill from my reading are less straightforward. In an attempt to arrive at some kind of clarity, I am tempted to conclude the following: one, the glass seems only half full (or half empty if you prefer); two, there is a striking degree of convergence in the Bismarckian nations' adaptation profiles; three, and rather paradoxically, almost all nations' reform endeavors look rather incoherent. They are moving in a similar direction, but whereto? Is it just the same old model in new packaging? Are they forging a new, hitherto undefined, model? Are they closing in on either the Liberal or Social Democratic alternative? Or will they emerge as hybrids? In order to assess where the Bismarckian model is heading we obviously also need to keep in mind that its regime-competitors are in the midst of transformation, too.

What above all else strikes the reader is how similar the sequencing and overall thrust of nations' adaptation has been over the past decades. One might be led to believe that an invisible coordinating hand reigned supreme. To an extent, as many chapters emphasize, the Maastricht accords, EMU and the common currency no doubt set the stage in terms of imposing identical constraints as well as signaling the urgency of financial reform. My impression, nonetheless, is that the invisible hand was primarily given by the increasingly dysfunctional logic of the model itself. Its dysfunctionalities came to the fore on three key dimensions.

Firstly, population aging in tandem with the labor shedding, early-retirement strategy of the 1980s-1990s overburdened the system because they produced adverse effects on the financial nominator and denominator simultaneously. The nominator became bloated with benefit recipients; the denominator shrunk because of the smaller post-baby boom cohorts, sluggish growth of female participation, and because of high youth unemployment. One result was sky-rocketing social contribution rates that, in turn, depressed demand for labor.

Rather than courageously breaking this Gordian knot, the common response was to save the model with policies aimed at restoring financial equilibrium: shifting some welfare financing towards general revenue taxation, and adjusting contribution and benefit calculations, especially in pensions and unemployment benefits. These steps were paralleled in labor market policy: partial employment deregulation and a few cautious steps towards an activation approach.

Secondly, the model proved ever more dysfunctional because the two main pillars that sustained the edifice, namely familialism and a full-employment, male breadwinner-based labor market could no longer be counted on to ensure against the risks not covered by the welfare state. Lack of jobs meant that the outsiders, primarily youth and women, came to rely on family support. The lack of affordable market alternatives mean that families cannot realistically purchase care services. And this, in turn, implies repressed female labor supply and, indirectly, less tax revenue.

Thirdly, as many chapters highlight, the Bismarck model is inherently ill-equipped to confront 'new' risks, such as frailty and long-term dependency or labor market exclusion. Attempts to manage these within the standard insurance logic, as Germany attempted, proved sub-optimal. Hence, the search for alternatives, be it an approximation to the Scandinavian model, as in the case of long-term care in Spain, or a more familialistic version, as in the case of Austria's general revenue financed cash-for-care approach. As far as early childhood care is concerned, most Bismarckian countries remain essentially familialistic, providing either no support at all or using cash payments to induce mothers to stay home with their children.

Where is the Bismarckian Welfare State Heading?

The catalogue of adjustments and reforms that are documented in this book points, it would seem, in all directions. Hence the apparent lack of policy coherence. Most country chapters highlight changes in contribution and benefit schedules, particularly those related to pensions. The common story here is a move towards defined contribution plans and changes in the assessment of pension accruals, the latter primarily meant to postpone the retirement age. Such reforms present, in my view, no departure at all from Bismarck. To the contrary, they simply imply a return to the principles that guided the model prior to the 1970s, namely a tighter link between entitlements and contributions. In some respects, then, the aim seems to be to reconsolidate the core logic of the model. On other counts, however, key attributes of the model are weakening. Many countries have sought to diminish the 'corporativistic' character of social insurance by homogenizing both contribution requirements and benefit eligibility across social strata.

We are offered plentiful evidence of moves towards the liberal regime. Almost all Bismarckian countries are introducing some kind of basic non-contributory safety net, such as the French RMI, the social pension in Italy, or minimum retirement guarantees. These are invariably minted on the social assistance logic with income testing designed to target the needy. This approach is neatly captured in Maurizio Ferrera's concept of selective universalism. Via tax subsidies, governments are also encouraging citizens to embrace the market for supplementary private pensions. This seems to have been especially successful in Austria and, to an extent, also in Spain. It remains, nonetheless, a subsidy primarily for the top-income quintile populations and, as such, it installs new inequities that may replace the traditional inequities associated with narrow corporative risk-pooling. Many chapters highlight the convergence towards liberalism in the case of labor market deregulation. True, almost all countries have taken steps in this direction, albeit primarily at the margins, by relaxing conditions related to private employment exchanges, fixed-term contracts, part-time jobs and the like. But even if, as in Spain, partial deregulation produced massive effects – that were unanticipated – it has not attacked the classical notion of job security for insiders in any radical manner. These reforms seem, instead, to be motivated primarily by the need to provide bridges to the labor market for the outsiders, primarily youth and women.

And there certainly are moves in the Social Democratic direction as well. The principle of entitlement based on citizenship rather than employment has found its way into health reforms in many countries, including France, Italy and Spain. Despite income testing, the new minimum social guarantees, especially in pensions, signal a cautious shift in this direction, too. Indeed, we should remember that the universalistic 'people's pension' model in the Scandinavian social democracies has its roots in the social assistance tradition. The Bismarck countries are indisputably weakening their traditional male breadwinner bias, and we detect a trend towards defamilialization on many fronts. All countries have introduced job security provisions for mothers and have, rather cautiously, begun to encourage fathers to take childcare leaves. Traditional familialism, such as the obligation to support kin in need, is eroding. Germany, a stalwart case of familialism, has abolished this criterion in terms of eligibility for old-age assistance. But, with the only very partial exception of Spain, it is difficult to see any major social democratization with regard to family policy. Most countries prefer to give cash incentives to care for children (and the frail elderly) at home. With the exception of Belgium and France, no country provides early childcare that meets demand even remotely. This may, however, change in the coming decade. Both Germany and Spain are launching relatively ambitious childcare policies for the under-3s. As yet, however, the conventional male breadwinner logic remains basically intact in most Continental European welfare states.

It would appear accordingly as if the Bismarckian countries are converging, if perhaps only at the margins, with both rivals. But the convergence is perhaps less real than it seems, basically because they are chasing a moving target. The adoption of general revenue financed assistance programs would seem like a push towards the liberal fold. But it is actually towards a liberalism that is increasingly *passé*. The liberal welfare states have, over the past decades, shifted towards a work conditional, negative income approach, such as the US Earned Income Credit and the British family credit schemes. And the apparent shifts towards the Social Democratic paradigm seem, likewise, a bit dated and also hugely incomplete. The Bismarckian countries are, no doubt, adopting a more active family policy, at least in terms of child allowances and parental leave subsidies.

These steps will bring the Bismarckian group closer to Denmark or Sweden in the 1970s. But meanwhile, the Nordic countries came to prioritize family services which, as far as I can see, are only reluctantly – if at all – embraced by the Bismarckian countries.

Why Reform the Model?

There is a pervasive common thread in this book, namely that the Bismarckian logic is near-immune to any radical transformation. The social insurance system has created its own powerfully institutionalized veto points, and it enjoys huge popular legitimacy. But does the model really require any radical reform? The contributors to this volume cite numerous reasons for why it performs sub-optimally: it has great difficulties in responding to new emerging risks; it creates dualisms between the core of insured and the growing population that relies on assistance, a dualism that largely mirrors peoples' attachment to the labor market. The Bismarckian countries have developed a conception of social exclusion that has no direct parallel elsewhere. Many also cite the severe difficulties that women face in reconciling work and motherhood.

A Paretian optimality framework is as good as any in terms of gauging the workings of a model.[1] Would a reorganization of the welfare state help push these countries towards a superior Pareto frontier? This would entail both superior efficiency and equity outcomes. I would argue that there are several core attributes, shared by most (but not all) members of the Bismarckian model that, if reformed, would yield a superior Pareto frontier.

The first symptom is related to fertility and, by implication, to population aging. With few exceptions, the Continental European countries are stuck in a persistent lowest-low fertility trap. Their fertility rates hover between 1.2 and 1.5 which compares unfavorably with the Nordic countries, Britain (and France) where the rate is around 1.8. This difference has huge effects on population growth and, unsurprisingly, the projected aging burden is vastly greater in Germany, Italy and Spain than elsewhere. It has been popular to explain low fertility in terms of the advance of post-material values. It is, however, difficult to imagine that the Spaniards are more post-material than, say, the Swedes. The telling statistic comes from fertility surveys that ask citizens what is their *desired* number of children. Across all EU countries, people invariably embrace the 2-child norm. Any major deviation from this signals, I believe, a crucial welfare deficit. The irony is that the child-deficit is greatest where familialism is most ingrained. If institutional arrangements work against family formation they clearly need to be reformed. Helping citizens attain their desired number of children will, unquestionably yield efficiency and welfare gains.

The preconditions for higher fertility are now well-established: adequate parental leave provisions, job security and, above all, access to childcare. More generally, fertility in advanced societies depends on gender equalization, and major obstacles to women's employment are bound to harm fertility. All this suggests that the typical cash incentive for caring at home may be counter-productive and that a concerted servicing approach is *sine qua non.*

Secondly, repressed female labor supply related to motherhood not only widens the gender divide but also reduces potential economic growth. The employment gap of women due to motherhood is substantial in most Continental European countries – the activity rate typically drops by 20 percent among mothers with pre-school children while, simultaneously, mothers are overwhelmingly in part-time jobs, especially in Germany and the Netherlands. To provide an idea of the associated growth-opportunity cost, we have simulations that show that were Spanish women to adopt an employment profile identical to Danish women, the Spanish GDP would be roughly 15 percent larger. The absence of affordable childcare and too brief paid maternity leaves (typically four months in the Continental European member states) bear much of the responsibility for the employment and, thus, income gap. Universal provision of childcare is doubly Paretian because it can be shown that the initial cost to government is fully reimbursed via mothers' superior life-time earnings and tax payments.

The third instance, almost never examined in the welfare state literature, has to do with human capital investment. In this book we find repeated examples of moves towards a more active labor market policy. This is of course aimed at adult workers and it is rather clear that, by and large, remedial activation policies are costly and quite ineffective. There are two sets of evidence that suggest that the typical Continental European welfare state pursues a failed human capital policy. One, comparatively speaking, the correlation between social origin and destiny is substantially higher than in the Nordic countries. This is less the case for the Netherlands, but strongly so for France, Germany and Italy. Two, several of the Continental countries (Italy and Spain in particular) exhibit very high rates of early school-leavers. If the opportunity structure is very unequal and up to a third of each youth cohort fails to obtain the skills required for a knowledge economy, a large amount of potential productivity is lost while the demand for passive income support will increase.

Traditional familialism bears a major responsibility for these problems. It is now well-established that the key foundations for cognitive abilities and learning are laid in the pre-school ages. If the main impulse in these years comes solely from parents (or grandparents) it is to be expected that conditions in the family of origin predict so strongly how children fare later on. High quality early childhood programs have been shown to be extremely effective in evening the playing field – again a strong case for abandoning the familialistic ideology and moving towards a service-intensive welfare state. This case is additionally bolstered by the results of evaluation studies which suggest that the returns to every dollar invested in quality early childhood services yields a return anywhere between 5 and 12 dollars.

The upshot is that one of the core characteristics of the Bismarckian model, namely familialism, has adverse consequences for equity and efficiency. But I think we can push the argumentation yet further and conclude that a stubborn adherence to familialistic principles has become anathema to family well-being. Defamilializing care responsibilities is a precondition for functioning solidarities in the kind of society and economy that is emerging. This comes out very clearly in recent research on intergenerational care giving. If we distinguish between the frequency and intensity (hours committed) of caring we find, to the surprise of many, that Danes and Swedes care for their aged parents 50 percent more frequently than their Italian or Spanish counterparts. In contrast, the Italian and Spanish care less frequently but far more intensely. The profile is identical in terms of grandparents caring for grandchildren. It would appear that intergenerational solidarity suffers when the commitment becomes very heavy; it strengthens when the burden is lighter.

My search for a superior Pareto frontier has, so far, centered on family policy and here the conclusion is clear: defamilialize. There are, however, also aspects that are inherent to the social insurance model that will, over the coming decades, provoke ever more intense equity problems. Several of the chapters in this book have examined how Bismarckian welfare states have adjusted their pension insurance so as to stave off intergenerational inequities associated with aging. The move towards defined contribution plans and postponed retirement implies that the additional costs of aging will be allocated more fairly between the retired generations and the working age population.

So far, so good. I have, however, seen no serious discussion of the heightened *intragenerational* inequities that are inherent in Bismarckian pension systems. The problem has to do with strong – and growing – social differentials in life expectancy: a manual worker, at age 60, can typically expect to live five or six fewer years than a professional. Considering the financial logic of pension contributions, namely a proportional share of wages (usually capped at some income level), the result is a hugely unfair redistribution in favor of those who live the longest.

I can think of two solutions to the problem. The first would conform to the principles of the Bismarckian model; the second would, over the years, most likely produce a genuine 'regime-shift'. If the aim is to rescue Bismarck, policy-makers would have to adjust pension entitlements so that expected years of life expectancy are explicitly weighted into the formula. The most logical option would be to index age of retirement *positively* to lifetime earnings: high income groups would then have to retire later than their low-income fellows. The second option would be to uncouple total retirement income from workers' contribution record to a far greater extent than now. The case for a first tier universal 'people's pension', as in the Nordic countries is, in this respect, obvious. It gains added relevance when we consider the new risk structure and the foreseeable large proportion of future pensioners that will have accumulated insufficient retirement wealth. As we have seen in this book, the Bismarckian countries have in fact moved towards an assistance-type basic income support system.

Were the Bismarckian countries to emphasize family services, and were they to take the leap towards a universal 'people's pension' we would, I believe, have irrefutable evidence of change that goes beyond path dependency or, as it often seems, ad hoc kinds of adjustments. More generally, some convergence with the Social Democratic model appears far more realistic, and arguably also more Paretian, than going for genuine liberalism. Emulating the liberal model in any serious way would imply a massive process of dismantling; emulating the Scandinavians implies, in contrast, an extension of social citizenship in view of novel risks that most ordinary citizens face with growing intensity.

1 Ordering Change: Understanding the 'Bismarckian' Welfare Reform Trajectory

Bruno Palier

1.1 Introduction[1]

How did Continental European welfare systems change over the last 30 years? What have they become? Were they eventually able to address the main challenges that they have been confronted with since the mid-1970s? The central research questions of this book are based on a striking puzzle. It was an accepted wisdom of the comparative welfare state literature published on the threshold of the 21st Century that the Continental European welfare systems were the least adaptable. In the mid-1990s, when he compared the capacity of different welfare regimes to face the new economic challenges, Gøsta Esping-Andersen emphasized the rigidity of the Continental welfare state arrangements, speaking of a 'frozen Continental landscape' (Esping-Andersen 1996a). Since 'Conservative corporatist' welfare systems were 'the most consensual of all modern welfare states', their edifice would remain 'immune to change' (*ibid.*: 66-67). Esping-Andersen concluded that in Continental Europe 'the cards are very much stacked in favor of the welfare state "status quo"' (*ibid.*: 267). Fritz Scharpf and Vivien Schmidt (2000) similarly argued that even though all welfare states are in various ways vulnerable to increasingly open economies 'Christian Democratic' welfare systems based on social insurance not only face the greatest difficulties of all, but are also the most difficult to reform. Paul Pierson (2001a) also observed that significant welfare state reform has been rarest and most problematic in Continental Europe.

Since the advent of the new millennium, however, major changes have become highly visible in the welfare arrangements of Continental European countries. During the 2000s, as a comparison of reforms in different social insurance fields (old-age, unemployment, health insurance) has shown[2], all Continental European countries have implemented important structural reforms of their welfare systems. Employment policies and un-employment insurance systems have changed, shifting away from a 'labor shedding' strategy and towards the development of activation policies (Clegg 2007). Austria, France, Germany, Italy and Spain have each gone through several waves of pension reform, the last introducing innovations such as voluntary private pension funds and emphasizing increasing employment rates among the elderly (Bonoli and Palier 2007). In health care, reforms grafted two new logics onto the traditional insurance approach: a logic of universalization through state intervention, and a market logic based on regulated competition (Hassenteufel and Palier 2007). Furthermore, countries well known for their ingrained familialism and traditional approach to the gender division of labor have radically changed their child- and elderly care policies. Since the late 1990s they have developed formal caring facilities and parental leave schemes, facilitating the combination of work and family life for women – and the creation of 'low end' jobs in the personal service sector (Morel 2007).

Notwithstanding the best informed predictions, to the contrary, then, important welfare reforms have occurred in Continental Europe. This is not simply a question of a belated 'catch up', either. Even though these changes have only become fully apparent since the early 2000s, our claim in this book is that they must be understood as the culmination of a longer and more drawn-out reform trajectory, rather than the result of an abrupt political revolution or a sudden rupture in an institutional or political equilibrium due to exogenous crises. This book is devoted to substantiating this claim through detailed analysis of national welfare reform trajectories in 12 countries of Continental Europe – Austria, Belgium, France, Germany, Italy, the Netherlands, Spain, Switzerland and the Visegrad Countries, the Czech Republic, Hungary, Poland and Slovakia.

Taken together, the chapters that follow represent a systematic and comprehensive empirical account of the welfare reforms that have taken place across Continental Europe since the early 1980s. Empirically, the focus is mainly on the nature, politics, timing and magnitude of social policy change, though consideration is also given to their economic and social impacts. Subjecting these cases to systematic comparative analysis furthermore serves to reveal a second puzzle; not only have all these Continental European countries eventually been able to introduce structural reforms into well-entrenched social insurance systems, but they have done so by following a very similar route. Our common analytical framework, based on the most recent developments in neo-institutionalist theory, helps us to explain why.

The next part of this introductory chapter is devoted to the presentation of this analytical framework. In the following part the origins of Bismarckian welfare systems will be explored, as well as their functioning and characteristics from their creation up to the start of the more contemporary period – from the late 1970s to the present – that is the main focus of the chapters that will follow.

1.2   A Historical Institutionalist Framework for Analysis

It is recent developments in historical institutionalism that provide the tools that frame our approach to the long-term transformation of welfare systems in Continental Europe. In this literature, recent theoretical and empirical work has departed from 'institutional determinism' and been able to combine appreciation of the impact of institutions on policy development, with the possibility for substantial and transformative policy change, as a cumulative effect of successive smaller reforms (Streeck and Thelen 2005). Drawing inspiration from this insight, as well as from Peter Hall's work on policy change, a common analytical framework has been developed and applied to each national country study in this volume. Trying to adapt the general historical institutionalist perspective for our more specific purpose, this common approach is based on a particular understanding of 'Bismarckian' welfare systems, on the importance given to 'welfare institutions', and on the key notion of 'reform trajectory'.

'Bismarckian' Welfare Systems

There has been continuous and lively debate around Esping-Andersen's famous typology of welfare systems (for reviews, see Abrahamson 2003; Arts and Gelissen 2002). Despite a number of criticisms, recent research on welfare reforms inevitably comes back to this three-fold distinction. Indeed, most collective books either refer to the 'three worlds' in their choice of countries (Scharpf and Schmidt 2000; Pierson 2001b), or organize comparison explicitly through groups of countries that reproduce this division (Esping-Andersen 1996b; Sykes, Palier and Prior 2001). Moreover, findings from comparative studies usually suggest that there are 'three worlds of welfare reforms', concluding that different processes of welfare state adaptation are associated with each world of welfare (Scharpf and Schmidt 2000; Pierson 2001b). The three paths for welfare state change result from the different historical and institutional constraints associated with each welfare system.

Research that has been conducted to date has either included all types of welfare regimes[3] or focused on liberal or Scandinavian regimes.[4] Despite the existence of isolated national case studies[5], no systematic comparative research has been conducted on the recent developments of 'Bismarckian', 'Conservative corporatist' or 'Christian Democratic' welfare regimes. The aim of this book is thus to provide a systematic comparison of welfare reforms within the 'Conservative corporatist' world of welfare capitalism, with the idea that more has occurred within these systems than is usually recognized. In this context, a specific reading of Esping-Andersen helps to define the field of the research. We focus on reforms to existing social policies and the introduction of new types of social policies in welfare systems and specific social programs that share the common features usually associated with the 'Bismarckian' tradition of social insurance.

These features have already been characterized in the comparative welfare state literature. Titmuss (1974), Esping-Andersen and others have identified three main approaches to the conception, implementation and management of social protection. Instead of trying to read Esping-Andersen's typology as a description of 'real worlds' of welfare capitalism, it is useful to conceptualize it as isolating and distinguishing ideal-types, differentiated both in terms of policy goals (logics or conceptions) and policy instruments ('ways of doing', institutions). These ideal types define a body of principles and values and political, economic and social objectives, and can be associated with a prevailing institutional configuration determining the rights and benefits, the financing and the management of the social protection arrangements for individuals resident in a nation. They also help to identify the role and position given to social protection institutions in relation to other factors of social protection (the market, the family and the voluntary sector), as well as the objectives pursued in terms of individual welfare and social stratification. Such ideal-typical categories can help to situate the core features of any real welfare system, or even any welfare program, notwithstanding the complexities that inevitably characterize any empirical reality.

As is well known, with respect to policy goals, three political logics can be identified in Esping-Andersen's work: the Liberal, the Social-Democratic and the Conservative-corporatist. These logics have to be supplemented by consideration of the gender relationships underpinning each model (Lewis 1992; Orloff 1993). The underlying principle of the *Liberal* type of social protection is to give emphasis to the market rather than the state in resource allocation. The state only intervenes as a last resort and its means of action seek to encourage a rapid return to the market (benefits must not discourage beneficiaries from working). The liberal approach discourages the state from meddling in the private affairs of the family and therefore involves few family policy measures. The so-called *Social Democratic* model is designed to provide a truly universal system of social protection. The principal objective of the welfare state is to ensure the equality, cohesion and homogeneity of social groups within an all-embracing middle class. The underlying concept is based on the dual breadwinner model, without distinction between men and women (Lewis 1992). Though the main characteristics of Bismarckian welfare regimes will be developed in greater detail below, we can here recall that according to Esping-Andersen and many others the typical *Conservative-corporatist* goal is less to reduce inequality than to preserve status. In the name of subsidiarity, this type of welfare provision is also aimed at supporting a family structure based on the male breadwinner, implying that women are left with primary responsibility for care giving (Lewis 1992).

To achieve their different objectives, the various systems make use of a range of techniques, including: means-tested assistance benefits; flat-rate benefits or social services provided by universal systems and financed through taxation; and contributory benefits provided by social insurance on the basis of social contributions. From a comparative perspective, one can distinguish four principal parameters by which these techniques can be differentiated (cf. Ferrera 1998; Bonoli and Palier 1998), which will henceforth be referred to as 'welfare institutions':

1   the rules and criteria governing eligibility and entitlement: who is entitled to benefit?
2   the form taken by benefits: what types of benefits are provided?
3   the financing mechanisms: who pays, and how?
4   the organization and management of the scheme: who decides and who manages?

International comparisons have shown that each social protection system has its own specific and principal – though not exclusive – means of combining these four variables, which provide a basis for comparing and distinguishing between the various national systems. In most cases, the manner in which these four variables are combined is common and relatively similar across all the branches of the system. Each welfare regime associates a specific institutional configuration with a relatively coherent doctrine: residual benefits with the primacy of the market and the need to combat poverty; universal benefits with the quest for equality; and social insurance schemes with the protection of specific occupational categories. They have different impacts with respect to the quality of social rights, social stratification and the structure of the labor market.

In this book, we analyze and compare reforms that occurred in countries where welfare systems are mainly based on the 'Conservative-corporatist' approach to welfare, and where the ways of providing social protection share a number of commonalities in respect of the four key institutional variables:

1   Entitlements are associated with employment status, with modes of access to social protection based on work/contribution; as will be underlined below, these systems were primarily aimed at insuring industrial salaried workers who paid contributions.

2   Social benefits are in cash, transfer-based, proportional, earnings-related, and expressed in terms of replacement rates; in Continental Europe, such benefits are often called 'contributory benefits' (meaning that the right to and the amount of benefit is linked to the contribution previously paid).

3   Financing mechanisms are based principally on social contributions, or what in the USA are called payroll taxes.

4   Administrative structures are para-public, involving the social partners in the management of the social insurance funds ('Kassen', 'caisses', 'cassa'...). Because these systems are thus not organized in and by the public administration (as well as for historical and political reasons – see below), the notion of 'welfare systems' captures their essence better than the concept of the 'welfare state'.

Even though some of these characteristics exist elsewhere (but rarely all together, especially regarding financing and governance structures), welfare systems based on these four institutional traits are to be found mostly in Continental Europe. Indeed, as will be exemplified and demonstrated in the national chapters in this volume, most countries of the European continent, having followed the Bismarckian route to welfare state development, can be considered as 'social insurance states' and share these common welfare institutions. As the comparative welfare state literature has shown, and as this volume confirms, Germany, Austria, France, the Netherlands, Luxembourg, Italy, Spain, Belgium, the Czech Republic, Poland, Slovakia and Hungary have all developed welfare systems (more or less) close to this ideal-type.

In suggesting that these countries share a logic that is mostly or mainly Bismarckian, and their institutions mostly or mainly based on social insurance, it should be emphasized and acknowledged that no real welfare system is ever pure and always represents a complex mix of policy goals and institutions. For sure, family policies in France are universalistic, the health care systems in Italy and Spain are of Beveridgean inspiration and the Italian trade unions do not traditionally play an important role in the management of the welfare system (etc.). However, all these countries are closer to each other than they are to other welfare systems. The French, Austrian or Belgian welfare systems are thus certainly not identical to the German one, but they *are* considerably closer to it than to the Swedish system, and thus reflect both similar principles of welfare and comparable 'ways of doing' welfare. A central hypothesis of this research project is that these Continental European systems should therefore also experience some shared difficulties and show similar reform dynamics.

Our book identifies the welfare institutions that these Bismarckian welfare systems have to a greater or lesser extent in common as the central variable for understanding the politics of recent welfare reform. The basic hypothesis is that the similarity of welfare conceptions and institutions largely explains the similarities in the problem profiles and in the developmental trajectories of these welfare systems.

Welfare Institutions Matter

The most important contribution of new institutionalism to the current research on policy change is of course the insight that 'institutions matter'. The definition of institutions often varies according to the approach (Hall and Taylor 1996). In accounts of welfare state stability and change, the institutions which are most frequently referred to are macropolitical institutions such as state structures and constitutional norms (unitary versus federal state, the relationship between the executive and legislative powers, majoritarian versus consensual democracy) (for a review, see Bonoli 2001), or the profile of representative institutions and bodies (the party system, the electoral system and systems of interest intermediation) (See for instance Levy 1999; Ross 2000; Huber and Stephens 2001; Korpi and Palme 2003). In his edited volume, Paul Pierson and his contributors provide insightful institutionalist explanations of the politics of welfare reforms by focusing on how these kinds of institutions shape the 'new politics' of welfare reform (Pierson 2001b: parts two and three).

However, as Paul Pierson himself has elsewhere acknowledged, 'major public policies also constitute important rules of the game, influencing the allocation of economic and political resources, modifying the costs and benefits associated with alternative political strategies, and consequently altering ensuing political development' (Pierson 1993: 596)[6]. In this volume, we share the conviction that the structure and institutional design of social policies needs to be integrated into our explanatory accounts in order to understand the types of problems, politics and processes of change that welfare systems have undergone.

Constitutional and political system variables take very different values within the family of Bismarckian welfare regimes: for example, Germany has a federal political system and France a highly centralized one. As will be shown in the various chapters of this book, these types of variations explain much of the difference in the timing and political framing of reforms in the countries studied. However, our aim is also to highlight and understand the *similarities* in the politics of the reforms. Since these countries have such diverse political systems, macropolitical variables can hardly explain similar trends in the content and sequencing of reforms. To understand the politics of the reforms in these cases, it seems more promising to look at the kind of incentives that their similar social policy institutions create.

In our approach, welfare institutions play a central role and serve several analytical functions. First, they are used to both describe and situate specific national welfare systems in a comparative perspective and over time. No one country – not even Germany – has ever been purely 'Bismarckian' in the ideal-typical sense outlined above. Hence each national case will be specified by assessing 'how Bismarckian they are' at the beginning of the period under study (late 1970s, early 1980s) as well as at the end of it (late 2000s), by specifying the share of contributory benefits in the various social programs, the share of social contribution financing and the governance-mix in the social policy-making and management. This will allow for both better characterization of each 'real world' of the national welfare system, and for qualitative, but rigorous and systematic, measurement of institutional change.

Measuring welfare state changes is one of the major difficulties in the current comparative welfare state literature (Clasen and Siegel 2007). As we know, social spending measures tend to obfuscate rather than demonstrate welfare state transformations.[7] Our common reference to the four institutional variables allows us to measure institutional welfare state change through a much better set of indicators than social spending. Characteristics of a program before and after a reform – the specific combination of the four institutional variables – then serve as objective criteria to reveal change. These categories become benchmarks against which these changes can be assessed.[8]

As mentioned above, welfare institutions will also play a central role in our explanatory framework. As shown elsewhere (Bonoli and Palier 2000), welfare institutions structure debates, political preferences and policy choices. They affect the positions of the various actors and groups involved in reform processes. They frame the kind of interests and resources that actors can mobilize in favor of, or against, welfare reforms. In part, they also determine who can and who cannot participate in the political game leading to reforms, and thus the identity and the number of 'veto players'. Depending on how these different variables are set, different patterns of support and opposition are likely to be encountered. This will be illustrated in the various country chapters to follow.

Finally, our focus on welfare institutions helps reveal often neglected types of reform that in the long run have very profound consequences: institutional reforms. In this case, the factor that was determining the politics of other welfare reforms becomes an object of reform itself: changes in the entitlement rules, and even more importantly, changes in the financing mechanisms or in the structure and functioning of welfare governance.[9] We will emphasize how important these institutional reforms have been to divert Bismarckian welfare institutions from their 'path-dependent' reform trajectories.

Accounting for Social Policy Changes

Historical institutionalists claim that 'history matters', that the past weighs on the present and future. In the welfare state literature, this importance given to the past has most often been used to explain resistance to change and path dependency. Writing in 1994, Pierson emphasized the stability of American and British welfare arrangements in the face of Reagan and Thatcher's attempts at radical retrenchment. He explained this resistance to change with reference to the force of past commitments, the political weight of welfare constituencies and the inertia of institutional arrangements, factors which coalesce to engender a phenomenon of path dependency. Emphasizing the importance of negative policy feedbacks, he concluded that 'any attempt to understand the politics of welfare state retrenchment must start from a recognition that social policy remains the most resilient component of the post-war order' (Pierson 1994: 5).

Even when they acknowledge some changes, many comparative studies conclude that the reforms had little real impact on the structure of the different welfare states, since the very nature of each system has been preserved (Huber and Stephens 2001). Up to the late 1990s, reforms were seen as essentially reinforcing the logic of each welfare system. The liberal welfare states, through the different processes of marketization of their social policies, thus seemed to have become even more residual and liberal (Taylor-Gooby 2001). The Social Democratic welfare states, thanks to an egalitarian distribution of cuts and a rediscovery of 'the workline', had come back to their traditional road to welfare (Kuhnle 2001). As mentioned above, in the wave of comparative welfare state studies published at the turn of the century, most of the Continental welfare states were presented as having remained the same, not so much because reforms reinforced their characteristics, but rather because they seemed unable to implement any important reforms in the first place.

An emphasis on path dependence thus went hand in hand with the conclusions of prevailing continuity. But important structural reforms have been introduced in the 2000s, and most – like means-tested benefits associated with activation measures for the long-term unemployed, or fully funded pension schemes – clearly do not belong to the traditional logic and institutions of the Bismarckian welfare regime. How can one understand the process that led to these structural changes? Can we combine a framework of analysis that takes the weight of institutions into account, but also helps account for structural 'path-shifting' changes? In addressing this analytical challenge, we have drawn inspiration both from the general literature on policy change and the most recent advances in neo-institutional theory.

When emphasizing the inertia of institutions ('frozen landscapes' and 'path dependency'), current research often seems to ignore the structural impact that public policies may sometimes have. While integrating phenomena of path dependency in welfare state analysis is essential, this should not preclude an examination of the impact of different reforms on social policy. In other words, recent developments within the social protection systems are not only due to self-generating evolutionary dynamics, but also to the implementation of public policies. Incorporating public policy aspects of change into the study of the ways in which social protection systems adapt suggests a need to make better use of the tools of public policy analysis, such as Hall's seminal approach to issues of policy change.[10]

Hall (1993: 278) argues that we 'can think of policymaking as a process that usually involves three central variables: the overarching goals that guide policy in a particular field, the techniques or policy instruments used to attain those goals, and the precise settings of these instruments...' Using this approach, it is possible to recast our understanding of welfare regimes in terms of public policies. The *instruments* of social policy are mainly the four institutional variables outlined above (the mode of access, the benefit structure, financing mechanisms and management arrangements). The *overarching goals* can be related to the three different political logics that are associated with the three welfare state regimes (Esping-Andersen 1990); the centrality of the market in the allocation of resources and the residuality of state intervention in the liberal regime; the centrality of equality, social citizenship and 'harmonization' of the population in social-democratic welfare regime; and the centrality of security, work, status and occupational identity in Conservative-corporatist social insurance systems.

Elaborating his framework for analyzing macroeconomic policy changes, Hall (1993) distinguished between three different types of changes. 'We can identify three distinct kinds of changes in policy... First, [a change of] the levels (or settings) of the basic instruments. We can call the process whereby instrument settings are changed in the light of experience and new knowledge, while the overall goals and instruments of policy remain the same, a process of first order change in policy... When the instruments of policy as well as their settings are altered in response to past experience even though the overall goals of policy remain the same, [this] might be said to reflect a process of second order change... Simultaneous changes in all three components of policy: the instrument settings, the instruments themselves, and the hierarchy of goals behind policy... occur rarely, but when they do occur as a result of reflection on past experience, we can describe them as instances of third order change' (Hall 1993: 278-279).

This approach helps to distinguish the differential impacts that a reform will have, depending on whether or not it changes the instruments and the overall logic. It provides a grid for assessing the type of change beyond a purely quantitative approach (more or less retrenchment), and a means for judging the degree of innovation introduced by a specific reform. A first order change will not entail profound changes as far as a historical path is concerned; it simply involves a change in the setting of instruments (such as raising the level of social contributions, or lowering benefit levels without changing the mode of financing, the type of benefit or the mode of access), without a change in the general principles and logic. Second order changes involve the introduction of new instruments (i.e. the introduction of new calculation rules or new entitlement rules in pension). These types of changes also appear to be path-dependent, as new instruments are introduced in order to preserve the existing system and its principles. Yet, such reforms may lead to more substantial change once they have been put in place and developed over time.[11] More directly, however, a further type of reforms may introduce new instruments associated with new goals, and thus possibly represent in the long run what Hall has termed 'paradigmatic changes' (Hall refers to the shift from Keynesian to monetarist policies; an equivalent in social policy might be the shift from unemployment compensation to activation policies).

Visser and Hemerijck (1997) have added to these three categories of change by identifying an intermediary type between instrumental and paradigmatic change, which they call 'institutional change'. This is when a basic institution of a welfare system is reformed, such as through the privatization of a public service, or a change in the financing mechanism (taxes replacing social contributions, for instance). These institutional reforms are focused on institutions themselves, without explicitly mentioning the goals. As will be shown in the various chapters of this volume, institutional reforms – especially concerning financing and governance – played a crucial role in softening blockages and allowing for more structural substantive change.

Beyond quantitative criteria such as more or less spending, it is thus possible to distinguish different categories of change according to the innovation they entail for the social protection system, on the basis of qualitative, but objective, criteria. In the following chapters, each reform or phase of reforms is categorized according to the nature of the changes it introduced within the welfare system. This serves to define different sequences in the reform trajectory followed by each welfare system, with each sequence or phase being dominated by one specific type of social policy change.

From Social Policy Changes to Reform Trajectory

In addition to helping us differentiate among social policy changes, Hall (partly following Heclo 1974) also points our attention to the consequential linkages between the various types of policy change, with the consequences of 'first order' changes often leading to the development of 'second order' ones, and so on. First order changes can be understood as the initial response that governments turn to when faced with a difficulty, which at this stage is not necessarily perceived as a new problem as such. In only changing the settings of the usual instruments, it is 'old recipes' that are resorted to, repeating what governments are used to doing. Hall thus points out that in their first response to the first oil shock in the early 1970s, British governments applied 'traditional' Keynesian policies with the aim of boosting consumer demand. Similarly, we will see that in Continental Europe, governments first turned to available social insurance instruments when faced with the social consequences of the economic crisis.

However, in something which is little-by-little perceived as a new context, these old recipes start to produce unintended effects or 'anomalies'. Advised by different kinds of experts (among them, at times, comparative social policy analysts) governments gradually acquire the conviction that they need to abandon traditional ways of doing things, which are now perceived to be wrong. Faced with mounting difficulties, policy actors consent to introduce some instrumental innovations, provided that these will help to preserve the logic of the system (for example, in our field, the first retrenchments of the early 1990s).

But it may be that even these innovations do not produce the expected results. In the macroeconomic policy case studied by Hall, this led to the crisis of the whole policy paradigm (both the goals and the associated instruments of Keynesian macroeconomic policies were denounced as counter-productive), and from there to the emergence and implementation of a new policy paradigm (monetarist policies) by new political actors. The chapters in this volume show that things did not occur in exactly this way in the transformation of Continental European welfare systems. More reforms (including institutional ones) were necessary, and it is still hard to speak of a radical transformation of the entire welfare systems, even though we will show that political actors adopted a new social policy paradigm in the 2000s.

In our cases we see no instances of brutal departure from the Bismarckian ways of thinking and doing, but rather a progressive change of these. Starting from an initial reaction to crisis that was highly determined by the institutional logic of the Bismarckian system itself (labor shedding and increase in social contribution), the orientation of reforms has changed only progressively, by a succession of measures that build on the consequences of the preceding ones. In all the cases studied in this book, changes have been implemented through a succession of reforms and not through an abrupt paradigmatic change. Therefore, if we want to understand the more recent structural reforms and the general process through which Continental European welfare systems have been transformed, we cannot analyze any one (big or small) reform in isolation from the whole reform process. This reform process we refer to as the 'reform trajectory'.

As we have shown for pension reforms in Continental Europe (Bonoli and Palier 2007), the reform trajectory is made of a succession of reforms, with the new one being, at least partly, based on the consequences of the previous one. Each stage in the process opens up new reform opportunities, by changing the political context in which reforms take place. One cannot attribute the overall transformation of the welfare system to a single 'one-shot' reform. In this book, we demonstrate that the transformation of welfare systems happens instead through an incremental process, in which the adoption of given measures facilitates the acceptance and growth of certain policy options – that would otherwise have been extremely difficult, if not impossible, politically – and undermines others. Individuals and collective political actors can exploit the new opportunities that earlier – and apparently marginal – reforms open up, and through their actions come to change the whole system. In order to account for these processes, the contributions to this volume thus make heavy use of the various categories that have been elaborated by Thelen and Streeck (2005a) to grasp the variety of incremental but cumulatively transformative changes that characterize institutional evolution.[12]

Welfare Reforms: Their Dimensions, their Consequences

We therefore claim in this book that the process of welfare state transformation has to be understood as the result of a 'reform trajectory' made up of different phases, with each characterized by a predominant type of policy change or reform. Each national country chapter will analyze their specific national reform trajectory, making reference to contingent and particular national circumstances. But in order to distinguish, compare and analyze each phase, we have identified the various dimensions that are analyzed across all the cases.

As shown by Hall (1997) among others, governmental action is not a purely rational and neutral reaction to a problem that is 'out there', such as an economic shock or a social change. If socio-economic transformations like globalization or ageing are unquestionably the triggers of welfare state reform, the timing, the content and the politics of these reforms have to be understood with reference to many more variables than just the problems they are supposed to solve. In this context three sets of variables should be taken into account in particular: ideas, institutions and interests.

It is difficult to claim that reforms are purely social and political constructions with no link to 'real' developments. Socio-economic changes are obviously triggering welfare state difficulties and reforms. In our approach, socio-economic developments are considered to provide the *context* for reforms. These reforms, however, are also framed by policy ideas and interpretations. In this case, it seems crucial to look both at the national debates around macroeconomic and social policy paradigms, as well as the lessons that actors draw from previous reforms and their consequences (Hall 1993). We thus pay special attention to the *diagnoses* that actors develop regarding the main problems to be solved and the optimal policies to be implemented in consequence. The same problem can be understood in various ways, and each diagnosis leads to a specific policy response.[13]

As has been extensively developed above, governmental action is also shaped by its institutional environment (the broader political system as well as the prevailing programmatic structure of past policies). We therefore take into account the general political context of each national case, and of each reform, as well as the specific impacts of the welfare arrangements and of preceding reforms. As also detailed above, we claim that specific welfare reforms can entail more or less important changes for welfare systems. It is thus important to qualify the main characteristics of the reforms as far as principles and institutions are concerned. Hence the *type of policy changes* that a reform involves (which order of change?) and the *content of the reform* (according to its goals and instruments) are crucial objects of analysis, notably in order to assess the institutional changes they entail.

Finally, it is of course necessary to focus on the *politics of reforms*, that is the interests of the main actors, their positions and mobilizations, and the patterns of conflict and negotiation. Here, the political orientation of government is certainly one variable to take into account, but in the case of Continental European social policies, political actors are not the only actors to analyze. As Pierson has demonstrated, the politics of welfare reforms are heavily determined by the interests and reactions of 'programmatic constituencies', i.e. those who benefit from welfare programs and their representatives. This can of course be the beneficiaries of welfare systems themselves, those who receive (or will receive) social benefits, but it can also be those whose organizations depend on, or at least are linked to, the structure of the welfare system (Bonoli and Palier 1996). In our cases, due to the historical development of social insurances and their governance arrangements (see below), the 'social partners' (trade unions and employers' representatives) have long been in a position to act as the most important 'veto players'.[14]

Furthermore, in order to grasp the mechanisms over time and the consequential linkages between phases of reforms, we specify what the *consequences* of each phase of reforms are. The focus here is on policy feedbacks that are not only blocking further changes (as in the path dependency/ resilience theories), but also 'reform feedbacks' that are creating opportunities for further changes over time. Four types of consequences and feedback effects can be mentioned:

a) Policy outputs, institutional consequences: How much do the reforms change the welfare system?
b) Policy outcomes: Did the reform succeed in its objectives? Did it solve the problem(s) it was supposed to address?
c) Social outcomes: Who wins, who loses? What are the social consequences of the reforms?
d) Policy and political feedback effects: Does the reform lead to new opportunities? To new problems? Does it change the political strength and weakness of actors? What do the actors learn from it?

For each country chapter, authors summarize the reform trajectory in a table or figure laying out the various dimensions mentioned above (See table 1.1).

Table 1.1 – The main dimensions of welfare reform trajectories

The Problems		The reforms		The Politics of the reforms		Outcomes/Consequences of the reforms			
Context	Diagnosis	Content of the policy	Types of change	Who are the actors?	What are their relationships?	Changes in the welfare arrangement?	Results? Are problems solved?	Who wins, who loses?	Failures? New opportunities for new reforms?

Along with our common analytical grid, these tables are very useful for highlighting the commonalities and differences in the welfare reform trajectories followed across Continental Europe in recent decades, an issue to which I return in the concluding chapter. The final section of this introduction turns instead to look more closely at the origins of Bismarckian systems of social protection and at their basic characteristics and functioning through their 'heyday' up to the late 1970s, on the eve of the period that is covered by the contributions to this volume.

1.3 Bismarckian Welfare Systems as they Were[15]

This section will focus on the origins of 'Bismarckian' welfare systems, on the main goals they tried to achieve through their historical development, on the specific principles on which they rely and the institutional arrangements that characterized them in the late 1970s, just before the beginning of the period studied in all country chapters.

The Industrial Origins of 'Bismarckian' Welfare Systems

Using the notion of 'welfare state' to designate the social protection systems of Continental Europe is misleading, since the state did not create the social insurances, nor did it (and still does not) totally finance or implement them. The state's initial role was mainly to make social insurance compulsory. But social insurance bodies were created before the state intervened, at the firm or on an industry level, either by workers themselves or by their employers.

With the advent of industrialization, conditions of life changed. Most industrial workers lived in urban areas, far from their extended families and other traditional support networks. They had to sell their labor power to survive – in effect, as Marx and Polanyi amongst others have suggested, they were transformed into commodities. This meant, of course, that they confronted huge problems if they could not work for reasons such as old age and incapacity, sickness, accidents at work – frequent in the early stage of industrialism – or simply because there were no jobs to be found. In Continental Europe as elsewhere, these situations gradually came to be recognized as and named 'social risks'.

To cope with these circumstances, during the 19th century certain workers – usually the more politicized, educated and skilled ones – became organized. In certain urban occupations they copied the mechanisms that had existed under the guilds and corporations of the Middle Ages, and created what were called 'friendly societies' (in England), '*Hilfskassen*' (in Germany), '*Sociétés de secours mutuelles*' (in France). These were a kind of solidaristic club among people belonging to the same profession, who paid a contribution out of their wage in return for social support in the event of a 'social risk'. These societies also became places of political discussion, they could organize social movements and strikes, and were also part of the origin of the development of trade unions. As shown by the 'power resources approach' (Korpi 1983), the more workers were organized the more they could exert pressure on their employers to seek the improvement of their members' wages and working conditions.

Employers did not always seek to repress these organizations. On the contrary, some saw themselves as having an interest in developing or at least subsidizing these solidaristic societies, particularly for the provision of social insurance. Mares (2003) has shown that employers had two main interests in the provision of social insurance for their workers. First, they could pool the risks that they themselves were facing, for example the risk of having to pay compensation to those who suffered from industrial injuries. Once workers were organized and could sue for negligence, it often made sense to admit a degree of responsibility and collectivize risk by creating work accident insurance systems (Ewald 1986). Secondly, confronted with the volatility of labor markets and at a time before the widespread use of labor contracts, employers could not be certain of holding onto their 'good' workers, those who were peaceful, worked well and especially those in whom employers had invested heavily in terms of skills training. Offering higher wages was often not sufficient to retain the best workers, and so proposing social protection to skilled workers to ensure their attachment to the company became a tool of workforce management (Mares 2003).

For sure, it was not just German, French or Belgian employers who pursued their economic interest in promoting and financing social insurance schemes for their employees. Swenson (2002) has shown that American or Swedish employers also supported social protection for their workers, for similar reasons. What was specific to Continental Europe though – especially in Germany, France and Belgium, and, to a lesser degree, Austria and the Netherlands or Italy and Spain – was the type of social protection mechanisms chosen and the political context in which they were expanded thereafter.

While market solutions were chosen in the United States – with employers contracting with private pension funds or private health insurances for their employees – and *national* insurance was eventually set up in the United Kingdom and Scandinavia, Continental European countries preferred to rely on collective occupational social insurance funds (the German *Kassen* and the French *Caisses*), run not as private companies but as not-for-profit bodies headed by representatives of employees and employers (afterwards called the 'social partners'). These social insurance funds were not – and still are not – public bodies, their representatives seeking on the contrary to remain independent from the state as far as possible. Hence, when there was debate in mid-19th century France about whether the state should legislate to make social insurance compulsory, many MPs opposed the idea of *'l'Etat-providence'* because of their resistance to state interference in the social protection domain (Castel 1995). In the same vein, when after passing the three social insurance laws in 1883 (sickness), 1884 (accident) and 1889 (old-age and invalidity) Bismarck wanted to re-enforce the role played by the state in the administration and the financing of the insurance bodies, he was vigorously opposed by the social partners, who distrusted the authoritarian state and wanted to defend their autonomy of management (*Selbstverwaltung*) and the self-financing of the social insurance schemes they ran (through social insurance contributions levied on wages rather than through taxes).

This distrust of state or market solutions was echoed in catholic social doctrine as elaborated in the late 19th Century in reaction to the increased involvement of many European states in the traditional domains of church intervention, i.e. education and poor relief (on conflicts between church and state, see van Kersbergen and Manow 2009). This doctrine promoted subsidiarity as the main principle for distributing competences in respect of social issues, with family responsibility given precedence, religious charities and other communities (including working ones) intervening in the case of family failure, and the state playing a role only as a last resort if these other institutions failed. As demonstrated by van Kersbergen (1995), this social catholic doctrine was crucial in shaping the approach to social issues of the emergent European Christian Democratic parties, which were to become one of the driving forces for the expansion of welfare systems in Continental Europe over the course of the 20th Century (see also Huber and Stephens 2001; van Kersbergen and Manow 2009).

The Main Goals: Providing Income Security to Workers and their Families, Promoting Social Peace

This short historical account helps us better understand the main characteristics of these systems of social protection that survived after World War II. Born with industrial capitalism, these systems of collective social insurance were primarily focused on providing job and income security for male industrial workers. Security seems indeed the basic word, and appears in the name of the main social insurance schemes: *Soziale Versicherung, Sécurité sociale, seguridad social, sicurrezza soziale, sociální zabezpečení, zabezpieczenia społeczne*, etc.

Hence, as far as social justice is concerned, these schemes were less concerned with poverty or inequality than with ensuring the proportionality of benefits in respect of former wage levels and contribution records, with reinforcing the so-called equivalence principle (*Äquivalenzprinzip*). As Titmuss put it: 'the industrial achievement-performance model of social policy (...) incorporates a significant role for social welfare institutions as adjuncts of the economy. It holds that social needs should be met on the basis of merit, work performance and productivity' (1974: 31).

This is partly why these welfare systems are so often labeled Conservative: they are not aimed at changing the income distribution, but rather at securing people's position in the labor market and at securing their income. From a political point of view, these systems appear less as the result of workers' victory over employers than as initiatives by Conservative governments to guarantee social peace by building cross-class compromises. As Ebbinghaus reminds us in this volume, societies with Social-Christian orientations and worker wings of Christian Democratic parties provided a favorable political context for their expansion (van Kersbergen 1995). Esping-Andersen and Korpi (1984) argued that the weaker and fragmented labor movements of Continental Europe went together with Conservative occupationalist welfare regimes, a legacy of the divide and rule strategies of authoritarian states. Conservative elites introduced welfare reforms 'from above', in a bid to legitimate the national state (Flora and Alber 1981; Ferrera 2005).

As stated by Susanne Fuchs and Claus Offe (2008: 6):

> An essential feature of Bismarckian social security policies is that they are designed to prevent the outbreak of non-institutional distributive class conflict. They do so by installing three institutional features into social policy: (a) the selective provision of benefits to those segments of the population (i.e. the core working class) whose economic opposition would be most destructive to the orderly process of economic development, (b) the forging of interclass alliances (e.g. in the form of social security funding being shared by employers and employees), and (c) the creation of institutional arrangements that subdivide the clientele of social security into a number of administrative categories (defined by region, gender, and type of benefits, as well as by such divisions as the employed *vs.* the unemployed, blue collar *vs.* white collar workers, ordinary pensioners *vs.* early retirees, workers in core or 'heavy' industries *vs.* workers engaged in the production of consumer goods and agriculture, etc.), thus shifting the focus of distributive conflict from a conflict between encompassing *class* coalitions to a conflict between *status groups*.

In this framework, professional belonging is crucial in defining an individual's social identity; social rights are largely obtained through work and emphasis is given to collective protection and collectively negotiated rights. Social insurance schemes are less an arena of industrial conflict than an instrument of social partnership designed to address the issue of the social and political integration of industrial workers – *die Arbeiterfrage* in German, *la question sociale* in French. They are first and foremost a guarantee of social peace.

Full (Male) Employment as the Condition for Full Coverage and Full Income Guarantee

The expansion of Bismarckian welfare systems was based on a specific post-war compromise. While all the governments of Western Europe shared the view that everybody should be protected against the main social risks, the institutional basis for this differed. In the United Kingdom and in the Nordic countries existing state solutions were expanded. In Continental Europe, where Christian Democrats either dominated governments or played a pivotal role, post-war reforms also built on existing institutions and utilized 'Bismarckian means' to reach Beveridgean objectives, i.e. to protect all individuals for all social risks (Palier 2005a). Instead of radically changing the system of social insurance that had been inherited from the interwar period, they progressively extended these schemes to cover all the risks of all dependent workers and the self-employed (and their relatives), supposing that mainly men would be in the workforce while women would stay at home and care for the children and/or dependent elderly (Lewis 1992). Instead of a major rupture, the story of these systems' expansion during the *'trente Glorieuses'* (the Golden Era of the welfare state, from 1945-75) is thus one of progressive extension of both the coverage and the generosity of the various social insurance schemes that were already in existence.

As far as risks are concerned, social insurances protect people against events of life that may lead them to not be able to work and to lose their income, temporarily or permanently. From the interwar period for industrial workers, and for all professions after World War II, all of what are now called 'old social risks'[16] were progressively covered by compulsory social insurance schemes: old-age, invalidity, work accident, sickness and unemployment. Extra costs induced by having children were also compensated in some Continental European countries.

Regarding the scope of application of these schemes, instead of integrating the whole population within one unique and universal scheme, very often different occupational groups were eager to preserve or create their own schemes. As a result, these systems had become 'quasi-universal' (Leisering 2009) by the 1970s, that is providing social insurance to all workers and providing derived social rights to their relatives. Social insurance systems nonetheless remained fragmented and unequal, providing better benefits to some professions (core industrial workers, public servants) than others (agricultural workers or the self-employed). The aim was to render social assistance redundant by providing all workers with social insurance and by sustaining full (male) employment. The system covered everybody as long as all male workers would be employed with a full-time open-ended working contract, families remained stable, and unemployment was only frictional.

In terms of redistribution, in line with the 'equivalence' principle, the goal was not to reduce income inequalities or to prevent poverty, but to guarantee the highest replacement rate possible. Compulsory social insurance should replace lost wages, without the need for a privately provided supplement. During the 1960s and 1970s the aim became explicitly to guarantee total maintenance of living standards during temporary (unemployment, sickness) or definitive (old age, invalidity) periods of inactivity for all workers who met the required levels and duration of contributions. The levels of benefits were thus aimed at guaranteeing 'full income maintenance' to workers (*Lebenstandardsicherung* in German).[17]

The Institutional, Social and Economic Characteristics of Social Insurance Welfare Systems in their Heyday

As shown in the first sections of national country chapters in this volume, in the early 1980s, the Bismarckian welfare systems of Germany, France, Austria, Belgium and the Netherlands shared the same basic *institutional features* (with Switzerland, Spain, Italy and the Visegrad countries showing many more exceptions, see their respective chapters):
- old age, health and work accident insurance were compulsory for all dependent workers and for the self-employed (with the exception of the richest for the purposes of health care in Germany and the Netherlands), and unemployment insurance was generalized;
- access to social insurance was based mainly on prior contributions paid out of earnings;
- benefits were provided in cash, proportional to past earnings, expressed in terms of replacement rates and dependent on the prior payment of social contributions – hence their name 'contributory ben-

efits'. In the early 1980s, the share of contributory benefits ranged from two-thirds of all benefits paid in Germany to 80 percent in France. In Belgium, France, Germany, Austria and the Netherlands, even health provision was partly conceived of in terms of cash benefits, with health insurance covering or reimbursing the cost of health services as well as replacing wages during sickness. The Bismarckian welfare systems were thus strongly cash oriented, leaving services (such as care) to women or to the third sector, in the name of the subsidiarity principle;
- financing came mainly from social contributions – from almost 70 percent of all welfare system resources in Austria or Germany to more than 80 percent in France;
- administrative structures were para-public, with the social partners heavily involved in the management of the social insurance funds. Even if the state was often involved too, it had to share managerial responsibility; and in some instances, a state presence in the administration of schemes was wholly absent, such as in old age and health insurance in Germany, or in unemployment and complementary occupational pension schemes in France.

With separate insurance schemes in different industries or firms, Bismarckian welfare systems were highly fragmented and heterogeneous. As shown in the various chapters in this book, the strong fragmentation of these systems was – and still is – one of their defining characteristics. In the late 1980s, there were 1200 separate regional occupational or company-based health insurance funds in Germany, though pension provision was much more integrated, with two main schemes – one for blue-collar and one for white-collar workers – and special schemes for miners, civil servants and the self-employed. In France, there were 19 different health insurance schemes, over 600 basic pension schemes and more than 6000 complementary pension schemes. Italy, Switzerland, Belgium and Austria also manifested strong fragmentation. The Netherlands has a (Beveridgean) basic universal pension system, but many 'pillarized' complementary pension schemes and a number of health insurance providers. The Spanish system was much more centralized and not divided into various funds, even though occupational fragmentation, especially in pension and health insurance (before its universalization), was present. Despite developing under centralized Communist regimes after World War II, the Visegrad Countries maintained the organization of social protection in funds and retained some occupational fragmentation. In general, unemployment insurance is much less fragmented, but it still manifests a high degree of 'corporatism', being run either by both social partners or uniquely by the trade unions, as in Belgium.

Social assistance schemes were always strictly separate from insurance provision, generally being locally run, tax-financed and managed by the public authorities. Family benefits such as family allowances were sometimes well developed, as long as they supported families and did not 'de-familialize' caring roles; they were also generally not linked to previous contributions, but either given to all families or targeted to the poorest. Southern countries have however long been characterized by almost no family policies (Ferrera 1996; Guillén, this volume; Jessoula and Alti, this volume), while France and Belgium not only supported families with generous family benefits (like their northern Continental neighbors), but also provided families with childcare facilities that have allowed more women to enter the labor market (Lewis 1992).

In terms of *social outcomes*, these systems were traditionally characterized by medium levels of decommodification and a strong reproduction of social stratification (Esping-Andersen 1990) i.e. by quite significant levels of (income and gender) inequality. In these systems, the level of social protection offered depends on the employment situation, professional status, gender and age of the individual. As a result of the relatively generous replacement rate of social benefits (around 70 percent of net wages for old-age pensions in France, Austria or Germany and between 50 and 90 percent for sick pay or unemployment insurance), these systems guarantee insured individuals a certain level of independence from the market in the event of a contingency. Dependence on the market is indirect, in so far as the level of social benefits provided by these systems is itself related to prior employment (and family situation), and since benefits are proportional to earnings and contributions, high levels of inequality in the labor market (between blue and white collars, between skilled and unskilled workers, between men and women) are simply reproduced by social insurance schemes.

Due to the weight of the male breadwinner model in most of these systems, with France and Belgium being to some degree exceptions (Lewis 1992), most women obtained social protection mainly indirectly, in their roles as spouses and/or mothers. Children also obtained protection through derived benefits, and not as individuals, thus creating problems for young adults with no prior work record. Given that entitlements were heavily employment and contribution related, and given that women often did not have paid work but instead shouldered caring responsibilities, they often received far lower benefits throughout the pension-, unemployment-, accident- and disability insurance systems (Häusermann, this volume and 2010b). Although this strong gender bias and the inequalities in rights and benefits it creates have been strongly criticized by feminist scholars, it must be noted that many Continental European feminist movements have themselves been long-time advocates of freedom of choice (financial support either to care *or* to enter the labor market) rather than merely campaigning for support to enter the labor market (Naumann 2005).

From an *economic perspective*, the focus of social insurance on the 'standard employment relation' (Hinrichs, this volume) typical of industry and public service employment, was consistent with the type of capitalist development that characterized Continental Europe. The expansion of the Bismarckian welfare systems was linked to mass industrialization, and occurred largely in the context of the (post-war) heyday of Fordist, industrial capitalism. In this it differed both from the British welfare state, that was partly established earlier, and the Social Democratic welfare states, that only took off later, in a more post-industrial economic context (Bonoli 2007).

Continental European welfare systems must also be understood in the context of the development of the specific forms of 'coordinated market economies' (Hall and Soskice 2001) typical of some Continental European countries, and requiring patient capital, labor market stability, cooperation between employers and employees, and high skill levels. As Ebbinghaus notes in this volume:

> Neo-corporatist theory saw the post-war expansion of Continental welfare systems as part of an implicit *social pact*: social protection was expanded in exchange for the acceptance of the uncertainties of social market economies (Crouch 1993). In export-oriented economies, social protection became an important buffer against the cyclical proclivity of the international market, thereby helping to maintain the social consensus typical in corporatist, small European states such as Austria, the Netherlands and Switzerland (Katzenstein 1985). More recently, the Varieties of Capitalism approach (Hall and Soskice 2001) linked the development of *coordinated* market economies in Germany and its neighbours to the emergence of social welfare institutions that were beneficial to maintain a skilled labor force (Estevez-Abe et al. 2001). Recent historical research rediscovered the role of employers in providing corporate welfare and suggests that it was not always against the interests of firms to support public social policies (Mares 2003).

In sum, the Bismarckian welfare state in the post-war period assumed that men were working full-time, and that they would have long and uninterrupted careers leading up to a relatively brief retirement. In most countries on the continent, the concept of full employment involved primarily the male breadwinner. It was he who was supposed to provide support for the entire family; it was by virtue of his salary that social benefits were acquired. Indeed, steps were often taken to discourage women from working. This dependence by families on the income and social privileges of male family heads resulted in greater importance being given to job security and to guarantees of employment status (the seniority principle, regulation of hiring practices and employment termination) than to the development of employment for all (Esping-Andersen 1996).

It is precisely the assumption of 'full male employment' that has been undermined by the changes in the economic and social context since the 1970s. These changes (increasing capital mobility, intensified competition between economies, deindustrialization, mass and structural unemployment, population ageing, rising female labor market participation) have increasingly challenged the functioning of the Bismarckian welfare systems and called for adaptation and reforms. The following nine chapters trace the processes of reforms through which each Continental European country has tried to respond to these challenges. Chapters 10 and 11 focus on particular aspects of Bismarckian welfare systems (the governance and the financing of social protection) and their changes. Chapter 12 shows how the Bismarckian welfare systems have gone from a strategy based on labor shedding to implementing employment-friendly reforms and assesses the successes and limits of such a U-turn. In chapter 13, I propose a transversal reading of all the chapters in order to highlight the common characteristics of the Bismarckian welfare reform trajectories, and to contribute to the understanding of how the Bismarckian welfare systems have changed, what they have become, and what the main economic and social consequences of these transformations are.

2 A Social Insurance State Withers Away. Welfare State Reforms in Germany – Or: Attempts to Turn Around in a Cul-de-Sac

Karl Hinrichs

2.1 Introduction

Within the European Union, Germany is still *the* 'social insurance state' *par excellence*. In 2007, 46 percent of the *general* government's outlays ran through the various social insurance schemes, and they disbursed roughly two-thirds of total social expenditure (according to national calculations). Social insurance spending amounted to almost one fifth of GDP which demonstrates the substantial impact of these social security institutions on the economy and on people's living conditions. The predominance of the institutionally segmented social insurance system stems from the still effective Bismarckian legacy that made Germany the prototype for a comparatively large and, at the same time, transfer-heavy welfare state.[1] The strong reliance on earnings-related contributions – the combined rate paid by employers and employees standing at 40 percent in November 2008 – is widely regarded as the major weakness of the arrangement, impeding employment growth that, in turn, would ease the financial stress of social insurance and state budgets.

Since about the mid-1990s, we have observed intensified efforts to transform welfare state institutions. Three directions of change are distinguishable. First, wage replacement schemes, traditionally aimed at status maintenance, are reoriented towards basic protection for pensioners and unemployed. Furthermore, the strategy of reducing the labor supply in view of increased open unemployment after 1974 was abandoned in favor of activating social policy. Instead of income support, the focus is now on a maximum integration of (long-term) unemployed, older workers and mothers into paid employment. Finally, in order to make welfare state financing more employment-friendly, there is a shift away from social insurance contributions towards a higher share of tax-funding, mainly out of the federal purse.

Although we have witnessed *unprecedented* structural reforms, mainly after the millennium, political attempts to arrive at an employment- and family-friendly 'post-Bismarckian' shape of the welfare state have been hampered by a combination of unfavorable and interrelated factors which constrain the room to maneuver: low economic growth rates in almost all the years after 1992, picking up not before 2005, resulted in an almost stagnant employment level and enlarged the 'problem load'. The costs of unification remained an impediment to attaining an overall balanced public budget and narrowed the opportunities to further shift welfare state financing away from contributions. Finally, within given political structures in Germany, drastic (and sometimes even small) reforms require a high degree of consensus among the political actors involved, and party politics has notably slowed down (if not recurrently foreclosed) changes in the welfare state edifice. Larger leaps of policy change are only possible when, temporarily or on a certain issue, party competition is neutralized by a tacit or actual 'Grand Coalition' of the two large political parties, and that is the way the substantial reconstruction of the German welfare state occurred.

These structural reforms after the year 2000, emanating from paradigmatic changes, represent the latest stage of a sequential reform process that Germany shares with other Bismarckian welfare states (Palier and Martin 2007a: 542-50 and first chapter of this volume). This reform sequence will be analyzed in what follows. In the next section (2.2), traditional traits of the German welfare state arrangement around 1980 are highlighted in order to evaluate later how and to what degree the core elements of this arrangement have changed after the sudden death of full employment in the mid-1970s when the long phase of welfare state expansion largely came to a halt.

It will be shown (section 2.3) that the subsequent development until 2008 can be divided into three periods. During the first period, that lasted from about the mid-1970s until the mid-1990s, mainly 'first' or 'second order changes' (according to Hall's [1993] terminology) occurred. While the first period was thus marked by bounded, largely path-dependent changes within the established social insurance paradigm, the second one during the latter half of the 1990s may be characterized as a *transitional period* or phase of gradual 'defrosting' of the German *Sozialstaat*. Not least triggered by the fiscal costs of unification, the political discourse shifted from social insurance as an effective problem-solving technology to a perception of social insurance as a problem in itself. Thus, non-wage labor costs, globalization and generational equity emerged as catchwords for the 'social construction of an imperative' to reform (Cox 2001) and paved the way for an ideational change that materialized in substantial structural changes during the third period. It started around the year 2000 and, still unfinished, means a *transformation* of certain policy areas *within new paradigms*.

The fourth section will be an evaluation of the magnitude and the patterns of change compared to the shape of the welfare state arrangement around the late 1970s. In the fifth section I will search for factors that help to explain the cumbersome process of transforming the social insurance state as well as the leaps which occurred during the third period. The concluding section provides some propositions about the adopted change in direction away from the Bismarckian legacy, the political consequences, and whether Germany has (temporarily) entered a fourth period which might be called 'the end of impositions'.

2.2 The German Social Insurance State as we Knew it

Social Security Based on the Standard Employment Relationship

Right from the start in the 1880s, the social security system in Germany centered on wage laborers. It developed along the concept of a 'standard employment relationship' (*SER*), although this term was not coined before 1985 as a kind of yardstick for exploring changes, and concomitant risks in the labor market, and in the social protection system (Mückenberger 1985). Through the interplay of state intervention into the working of the labor market (regulatory policies), the achievements of collective bargaining and the rules of social custom, the labor contract was incrementally enriched with individual and collective status rights regulating dependent labor and its exchange (Hinrichs 1991; 1996). As a norm and the (once) predominant reality, the *SER* implies continuity and stability of employment with not more than short interruptions of gainful work. This is supposed to be dependent work, bound to directives and performed as a full-time job based on an unlimited contract from the end of education until retirement at a certain age. Resting upon employment at 'standard' conditions, but separately organized, *social insurance schemes* provide wage replacement for well-defined circumstances, namely, when typical risks of wage labor occur and workers are temporarily unable to earn a market income (sickness, unemployment) or are no longer expected to do so (invalidity, old age). These earnings-related benefits are also meant to marginalize *poverty policy*, i.e. to reduce the dependence on regularly lower subsidiary assistance benefits which are subject to a means test.

As a societal arrangement of production and reproduction the *SER* was clearly gender biased. It was assumed that, ensured by collective agreements, a full-time job (even at the lowest wage rate) delivers a 'family wage' which is an income sufficient to maintain the needs of a nuclear family. Social insurance schemes stabilized the emerging *male breadwinner family* because own and derived entitlements were usually high enough to also cover the needs of dependants. Thus, not much attention had to be paid to the social security of predominantly female workers in atypical or marginal employment, who provided merely a temporary or supplementary income. In this way, the *female homemaker family* was constituted as the opposite side of the coin, which largely rendered unnecessary state provisions for child and elderly care and thus impeded the continuous integration of women in the labor market. Instead, cash transfers (child and housing allowances, tax advantages) met the income needs of family households during certain phases of the life course.[2]

Social Insurance Schemes: Institutional Features

Social insurance schemes are the core of the Bismarckian welfare state. As with any other welfare state program, they can be analyzed along four dimensions (cf. Bonoli and Palier 1998). The information given below relates to the situation around the late 1970s which represents the end of expansionary development, but includes the long-term care (LTC) insurance scheme which came into effect not earlier than 1995 (see section 2.3).

(1) Starting with *financing*, the revenues of all social insurance schemes by definition stem mainly or completely from earnings-related contributions, unrelated to individual risk. They are equally divided between employers and employees. Contributions are levied up to certain earnings ceilings (higher for the unemployment and pension scheme) and above that no entitlements to cash benefits are earned. However, from the outset tax subsidies have been a funding component in the pension scheme and, recurrently, the federal government had to cover deficits of the unemployment insurance scheme. LTC insurance and the health care scheme (until 2003) always met their expenses solely out of contributions, and all schemes operate on the pay-as-you-go principle. On behalf of the recipients of cash benefits the respective scheme actually transfers contributions to other schemes (e.g. from unemployment insurance to the sickness funds, the pension and, nowadays, also to the LTC scheme). Due to this financial interdependence, rule changes in one scheme (e.g. of the contribution rate) often affect the financial status of other schemes as well.

(2) In general, *access to benefits* is dependent upon prior contributions paid out of actual earnings. Most members of the schemes are compulsorily insured. The sickness funds and the public pension scheme may also be joined voluntarily (e.g. by self-employed), and employees with earnings above a certain ceiling may either remain voluntary members of the statutory sickness funds or opt out and seek private insurance coverage. Beginning with blue-collar (industrial) workers in the 1880s, the extension of mandatory coverage to further categories of the gainfully employed was almost completed by the end of the 1970s. In contrast, LTC insurance started as an almost universal scheme, requiring membership even for those who had voluntarily taken out private health care coverage. This scheme and also the sickness funds provide in-kind benefits to dependent family members with no earnings or earnings below a certain ceiling. They are exempted from contributions as their eligibility rests upon the coverage of the principal person insured. The pension scheme also offers 'derived' benefits for survivors of a deceased worker/ pensioner.

(3) Regarding *benefit structure*, cash benefits clearly prevail (nearly two-thirds of the social insurance schemes' expenditure in 1980), and in all schemes they are related to former earnings. The equivalence principle (individual equity) is most strictly applied in the pension scheme because the length of covered employment counts as well. Nevertheless, before the implementation of a series of pension reforms beginning in 1992, several provisions were included in the benefit formula which, in order to attain a socially adequate pension, produced additional entitlements for periods with zero or low earnings. The *level* of earnings-related benefits is meant to ensure status maintenance, although the replacement ratio varies across the schemes. No income losses occur to workers whose sickness lasts less than six weeks and, after the employer's wage continuation ends, sick pay regularly amounted to 90 percent of net earnings in 1980. That year, the target replacement rate (*net*) for a 'standard pensioner' – which assumed an insurance career of 45 years and always having earned the average wage – stood at 70.3 percent. Unemployment insurance benefits, paid up to a maximum of 12 months, amounted to 68 percent of former net earnings until 1984 (the level of indefinitely paid *tax-financed* unemployment *assistance* benefits was 58 percent). All four social insurance branches also or solely grant in-kind benefits – rehabilitation (pension scheme), training (unemployment insurance), medical care (which makes up 95 percent of the sickness funds' expenditure) and long-term care (100 percent). Here we find a dualism of principles.

Contributions are levied according to earnings capacity, whereas in-kind benefits are awarded depending on ascertained (medical) need or appropriateness to facilitate the return to employment (rehabilitation and active labor market policies). Thus, interpersonal redistribution within the risk pool of insured is more pronounced than in the realm of cash benefits.

(4) Finally, regarding *administrative* and *organizational* structures, all social insurance schemes are para-public entities with separate budgets. Right from their inception, corporatist self-administration has been a central feature and a correlative of contribution financing. However, the composition of the respective governing bodies varies. In the Federal Labor Agency (*FLA* – unemployment insurance), beside the social partners, representatives of public authorities (e.g. from the states) are involved. The pension scheme is administered solely by the employers and the insured (predominantly: trade unionists). This is also true for most sickness funds and the LTC insurance units which are organizationally tied to them.[3]

While participation in self-administration may have provided organizational support for trade unions in the late 19th century and still offers both social partners a legitimate right to put forward their point of view in public and to be heard in legislative procedures, self-administration as such has lost much of its relevance (except for the health care scheme). Ever more detailed legislation has hollowed out the scope for autonomous decision-making by the respective (corporatist) bodies and largely made self-administration a symbolic feature (see Ebbinghaus, this volume). Moreover, the social insurance units have been forced to adopt a more managerial structure of governance for the day-to-day matters. Representatives of employers and employees are confined to supervisory boards, similar to those in joint stock companies. These organizational changes aim at higher efficiency and lower administrative costs, and the same is true for mergers within the social insurance branches. The formal separation of public pension schemes by occupational status was finally abolished in October 2005 when they were merged into one. Due to voluntary mergers of sickness funds into larger units their number has been drastically reduced (1992: 1,223; 2008: 210) and will further decline. Recent *administrative* and *organizational restructuring* was a relatively low-profile issue and has not played a central role in *substantively* changing the German social insurance state. Therefore, this dimension will not be dealt with further.

2.3 A Sequential Reform Trajectory

Germany's social protection system has been confronted with an almost continuously increasing 'problem load' since the early 1990s, while
political institutions have constrained the timely adjustment of policy
goals and instruments. Thus, the large German welfare state may be
typified as a truck steadily moving further into a cul-de-sac, hence, facing ever more limited opportunities to turn around and get a clear run
again. Figure 2.1 depicts the overall reform trajectory as a U-turn divided into three phases. Factually, the sequential process does not fit neatly
for all social policy domains looked at in the following. There was some
overlap, development was not always straightforward, and the modes of
institutional change varied between policy areas. However, except for
the domain of health and long-term care policy, the process has arrived
at structural reforms following a conception clearly different from the
past.

Figure 2.1   Welfare State Turnaround in Germany

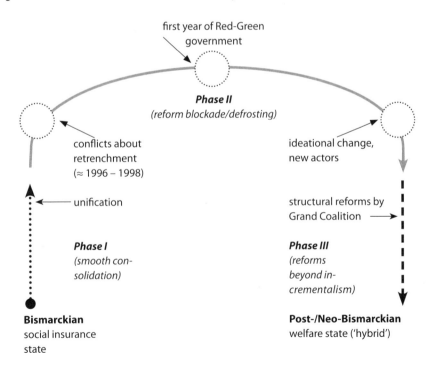

first year of Red-Green
government

Phase II
(reform blockade/defrosting)

conflicts about
retrenchment
(≈ 1996 – 1998)

ideational change,
new actors

unification

structural reforms by
Grand Coalition

Phase I
(smooth con-
solidation)

Phase III
(reforms
beyond in-
crementalism)

Bismarckian
social insurance
state

Post-/Neo-Bismarckian
welfare state ('hybrid')

Period I (1976-1995): Smooth Consolidation and a Last Victory for Social Insurance

Increasing unemployment figures in 1974/75 and again after 1980 put financial pressure on the social insurance schemes. The most obvious response to cost increases in health care and more spending on the unemployed and on early retirees was to raise revenues. Thus, the total contribution rate rose by 5.3 percentage points between 1975 and 1990 (see Table 2.1). However, there were also retrenchments. Up to the end of the 1980s, they remained moderate and amounted to nothing more than 'smooth consolidation' (Offe 1991). Those restrictions of benefit generosity were concluded in consensual manner and if not, the respective political party in opposition expressed hardly more than 'dutiful protest'. At that time, the two large 'people's parties' (*Volksparteien*), the Christian Democrats and the Social Democrats, were both committed to preserving the structures of the social insurance state and to retaining a high level of state-guaranteed protection.

Table 2.1	Combined Contribution Rate (Employer + Employee) to Social Insurance Schemes
1960	24.4%
1970	26.5%
1975	30.5%
1980	32.4%
1990	35.8%
1995	39.3%
1998	42.1%
2000	41.0%
2003	42.1%
2005	42.3%
2007	40.6%
2008	40.0%

Almost immediately after unemployment figures started to soar, a series of incremental changes (moderately) increased the pressure on unemployed people to accept job offers, 'nibbled' on the eligibility criteria for claiming unemployment benefits and impaired the entitlements in various way over and above the reductions of the replacement rate in 1984 and 1994 (for further details, see Clasen 2005: 54-76). In contrast, benefits in case of early retirement remained generous and the corresponding options were even extended. All actors – the government, trade unions, employers and the older workers themselves – preferred a premature exit from the labor market to higher open unemployment. Thus, early retirement was widely utilized and, factually, a reversal set in not long before the year 2000.

Since the late 1970s, numerous reforms of the *statutory health insurance* (SHI) scheme stopped mainly supply-side driven spending hikes only for a few subsequent years. The health care providers who held numerous veto points within the institutional setting of this policy domain were able to ward off more ambitious reform proposals affecting their income or autonomy. Comparatively successful in stabilizing the average contribution rate was the 'Seehofer reform' that went into effect in 1993. Different from the largely ineffective 1989 reform, it came about as a negotiated compromise between the Christian-Liberal government and the Social Democrats whose majority of votes in the *Bundesrat* (since 1991) was crucial for pursuing a comprehensive reform approach. Two organizational changes stimulated *competitive pressure* on the sickness funds and paved the way for further intensification in the latest reform of 2007. First, cross-subsidies between sickness funds were introduced so as to balance varying risk profiles of their membership (according to age and sex) and differences in their revenue structure. These risk-adjustment subsidies narrowed the hitherto broad range of contribution rates levied by the different sickness funds. They were a prerequisite for the second change: all members (and not only the white-collar workers as before) were allowed to choose from nearly all sickness funds and applicants could not be rejected. The idea was that sickness funds should compete for members on the basis of efficiency and service quality, particularly when given more latitude to negotiate with service providers, and the reform indeed resulted in a declining number of sickness funds due to mergers (see above).

In comparative perspective, the *pension reform* of 1989 (becoming effective in 1992) was an early response to imminent population aging and a highlight of corporatist incrementalism, as well as a continuation of consensual pension politics including the social partners and the major political parties. As a change of *instruments*, it formally introduced net wage indexing of new and current pensions. *De facto* it had been applied already since the late 1970s due to arbitrary manipulations of the adjustment formula. After 1992 a *net* replacement level of 70 percent for the 'standard pensioner' was ensured. Moreover, in the long run workers taking out a first pension before reaching the normal retirement age (65) would have to face permanent deductions. Federal subsidies to the public pension scheme were increased and expected to durably amount to 19 percent of the scheme's spending. Finally, credits for childcare that had been first recognized as an equivalent to waged work in 1986 were improved (three instead of one year for births after 1991). The cumulative effect of the various reform elements was expected to facilitate a contribution rate of 26.9 percent instead of 36.4 percent in 2030 (Sozialbeirat 1998: 242). Among all relevant political actors the assessment prevailed that no substantial readjustments had to be considered before the year 2010.

The legislation of the *long-term care insurance* (LTC) in 1994 was the last manifestation of consensual reform policy carried out by the two *Volksparteien* until 2001, and it was the last expansionary reform within the social insurance approach, although this institutional innovation to a large extent replaced previous spending on means-tested care benefits. In view of this social risk becoming ever more virulent in an ageing society, the proponents within both parties almost unanimously regarded the LTC scheme as the completion of the social insurance state. However, the new scheme had not come off without the states' and municipalities' insistence on being relieved from rising social assistance spending on the needy elderly. While a compromise on the contours of the benefit side (graded according to need classes with no full-cost coverage) emerged quite early, legislation was delayed for many years by the struggle over organizational form and, hence, how to finance such fundamental reform – concretely, whether to opt for a tax-transfer scheme, a mandatory private insurance, or an additional social insurance scheme. It was a principled conflict over either creating or warding off a precedent for future social policy development. Ultimately, the two large parties compromised upon a variant that was most faithful to the traditional social insurance path, namely, a separate branch under the roof of the sickness funds. In this way it avoided further burdening the federal budget, circumvented the 'double payment problem' of a private funded LTC insurance, and applied the technique most familiar and comprehensible to the public as contribution payments entitling to non-means-tested benefits in the case of risk occurrence (Götting et al. 1994).

Nevertheless, the new scheme included two unprecedented features: *factually*, employers are burdened with less than half of the contribution rate since one paid holiday was abolished. Furthermore, the contribution rate (1.7 percent) *and* the (maximum) benefit levels were fixed by law. That way a dilemma was created when the number of beneficiaries increases (as it in fact happens): Either a higher contribution rate has to be legislated or a deterioration of the benefits' real value due to rising costs of care services must be accepted. It was not until 2007 that the government decided to depart from a stable contribution rate (plus 0.25 percentage points to be balanced by a lower rate to unemployment insurance) in order to upgrade benefit levels in 2008 and thereafter. Thus, by resorting to higher contributions the 2008 reform partly reversed the 'policy drift' (Streeck and Thelen 2005a) of the scheme. In view of rising numbers of frail elderly, a structural reform of financing (a departure from pure pay-as-you-go) is being debated, but no contours are recognizable as yet.

Germany participated in the worldwide recovery of economic growth during the 1980s. As a result, the employment level increased, the public deficit dropped from 3.9 percent of GDP to zero in 1989, and the social spending/GDP ratio went down from 30.4 percent (1981) to 26.9 percent (1990) (BMGS 2005: 192). This altogether favorable situation on the eve of unification supported the belief that the social and economic consequences of this singular event could be mastered. After implementing the pension (1992) and health care reform (1993), still in the mid-1990s, there was broad-based confidence in the ability to modernize the single social insurance schemes one by one, to improve their poverty alleviating function and to maintain the schemes' financial viability in the long run (Nullmeier and Rüb 1994: 60-3; Leisering 1995). Moreover, the passing of the LTC scheme had obviously proven the social insurance technology to be capable of becoming applied to new social risks.

Period II (1996-2000): From (Unfounded) Optimism to 'Reform Blockade'

The second period was characterized by a not unanimously shared ideational change. Rather, adversarial politics prevailed between the two party blocs — the Social Democrats and the Green party in one camp, the Christian Democrats and the Liberal party in the other. Within Germany's specific political institutions such a constellation provided ample incentives for blame generation and stalemate. In view of retrenchments only partly implemented or revoked and the absence of structural changes, the term 'reform blockade' was frequently used during the second half of the 1990s (cf. Manow and Seils 2000).

When the LTC insurance went into full effect in July 1996 optimism regarding the ability to safeguard the social insurance state by incremental adjustments had vanished. The fiscal costs of unification came to the fore and strongly influenced the reform trajectory after 1995. Contrary to expectations in 1990/91, it would trigger a replication of the 'economic miracle' of the 1950s and early 1960s (Abelshauser 2004: 402-7), the 'unification boom' was short-lived, and more than one third of jobs got lost in East Germany between 1989 and 2000. The advancing deindustrialization process in West Germany put additional strain on both unemployment insurance and, due to massive inflows into early retirement in both parts of the country, also on the public pension scheme. The result of the 'welfare without work' syndrome (Esping-Andersen 1996a) was that the total contribution rate rose from 35.8 percent in 1990 to 39.1 percent in 1996 (plus 1.7 percent for LTC insurance after June 1996).

Consequently, the discourse on social policy reform altered dramatically after 1995. At that time *globalization* spread as a term in the political debate and was immediately related to high *non-wage labor costs* as a threat to international competitiveness and job growth. Social insurance contributions has become a central topic in almost any reform debate since then and favored strategically interested interpretations about the detrimental effects. Those arguments had not been absent in the debate before the mid-1990s, but as the new diagnosis of the problem came to the fore they condensed into irrefutable facts justifying more serious social policy changes. One quotation from the spokeswoman of the Liberal Party, Gisela Babel, may suffice to show how the interpretative pattern had changed. When the 1997 pension reform bill was read in the *Bundestag* she referred to the reform of 1989 and said: 'At that time no discontent with a contribution rate to the pension scheme of 26 percent or 28 percent was discernible. That was flatly considered acceptable then. Today we do not consider it acceptable anymore' (Deutscher Bundestag 1997b: 16780-1).

Similarly, causal beliefs regarding the unemployment problem moved further away from macroeconomic constellations as a prime cause. Instead, too little labor *market* — due to excessive state intervention and the effects of industry-wide collective bargaining — was identified as root cause (Bleses and Seeleib-Kaiser 2004: 110-3, 121-3). Consequently, removing rigidities through deregulation was the answer as well as extended recommodification, i.e. more incentives for the unemployed to take up job offers and stricter sanctions if they refused. Later, a somewhat biased interpretation of 'employment miracles' abroad (the Netherlands, Denmark), already applying stricter activation policies, was utilized to emphasize the necessity of further changes.

Although official estimates on demographic ageing had hardly worsened since the legislation of the pension reform in 1989, they were perceived as more dramatic than before. *Generational equity*, hitherto absent in the German discourse, became an issue for the first time in 1997 when it appeared in the explanatory statement to the draft law of the pension reform that was legislated the same year (Deutscher Bundestag 1997a: 1, 47). A declining replacement ratio for present and future pensioners was justified in order not to overburden the younger generations. Interested actors, like the financial market industry, and policy entrepreneurs reinforced arguments about the non-sustainability of the PAYG pension scheme and the exhaustion of the one-pillar approach to deliver appropriate retirement income and thus prepared the ground for the multi-pillar paradigm to become ever more predominant.

In reaction to previous reforms regarded as insufficient, the new interpretative patterns were most energetically advanced by the government parties (and the employers). The Social Democrats, the smaller opposition parties (the Greens and the left-wing PDS) and the labor unions – none of them suitably prepared to enter a social learning process – did not adopt them. Therefore, the Christian Democrats departed from the commitment to a strong welfare state they hitherto had shared with the Social Democrats for electoral reasons and because of the strong stance of the Labor wing within the party's membership. Largely because of pressure from the Liberal party, the coalition government turned to a unilateral approach, and no longer actively sought a compromise with the Social Democrats, who then utilized the *Bundesrat* to block policy changes wherever possible. In the run-up to the 1998 federal election they promised to undo the 'social atrocities' the Christian-Liberal government had committed (and actually repealed several policy changes immediately after coming into office). Thereafter, the Christian Democrats turned the tables when they attempted to bloc reform legislation of the Red-Green government.

It meant that all health care reforms from 1996 until 2003 were highly contested between the respective government and opposition. Because of the required consent of the *Bundesrat*, the hospital sector, the largest spending component, was hardly tackled. Nonetheless, these reform packages put a temporary brake on expenditure increases. The incoming Red-Green government never implemented some 'privatization' measures legislated by its predecessor and partly revoked increased co-payments for patients.

Changes in the public pension scheme were no less controversial. In view of a steep rise of elderly unemployed prematurely claiming an old-age pension (at age 60), the phasing-out of early retirement options without permanent deductions was accelerated in 1996. Moreover, various entitlements, not based on individual contributions out of earnings, were further reduced and thus strengthened the link between contributions and benefits. These retrenchments were a prelude for a more substantial reform legislated one year later and, once again, bitterly opposed by the Social Democrats who were closing ranks with the labor unions. In particular, they resisted impairments for disability pensioners and the inclusion of a 'life expectancy factor' in the benefit formula (that would have led to a gradually declining replacement rate). After coming into office, the Red-Green government suspended both controversial elements and passed a more moderate reform of disability pensions in 2000 instead.

However, the Social Democrats agreed to one element of the 1997 pension reform, namely, higher federal subsidies to be financed out of an increased VAT rate. Consensus on this issue (*Bundesrat* approval was required) marks a turning point as well as the start of an *institutional reform* that subsequently extended to the health care and the unemployment insurance scheme. Before, by an artfully arranged cost- and revenue-shifting game between the different social insurance branches and the federal purse, the scheme most pressured was relieved at the expense of those in less financial straits but, predominantly, the social insurance system at large became burdened by the relief of the federal budget. Particularly, after 1990 significant parts of unification costs had been shifted onto the unemployment and pension scheme. Since the mid-1990s, the social insurance institutions demanded a reversal, arguing that benefit components not based on contributions out of own earnings (*versicherungsfremde Leistungen*) should not be borne by the community of insured, but rather, the general public was financially responsible for redistribution of this kind. Thus, in order to attain the front-ranking objective of a combined contribution rate below the 40 percent threshold, infusing (more) tax revenues into the budgets of social insurance schemes immediately facilitated a lower contribution rate without (further) reducing benefits. To that end, the Red-Green government introduced (and subsequently hiked) an energy tax (*Ökosteuer*) and transferred the revenues into the budget of the public pension scheme. Such a refinancing eased reforms in other Bismarckian welfare states as well (see Palier, chapter 13, this volume).

Period III (2001-2007): New Momentum for a Reform Process 'Beyond Incrementalism'

The 'reform blockade' was not dissolved before 2001 when a tacit consensus re-emerged. Subsequently, a number of institutional changes and structural reforms passed after compromises had been negotiated between the Red-Green government and the opposition.

Health Care: More Efficiency through More Competition

The new Red-Green government was unable to carry through a comprehensive health care reform after the majority in the *Bundesrat* had shifted to its disadvantage in 1999. It could, however, legislate a pared-down package in 2000 that focused on the governance structure. The reform aimed at more efficient and qualitatively improved delivery of medical services, and this attempt was continued in 2003 when the government turned to the Christian Democrats and negotiated a compromise on another reform package that was approved by the *Bundesrat* (Gerlinger 2003). It also included tax revenues from an increased tobacco tax that were funneled into SHI and meant to cover spending items 'alien' to this scheme (like maternity benefits). Again, the 2003 reform further shifted the costs of health care to the *patients* (among others, they have to pay an 'entrance fee' of 10 euros per quarter when seeing a doctor in private practice) and to the *insured*. Since July 2005 the contribution rate is no longer equally shared between employers and employees, but rather, employees have to pay an additional 0.9 percentage points, and employers are relieved correspondingly.

Further reforming the health care system was announced to be a central project of the new 'Grand Coalition' government that came into office in autumn 2005. It was legislated in February 2007 after substantial controversies between the government and all other actors involved in this policy domain, and among the government parties. Prior to the 2005 elections, both the Christian Democrats and the Social Democrats expressed their determination to change the financing of health care but in an entirely different way. The compromise does not foreclose the realization of one or the other concept after the next federal elections. The core element is a newly established 'health fund' which, beginning in 2009, collects all contributions at a uniform rate fixed by the government (i.e. no longer determined by the self-governing bodies). Additionally, the federal government contributes to the 'health fund'. Tax subsidies will increase to 14 billion euros per annum and effectuate a lower contribution rate than would have to be raised otherwise. Transfers to the individual sickness funds are allocated according to the risk structure (age, sex and morbidity) of the respective membership. In case revenues do not meet their expenses, those sickness funds have to raise a supplementary contribution from which the employers are exempt while others may refund surpluses to their members. This element of the 2007 reform package shows its main thrust, which is to further strengthen competition within the health care system, a development opened up by the institutional reform of 1993.

Strengthened competition is moreover expected to improve efficiency and quality of health care delivery. To that end, provisions that have been legislated during Red-Green incumbency in 2000 and 2003 and which allow for more flexible contractual relationships between sickness funds and providers, are extended.

Pension Policy: Adopting the Multi-Pillar Approach

In pension policy the Red-Green government executed a *paradigmatic change* when it departed from the supposedly 'exhausted' social insurance approach (Bönker 2005) in 2001. Three innovations included in the reform package are most important (Hinrichs 2005). First, the reference point shifted from the benefit to the revenue side: the standard replacement ratio of 70 percent (net), established in 1992, was replaced with a fixed contribution rate that is not supposed to exceed 20 percent until 2020 and 22 percent until 2030. In order to keep to these targets, 'brake mechanisms' were included in the benefit formula. The expected decline of the standard replacement ratio meant a clear departure from the dogma of status maintenance (after a complete full-time career) to be attained by public pensions alone. Second, in order to close the arising pension gap, the core of the 2001 reform was the institutionalization of the so called *Riester-Rente.* The voluntary take-up of certified savings plans is encouraged by offering tax advantages or direct subsidies. Such an extension to *retirement income* policy has irrevocably put the German pension system on a multi-pillar track again, since 1957 having been equivalent to a *public pension* policy and a one-pillar approach.

Finally, old-age (and disability) pensioners with insufficient resources are no longer referred to the general social assistance scheme, but rather are entitled to benefits from a special basic security scheme which are still means-tested and not higher than before. However, the traditional obligation of adult children to financially support their elderly parents is lifted. This third innovation may be regarded as a pre-emptive policy; eased and less stigmatized access to benefits from the new scheme will make the combined effects of a more flexible labor market (fewer regular full-time employment careers) and of past and future pension retrenchments socially more bearable (see section 2.4).

The 2001 reform gained a majority in the *Bundestag* after the labor unions and the 'traditionalists' within the SPD were acquiesced by some (symbolic) concessions (Trampusch 2006). A tacit interparty consensus emerged after further accommodations were granted to the CDU/CSU so that the party abstained from determined efforts to close the ranks in the *Bundesrat* and, actually, no unified bloc of states with the CDU in government obstructed the reform package.[4] A similar pattern of conflict and, ultimately, of conflict resolution occurred in 2004. Calculations made prior to the 2001 reform had proven overly optimistic, and so as not to miss the contribution targets, the benefit formula was changed again. Following the recommendations of a reform commission, the inclusion of a so called 'sustainability factor' (the changing ratio of pensioners and insured) will lead to a further decline of the replacement rate when the adjustment of the value of one 'earnings point', relevant for both new and current pensioners, will lag behind the growth of average covered earnings (cf. Schmähl 2007). The *net* standard replacement rate is going to drop from about 69 percent at the beginning of this decade to about 52 percent in 2030.

In order to ensure adherence to the contribution rate targets, the reform commission further proposed a higher standard retirement age (Kommission 2003). The Red-Green government abstained from including this most controversial and unpopular issue in the 2004 legislation, but closed the last loopholes for early retirement at age 60. Therefore, it was the 'Grand Coalition' government who decided in 2007 to lift the normal retirement age from 65 to 67 years between 2012 and 2029. This implies lower benefits for future retirees who, for whatever reason, (have to) claim their public pension at an earlier age.

Protecting the Unemployed: Bifurcated Benefits

A second *paradigmatic change*, again meaning a departure from the Bismarckian principle of status maintenance, took place in labor market policy when the 'Hartz laws' were implemented between 2003 and 2005 (Hinrichs 2007; Konle-Seidl et al. 2007; Oschmiansky et al. 2007). They emanated from proposals of the reform commission named after its chairman Peter Hartz (Kommission 2002). A compromise with the *Bundesrat* (concretely: the Christian Democrats) had to be attained on the most important provisions.

The *Hartz* laws came in four parts. The first three included changes in the governance structure of the Federal Labor Agency (*FLA*) and measures to improve the services provided to its clients, new instruments of labor market policy, stricter 'activation' of the unemployed, and a curtailment of insurance benefit eligibility for the unemployed age 55 and older (with a maximum 18 months instead of 32). Most controversial was the *Hartz IV* act which implied lower benefits for many long-term unemployed. It abolished the awkwardly constructed unemployment assistance scheme that was tax-financed (federal budget) and means-tested, but at the same time, earnings-related. This benefit had meant to (indefinitely) ensure status preservation at a lower level of provision than did unemployment insurance benefits. In fact, after 1999 it was contingent on prior contribution payments because only those (long-term) unemployed who had received unemployment insurance benefits before were entitled to claim unemployment assistance.

The *Hartz IV* reform fused the unemployment and social *assistance* schemes into one institution (and renamed the *insurance* benefit as *ALG I*). Eligible for the new benefit type *Arbeitslosengeld II* (*ALG II*), in place since January 2005, are people of employable age who are 'able to work' (defined as at least three hours per day) *and* obliged to seek employment. For their dependants 'not able to work' (mostly children) there are supplements. Flat-rate *ALG II* is contingent upon a comprehensive means-test. As of July 2009, the monthly *cash* benefit amounts to 359 euros for a single person and, additionally, the actual costs of 'appropriate' housing (rent plus heating costs) are covered. If a long-term unemployed person has received a sufficiently high *ALG I* the transition towards the lower *ALG II* income is smoothed out over a two-year period. Thus, only the unemployed with no prior or insufficient *ALG I* entitlements are dependent on the flat-rate benefit from the very start. *ALG II* is not merely a basic security scheme for the registered unemployed: rather, it is designed to serve all needy people of working age. As with social assistance before, *ALG II* may be paid as an in-work benefit if income from employment is too low to meet the needs of the household.

The *Hartz* reforms have not only changed access to and the structure of benefits. They have also shifted the financing of unemployment, foremost at the expense of the federal budget and to the benefit of contributors to the unemployment insurance scheme and the municipalities. The latter gained because the federal government fully covers the expenditure on *ALG II* cash benefits and social insurance contributions on behalf of the recipients, and because the government partakes in spending on housing costs. Prior to the implementation of *ALG II* the *FLA* also had to bear in full the costs of active labor market policies for beneficiaries of unemployment *assistance* and related administrative expenses. As of 2008, it has to cover only half of the costs of the reintegration measures provided to *ALG II* recipients, while the other half is taken over by the federal purse. Furthermore, the *FLA* saves on unemployment insurance benefits (*ALG I*) due to the shortened eligibility period. Finally, since 2007 the revenues of one percentage point from the increased sales tax (VAT) are transferred to the *FLA* (about 7.2 billion euros in 2007). For this reason, though more importantly because of declining numbers of *ALG I* recipients after 2005, it was possible to lower the contribution rate to the unemployment insurance scheme from 6.5 to 4.2 percent in 2007 and once more to 3.3 percent in 2008.

Family Policy: Overcoming the Male Breadwinner Family
Another reorientation which may also be termed a *paradigmatic change* happened in family policy which traditionally focused on stabilizing the 'female homemaker family'. The reorientation that has yet to fully materialize is part of what Bleses and Seeleib-Kaiser (2004: 89-93) have called the 'dual transformation' of the German welfare state arrangement, namely, the aim to shrink social policies centered on the (male) wage earner and to expand policy areas that help to reconcile paid work and family life. The expansion during the Christian-Liberal government (see Clasen 2005: 153-66; Ostner 2006), however, was based on the concept of sequencing parenthood and employment: one parent (read: the mother) should take a parental leave for the first three years after giving birth to the (youngest) child and return to (part-time) employment thereafter (the job being guaranteed in the meantime), when the child is entitled to a place in the (part-time) kindergarten. Social transfers should (partly) compensate for the loss of earnings and improve the income situation of young families. To that end and beginning in the second half of the 1980s, the government introduced or increased various cash benefits (e.g. child allowances, pension credits for child and elderly care, parental leave benefits), and on that account Germany is nowadays spending more than most European countries (Bundesregierung 2006: 38-40).

In contrast, the Red-Green government regarded any long interruption of employment as being detrimental for utilizing and expanding the human capital of mothers and, thus, their career prospects. It therefore provided incentives for a speedier return into paid employment (e.g. higher parental leave benefits when taken out for a shorter period or, with regard to pension credits, a revaluation of covered earnings until the child reaches age ten) and offered federal subsidies to create facilities for full-day schooling, thus easing mothers' full-time employment. The unfinished project to reform parental leave benefits (*Elterngeld*) was continued by the 'Grand Coalition' government and put into effect in 2007. The new benefit type is paid for merely 12 months (plus an additional two months if the other parent also goes on leave; always 14 months for single parents). The *Elterngeld* is most advantageous for middle-class women (Henninger et al. 2008) because it amounts to two thirds of former net earnings (up to a maximum of 1,800 euros per month; minimum benefit: 300 euros), is financed out of federal taxes, and is no longer income-tested (as the former flat-rate benefit of 300 euros). In order to render possible a higher employment rate for mothers, along with increased fertility rates and lower child poverty rates (like in Scandinavian countries), the supply of affordable day care has to be substantially expanded. Therefore, by 2012 places for one third of the children below the age of three will be created. Spending on those 'defamilialization policies' is largely financed out of the federal purse.

The shift towards a 'sustainable' family policy — i.e. one that is pro-natalist, promotes gender equality and the life chances of children coming from deprived and migrant families — is generally accepted. However, the coalition parties still differ on how rigorously an 'employment-centered family policy' should be pursued. The Conservative factions among the Christian Democrats want to facilitate a *choice* between the 'female homemaker family' and the 'dual earner family' pattern (e.g. by insisting on a home care allowance). In contrast, the Social Democrats, all the opposition parties, and both social partners give clear priority to the latter concept, which is in line with (but was not explicitly influenced by) the supported 'adult worker model' as emphasized in the revised Lisbon Process (Annesley 2007).

2.4 The Consequences of Maneuvering out of the Cul-de-Sac

The intensification of the reform process after the year 2000 has brought about significant institutional changes in the German welfare state arrangement which mainly correspond to the mode *'conversion'* (Streeck and Thelen 2005a). Assigning a new mission or objective to a given institution has clearly taken place in family policy (supporting the dual-earner instead of the male breadwinner family), in the protection of the jobless (abolition of earnings-replacing benefits for long-term unemployed coming as a 'big bang'), and in the public pension scheme (relinquishment of status maintenance through a series of incremental changes – cf. Hinrichs and Kangas 2003). For the old-age security system at large, the turn towards the multipillar approach in 2001 has also set in motion path-altering dynamics through a mechanism of *'differential growth'* (Streeck and Thelen 2005a: 23) as a voluntary private pension scheme, small in the beginning, was *layered* upon the public system and will grow comparatively faster than the public one. Starting from zero in 2002, meanwhile (December 2009), about one third (13 million) of all eligible employees have taken out a savings plan for the *Riester-Rente*. In health care policy we have seen institutional reforms beyond retrenchment (strengthened competition) but not yet changes that come up to '*conversion*', and the 2008 reform has saved the LTC insurance scheme from further '*policy drift*'.

Contrasting the institutional conditions of the German welfare state at around 1980 (see section 2.2) with those after the more recent reforms, the changes are most clearly visible in the *financing* dimension. Despite substantial increases of the combined contribution rate to social insurance schemes (see Table 2.1) there is an ongoing shift away from this mode of funding. The share of total social spending that is financed out of contributions has decreased from 65.7 percent in 1991 to less than 60 percent since 2003 (BMAS 2008b: 12). This is largely the result of more tax money being infused into the social insurance schemes. To that end, indirect taxes have been increased (VAT and tobacco tax) or newly introduced (ecology tax). The shift in financing has gone farthest in the public pension scheme. In 2007, payments out of the federal budget (including contributions for childcare credits which currently facilitate a lower rate being levied on earnings) covered about one third of the annual expenditure of this basically contribution-financed pension scheme, whereas in 1992 they delivered only 21 percent. These subsidies amounted to 29 percent of the federal budget in 2007 (Bundesrechnungshof 2007: 90, 95). Tax expenditure on the *Riester-Rente* still comes at the top of these figures.

It is the *raison d'être* of all refinancing measures to push the combined contribution rate to the social insurance schemes permanently below the 40 percent threshold and, in particular, to exempt employers from any further increase of this type of non-wage labor costs. To that end, recent reforms have also dissolved the 'iron principle' of social insurance contributions being equally shared between employers and employees. As of November 2008 a childless worker who puts in the recommended rate of 4 percent of her earnings into a *Riester-Rente* contract is burdened at a rate of 24.8 percent while the employer pays 19.6 percent on top of the gross salary. That is about the same level as in 1994.

What has continued, however, is an opportunistic 'switchyard policy', namely, to raise the contribution rate in a scheme that is in dire need of additional funds and to lower it in another which is under less pressure at the moment (as happened in 2008 when the unemployment insurance contribution was lowered and increased for LTC insurance). Similarly, tax subsidies to social insurance schemes are not stable, even if ostensibly rule-based. They vary according to the constraints of the federal budget and the respective scheme's pressure (or: opportunity) to change its contribution rate.

Access to benefits has changed as well. Although *need* and *citizenship* as criteria of benefit receipt have gained greater weight, no definite trend away from predominant contribution-based entitlements can be observed. However, coverage has become more universal. As mentioned before, LTC insurance obligatorily included all people with health insurance cover right from the beginning. After the latest health care reform (2007) all uninsured people are required to either join the statutory system or to seek private health insurance (depending on individual circumstances). Moreover, mandatory pension provision of some kind for all self-employed who are not yet obliged to join the public or special private schemes is widely supported although not yet concluded (Sachverständigenrat 2006: 263-75). Finally, the introduction of *ALG II* has made all recipients become members of the health care, LTC and pension schemes because contributions out of the federal purse are paid on their behalf. Sufficiently high earnings from employment prior to child birth but not contribution payments are a precondition for receiving an income-related and tax-financed parental leave allowance higher than the minimum amount of 300 euros per month. It makes this benefit type a somewhat strange element within an otherwise citizenship-based system of a family policy that provides flat-rate benefits (and services). Here we find another improvement in benefit access: unremunerated family work – raising children or taking care of frail people – has been acknowledged as equivalent to paid work. It increases pension entitlements and also offers some advantages with regard to eligibility for unemployment benefits and labor market services.

The growing relevance of the needs principle is related to changes in the *structure of cash benefits* based on prior contributions and meant to secure one's acquired status. As Bleses and Seeleib-Kaiser (2004: 92) correctly observe, 'the principle of *publicly* guaranteeing the achieved living standard is on the retreat, while the principle of publicly securing a minimum of existence is increasingly gaining importance'. Such development, amounting to paradigmatic or 'third order' changes (Hall 1993), shows up most clearly in the protection of long-term unemployed and pensioners.

The replacement of the earnings-related (though means-tested) unemployment assistance benefit with a flat-rate benefit (*ALG II*) that entails stricter eligibility criteria broadened the range of unemployed claimants entitled merely to basic security. Among them those who lost out from the change outnumbered the winners (Goebel and Richter 2007). In old-age security the needs principle has not been strengthened directly, apart from survivors' pensions now being tested against all income of the survivor above a threshold. The introduction of the special basic security scheme for the elderly and disabled has led to a higher take-up rate (as intended). In 2007, 2.4 percent of the population aged 65 and older received this type of benefit.

However, future retirees can be expected to be the main *losers* from the combined impact of pension reforms and changes in the labor market, meaning that more elderly will become dependent on means-tested basic security (Hinrichs 2008). The deterioration will arise from the declining standard replacement ratio, the abolition of elements in the benefit formula that once ensured socially adequate pensions, and the permanent pension deductions in case of early retirement now almost fully effective. Therefore, limited earnings inequality and stable employment careers, preconditions for the functioning of social insurance schemes, are becoming ever more relevant.[5] However, rising income inequality thins out the middle class (Grabka and Frick 2008), and even a full-time job no longer insures against poverty. In 2006, 14.3 percent of full-time and 23.4 percent of (covered) part-time workers earned an hourly wage of less than two-thirds of the median (Bosch et al. 2008). The spreading of the *working poor* is only one aspect of increasing labor market flexibility. Furthermore, fewer employment careers corresponding to the *SER* model result from more frequent spells of (long-term) unemployment, (marginal) part-time work or periods of uncovered self-employment. Very often, workers in low-paid or precarious jobs lack the funds to additionally save for a *Riester-Rente* that becomes indispensable to ensure a modest standard of living after retirement.

For the time being, however, poverty among the elderly population is a relatively minor problem compared to the increased number of poor children (BMFSFJ 2008). Unemployment of their parents and single parenthood are the primary reasons. In January 2008, three years after the implementation of the *Hartz IV* act, about 1.9 million children below the age of 15 lived in households of *ALG II* recipients (*Bedarfsgemeinschaften*), i.e. every sixth child received means-tested benefits (Bundesagentur für Arbeit 2008: 35). Nevertheless, families with (small) children are the *winners* of welfare state reconstruction. The expansion of childcare facilities offers (lone) parents the chance to earn a (second) income already after the youngest child's first birthday, and before they benefit from the wage-replacing parental leave allowance. Moreover, the reorientation of family policy may attain more equal educational opportunities for children from disadvantaged families when they are taken care of outside the home already during infancy and after half-day schooling.

2.5   The Bumpy Road out of the Reform Blockade: How was it Possible?

Within the tripartite sequence of reforms, the first period (section 2.3) is the least interesting one because Germany — like other Bismarckian welfare states — responded to new challenges in a 'quasi-natural' way. In order to understand why, after a (second) period of controversial retrenchments and reform blockade, the reconstruction process finally arrived at structural reforms, it is important to consider the consequence of *unification* and the *change in social policy-making*.

The relatively favorable economic and fiscal situation around 1989 nurtured self-confidence to maintain the social insurance state by incremental reforms and to master the social and economic consequences of *unification*. It retarded social learning in Germany at a time when in Sweden, Finland and, even earlier, in the Netherlands, a universally shared perception of an 'acute crisis' helped to reframe social policy issues and to arrive at substantial welfare state reforms (Hinrichs 2002). Unification was a singular mega event but meant no immediate 'crisis', and all collective actors were anxious to avoid or limit repercussions on the established institutional structures that had been extended to East Germany. The weak economic position of the East German *Länder* required continuous net interregional transfers out of public purses (federal, state and social insurance budgets). In 2003 still, the West-East transfers amounted to 3.2 percent of GDP which roughly matched the total public deficit in the same year (Lehmann et al. 2005). Those transfers contributed to the slowdown of overall economic growth in Germany and aggravated the 'problem load' while at the same time they limited the fiscal and political space available to make reforms suitable to mitigate pressures (e.g. a more impressive shift away from contribution towards tax financing).

Exacerbated 'problem load' has also meant a scissor-like growth of transfer recipients and fewer workers contributing to the social security system. The number of gainfully employed people in Germany has hardly changed between 1991 (38.6 million) and 2005 (38.8 million). However, the number of employees liable to social insurance contributions dropped by about 3.8 million due to the increase of self-employed and marginal workers. Additionally making things worse, among them there was a shift towards part-time workers (+ 1.7 million) who contribute less to the schemes' revenues than do full-time employees whose total number decreased by 5.5 million. The declining share of compulsorily insured workers, down from 77.7 percent (1991) to 67.4 percent (2005) of all gainfully employed persons, is partly due to structural shifts (towards service sector jobs) and cyclical reasons, but also stems from policies to attain a more flexible labor market (Bach et al. 2005; BMAS 2008a: Table 2.4 and 2.6A).

The almost continuously increasing 'problem load' was not matched by a corresponding reform intensity until the end of the 1990s. The ideational change that emerged around the mid-1990s had left the Social Democrats largely unaffected and the incoming Red-Green government (autumn 1998) even revoked several reform pieces enacted by its predecessor. After a short-lived economic upswing (1998-2000) and somewhat influenced by the reform concepts of *New Labour* in the UK, Chancellor Schröder and the now dominating 'modernizers' within his party finally adopted the new interpretative patterns (the Greens as well) and got 'in line with the dominant social policy agenda set at the international level' (Palier and Martin 2007a: 535). Consequently, at this 'critical juncture' the course was changed.

Thereby, the government further shifted the *mode of policy-making* that had already begun during the late years of the Christian-Liberal government: it no longer left the initiative to reform and compromise-building to corporatist bodies (of which the pension reform of 1989 was a prime example), but rather, took the lead and partly ignored the social partners. To a large extent, augmented autonomy in relation to the system of interest organizations after the year 2000 and stronger reliance on state power was due to a *generational change* of the elite of 'social politicians'. Previously, politicians and bureaucrats with (long-standing) careers in the labor unions, charities or other associations dominated in the Ministry of Labor and Social Affairs and the responsible committee of the *Bundestag*, and defenders of the traditional social insurance approach also prevailed in advisory councils (like the *Sozialbeirat*). They have been superseded by professional 'party politicians', being less committed to traditional values, but rather, more concerned with electoral considerations and economic liberalism (Trampusch 2005; Hassel and Trampusch 2006).

'Government by commission' was another feature of social policy-making after the year 2000 and also meant to take agenda-setting out of the hands of (remaining) 'old politics' actors. The preparation of concrete reforms was delegated to commissions (largely staffed with 'friendly experts') for the sake of mobilizing consensus and relieving the government from the task of gaining legitimacy (Czada 2004). However, since 1999 reform efforts of the Red-Green government were constrained by an adverse majority in the *Bundesrat* that, among others, foreclosed a more comprehensive health care reform in the year 2000. Thus, it was not before 2001 that an informal consensus between the government and the Christian Democrats re-emerged on reforms that involved no principled dissent and of which the pension reform of 2001 was the first case (see section 2.3).

Because the German political system is susceptible to both lasting blockades and sudden reform leaps, it can be concluded that all milestones in changing the social policy arrangement only came about when, on a certain issue, competition between the two large political parties was suspended and the respective party in opposition was prepared to negotiate a compromise (the introduction of LTC insurance, health care reforms 1993 and 2003, the *Hartz* reforms) *or* a 'tacit consensus' emerged. The pension reforms of 2001 and 2004 were based on such a 'tacit consensus' and meant not to utilize the veto potential of the *Bundesrat* but nevertheless attaining concessions from the government. In all these cases, key social actors (health care providers and labor unions) hardly had a chance to significantly influence or even obstruct the legislation process or were fobbed off with symbolic concessions (like the labor unions at the final stage of the 'Riester' reform in 2001 – see Hinrichs 2005). The results of the premature federal elections of 2005 left hardly any other option but to form an unloved 'Grand Coalition' government. This constellation largely neutralizes all veto powers (although individual state governments may still exert 'voice') but shifts conflicts about social policy change into the government itself where party competition between the CDU/CSU and the SPD is not put to rest.

2.6 Conclusion

The analysis in the preceding sections has shown that in a less stable environment the contribution and transfer-heavy German welfare state increasingly came under pressure. At the same time, there was a limited, but flexible adjustment to internal and external challenges. The micro-institutional contexts of social insurance schemes were less an impediment to reform than were macro-institutions. Germany's specific political structures allow for determined reform steps only if an overt or tacit consensus between the two large political parties can be brought about. Most significant structural reforms, following from paradigmatic changes, happened after the year 2000 and produced corresponding effects for citizens financing the welfare state or receiving social benefits.

The institutional redirection of the German social insurance state has not followed a coherent design for a 'new welfare state'. Nevertheless, the contours of a still unfinished 'post-Bismarckian' welfare state arrangement – a hybrid of the Anglo-Saxon and the Scandinavian model – are recognizable. Reduced levels of income security through wage earner schemes, accompanied by demands for self-responsibility and more private provision, stronger reliance on means-tested benefits, and stricter activation measures signify the turn towards the Liberal model. Activation is also a central trait of the Scandinavian policy design, but more important reform trends related to that model are increased tax-financing (the prime direction of reform efforts) and more spending on family-oriented services. Therefore, transformation of the 'Bismarckian' welfare state in Germany may come down to a zero-sum situation (at best): what families gain as parents they lose as wage earners (higher social insurance contributions and expenses on private provision) or when out of waged work, i.e. being unemployed or of old age.

While appreciating the expansion of family policy, the public strongly disliked the reform of labor market policy, perceived as a threat not only by the currently unemployed but also by the (lower) middle classes. Thus, the legislation of the high-profile *Hartz* reforms came at a high *political* price for the Social Democrats. A flat-rate benefit for long-term unemployed was disapproved by a large majority within the population because it violated established notions of social justice (Krömmelbein et al. 2007: 123-4, 145-6, 176), and the Red-Green government was unable to communicate that the reform was not exclusively a 'cut' of just entitlements, accompanied by harsher sanctions. Additionally, *Hartz IV* was enacted when there were only scant prospects for an improved labor market situation (Eichhorst and Sesselmeier 2007). The implementation was accompanied by mass protests (foremost in East Germany), and it contributed to several defeats for the Social Democrats in subsequent state elections, eventually leading to premature federal elections in September 2005. Numerous left-wingers turned away from the party, and the weakly organized splinter group (*WASG*) joined forces with the (mainly East German) Left Socialists (*PDS*). Under the label *Die Linke*, they gained 8.7 percent of the votes in 2005 and attained a foothold in West Germany.

The various reforms put through during the 2002-2005 legislature and active participation in enacting a higher standard retirement age in 2007 have also alienated the traditional allies, the labor unions and the Social Democrats. Some unions or, at least, strong internal fractions openly sympathize with the party *Die Linke*. Thus, in view of this no longer negligible radical Left party and a dissatisfied rank and file, the Social Democrats were first to pronounce the 'end of impositions'. Within the 'Grand Coalition' government they successfully pressed for another extension of the eligibility period for *ALG I* benefits. As of January 2008, unemployed of age 58 and older are entitled to a maximum duration of 24 months (instead of 18). Moreover, in order not to further exasperate the pensioners, both government parties agreed not to apply the legally fixed adjustment formula in 2008 and 2009, but rather, to arbitrarily raise public pensions by (a still meager) 1.1 percent in July 2008, instead of 0.46 percent according to the formula. It remains to be seen whether the 'end of impositions' in 2007 will mark the start of a *fourth period* in a continuing sequence. After the economic upswing and the decline of unemployment figures suddenly came to a halt in fall 2008, welfare state reform also reached a standstill – at least until the next federal elections in fall 2009.

3 The Dualizations of the French Welfare System

Bruno Palier

3.1 Introduction[1]

The main components of the French welfare system clearly reflect the Bismarckian tradition of social insurance. From 1945 to the late 1970s, social policies expanded as one of the important parts of the Keynesian compromises that underpinned the *'Trente Glorieuses'*. Social spending was seen as favoring economic growth and employment, social insurance transfers as consolidating social integration and (occupational) solidarity, and welfare state institutions as supporting social peace. Subsequently, however, the economic, social and political functions of the social protection systems have been progressively undermined. After a long period of crisis and resistance throughout the 1970s and 1980s, French social programs are since then being progressively reformed to adapt to the new economic and social environment. As this chapter will show, though, this adaptation is only partial, since it has been implemented through a dualistic strategy of reform. This has divided French welfare and society into two worlds: those still insured by an increasingly contributory complex of public and private insurances, and those dependent on a new tier of basic social protection.

This chapter will first recall the content of post-war compromises on which French social protection was based. It will then analyze the four different phases of the French welfare reform trajectory, focusing on the intellectual, institutional and political mechanisms through which the French welfare system is being progressively transformed. The conclusion will map out the main characteristics of the new social policy institutions and paradigm of the French welfare system.

3.2 The Institutional Arrangements Reflecting the Post-War Compromises

In 1944, the *'Union nationale'* French government had the ambition of generalizing social protection and achieving universal and uniform coverage. At the time, however, there was a strong distrust of state solutions in social protection among groups who already had access to specific social insurance schemes, within the workers' movement and even from some senior civil servants who held corporatist views, including Pierre Laroque, the so-called 'founding father' of the French *Sécurité sociale* (Merrien 1990). It was therefore decided to generalize social protection within an employment-related social insurance framework rather than a universal state-run system, an uneasy compromise between Beveridgean goals and Bismarckian means. As the following overview shows, this compromise led to a welfare regime that almost epitomizes the typical institutional characteristics of Bismarckian welfare systems: employment-related entitlement, earnings-related benefits, a system focused on the needs of the male breadwinner, contribution-financing and decentralized control.

Entitlement: Social Rights for Workers and their Families
The main goal of the founders of the French social security system in the mid-1940s was the economic and social integration of the working class as a means of preventing any revolutionary movement at a time when the Communist Party was mobilizing around 25 percent of the popular vote in general elections. They therefore first developed a social insurance system for dependent workers in the private sector (the *'régime général de la Sécurité sociale'*), and in the following years social protection was expanded through the multiplication of similar but distinct and specific schemes (*'régimes'*) for other occupational groups. When a law declaring the generalization of social security to the whole population was passed in 1978, social rights were based on occupational status and acquired through the payment of social contributions, with indirect social rights given to family members (*'ayant-droits'*) of the (mainly male) worker.

Benefits: Contributory Benefits Aimed at Income Maintenance
The main goal of the system was to guarantee income security for workers (*'garantir la sécurité du lendemain'*: guaranteeing tomorrow's income), an aim realized through cash benefits proportional to former income. In the early 1980s contributory cash benefits represented 70 percent of all

French social expenditure (IRES 1983). Benefits delivered by *la Sécurité sociale* were limited by a ceiling equivalent to roughly 133 percent of the average wage in pensions, and there was a co-payment in health insurance (called '*ticket modérateur*'). In order to improve its coverage, the first tier social security schemes were complemented by complementary private but non-profit pensions ('*retraites complémentaires*') and health insurances ('*mutuelles*').

A worker having worked full-time for the required number of years (37.5 since 1971) could expect a pension worth 50 percent of the average best 10 years of income, plus some 25 percent from complementary pension schemes. Unemployment benefits were raised to quite generous levels in 1979, when 50 percent of the insured unemployed could receive 90 percent of their former wage for one year (Palier 2005a). In health care, the main concern was to replace the income lost during sickness (sick pay represented 60 percent of health expenditure in the early 1950s), and it was chosen to reimburse the cost of treatment instead of providing public health care. This allowed people to choose their doctors freely, pay them directly and afterwards be reimbursed by their health insurance fund and, for some, by their *mutuelles* for the co-payment.

Financing: Social Contribution as a 'Deferred Wage'

From the outset, the creators of the French social protection system wanted it to be as independent as possible from the state, and thus financed it only through specific social contributions. General (income) taxes have always played a marginal role in the financing of social insurance, and as early as the 1950s the social partners accused the state of unduly burdening the system by asking social insurance funds to pay for non-contributory benefits.[2] On the other hand, the social partners have always wanted to avoid the 'fiscalization' of social insurance, since it would have meant questioning their role as managers of the social insurance funds (Palier 2005a: chapter 3).

In 1982, 82.5 percent of social expenditure was financed through social contribution, which represented 45 percent of the gross wage of workers. These social contributions are split into employees' social contribution (20 percent of all social contributions) and employers' social contribution (80 percent) (IRES 1983). The French conception is that social benefits are earned through the payment of social contribution and benefits have long been called a 'deferred wage'. Social rights obtained through work are as result extremely legitimate: people work and pay for their own social security. Benefits are considered as 'acquired rights' in a double sense:

acquired thanks to workers' mobilizations throughout history (*'acquis so-ciaux'*)[3], and through individuals' payment of social contributions (i.e. the 'equivalence principle').

Organization and Governance: A Fragmented Corporatist System

The French system is divided into a number of different programs (*'branches'*). The *'régime général'*, which covers the dependent workers of the private sector in trade and industry (60 percent of the working population), comprises four branches: health care, old age, family and financing. In order to complement its benefits, numerous complementary private collective insurances have developed, such as the complementary pension funds for the salaried workers of the private sectors[4], which became compulsory in 1972, and *mutuelles*, complementary health insurance funds. The latter are not compulsory, but by 1980 75 percent of the French population was covered by one (IRES 1983). In 1958, unemployment insurance was negotiated as a national level collective agreement and thereafter managed by the social partners with no state intervention. Many other social insurance schemes have been created alongside the *régime général*, for different occupational groups. In 1980, there were 19 different health care schemes, 600 first tier old-age insurance funds, more than 6000 complementary pension schemes, and thousands of *mutuelles* (IRES 1983). Only family allowances (*'caisses d'allocation familiale'*) and unemployment insurance (UNEDIC – *Union nationale pour l'emploi dans l'industrie et le commerce*) cover the whole population within one scheme.

French social security schemes are made up of different funds (*'Caisses'*) organized at national, regional and local levels. Their staff is neither paid by the state nor is it under its authority. Until the mid-1990s each fund was headed by a governing board comprising representatives of employers and employees, with a chairman elected from their ranks, and a director of the Fund, who was appointed by the governing board in liaison with the Ministry of Social Affairs. The system was supposed to be managed by those who pay for it and have an interest in it, subject to only limited control by the state. In fact, the state has always decided the level of benefits and contributions for compulsory health insurance and for first tier old-age insurance; only in the complementary pension schemes and unemployment insurance do the social partners really decide (see also Ebbinghaus, this volume).

The participation of workers' representatives in the management of the social protection system is called *'la démocratie sociale'*, and aims to guarantee the social and political integration of the workers within the society as well as the collaboration between workers and employers, hence social peace (Merrien 1990; Castel 1995). French unions have compensated their increasing weakness in the realm of production – unionization in France has become the lowest among the developed countries – by the material and symbolic resources provided by their managerial role within the social protection system (Jobert 1991).

One of the most important of these resources was the control of staff working for insurance funds. Responsibilities for staffing had long been devolved to the governing boards of the funds and belonging to the trade union that was chairing the fund became a criterion to be hired. The funds often provided pseudojobs and actual wages for people actually working for the trade unions (Catrice-Lorey 1995; Duclos and Mériaux 1997; Cour des Comptes: various years, notably 1990 and 2000). Other resources were more symbolic: the trade unions came to be seen as the defenders of the system and of the *acquis sociaux* associated with them in the eyes of the French population.

During the *Trente Glorieuses*, the French social protection system was seen as favoring economic growth and employment, promoting social progress and social integration, aiding the political legitimization of social order and as sustaining social peace. Step by step, these positive connections between the social protection system and the economy, society and the polity have been questioned and transformed.

3.3 The French Reform Trajectory

As in most of its Bismarckian neighbors, the French welfare reform trajectory comprised four main sequences. Governments first responded to recurrent social security deficits with increases in social contribution rates. Meanwhile, various plans for industrial restructuring, also partly financed by social contributions, were launched. In the context of intensified European constraints in the early 1990s, difficult and contested retrenchment was attempted in unemployment, old-age and sickness insurances (2nd sequence). But faced with the increasing inadequacy of the French social insurances in the new economic and social context, governments also launched more institutional reforms that created new benefits, new sources of funding and new governance rules (3rd sequence). The cumulative effect of the three previous waves of reform led to a fourth sequence, starting in 2001, which implemented activation in (un)employment policies, multi-pillarization of pensions and a restructuring of the French health care system. The main components of these four sequences are summarized in table 3.1.

Plans for Rescuing the System

With the economic crisis of the 1970s, the social protection system encountered a vicious combination of declining resources and spiraling costs. These resulted in huge and recurrent deficits in the social protection budget, the famous '*trou de la Sécu*'. Furthermore, these deficits were no longer perceived as temporary ones that could be reabsorbed through reflationary measures. At the turn of the 1980s, two French governments – Jacques Chirac's in 1974-76 and Pierre Mauroy's in 1981-82 – learned the hard way that the traditional Keynesian chain was broken. In both cases, these governments raised social benefits in order to boost private consumption and economic activity, and both gained only larger public deficits, a negative trade balance, inflation and increases in unemployment and taxation. Henceforth the Keynesian use of social benefits was delegitimized for governments of both Left and Right.

Subsequent governments thus all share the idea that the social security deficits had to be balanced. However, of the two solutions available – increasing resources or cutting expenses – only one was seriously considered during the 1970s and the 1980s. For at least 15 years, governments avoided major retrenchments and preferred to increase social contributions to balance the social security deficit. Instead of developing an accusatory rhetoric against the welfare system that would have provoked the whole population and trade unions, they acknowledged the importance of the *Sécurité sociale*, while at the same time underlining the dangers of its current situation and presenting measures to restore its viability.

From 1975 to 1995, unless an election was imminent, each announcement of a deficit in *Sécurité sociale* was followed by the presentation of a '*plan de redressement des comptes de la Sécurité sociale*' (i.e. program for balancing the social insurance system's budget[5]). These plans typically consisted of increases in contributions paid by employees and some limited economizing measures, mainly in health, where the level of reimbursement of health care expenditure was lowered.[6] However, during the same period, the rates of all the contributory benefits were increased or at best stabilized. Social benefits were perceived as a good buffer against the toughest social consequences of the crisis (Levy 2005). Consequently, social expenditure continued to increase, rapidly until the mid-1980s, but more slowly ever since. The proportion of social protection expenditure in GDP grew from 19.4 percent in 1974 to 27.3 percent in 1985 and 27.75 percent in 1992.[7] Social contributions increased from less than 20 percent of French GDP in 1978 to almost 23 percent by 1985, and have stabilized at that level ever since. While social contributions amounted to 45 percent of gross wage in the early 1980s, in 1996, they amounted to more than 60 percent for a wage above 1.3 times the minimum wage (Palier 2005a).

In order to avoid conflict with social partners and with the population, governments applied 'good old recipes' and were thus able to maintain a high level of social protection in a period of crisis. This response was also in line with the labor shedding strategy adopted at this time in France, as in other Continental European countries (Esping-Andersen 1996a). Indeed, during the 1980s governments used social expenditure to soften the hardest social consequences of industrial restructuring and mass redundancies that followed, a strategy called 'le traitement social du chômage' (the social treatment of unemployment). These policies were designed to remove the oldest workers from the labor market by lowering the legal age for retirement (from 65 to 60 in 1981) and encouraging early retirement. 84,000 people retired early in 1975; 159,000 in 1979; 317,000 in 1981 and 705,000 in 1983 (Bichot 1997: 132).

Mastering Social Expenditure: The First Attempts at Retrenchment

In the 1990s, this strategy became increasingly problematic in the new European environment, characterized by the creation of the single currency and the imposition of the Maastricht criteria. The single market increased competition between European firms, in which labor cost played an important role. French employers increasingly focused the debate on the need to stop the increase in social contributions, hence pushing towards a diminution of social benefits. After 1992/1993, retrenching social expenditure was included in the government strategy of reducing public deficits in order to meet the Maastricht criteria. This new European context led to reforms in unemployment insurance in 1992, old-age insurance in 1993 and health care in 1995. These reforms were all made 'in the name of European constraints', but were also possible thanks to one trade union, the CFDT (*Confédération Française Démocratique du Travail*), who chose a reformist position and new alliances with the employers' movement in order to outmaneuver its two main competitors, the CGT and FO (*Confédération générale du Travail* and *Force Ouvrière*).

The unemployment insurance system was reformed in 1992 through an agreement between the CFDT and the employers' association. The reform replaced all existing unemployment insurance benefits with a new '*Allocation Unique Dégressive*' (AUD), payable only for a limited period of time, depending on the contribution record. The amount of this benefit was to decrease with time, and entitlement was to expire eventually after 30 months. Afterwards, unemployed people had to rely on tax-financed income-tested benefits. The level and the volume of unemployment benefits started to fall after 1992, the reduction being larger for the means-tested benefits than for AUD (Daniel and Tuchszirer 1999).

In 1993, the Balladur government reformed the first tier pension scheme, covering private sector employees (*régime général*). The indexation of benefits was based on prices, as opposed to earnings, initially for a five-year period but has since been extended indefinitely. The qualifying period for a full pension was extended from 37.5 to 40 years, and the period over which the reference salary was calculated from the best 10 years to the best 25. These changes were introduced gradually over a 10-year transition period. Surprisingly, this reform did not provoke very much opposition. This was possible because the reform was limited to the private sector general scheme and because of the introduction of a package that 'traded' benefit cuts against the tax financing of non-contributory benefits (Bonoli 1997). In exchange for the trade unions' acceptance of the reform, the government created a '*Fonds de solidarité vieillesse*' for the funding of non-contributory benefits. The state thereby agreed to pay for the 'undue charges' and thus reassured the social partners of the continuity of PAYG old-age insurance schemes. In 1995, the new prime minister Alain Juppé tried to impose the same conditions on public sector employees without negotiation, but had to withdraw this measure in the face of massive strikes (Bonoli 1997).

In the health sector, the numerous plans implemented during the late 1970s and the 1980s were not successful in limiting the unstoppable growth in demand for health care. They could only increase the co-payment paid by the patients, which for many was reimbursed afterwards by the *mutuelles*. After 1990, governments decided to force the medical professions, the health insurance funds and the state to elaborate a '*convention médicale*' (medical care agreement) to help control the evolution of expenditure by setting a provisional target for the evolution of the health care spending, practitioners' remuneration and additional expenses. Between 1990 and 1995, though, doctors did not sign any of the proposed convention and the targets set for other paramedical professions were not met. In 1995, in his extensive reform of social security, Juppé forced the social partners to sign an agreement by threatening state intervention. The Juppé plan also empowered the state within the health care system by the creation of many new state-headed agencies. Finally, the management of health care funds was reformed, giving more power to the director and less to the president (representing the social partners). Unlike Juppé's pension plans, all these measures were maintained and implemented; however this was not sufficient to fundamentally check the increase in health expenditure (Hassenteufel and Palier 2007).

The Politics of First Retrenchments

All these reforms shared some features that are related to the specific institutional settings of welfare systems based on social insurance. First, the retrenchment reforms were not presented as a means to dismantle the welfare system, but rather to preserve or consolidate it. Since the benefits to be retrenched are extremely legitimate, these reforms were introduced in the name of European constraints, but were also claimed to be necessary to restore the system's viability. Second, the reform proposals were put together in such a way that the social partners could accept them. As illustrated in 1995, the social partners have the power to block reforms they do not agree with. The acceptance by the social partners of reductions in benefits relied on a *quid pro quo* (Bonoli 1997) based on the distinction between what should be financed through contribution and what should be financed through taxation. The government committed to paying for the '*charges indues*' through the financing of non-contributory benefits – flat-rate social minima for the elderly, the handicapped, the long-term unemployed; and contribution credits for periods out of work because of unemployment or child rearing – in exchange for a reduction of social insurance benefits (Bonoli and Palier 1996). Finally, for old-age and unemployment insurances, these reforms reduced the level of protection by the strengthening of the link between the amount of contribution and the volume of the benefits. This of course relied on the already existing logic of these social insurance schemes.

These changes were based on new instruments (changes in calculation rules, creation of new state subsidies, etc.), but were perceived as preserving the very nature of social insurance, and in some ways even as reinforcing it. They did not really challenge the principles of social insurance and can be considered 'second order changes' (Hall 1993). However, since these reforms diminished the coverage and generosity of social insurance, ever more space was created for the development of new benefits, whether on top of compulsory social insurance, or 'beneath' it, for those who lost (or never gained) their rights to social insurance. As analyzed in the next section, these developments led to criticism of social insurance and to the emergence of a new world of welfare in France.

The Institutional Reforms: New Benefits, New Financing, New Distribution of Power

The reforms presented above had spillover effects. The plans to balance the social security budget increased the level of social contributions, thus re-enforcing economic difficulties. Retrenchment measures meant less generous benefits and more people left out, contributing to social exclusion. All these reforms were difficult to implement and accompanied by demonstrations and strikes, putting an end to social peace. In the 1990s, new diagnoses of the difficulties began to gain popularity among experts, politicians and even trade unionists, which implied that the system was not a victim of the crises, but part of the causes of France's social, economic and political difficulties.

With these new diagnoses, the very characteristics of the system came to be seen as the cause of these difficulties, and all the bases of the post-war compromise were undermined: protecting workers no longer supports social integration, but leads to social exclusion; the system no longer contributes to economic growth, but impedes it through its financing mechanisms; *démocratie sociale* no longer sustains social peace, but allows demonstrations and blocks reform. These new analyses underpinned a change in the political discourses and agendas of all governments during the 1990s: from rescuing the *Sécurité sociale*, the aim became to transform it. This has been done through incremental institutional reforms that are often neglected in analysis of welfare retrenchments. These reforms aimed to change the politics of social protection, and although often marginal in the beginning their importance has grown more visible over time (Bonoli and Palier 1998). In the following, the four most important aspects of these reforms are analyzed. As will be seen, the reforms changed core aspects (eligibility, benefits, financing, management) of the Bismarckian institutional structure of the French welfare regime.

The Social Crisis of the French Welfare System: The Problem of Social Exclusion

Since the late 1970s, France has seen a considerable increase in unemployment. Unemployment rose from 4.1 percent of the active population in 1974 to 10.5 percent in 1987, fell slightly in the late 1980s, but then rose again to 12.5 percent by 1997. It fluctuated again but has decreased ever since, until recently (see Hemerijck and Eichhorst, this volume). Long-term unemployment also increased, supporting the idea that France had high structural unemployment. In 1974, 16.9 percent of the unemployed were jobless for more than one year, 2.5 percent for more than two years. These proportions had risen to 42.7 and 21.0 percent by 1985. The average length of unemployment was 7.6 months in 1974, 15 months in 1985, and 16 months in 1998 (*L'état de la France* 2000-2001).

The social insurance system set up in 1945 was not designed for mass unemployment. This predominantly contributory system is especially unable to deal with those who have never been involved in the labor market (young people) or who have been removed from it for a long period (long-term unemployed), because they have not contributed to social insurance, or because they are not contributing any more. Moreover, because of the 1992 reform of unemployment insurance, more and more unemployed could no longer rely on unemployment insurance. The number of 'excluded' people kept increasing during the 1980s, and this became one of the most pressing social issues. During the 1980s, attention was drawn to 'new poverty' by the media and groups from civil society, who denounced the incapacity of socialist governments to face the new social problems. The 1987 Wresinski report[8], '*Grande pauvreté et précarité économique et sociale*' suggested that some 400,000 people were living in France without social protection.

In this context, the social protection system could be accused of reinforcing the mechanisms of social exclusion, because of the gap between 'insiders' included in the labor market and who could rely on the insurance system, and 'outsiders' who obtained a much lower level of protection despite needing it most. The issue finally entered the political agenda, leading to the introduction of 'insertion policies' to fight social exclusion. Social exclusion was framed as a problem of lack of support rather than of lack of work, and required a response in term of new social rights, rather than labor market reform (Paugam 1993).

New Benefits

In order to cope with new social problems that social insurance was unable to deal with, governments developed new social policy instruments, with reference to new social policy goals. Faced with growing numbers of jobless, youth or long-term unemployed and single parents, new benefits were created or formerly marginal benefits developed (Palier 2005a: chapter 6). The creation of the RMI (*Revenu Minimum d'Insertion*) is the most important of these new social benefits. This new non-contributory scheme, meant for those having no or a very low income, was introduced in December 1988. Its main features are the guarantee of a minimum level of resources to anyone aged 25 or over, taking the form of a means-tested differential benefit. In addition, the RMI has a re-insertion dimension, in the form of a contract between the recipient and 'society'. Through a contract signed between them and a social worker, recipients must commit themselves to take part in a re-insertion program, which can entail either job seeking, vocational training or activities designed to enhance the recipient's social autonomy. When it was created, this new benefit was supposed to be delivered between 300,000 to 400,000 people. Since the late 1990s, more than one million people receive the RMI (1.1 million in 1992, 1.2 million in 2008). Including spouses and children of recipients, 3.5 percent of the French population is involved (DREES, various years).

Besides the RMI, France now has eight other social minimum incomes, and more than 10 percent of the French population is currently receiving one of these (Palier 2005a). The use of this new repertoire of social policy has also been extended to health care. In 2000, a new income-tested benefit was created to provide the poorest with free access to health care (*Couverture Maladie Universelle*, CMU) and to provide free complementary health insurance for those who could not pay for complementary health care (*CMU Complémentaire*).

The development of benefits targeted at poverty alleviation has gradually encouraged an accompanying logic that was entirely absent from the French social protection system previously. In Liberal welfare states, these benefits are traditionally accused of creating a dependency culture and generating unemployment traps. By the late 1990s more and more analyses in France emphasized that people receiving social minima, especially the RMI, would lose money and social advantages if they took a part-time job paid at minimum wage level. In response, people receiving RMI who found a job were first allowed to receive both the RMI and a very low wage for a short period, so that they did not lose out when taking a job. In 2001, in order to augment the incentives to return to work, the Jospin government created a tax credit called *'Prime pour l'emploi'*, which is a negative income tax for low-paid workers. In the same vein, in 2003 the Raffarin government tried to transform the RMI into RMA (*Revenu Minimum d'Activité*), an in-work benefit for those having received the RMI for two years aimed at increasing incentives to work. This new scheme performed poorly, though, and in 2009 was replaced by a new scheme, *Revenu de Solidarité Active* (RSA), which provides social contribution exemptions to employers hiring RMI beneficiaries or long-term unemployed, and guarantees a permanent negative income tax to the new low-wage workers so that they get at least 200 euros more than what the RMI would have provided them with. Both a totally new rhetoric (unemployment trap, work disincentive) and a totally new type of social policy instrument (in-work benefit such as RSA) have thus been imported during the development of the world of poverty alleviation in France.

Changes in the Financing of the French Welfare System

Attempts to render the system more 'employment friendly' were also behind shifts in the financing of the system. Until 1996, 80 percent of social protection was financed through employment related contributions and as seen above the weight of social contribution has been increased during the 1980s. But during the 1990s, the system was increasingly assumed to be producing unemployment and to be economically unsustainable. The employers' representatives, as well as more and more economists, criticized the excessively high level of social contributions in France, especially at the lower end of the salary scale. These groups claimed that in the European context, firms could simply not afford such a high level of social contributions (Palier 2005a: chapter 7).

Governments started to focus on this issue, and during the 1990s, lowering the level of social contribution became the main employment policy in France. Measures were first targeted on contracts for some particularly disadvantaged groups, such as the long-term and youth unemployed, or on small companies, which were considered to be the most affected by the relatively high cost of unskilled labor. But in 1993, with the Balladur *'plan quiquennal pour l'emploi'*, all wages below 1.3 times the minimum wage were partly exempted of social contributions (DARES 1996). This new strategy contributed to the push for retrenchment measures, since the other solution to deficits, i.e. increasing social contributions, was now perceived as damaging economic efficiency and job creation.

In order to generalize the movement to lower labor costs, governments have also tried progressively to replace some contributions with taxation. A new tax, originally aimed at replacing the social contribution financing non-contributory benefits, was created in 1990: the *Contribution Sociale Généralisée* (CSG). Unlike social insurance contributions, the CSG is levied on all types of personal incomes, including wages (even the lowest ones), but also extending to capital revenues and welfare benefits. Unlike income tax in France, CSG is strictly proportional and earmarked for non-contributory welfare programs. In the early 1990s, the CSG appeared to play a marginal role, and when it was introduced, it was levied at only 1.1 percent of all incomes. However, in 1993 the Balladur government increased the CSG to 2.4 percent of incomes. The 1995 Juppé plan set it at 3.4 percent and since 1998 the rate is now 7.5 percent, replacing most of the health care contributions paid by employees. As of the early 2000s, the CSG provides more than 20 percent of all social protection resources and represents 35 percent of the health care system's resources (Palier 2005a: chapter 7).

The introduction of this earmarked tax enabled a shift in the financing structure of the system towards more state taxation. This new instrument has two main consequences, which entail a partial change in the logic of the system. First, since financing does not come only from the working population, the CSG breaks the link between employment and entitlement. Access to CSG-financed benefits cannot be limited to any particular section of society. The shift in financing has thus created the conditions for the establishment of citizenship-based social rights, especially in health care. Second, the shift leaves the social partners with less legitimacy to participate in the decision-making and management of social provision. In this respect the shift towards taxation constitutes a pressure for a transfer of control from the social partners to the state, an evolution that is in line with other important political changes that have occurred since the mid-1990s, as shown below.

A New Distribution of Power

During the 1990s, the management arrangement of the French social insurances started to be increasingly criticized. In 1945, the management of the social insurance system was given to the social partners to avoid bureaucratization and the subordination of social policy to purely budgetary considerations. As budgetary control became an important issue during the 1980s, the devolved management of social insurance also became problematic: experts and civil servants accused the social partners of having hijacked the social security funds, of abusing their position within the system at the expense of the common good and of not taking responsibility for containing costs (Bonoli and Palier 1996). As seen above, the strongest opposition to retrenchment was not through political confrontation, but through social and trade union mobilization. If they wanted to implement any change, governments had to take the unions' views into account, limiting the scope for reform. Within the governmental sphere, the perception developed that the state would be better at containing the expenditure increase (Bonoli and Palier 1996).

Reforms have been gradually implemented in order to empower the state within the system at the expense of the social partners, mainly since the Juppé Plan of 1995. Next to the new agencies and power given to state civil servants, the most important reform was the vote in February 1996 of a constitutional amendment obliging the Parliament to vote every year on a social security budget. For the first time in France, Parliament is taking part in the debate on the *Sécurité sociale* budget, which before was not seen as being part of the state budget. The use of the new parliamentary competence helps the government to control the social policy agenda. Instead of always having to legitimize their intervention in a realm under the purview of labor and employers, they are now able to plan adaptation measures regularly, especially relating to cost containment. This new instrument also introduces a new logic of intervention. Instead of trying to find resources to finance social expenditure driven by insured persons' demand, the vote of a *loi de financement de la Sécurité sociale* implies that a limited budget should be allocated for social expenditure. Since most of the social benefits are still contributory, it is impossible to define a limited budget completely *a priori*, but governments are entering this new logic and Parliament has since then voted new instruments aimed at this purpose, such as limited global budgets for the hospitals and for ambulatory doctors, ceilings and growth limits for social expenditure.

The Politics of Institutional Reforms

Contrary to the way some important policy changes have been implemented in other countries or fields (Hall 1986; 1993), these institutional reforms were implemented in a very ambiguous and incremental way in France. Analysis of the politics of such reforms shows similarities between the different political processes (Palier 2005b). First, it is impossible to claim that one specific group of actors has been the main, unique and causal agent of all these changes. Changing a welfare system as legitimate as the French necessitates 'carrying' almost all the actors involved in social policies in the reform process. Led by a coalition of high civil servants sharing new analyses and perspectives on welfare, governments, employers and some trade unions have participated in these reforms. Among the trade unions, the CFDT again played an important role, while FO and the CGT remained in a very defensive position, opposing most reform proposals. The CFDT was one of the most active proponents of re-insertion policies, and above all of CSG (and afterwards of 35 working hours and activation policies). During the 1980s, the CFDT had changed its political and strategic position, leaving calls for '*autogestion*' and adopting a 'responsible' and 'cooperative' approach to social policy issues. Outside the management of social insurance funds since 1967, the CFDT's changed economic and social position has allowed this union to gain control of important responsibilities over social insurance funds, in alliance with the employers and at the expense of FO (Palier 2005a: chapter 8).

Second, all of these changes have been based on the collective acknowledgment of past policy failures. The development of each new measure started with the politicization of a 'new social problem', which was interpreted as resulting from a failure of past policies: social exclusion, which social insurance is unable to deal with and can even reinforce; low-skilled unemployment, due to the weight of social contributions and a passive unemployment compensation system; and the inability of the welfare system to be changed because of the blurred assignment of responsibilities within the systems. These shared diagnoses of policy failure were essential for gathering people on a new policy track. As long as the problem was not perceived in the same way, it was difficult to change the path of action. Acknowledgments of failures led to a re-interpretation of existing social and economic difficulties, and in the new explanations for the existing problems, the position of the social insurance system shifted from one of a victim to that of a villain. It took quite a long time before all actors came to share similar diagnoses of the problems, a process facilitated by the multiplication of commissions and reports, where the partners involved progressively shared the same approaches.

Third, although a large majority of the actors concerned about social protection problems agreed with the new structural measures (RMI, CMU, CSG, etc.) they did so for reasons that were often very different and sometimes contradictory. Many reforms were implemented in the name of the distinction between insurance and assistance (called 'national solidarity' in French). However, trade unions wanted this rationalization in order to preserve their realm of social insurance, whereas governments and civil servants expected more responsibilities in social protection through these changes, at the expenses of social partners. Similarly, the RMI was seen by the Left as a means to provide money and social help through the contract, while the Right supported it as a new kind of conditional benefit. The Left supported the CSG because it was a fairer tax than social contribution for the employees, whereas the Right saw it as a means to lower social charges for the employers; civil servants supported CSG because it increased state control over social expenditure, while the employers and the CFDT argued that it would allow the social partners to preserve the 'purity' of social insurance, non-contributory benefits being financed by taxes. An important element for the acceptance of a new measure thus seems to be its capacity to aggregate different – and even contradictory – interests, based on contrasting interpretations of the consequences of implementing the new instrument. Structural changes in social policies were achieved through 'ambiguous agreement' on new measures, rather than via a clear ideological orientation (Palier 2005b).

Finally, these types of change were introduced at the margins and gradually extended, their expansion often leading to a change of their meaning within the system. They were first introduced to complement the system, but they gradually became the base for a new pillar in the social protection system. The introduction of new measures at the margins facilitated their acceptance by the major defenders of the core system, either because they did not feel concerned by them (the RMI was not for the salaried workers that trade unions defend), because they were targeted at those least able to protest (the low-skilled were the first to have their income exempted from social contributions, they were also the first to be targeted by activation policies) or because they believed that these new measures would help them to defend the very nature of social insurance (tax financing of non-contributory benefits). However, the French experience shows that the growth of initially marginal new measures can lead to a paradigmatic change for the whole system.

Changing the Structures of the French Welfare System

The accumulation of the reforms analyzed in the previous sections created the conditions for a series of structural reforms that have been implemented in the French social protection system since the early 2000s.

From Passive to Active Labor Market Policies

The problem of unemployment has been understood and dealt with in two different ways in France since the late 1970s. In the 1980s and early 1990s it was perceived as an unavoidable consequence of new economic policies and thus treated passively, especially through the development of minimum income benefits, early retirement schemes and *traitement social du chômage*. In the early 1990s, governments started to change their policies to improve job creation and to develop 'active labor market policies'. As we have seen, governments started to reduce insurance contributions on low-paid work. After 1998, and as a consequence of the debates and changes associated with the insertion policies (see above), the Jospin government introduced explicit 'make-work-pay' strategies to reduce the risk of unemployment traps for socially excluded people. The most important measure is the *prime pour l'emploi* (PPE). In 2000, some of the social partners (mainly employers and CFDT, with fierce opposition by CGT and FO) signed a new agreement reforming the unemployment insurance, eliminating the degressivity of the unemployment insurance benefit (ex AUD) but creating a new individualized contract to ensure that each jobseeker is accompanied in their search for work (the *Plan d'aide et de retour à l'emploi* – Pare). The social partners who signed this new convention explicitly agreed upon the idea that unemployment insurance benefits should not only compensate the loss of income, but also encourage people to find a new job (Clegg 2007). The 2009 merger of the national employment agency and the unemployment insurance fund, as well as the creation of RSA (see above), have taken France yet further down this path towards activation.

Changing the Incentives in the Pension System

In pensions, the solutions that are currently being promoted to solve the future crisis of the PAYG system are not only based on the changes in calculation rules, but also on creating new incentives so that people contribute and work longer, and so that people also rely on private savings in addition to the public scheme.

Since the late 1990s, measures have been implemented to increase the activity rate of older workers and reverse the early exit trend of French 'employment' policies. A new early retirement scheme was established in 2000, restricted to workers who had difficult working conditions.[9] The idea was that the new scheme would progressively replace all the old, less selective ones. The early exit scheme for civil servants was closed in 2002, and another scheme, the Job Substitution Allowance Scheme, was terminated in 2003. The contributions paid by firms to early exit funds were raised in 2001, increasing the direct costs for all schemes.

In 2003, the Raffarin government launched a second big pension reform, aimed, first, at aligning the situation of the public sector to the private one and, second, at expanding the length of contribution for all workers to get the right to a full pension. As planned in 2003, the period of contribution was increased for everybody (public and private sector) to 41 years in 2008, and is planned to increase to 42 years by 2020. It was also announced that the indexation of pensions would be based on prices for everybody, civil service pensions having previously been indexed on wages. A new system of incentives for people to retire as late as possible was also created: a bonus ('*surcote*') will be given if people retire after the legal age, and a sanction ('*décote*') applied in case of retirement before this age and in case of missing years of contributions.

Since the announcement of these measures created fierce opposition by trade unions and many demonstrations, the government announced some concessions but only to certain unions (CFDT mainly, but also CFTC and CGC, see Häusermann 2010b), such as guaranteeing a replacement rate of 85 percent of SMIC – minimum wage – for the lowest pensions (the average rate of replacement in France in 2003 was 74 percent). It allowed workers who have worked more than 40 years before the age 60, and/or who had begun to work between 14 and 16 years old, to retire at 58. The reform also increased educational credits for civil servants. Furthermore, it unveiled the creation of a supplementary regime by points in order to take into account the bonus for the calculation of the pensions of the civil servants, and also announced an increase of 0.2 percent in social contributions after 2006 in order to finance retirement before age 60, counting on the decrease in unemployment to finance the deficit of the pension systems. But in 2007, it was announced that the very specific pension schemes of public firms would also be progressively aligned to the new general rule. By then, trade unions appeared to be too weak to oppose the reform, and could not oppose the confirmation of the new path taken when discussed in 2008.

Reforms also tried to encourage the development of 'saving' through tax exemptions. Two systems of voluntary saving were created in 2004, one individual (PERP: *Plan d'épargne retraite populaire*, which can be proposed to individuals by any bank or private insurer), and PERCO: *plan d'épargne retraite collective*, to be organized within firms or by the social partners at sectoral level. In both cases, the government was explicit that people should try to compensate the future decrease in compulsory PAYG pensions with their own savings. At the end of 2005, 1.7 million people had entered into a PERP contract, while 102,000 wage earners were members of a PERCO plan. However, the growth rate in 2005 was much higher for PERCO plans (66,000 new members, i.e. a 168 percent annual growth rate) than for PERP plans (450,000 new members, i.e. a 36 percent annual growth rate). Moreover, the contributions paid into PERCO plans were four times as high as those paid into PERP plans (DREES 2007).

A Profound Reform of the Health Care System

During summer 2004 a new law on health insurance ('Douste Blazy reform') was voted by the Parliament in a context of a huge deficit in the health insurance system (10.6 billions euros in 2003, 11.6 billions expected for 2004). As with previous plans for health care, this reform continued to increase co-payments for the patients, through an increase of the fee payable for each hospital stay, and the creation of a non-reimbursable fee of 1 euro on each consultation (this type of fee was extended to drugs, exams and transportation in 2008).

The Douste Blazy reform also initiated a profound reorganization of the French health care system, moving towards both more direct management of the system by state representatives at the expense of the social partners (*étatisation*) and more control over patient behavior. This structural reform, which introduced some basic features typical of National Health Services within the French health insurance system, was made possible by the changes that occurred progressively over the previous years, notably the extension of health care to all (through the CMU, see above), and the increasing role played by taxes instead of social contribution (through the CSG, see above).

The 2004 reform instigated the merging of the various health insurance schemes into one body – the national union of sickness funds[10] – directed by a senior civil servant nominated by the government. The new director now leads negotiations with the different medical professions and has the power to nominate directors of local sickness funds. As a consequence, the power of the trade unions has been considerably diminished; the law disbanded the administrative boards on which they sat and replaced them with simple advisory councils. In 2009, new legislation was passed that reorganized the health care system at the regional level, here too creating a single body[11] to replace the various schemes and administrations formerly in charge of health care provision. The circulation of patients within the system has also been streamlined in recent years, and since

2004 French patients must choose a 'treating doctor' ('*médecin traitant*') who must be seen before any other specialist is consulted. The level of re-imbursement by the health insurance is much lower if one does not go through this gate keeper.

The level of re-imbursement of non-acute/non-chronic care (mostly primary care) has gone down dramatically over the last 30 years. While more than 70 percent of primary care costs were reimbursed in the early 1980s, today the figure is under 60 percent, part of the difference being covered by voluntary private health insurance. However, only 84.9 percent of French people have a complementary health insurance, while 7.4 percent are covered by the complementary universal sickness scheme (CMUC) and 7.7 percent have no complementary cover (IRDES 2008).[12] Moreover, though the reimbursement rates are based on the prices set by the compulsory health insurance system, many doctors actually overcharge their patient, with the extra cost being covered only by expensive *mutuelles* or private health insurances. Private health insurance thus plays a bigger and bigger role in the primary care sector, which represents half of health care expenditure, as the basic health insurance retreats from its comprehensive coverage. The development of the French health system can thus been characterized by both *étatisation* and 'rampant privatization' (Hassenteufel and Palier 2007).

Divisive Reforms

During the 2000s, the politics of these most recent reforms were characterized by strong controversies among the trade unions, with strikes and demonstrations being supported by some of them (led by CGT, FO and public sector unions) while others (led by CFDT) sought to find agreement. Clearly, the governments played on this division within the trade union movement to weaken the mobilization and gain support for their reforms. In 2001, the agreement between CFDT and employers was strongly criticized by CGT and FO. In 2003, when demonstrations brought two million people out against the public sector pension reforms, the government agreed to all the demands of the CFDT, but denied all those of the CGT, despite the more conciliatory attitude of its new leader. The health care reform was less controversial since it has been (implicitly) agreed since the late 1990s that the social partners would withdraw from their responsibilities in the health care sector. However, when the first agreement between UNCAM and the medical profession was discussed in 2005, the specialists signed it when the generalists opposed it.

Table 3.1 – Summary of reform trajectory: France

Types of change	Context	Diagnosis
Before retrenchment (1975-1992) *'Les plans de sauvetage de la Sécurité sociale'*	– Economic downturn (mid-1970s onwards) – Massive unemployment – *Trou de la Sécurité sociale*	– One needs to save the national champions – *Traitement social du chômage*
First wave of Retrenchment The 1990s *'Les politiques de maîtrise des dépenses'*	– Failure by both the Right and the Left of Keynesian reflation plans – Non-explicit conversion to macro-economic supply-side policies -Economic recession (early 1990s) – Huge unemployment insurance deficit – Explosion of health insurance expenditures – Single market – Preparation of the single currency	– *La Sécurité sociale est en danger* – The system has to be rescued – A high level of social contribution hinders both competitiveness and job creation.
Institutional reforms	– increasing social exclusion – social partners have been able to block important reforms – among the highest level of social contribution in Europe	– *La Sécurité sociale* is causing trouble and contributes to the crisis – Social insurance schemes cannot deal with social exclusion – Social contributions damage competitiveness and create unemployment – The social partners are not ready to take difficult decisions
The second wave of reforms Path-breaking changes The 2000s	– Domination of employers and right-wing party – European single market – European Monetary Union	– Welfare systems need a profound adaptation to the new economic context – Diffusion of the OECD, EES, OMC ideas

Content of the policy	Politics of the reforms	Consequences
– Massive early exit plans – Creation of subsidized jobs – Rise in social contributions – Change in the generosity of some benefits in sickness insurance	– Right-wing and then left-wing government implement Keynesian reflation plans – Protest against 'Plan de sauvetage de la Sécurité sociale'	– Increase in labor cost – Declining employment rate among elderly and youngsters – Persisting unemployment and social deficit
– Stricter contributivity rules for unemployement and pension benefits – Patients need to contribute more for their healthcare costs – Creation and development of tax financing of non-contributory benefits	– Massive protest against direct retrenchment plans – The state is ready to pay for 'charges indues' – Reforms are implicitly negotiated on the basis of clarification between 'solidarité professionnelle' and 'solidarité nationale'	– More and more people are excluded from social insurance schemes – Less and less 'social' insurances – Those who are still insured need to complement their compulsory insurance with private health mutuelles and complementary pension plans
– New benefits, (universal or targeted), tax-financed, managed by the state (RMI, CMU) – Expansion of private provision – New mode of financing: A new tax for social expenditure (CSG) – Étatisation: More power for the state	– 'Virus' strategy, layering – New provisions, new institutions are implemented at a marginal point, on the base of an ambiguous agreement – Still conflictual on governance issues, but the social partners lose various battles	– Weakening of social insurance mechanisms and actors – Although initially marginal, new measures progressively develop into a second pillar of the system (e.g. RMI as the unemployment benefit of last resort; e.g. the CSG as the main resource for health care sector; e.g. the empowerment of state representatives within the system)
– PARE: Activation of unemployed – PERP: new private pension funds – Empowerment of the state and of private insurances within the health care system	– Employers take the lead in welfare reforms (La refondation sociale) – Divided unions – Governments play certain unions (CFDT, CGC and CFTC) against others (CGT, FO); workers' mobilization fails to prevent the reforms	– A more mixed economy of welfare, focused on employment-friendliness – Shrinking of social insurance programs, further activation of the assisted – Dualization of the system (social and private insurances/assistance) – We are all supply-siders now, but not everybody will pay the price of this turn

3.4 Conclusion: Dualisms in the French Welfare System

Compared to its features in the early 1980s, one can see that the French welfare system has gone through important changes that are summarized in tables 3.2 to 3.4. However, these changes have not had the same consequences for the whole population, since one of the main outcomes of the reform trajectory has been a progressive dualization of the French welfare system (and society).

We have seen that at its inception the French *Sécurité sociale* was meant to attain Beveridgean goals of universality through the social insurance means of Bismarck. Because of the reforms implemented during the last thirty years, France's compulsory social insurances are no longer all-encompassing. This has opened up a space for the development of other types of social protection mechanisms, both public (state-run) and private. These changes have resulted in multiple dualizations in the French welfare system: the development of two worlds of welfare within the public system; the addition of a private component to the public one; and the division of the population between the insured insiders and the assisted or activated outsiders.

Two distinct worlds of welfare have come to coexist in the public system. One is the remaining realm of social insurance, comprised mainly of old-age pensions and unemployment insurance, where what is called in France, 'professional solidarity', is central and benefits are still acquired through work, albeit linked more closely than before to the amount of contribution paid. The social partners have kept their hands on the development of these insurances, even though the 'shadow of hierarchy' is ever more visible. This world of social insurance can no longer offer comprehensive coverage i.e. cover the whole population and provide the insured with sufficient benefits to sustain their standard of living. The second world of welfare is one of what is called in France, 'national solidarity', comprised of health care, family benefits and policies aimed at fighting social exclusion. Here, eligibility is based on need and citizenship, benefits are either universal (for health and family allowances) or means-tested (CMU, RMI and other minimum incomes), and they are financed from national taxes (especially CSG) with the state playing a central role.

In France, retrenchment consisted mainly of stricter eligibility criteria in social insurance, and as a consequence fewer people are covered by social insurance and those covered are less well covered. This shrinking of social insurance leaves space both underneath – for covering the poorest with minimum incomes – and above – for private voluntary components (private pension funds and private health insurances) – the public system. This is a new architecture for the French welfare system, with social insurances still central but no longer hegemonic.

This new architecture has created new forms of vertical dualism in society. The French population itself seems to be increasingly divided into, on the one hand, those who can rely on a rather generous social insurance program and continue to have access (thanks to their employers or their own wealth) to private complements, and on the other hand, those who have fallen out of that system and are dependent on minimum benefits. To the latter group, one should probably add those being 'activated' into atypical contracts under which they benefit from second rank labor and social protection (Clegg 2007; Palier and Thelen 2010). Between those on minimum incomes (10 percent of the French population) and the 25 percent of the working population with an atypical working contract (fixed term, part-time, with lower wage than normal, RSA and other subsidized jobs), it seems that around a third of the French population does not participate in the 'normal' labor market and social protection arrangements. French social protection reforms have thus contributed to increase inequalities and divide society between insiders and outsiders (Palier and Thelen 2010).

These trends have been accompanied more than they have been truly contested by the social partners. As seen before, most of the retrenchments in social insurance benefits were negotiated on the basis of a distinction between 'insurance' and 'solidarity'. This led to the separation of the two worlds that were once associated when the system was aimed to reach Beveridgean goals through Bismarckian means.

We are all Supply-Siders Now!

If the French social protection system has gone through important institutional changes (see tables 3.2 to 3.4), the objectives of social policy have also undergone fundamental changes. Before, social protection was mainly conceptualized as a way of guaranteeing a substitute income for people who could no longer work, temporarily or permanently. Benefits were conceived as an entitlement, earned over years of social contributions. More and more, social policies are conceived as instruments for modifying individual behavior, in particular with regards to employment, and as a tool for spurring the economy – not by supporting household consumption, but by encouraging citizens to work as much as possible and by developing private social protections. This should, in principle, foster new economic activities in pension funds, the insurance industry, medical research and personal services. The French social protection system is gradually supposed to become an instrument of competitiveness: in business (decreases in employer social contributions, development of private social protection activities), of the state (decrease in taxation, control over the rise in public social expenditure), and of individuals (activation policies).

In France, the *sécurité Sociale* was part of an overall economic policy that both promoted and relied on full employment – essentially a Keynesian policy, focused on the demand side. After 30 years of change, one can say that French social protection is now adapted to the new dominant macroeconomic paradigm, focused on the supply side (Hall 1986; 1989). The turn of French social protection towards activation and employability (so that the unemployed go back to the labor market), the lowering of social contributions to help private companies supply more jobs, and the development of the market of social protection all play a part in this paradigmatic change. Whether this turn fits with the new economic and social conditions created by the 2008 financial crisis looks, however, increasingly questionable.

Table 3.2   Institutional changes in old-age insurance (changes in italics)

	Early 1980s	*Mid-2000s*
Eligibility	Status based access to old-age pension (37,5 years of contribution, 50% of the means of 10 best years); contribution-based access to compulsory complementary occupational pension; means-tested access to minimum pension; selective access to private occupational pensions	*Contribution*-based access to old-age pension (*41 years of contribution, 50% of the means of 25 best years*); contribution-based access to compulsory complementary occupational pension; means-tested access to minimum pension; selective access to private occupational pensions; *increased fiscal privileges for private pension savings*
Benefit structure	Contributory benefits; means-tested differential minimum income	Contributory benefits; means-tested differential minimum income; *increased funded benefits*
Financing	Old age insurance contributions (even for minimum pension)	Contributions; *taxes for minimum pension; private occupational pensions are funded through tax exempted employee's and employers payment*
Management	Tripartite (*régime général*), social partners only for compulsory complementary pensions	Tripartite (*régime général*), social partners only for compulsory complementary pensions; *firm or branch level agreements and private companies (supplementary occupational pensions)*

Table 3.3   Institutional changes in health care policy (changes in italics)

	Early 1980s	*Mid-2000s*
Eligibility	Status and 'personal insurance', voluntary facultative 'mutuelles'	*Universal health insurance;* voluntary facultative 'mutuelles' *or private insurances*
Benefit structure	Re-imbursement (100% for hospital care, 75% for ambulatory care)	Re-imbursement *(95% for hospital care, 60% for ambulatory care)*
Financing	Health insurance contributions	Employers' contribution; *CSG (for the employees), taxes.*
Management	Tripartite, mutuelles	*Central and regional government,* mutuelles *and private insurance companies*

Table 3.4   Institutional changes in unemployment insurance (changes in italics)

	Early 1980s	*Mid-2000s*
Eligibility	Mandatory insurance for employees	Mandatory insurance for employees; *tightened eligibility (longer contribution period); benefits partly dependent on job seeking activities*
Benefit structure	Income replacement (about 79% during the first year)	*Lower and degressive* income replacement; *activation policies*
Financing	Contribution payments	Contribution payments
Management	Bipartite	Bipartite *(in the shadow of hierarchy); merger of the employment agencies and the unemployment insurance funds.*

4 Janus-Faced Developments in a Prototypical Bismarckian Welfare State: Welfare Reforms in Austria since the 1970s

Herbert Obinger and Emmerich Tálos

4.1 Introduction[1]

Austria is nowadays widely seen as possessing a highly developed, albeit mainly employment-related, social security system strongly based on the idea of status preservation of wage earners (Obinger and Tálos 2006). The foundations of this model date back to the late 19th and early 20th century when core branches of social insurance such as accident insurance (1887), health insurance (1888) and old-age pensions for white-collar workers (1906) were introduced in the Austrian-Hungarian Empire in an attempt to settle the 'labor question' (*Arbeiterfrage*). The basic objectives of public intervention in social affairs, the organizational principles (self-administration), the mode of financing (social security contributions), and the structural make-up of the welfare system laid down at that time provided the guiding principles that underpinned the expansion of the welfare system in the 20th century (Hofmeister 1981; Tálos 1982). Benefits are tied to labor market participation, while the legacy of paternalist authoritarian policies is mirrored in occupationally fragmented and mandatory social insurance. Status preservation via earnings-related transfer payments, a lack of social services and the preservation of the male breadwinner model are core elements of the Austrian social security system giving rise to strong stratification effects in terms of gender and occupational status. With few exceptions, social insurance related benefits are financed entirely through social security contributions. Social assistance, by contrast, is a social safety net of the last resort based on subsidiarity and tied to a means-test.

Given this structural make-up, the standard account in the comparative welfare state literature depicts the Austrian welfare state as a prototypical Bismarckian or corporatist-Conservative welfare regime (Esping-Andersen 1990). The expansion of the Austrian welfare state during the *trente glorieuses* mainly affected the personal coverage and the level and spectrum of benefits offered by the various programs. Based on a Keynesian post-war consensus and building on the inherited Bismarckian system of social security, the goal of income support was universalized during the post-war period. A duopoly of pro-welfare state parties, consociational democracy and corporatism, as well as a Federal Constitution lacking institutional veto points, provided a political configuration highly conducive to welfare state expansion in the aftermath of World War II.

Though a U-turn in social policy occurred later than in many other West European nations, the speed of reform has remarkably accelerated during the past two decades. We show in this chapter that the contemporary Austrian welfare state still manifests salient Bismarckian traits. The contemporary arrangement of social security should not, however, be seen simply as a frozen landscape inherited from the past, but rather as what might properly best be described as a 'partially defrosted' Bismarckian welfare state.

4.2   How Bismarckian was the Austrian Welfare State?

In the early 1980s, the Austrian social security system was based on the following principles and objectives (Obinger and Tálos 2006):

Eligibility to Social Benefits
From the 1880s onwards, labor market participation has been the crucial qualifying condition for drawing benefits from social insurance. The main objective of social insurance was to protect wage earners against losses of income in case of sickness, occupational injury, unemployment and old age. Non-employed spouses and dependent children were entitled to free co-insurance and survivors' benefits. Initially, social security was strongly occupationally fragmented with the major dividing line running between blue-collar and white-collar workers on the one hand and private sector employees and civil servants on the other. The self-employed and farmers were integrated into social insurance only in the aftermath of World War II.

Eligibility to benefits on a universal basis applied only to a limited number of programs such as family allowances and the long-term care allowance introduced in 1993.

Subsidiarity was and still is the guiding principle of social assistance and unemployment assistance (*Notstandshilfe*). Public assistance in case of hardship could only be claimed if all other sources of income maintenance such as employment, family support and existing social benefits either had been exhausted or were not sufficient to guarantee a decent standard of living (Pfeil 2000; Dimmel 2003). Social assistance was a means-tested benefit that was controlled and funded by the nine *Länder*.

Type of Benefits

Given the predominance of social insurance, benefits were mostly offered in cash. Wage-centered social security was strongly imbued with the principle of equivalence. Social insurance as the most important pillar of the welfare state therefore reproduced the inequalities inherent in the labor market and the employment record of individuals. A final salient feature of the Austrian welfare state was that benefits were mostly publicly provided. Markets, therefore, have been largely crowded-out as an alternative route to benefit provision. Until the 1990s, for example, 90 percent of all pension benefits were provided by the statutory public pension scheme.

Self-Administration

The pronounced occupational fragmentation typical for Bismarckian welfare states was mirrored in the organization of social insurance, which, from the very outset, has been based on the principle of self-administration. Between 1947 and 1999, board members of the insurance agencies and funds providing insurance cover were nominated by the Austrian Trade Union Federation and the so-called chambers, i.e. the statutory interest organizations of labor, capital and peasants. Implementation of social insurance affairs was the responsibility of the respective insurance carriers which were organized along territorial (health care) and occupational principles. Since the 1980s, their number has declined from 28 to 22 in the wake of a few mergers.

Unemployment insurance was directly administered by the Ministry of Social Affairs until the mid-1990s. In 1994, the administration was decentralized and outsourced to the Austrian Labor Market Service (AMS), which is also responsible for job placement. The AMS has offices in each *Länder* and 96 regional offices. The social partners are strongly represented in these bodies.

Funding

The mode of financing reflected the overarching principle of wage-centered social policy. *Social insurance* was primarily funded through earmarked contributions paid by employees and their employers on a pay-as-you-go basis. Only pensions and health care (mainly hospitals) were to some extent co-financed from the public purse. In 2004, about two-thirds of total social expenditure was financed from contributions, whereas the remaining share was covered by federal grants (BMSK 2007: 195).

The profound occupational fragmentation enshrined in the Austrian welfare state was mirrored in occupationally fragmented contribution rates, contribution ceilings and co-payments (e.g. health care) which differed between blue- and white-collar workers[2] on the one hand and between employees, the self-employed and civil servants on the other. Other sectors of the welfare system beyond social insurance showed different funding patterns. Long-term care allowance (introduced in 1993) and social assistance benefits were entirely tax-funded, whereas family cash benefits were financed by employers and the public purse.

4.3   Welfare State Change since the 1970s: Reform Sequences

The development of the Austrian welfare state over the past 30 years can be divided into three phases, which are characterized by increasing reform intensity over time.

– Whereas the early 1970s were still characterized by a substantial expansion of the welfare state, the first half of the 1980s witnessed a turnaround towards stabilization and retrenchment. On the funding side, the major response was to increase social security contributions. However, this policy shift only included gradual or first order changes (Hall 1993) which did not affect the basic principles of the existing welfare state settlement.

– Against the backdrop of profound political and socio-economic transformations (e.g. a revival of the Grand Coalition in 1987, EU membership and the formation of the EMU), a policy course aimed at fiscal stabilization was continued in the second half of the 1980s and early 1990s. The EU accession in 1995 marked a watershed as the measures launched in the second half of the 1990s mainly had a restrictive impact and included a number of second order changes. Nevertheless, the basic principles of the welfare state remained largely intact in this period.

- The new millennium, by contrast, which in political terms was marked by the advent of a center-Right government (2000-2006), led to more far-reaching reform efforts which, in consequence, produced third order changes in some policy sectors, notably pensions. In addition, the center-Right government imposed far-reaching institutional changes by altering the rules of the political game.

The 1970s and Early 1980s: From one Last Expansionary Flash in the Pan to a Reorientation in Social Policy towards Stabilization

In 1970, a Social Democratic single party cabinet came to power. The new government was committed to the idea of societal and political modernization, which included not the least plans to expand and remodel the welfare state. *Family policy*, for example, was considerably restructured and expanded. The approach taken to increase vertical redistribution was to roll-back family-related tax allowances in favor of tax deductions and higher transfer payments such as family allowances, parental leave allowance and birth allowance. New benefits in kind included free school books and free transport for schoolchildren and apprentices.

In terms of *health care*, the Social Democrats introduced general medical check-up examinations (1972) and mother and child examinations (1974) to strengthen preventive medicine. The coverage of *accident insurance* was considerably enhanced when school children and students were integrated into this program in 1976.

The benefit spectrum of the *pension system* was also enhanced. Widows' pensions (1970) and minimum pensions (1973) were raised, while spells of tertiary education, sickness and unemployment were considered for benefit calculation (see Tálos 1986: 99).

A similar expansion took place in the realm of *unemployment insurance.* Unemployment compensation as well as family supplements were raised, while eligibility was relaxed through the abolition of waiting days (1976).

A remarkable attribute of this period was that most reforms were based on compromises between the social partners. The negotiation-based style of *politics* did of course not rule out sporadic political conflicts in social policy with collective labor law as the prime example (Tálos 1982). Nevertheless, the compromise-based pattern of decision-making prevailing in this period demonstrates that social partnership was widely practiced even in periods dominated by a single party government.

The occurrence of the oil price shocks marked a turning point. Even though macroeconomic performance had worsened in the wake of the oil shocks, Austria outperformed most Western democracies in terms of macroeconomic and labor market performance in the crisis of the 1970s (Rothschild 1985; Scharpf 1987). The political strategy to cope with the repercussions of the oil shocks is captured in a famous quote by the then Federal Chancellor, Bruno Kreisky, who said in the run-up to the general elections of 1979: 'A few billion Schillings more debt gives me fewer sleepless nights than would a few hundred more unemployed.' The adopted policy package labeled as Austro-Keynesianism included coordinated wage policies, labor hoarding in state-run industry, labor shedding via early retirement benefits, anti-cyclical deficit spending and public promotion of investment and exports. A further response to the crisis of the 1970s was to increase social security contributions and to raise contribution ceilings for all professions and insurance branches (Talos 1982: 360-61). Keynesianism had its price, however. The level of debt skyrocketed from 20.4 percent in 1970 to almost 50 percent of GDP in 1985. Whereas the Social Democrats and the trade unions advocated the continuation of welfare state expansion and Keynesian economic policies, the deteriorating economic situation also increased skepticism concerning the welfare state, particularly among employers associations. Leading representatives argued, for example, that 'the welfare state has reached its outer limits if it has not already crossed them' (Stummvoll 1977). Moreover, the welfare state was seen as an integral part of a 'democracy of complaisance' (*Gefälligkeitsdemokratie*) and blamed for having contributed to a financial calamity, since its expansion continued regardless of economic capabilities. Mounting anti-welfare rhetoric in combination with increasing economic difficulties triggered a trend reversal in social policy which was further accelerated by the Social Democrats' loss of their absolute majority in 1983. From 1983 to 1986, the Social Democrats (SPÖ) formed a coalition with the Freedom Party (FPÖ). Austro-Keynesianism was gradually renounced in this era of transition (Tálos 1987; Unger 2001; Lauber and Pesendorfer 2006).

Against the backdrop of rising unemployment in the early 1980s, the reform debate initially focused on labor market policy (Tálos 1986; 1987), but increasingly also on pensions. Rather than demographic problem pressure it was budgetary pressure why the first departure from the expansionist route occurred under the SPÖ/FPÖ government. In 1984, a restrictive pension reform was adopted which aimed to curb expenditure via changes in the pension formula.

Full employment ceased to exist in 1982/83 and the rate of unemployment went up to more than 5 percent over the next years. The resulting rise in expenditure devoted to this program (Tálos 1987: 153) evoked mounting criticism from employers. The turning point towards retrenchment occurred in 1983 (Tálos 2004), when the SPÖ/FPÖ government suspended unemployment compensation in case of compensation payments after dismissal. Nevertheless, the government responded to the rise in unemployment mainly with higher contribution rates and various supply-side oriented measures rather than with large-scale benefit cutbacks. Active labor market policy was enhanced and the stock of the foreign labor force was slashed. From the late 1970s, early retirement served as an instrument of labor shedding and therefore helped to cushion the mounting labor market problems in the short run. The spread of early retirement programs led to a remarkable decline in the effective retirement age from the mid-1970s onwards (see Figure 4.1). However, labor shedding created negative fiscal feedback effects in the longer run which, in consequence, led to more far-reaching reforms in subsequent years and contributed to a staged reform process in pension policy (cf. Bonoli and Palier 2007).

Figure 4.1   Development of the effective retirement age contingent upon pension type and gender, 1970-2005 (5 year intervals)

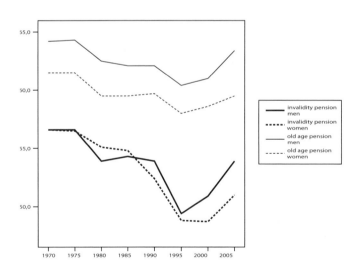

Source: Hauptverband der österreichischen Sozialversicherungsträger: Handbuch der österreichischen Sozialversicherung, Vienna (various issues).

A first path reversal is also visible in *family policy* and *health care*, albeit to a lesser degree. The policy strategy in health care to cope with rising health expenditure was to extend co-payments. The SPÖ/FPÖ government introduced new out-of-pocket payments for in-kind benefits such as glasses or prostheses in 1983, while the expansion of family-related benefits virtually came to an end. Some benefits such as the birth allowance have even been subject to moderate cutbacks.

In sum, the early 1980s witnessed a trend reversal in social policy which was mainly triggered by increasing economic problems. With the exception of early retirement, the expansion of the welfare state not only came to a halt in this period, but was also, in some measure, put into reverse gear. Labor market problems were papered over by means of the pension system, while some first order policy changes aimed at financial stabilization were implemented in pension and unemployment insurance. These measures, however, did not undercut the traditional core principles underpinning the welfare state. Neither its basic objectives nor its fundamental structures were contested in this period.

Adaptation to a Remarkably Changed Environment (1987-1999)

In 1987, a Grand Coalition resumed office for the first time since 1966. The pragmatic modernizers led by Chancellor Vranitzky got the upper hand in the social democratic camp, while the Christian Democrats (ÖVP) increasingly advocated neoliberal ideas. State intervention in economic affairs and the welfare state were seen as part of the causes of the mounting economic difficulties. In the following years, the SPÖ/ÖVP government initiated a reorientation in economic policy by adopting a moderate supply-side oriented strategy committed to debt containment, liberalization and privatization of state-owned enterprises. This policy shift was triggered by declining economic performance as well as by the cabinet's intention to join the EU, which was finally accomplished on 1 January 1995.

Macroeconomic performance further deteriorated from the mid-1980s onwards. Economic growth was significantly lower compared to previous decades (Stiefel 2006: 73) and the rate of unemployment increased from 5.2 (1986) to more than 7 percent in 1999. This development was paralleled by an increase in the number of the long-term unemployed and a spread of atypical work (Stiefel 2006: 77f; Tálos 2005a: 44 ff). Budgetary pressure and labor market problems grew more acute with the de facto bankruptcy of large parts of state-run industry[3] in the mid-1980s. In consequence, the level of public debt increased from 49.8 percent (1985) to 69.2 percent of GDP in 1995. Austria therefore actually went over the critical 60 percent Maastricht threshold at just the time of its entry into the European Union. Soaring public debt plus high real interest rates in the 1980s increased the pressure to impose austerity policies. The commitment to EU membership, the liberalization of capital markets in the late 1980s and early 1990s as well as the formation of the EMU sounded the death knell for Austro-Keynesianism (Winckler 1988). Under these circumstances, the policy route of incremental adjustment and financial stabilization practiced in the early 1980s was not only continued by the Grand Coalition but also rather implemented with greater intensity and speed (Tálos and Wörister 1998).

Pensions

The latter is apparent from the shorter intervals between the various reform initiatives pursued by the SPÖ/ÖVP government in the field of pensions (e.g. 1988, 1990, 1991, 1993, 1995, 1996 and 1997). The various pension reforms were largely triggered by increases in federal funding of the pension system on the one hand and by mounting pressure to contain budget deficits on the other. In terms of the expenditure/GDP ratio, the Austrian pension system was, in the 1990s, one of the most expensive in the world, not least because the effective retirement age was one of the lowest. The pressure to impose austerity policies resulting from derailing budget deficits led to various retrenchment measures and higher contribution rates. The assessment basis was extended stepwise from 5 to 15 contribution years and the increment factor was fixed at 2 percent for all pension types in 1997. In addition, eligibility to early old-age pensions was tightened (1996), while the contribution rate for the self-employed and farmers was raised in 1995. Moreover, the Grand Coalition enacted measures to harmonize the calculation of civil servants' pensions with that of general pensions.

The government also changed the indexation of benefits (adjustment based on net rather than gross wages) and introduced deductions in case of early retirement. Moreover, spells of higher education were no longer considered for benefit calculation. The inclusion of the new self-employed in the health and pension insurance systems was less an attempt to manage problems related to the 'new social risks', but rather was motivated by financial considerations, i.e. to secure an increase in contribution payments.

Improvements in benefits, in contrast, remained few and far between. Examples included the upgrading of spells devoted to child raising for benefit calculation, a modification of the assessment period in 1993 (with the so-called 'best' 15 years as basis for benefit calculation) and the possibility for employees with a non-standard employment contract to take out voluntary pension and health insurance.

The federal government increasingly dominated the policy-making process in this second phase, whereas the traditionally strong influence of the peak associations of labor and capital steadily declined (Karlhofer 1999: 16 ff.). Tensions between the social partners increased and the balance of power between them became more asymmetric over time, given the deteriorating economic situation and the greater exit options for capital. Moreover, EU membership further undercut the influence of the social partners, since traditional bargaining instruments were either restricted or became, like price regulations, entirely obsolete. In consequence, tripartite interest mediation became less important as compared to the heyday of corporatism, as it was not only practiced less frequently but also restricted to fewer policy sectors (cf. Tálos 2005b).

Labor Market Policy

Retrenchment in unemployment insurance also became more pronounced in the second period. Until 1993, however, both retrenchment and expansive measures were adopted. Benefit enhancement included the abolition of a clause discriminating against women with regard to unemployment assistance (females were not entitled to unemployment assistance if the partner was in full-time employment), the introduction of a uniform net replacement rate of 57.9 percent, the integration of foreigners into unemployment assistance and, finally, the extension of benefit duration for older unemployed with long insurance records.

The mid-1990s witnessed a turnaround in labor market policy. While contribution rates were stabilized at 6 percent in order to freeze non-wage labor costs, the government increasingly relied on benefit cutbacks and the activation of the unemployed from 1993 onwards. The restrictive course is apparent from the *Beschäftigungssicherungsgesetz* (1993) and the two so-called austerity packages launched in 1995 and 1996. The latter entailed a series of benefit cuts in order to meet the Maastricht convergence criteria after the budget deficit exceeded 5 percent of GDP in 1995. Qualifying conditions for unemployment benefits as well as sanctions have been tightened. The already low net replacement rate was further scaled back, unemployment assistance was subject to cutbacks and the base period of unemployment compensation was extended from 6 to 12 months. Despite all these kinds of retrenchment, the reforms legislated in the 1990s did not lead to any real departure from established policy routines.

Health Care

In the health care sector, demographic changes, medical and technological progress, and an increasing numbers of doctors produced an increasing expenditure trajectory after 1970. Concerns about rising costs dominated the political discourse with cost containment serving as the major impetus for health care reforms. One approach to curbing public health expenditure was to increase the public control of the territorially fragmented health care system and to reorganize both organization and financing of the hospital sector. The reform trajectory adopted was to strengthen health care planning in order to reduce the oversupply of hospital beds and large-scale medical equipment. Given the distribution of competencies in this sector[4], all these efforts had to be negotiated between different branches of government and were formally based on a state treaty. In 1997, the remuneration for medical services provided in hospitals was fundamentally restructured when a payment system based on diagnosis related groups was introduced. As in many other countries, the main idea was to shorten hospitalization by adopting a performance-oriented remuneration system. Moreover, the government not only raised health insurance contributions and contribution ceilings for most occupational groups as well as retirees, but also introduced new co-payments and deductibles.

However, the 1990s also witnessed the introduction of new benefits. The most important expansive measure in cost terms was the introduction of a federal long-term care allowance in 1993. Strongly pushed by various organizations of disabled people, the adoption of this program has anchored a structurally unique pillar as part of the Austrian social security system. In contrast to the German counterpart, the Austrian program is entirely tax-funded. This mode of financing was less a deliberate decision to lower non-wage labor costs and is rather a legacy from the past, as the new scheme has replaced special supplements for handicapped people offered by pension insurance. The new program is designed to cover additional care-related costs. Entitlement is independent of income and the benefit is paid regardless of the cause for the need of long-term care. The care allowance is a lump sum benefit that is staggered (seven levels), contingent upon the extent of the care required. Based on a state treaty, the nine *Länder* have agreed to guarantee nation-wide provision of social services until 2010 and to provide a similar care allowance for people not qualified for a care benefit under federal law.

Family Policy

Family policy was considerably enhanced during the first legislative period of the Grand Coalition. As in most other Continental countries, Austria has experienced a dramatic decline in fertility rates over the last three decades. Once more, however, the policy route taken was to increase cash benefits. Parental leave allowance was enhanced from 12 to 24 months and extended to fathers in 1990. In addition, tax deductions and family allowances were raised several times. In the mid-1990s, family policy experienced a backlash. As in the other welfare state sectors discussed above, the exploding budget deficit together with EU accession increased the pressure to stabilize public finances. The government passed two so-called austerity packages, which included the abolition of birth allowance and free public transport for students, the introduction of co-payments for school books, cutbacks in family allowances and a reduction of parental leave entitlement for one parent from 24 to 18 months (BMUJF 1999: 414-418).

Family policy has traditionally been shaped by the political parties, with the social partners playing only a minor role. In the 1990s, however, family policy was considerably influenced by the Constitutional Court. The Court ruled in two judgments that maintenance costs for the better-off are not adequately compensated through the tax system. In 1999, the Grand Coalition responded to the Court's rulings with a comprehensive family policy package including increased tax credits for families as well as higher transfer payments. As a result, the present system of income support for families is again based on a more balanced dual system consisting of transfer payments and a variety of tax breaks.[5] The late 1990s also witnessed increased efforts to overcome massive shortcomings with regard to day care facilities for children. Austria has traditionally been an extreme laggard in terms of the provision of public childcare facilities, especially children of nursery age. In 1995, the proportion of children aged zero to three in child care was about 3 percent (Badelt and Österle 1998: 156). Since the provision of formal childcare is the responsibility of the *Länder* and municipalities, the Grand Coalition provided special grants to subordinate governments from 1997 to 2000 in order to increase the number of childcare facilities at the local level. Nevertheless, the coverage for toddlers is still very low from a comparative perspective and there exists a substantial divide in coverage between rural areas and urban agglomerations.

Even though some second order changes were implemented, the basic patterns of the welfare state remained intact in this phase. From the mid-1990s onwards, the ÖVP and the employers' associations increasingly advocated policies aimed at deregulation, flexibilization and the containment of non-wage labor costs to increase the competitiveness of the economy. Though the influence of the social partners declined with mounting economic problem pressures and the resulting diminished scope for (re)distribution, the interest organizations of labor remained powerful enough to block far-reaching retrenchment. Tensions between the social partners spilled over to the coalition parties which became increasingly obstructive – something the general public viewed as producing a 'reform jam'. Along with the benefit cutbacks imposed in the second half of the 1990s this contributed to the rise of right-wing populist Jörg Haider. The general elections of 1999 brought painful losses for the coalition parties, while Haider's FPÖ gained almost 27 percent of the vote. Although his party only ranked third in the 1999 general election, ÖVP chairman Wolfgang Schüssel exploited this window of opportunity and formed a coalition with the Freedom Party. Accompanied by fierce national and international protests, a center-Right government came to power for the first time since 1945.

Towards Institutional Reforms: The 2000s

The turning point in social policy occurred in 2000 when the ÖVP/FPÖ coalition entered government. The lesson learnt by the ÖVP in the 1990s was that a major social policy change could only be implemented *against* but not together with the Social Democrats. For leading representatives of the ÖVP (cf. Khol 2001) it was the veto power of the unions that impeded far-reaching reforms in the past. Given that diagnosis, the center-Right government launched institutional reforms in order to bypass the informal veto powers held by the unions within the system of social partnership. Hence, the government changed the traditional rules of the game in order to realize a shift in the balance of power. Labor's former quasi-institutional role in the decision-making process ceased and the coalition utilized majority rule to pursue its neoliberal agenda. Based on the slogan 'speed kills' coined by the ÖVP party whip Andreas Khol, reforms were literally pushed through so that the opposition and the unions were repeatedly confronted with a series of *faits accomplis*. As a consequence, consociational democracy and corporatism virtually came to an end at the turn of the new millennium (Tálos 2005b; Karlhofer and Tálos 2006; Obinger and Tàlos 2006). The 'meta-reforms' adopted to realize the envisaged policy change also involved the removal of Social Democrats from power positions and attempts to increase the government's influence on the self-administered social insurance bodies.

The overriding goal of the center-Right coalition was to realize a paradigm shift in economic and social policy. The ÖVP/FPÖ government stepped into the arena with a program aimed at a fundamental reform in economic and social policy in order to 'halt a misunderstood Keynesianism, presented as Austro-Keynesianism, that had served as a smokescreen for soaring debt, and to free the nation of debt altogether' (Government Program 2000). Strong emphasis was put on a largely expenditure-based restructuring of state finances with a balanced budget as the prime objective. 'A good day begins with a balanced budget', a slogan coined by finance minister Karl-Heinz Grasser, became the government's new leitmotif in fiscal policy. With a view to taking a new approach in social policy (labeled as *Sozialpolitik neu*), which was mainly committed to improved targeting and to combat the misuse of social benefits, the coalition announced far-reaching welfare state changes (see Obinger and Tálos 2006: 25-34). In order to improve the competitiveness of the Austrian economy, the government announced a freeze in non-wage labor costs and planned various measures aiming at deregulation and flexibilization (Fink and Tálos 2004).

Pensions

Pensions were a main target of reform in the government program. Like in other Continental countries (cf. Bonoli and Palier 2007), the government envisaged the transformation of the pension system into a multi-pillar system and announced the abolition of existing early retirement programs. Several factors were used by the government to justify this radical turnaround in pension policy. The most important was the need for a strict austerity course in order to achieve a balanced budget. Pension reform was also motivated by efforts to make the system sustainable in light of prospective demographic changes and to improve the fairness within the system (i.e. to level out the differences resulting from occupational fragmentation) as well as between generations (i.e. to reduce the financial burdens on the economically active generation).

In the beginning, the government abolished early old-age pensions based on disability, reduced the replacement rate of widows' pensions and increased deductions in case of early retirement. The envisaged restructuring of the pension system was finally realized from 2003 onwards and occurred in three steps.

The *first step* was the so-called 'Pension Reform Act 2003'. This reform abolished the various categories of early retirement benefits in a series of stages, while the annual pension deductions imposed for those taking early retirement were raised to 4.2 percent of the gross pension. From 2004 on, the assessment base was to be gradually lengthened from 15 to 40 years, implying that pensions would henceforth be calculated on the basis of a life-time work record. Moreover, the increment factor was reduced from 2 to 1.78 percent and the number of years required to qualify for the maximum pension was extended from 40 to 45 years. In addition, the first benefit indexation will now only take place after two years of retirement. This reform led to massive and, at least for Austria, atypical protests. Since even the government was divided on this reform, the coalition watered down the proposed changes to some extent by imposing a cap on the losses resulting from the reform. A further compensatory measure was to credit 24 instead of 18 months devoted to child raising as contribution periods (with an upgraded rate). Finally, a special fund was established to provide assistance in case of hardship, while workers in heavy industries were exempted from some of the restrictive measures.

The *second step* in redesigning the pension system was the harmonization of the different occupational pension schemes. The General Pension Act of 2005 included the following measures: with the exception of civil servants employed by the *Länder* and municipalities, the new unified pension law applies to all employees born 1954 or later. An individual pension account was established for every insured person showing the contribution record and the accumulated claims. In contrast to initial plans proposed by the government, a benefit-defined rather than contribution-defined pension account was established. To address the foreseeable graying of society, a so-called demographic factor was adopted. Deviations from the forecasted increase in life expectancy will automatically affect the contribution rate, the retirement age, benefit indexation and the federal grant. Retirement will be possible within a 'corridor' at an age between 62 and 68. Pension benefits are reduced by 4.2 percent per annum if a person retires before the statutory retirement age of 65. The bonus for delayed retirement is calculated accordingly. For insured persons who have already earned contribution periods, a so-called 'parallel calculation' will be made. More specifically, the benefits will be calculated on the basis of the legal situation before and after the harmonization of the pension system. The pension is then calculated as a weighted average of the entitlements earned under both schemes.

The *third step* taken to overhaul the pension system will lead to a multi-pillar system in the long run. Even though the government did not introduce a formal 'Three-Pillar System' as originally proposed, two reforms launched by the center-Right coalition nevertheless have, de facto, paved the way for a move in this direction. Irrespective of partisan conflicts, the National Council unanimously adopted the Federal Act on Corporate Staff Provision in 2002. The main idea of this bill was to adapt the traditional severance pay scheme to modern worklife circumstances and to convert severance pay into supplementary private pensions ('Abfertigung neu') that, in the long run, should serve as a sort of second pillar. A similar conversion of severance pay into occupational pensions took place in Italy (cf. Jessoula and Alti, this volume). Employers pay 1.53 percent of the monthly salary to special funds in charge of program administration. All private sector employees (including apprentices and employees with marginal jobs) are covered under this program from the first working day onwards. The benefit is due after the termination of the employment contract. Individuals either can draw a lump-sum payment equivalent to the accumulated capital or claim a pension. The latter option, however, is more appealing since no taxes are levied.

The third pillar of the future pension system will consist of subsidized individual savings (Prämiengeförderte Zukunftsvorsorge). This pillar is based on public subsidies paid to private forms of saving such as life insurance. Contracts must have a policy period of at least 10 years and cannot be signed by a person aged 62 and over. In a manner similar to the pensions derived from the second pillar, the accumulated capital is tax free unless the capital is claimed before the 10-year period. The take-up of this program is high. In 2007, already more than 1 million contracts (equivalent to about 30 percent of the economically active population) have been closed. The succeeding SPÖ/ÖVP government, which came to office in 2007, made no major efforts to undo the overhaul of the pension system.

Unemployment Insurance

The changes implemented in the realm of unemployment insurance were also far-reaching as the ÖVP/FPÖ government has further intensified retrenchment of cash benefits and increasingly relied on the activation of the unemployed. These changes in labor market policy have been increasingly shaped by European employment policies. The goals spelled out in the Lisbon agenda, such as activation, employability and a higher labor market participation of women and older persons, have certainly influenced the recent reform trajectory, with the OMC serving as major transmission mechanism. In its government program, the coalition repeatedly heralded measures to eliminate fraud and to combat the misuse of unemployment benefits (see Government Program 2000: 19, 33, 24). Closely connected to this approach was the announcement of the intention to improve the targeting of social benefits: 'Targeting of benefits is low and has to be subject to a permanent audit' (ibid.: 17, 23). Already in 2000, the previous settlement in unemployment insurance was modified in several respects: the surcharge for families was reduced by more than one third, the replacement rate was lowered once more, the qualifying period was extended and sanctions were tightened. The government also increased the pressure on the unemployed to accept a job. Regulations concerning suitable job offers and a reasonable time span to commute to and from work were tightened. The so-called job protection clause (*Berufsschutz*), a provision preventing individuals being required to accept a job falling short of his or her skills, was limited to 100 days and supplemented by a system aiming to preserve previous salary levels (*Entgeltschutz*). In addition, unemployed individuals have to provide evidence of active engagement in job search. At the end of its office term, however, the government, in part, shied away from retrenchment in this area, as a supplementary allowance was established to top up the unemployment benefit for low-income groups.

Since the labor market participation of the elderly labor force is traditionally very low, and given the fact that the ÖVP/FPÖ government has radically curtailed early retirement, the government has enacted some measures to enhance the employment opportunities for this group. The main approach has been to reduce non-wage labor costs for the elderly, with females aged 56+ and males aged 58+ henceforth exempt from unemployment insurance contributions, which are covered by general funds devoted to labor market policy. Moreover, the ÖVP/FPÖ government has also increased (in nominal terms) expenditure devoted to active labor market policies. Special emphasis has been put on education and training measures to improve the skills of women and to combat youth unemployment.

Given the tighter eligibility to unemployment benefits and a stronger reliance on activation policies, the government increased efforts to create employment opportunities for the unskilled labor force in order to keep the number of unemployed down. With its Job Promotion Act passed in 2005, the government has made an attempt to create new jobs in the low-wage sector. The coalition has introduced a so-called service check to create (legal) jobs in private households and to provide minimum social security for the home help. The service check can be bought at the tobacconist or post office. The remuneration must not exceed the maximum of 456 euros per month. So far, however, the take-up rate was low. Finally, the government has paved the way for in-work benefits, albeit on an experimental basis only. The program adopted consists of wage subsidies (*Kombi-Lohn*) paid to younger and elderly long-term unemployed who may receive half of their previous unemployment assistance as a subsidy in a new job up to a maximum of 1,000 euros per month.

By and large, but with some notable exceptions, this policy course was continued by the Grand Coalition between 2007 and 2008. In strong contrast to the center-right coalition, however, the social partners were involved in the decision-making process (Tálos 2008; Obinger 2009). Unemployment insurance was revised in two important ways. Employees with earnings up to 1,100 euros per month were exempted from unemployment contribution payments (the resulting revenue shortage is covered by the federal budget). Quasi-freelancers (*freie Dienstnehmer*) were incorporated into unemployment insurance, whereas some categories of self-employed were included on a voluntary basis. Moreover, the peak associations of the social partners agreed to establish a (gross) minimum wage of 1,000 euros per month for full-time employees.

Health Care

Cost containment was once again the major impetus for the reforms that have taken place in the health care system. Out-of-pocket payments in case of hospitalization and prescription charges were raised and the ÖVP/FPÖ government replaced the sickness insurance certificate by an e-card for which patients have to pay a so-called service fee of 10 euros per year. As a result of ever-increasing co-payments, the share of private health expenditure as percentage of total health expenditure has increased continuously and is now one of the highest in Europe.

The ÖVP/FPÖ coalition also intended to harmonize the contribution rates of blue- and white-collar workers. To achieve the latter goal, however, the contribution rate for white-collar workers was raised. Moreover, and in accordance with policies previously realized by the Grand Coalition, the contribution rate for old-age pensioners was raised. Finally, a new surcharge on health insurance was imposed for all insured to cope with the rising costs resulting from non-occupational injuries.

Some funding measures imposed by the ÖVP/FPÖ government led to a slight path departure in health insurance. Free co-insurance for childless couples was abolished and the government deviated from the traditional principle that health insurance contributions are paid in equal parts by employers and employees. In an effort to reduce non-wage labor costs, the contribution rate for employers related to health insurance of blue-collar workers was reduced.

Hospital funding was again a major site of reform activities. A new state treaty adopted in 2004 set the basis for the Health Care Reform Act of 2005 (Hofmarcher 2006). At its center stood an organizational reform (involving the establishment of a Health Care Agency plus a Health Care Commission at the federal level and the establishment of nine Health Care Boards plus nine Health Care Platforms at the *Länder* level), the extension of performance-oriented remuneration to the outpatient sector (at least in the long run), the integration of all health sectors into an integrated system of medical planning, efforts to reallocate the supply of medical services from the hospitals to the outpatient sector, quality management and an electronic modernization of the health system. Moreover, the federal and the *Länder* governments agreed upon cost-containment measures and revenue increases (e.g. higher taxes on tobacco) equivalent to 300 million euros in each case. Enhancement of benefits has remained rare throughout this period. For example, the ÖVP/FPÖ coalition improved the social security of caregivers (e.g. pension insurance) and strengthened efforts support medical prevention in the wake of the 2005 Health Care Reform Act.

The succeeding Grand Coalition achieved some improvements in terms of long-term care. Since households often had illegally employed (cheap) nursing staff from Eastern Europe, the Grand Coalition created the basis for the legal employment of qualified nursing staff in order to ensure round the clock (24 hours) care of severely handicapped persons in private households. By contrast, a comprehensive reform of the health care system failed. This reform failure contributed to the collapse of the Grand Coalition in July 2008.

Family Policy

The change of government in 2000 was also paralleled by a Conservative turnaround in family policy. The most important measure in this respect has been the replacement of the parental leave allowance by a universal child care benefit in 2002. Compared to the insurance-based parental leave allowance, entitlement is detached from labor market participation and the maximum duration of entitlement has been increased by one year to 30 months where only one parent draws the benefit. If both parents take care of the children, the maximum duration is three years. The new benefit offers a lump sum payment of 436 euros per month and can be combined with earnings up to a particular ceiling. Given the lack of child-care facilities for the under-threes, the child care benefit was designed to bridge the gap caused by the lack of formal provision for this age cohort.

The government's frequent emphasis of freedom of choice for families (cf. Morel, 2007) has been more a rhetorical exercise than a reality, as the center-Right coalition has not made any major effort to increase the number of child care facilities.

During its second term of office, however, the government did enact some reforms to reconcile work and family life with measures aimed at making workplace arrangements more flexible. In 2004, the coalition launched a bill that introduced a right to part-time work for parents up to the seventh birthday of the child. Yet, the legal right to part-time work was restricted to parents with an employment record of three years in companies with at least 20 employees. In 2002, a so-called family hospice leave was introduced which allows wage earners to quit their job up to six months in order to nurse a severely sick or dying relative. However, this leave is neither remunerated[6] nor are those in homosexual partnerships entitled to take hospice leave. Though the opposition criticized these provisions, the bill was passed unanimously by Parliament.

Overall, the center-Right cabinet has further strengthened the classic male breadwinner model. With the exception of a right to part-time work for parents, the measures adopted were mainly based on traditional population policies encouraging women to leave the labor force. It therefore comes as no surprise that the Grand Coalition agreed upon an adaptation of the childcare benefit in 2007. In addition to the existing (maximum) entitlement of 36 months it is now possible to receive a higher childcare benefit for a shorter period. For example, the benefit amounts to 798 euros per month if the benefit is claimed for 18 months only. Moreover, the *Länder* and the federal government will provide 60 million euros each to increase the number of childcare facilities until 2010.

4.4 Bismarck is Dead. Long Live Bismarck

In retrospect, social policy development since the late 1970s can be separated into three phases. What distinguishes these three phases from each other is the scope and intensity of the reforms implemented, the underlying mode of decision-making and the ways in which socio-economic problems were perceived and addressed (Table 4.1).

Table 4.1   The four phases of social policy development in Austria, 1970-2008

Phase	Context	Diagnosis and solutions	Politics	Content of economic and social policy	Consequences
Before retrenchment 1970-86	Social Democrat single party government and SPÖ/ΓPÖ coalition, relative economic success despite oil crisis	Social benefits can help the victims of the crisis, welfare state as automatic stabilizer	Negotiation-based	Austro-Keynesianism, expansion of the welfare state, labor shedding, higher social security contributions	Low unemployment but mounting public debt, labor markets problems were masked and shifted to the pension system
Towards retrenchment 1987-99	Rising public debt and unemployment, de facto collapse of state-run industry, EU-membership and EMU formation, Grand Coalition	Modernizing and adapting the welfare state to a new environment, cost containment to meet convergence criteria (since mid-1990s)	Negotiation-based with declining role of corporatism in the 1990s	Moderate supply-side oriented course in economic policy, benefit-contribution nexus was tightened, co-payments (health care), long-term care allowance, benefit cutbacks since EU accession	Mounting public debt, far-reaching structural reform failed because of conflicts within Grand Coalition and social partners
Path-breaking changes 2000-2006	Center-Right government committed to neoliberal agenda and debt containment, EMU and European single market, EU eastern enlargement	Structural reforms to make the welfare state viable in a more competitive environment: containment of non-wage labor costs, better targeting of benefits needed, deregulation and flexibilization	Majority rule to bypass veto power of unions, big-bang strategy ('speed kills')	Pronounced supply-side oriented course, multi-pillarization and harmonization of pension, activation of unemployed, neo-Conservative family policy	Pronounced supply-side orientation, dualization between insiders and outsiders, recommodification, higher inequality in the long run

Table 4.1 The four phases of social policy development in Austria, 1970-2008

Phase	Context	Diagnosis and solutions	Politics	Content of economic and social policy	Consequences
2007-08	Grand Coalition, economic boom but high inflation	Increased efforts to compensate the losers of previous social policy reform, compensation for price inflation	Negotiation-based	Some measures to cope with poverty and new social risks (e.g. minimum wage), continuation of supply-side oriented economic and labor market policy ('flexicurity')	Funding of health care system unsolved due to failure of health care reform

While the 1970s were characterized by an expansion of social benefits under a Left single-party government, welfare state expansion came to an end with the short-lived SPÖ/FPÖ government (1983-1986), which simultaneously marked the crossover to the second phase in which welfare state retrenchment began to exert a real influence in Austria.

This second period was shaped by a renewed Grand Coalition and lasted from 1987 until 1999. Framed by mounting economic problems, deep changes in the international political economy (Scharpf 2000) and EU-accession in 1995, the Grand Coalition bid farewell to Austro-Keynesianism and adopted a moderate supply-side-oriented course in economic policy. Nevertheless, the incumbency of the SPÖ/ÖVP government can be divided into two sub-periods with EU accession as the major watershed. Until the mid-1990s, mostly balanced reforms were legislated. Expansion measures such as the introduction of long-term care allowance and enhanced family cash benefits even outweighed benefit cuts, albeit at the expense of soaring public debt. The imperative of budget stabilization in the shadow of the Maastricht Treaty led to progressively larger benefit cuts in the second half of the 1990s. Despite their restrictive impact on beneficiaries, the reforms enacted in this sub-period were highly path-dependent and can be classified as first and second order changes (Hall 1993). This outcome was also a result of corporatism. Though the Austrian *Sozialpartnerschaft* showed symptoms of decline during the second period, corporatism nevertheless remained basically intact in the

1990s and the trade unions remained strong enough to block more radical reforms.

The advent of the third period coincides with the take-over of government by a center-Right coalition in 2000. In an effort to realize a paradigm shift in economic policy towards a pronounced supply-side strategy, social policy was subordinated to labor market flexibility, structural competitiveness, and debt containment. In order to achieve these goals, however, the government had to change the politics of welfare reform. Hence the negotiation-based adjustment path characterizing previous periods was abandoned. Instead, the ÖVP/FPÖ coalition increasingly relied on majority decisions and deviated from corporatist policy-making in order to bypass the informal veto power held by the trade unions under this setting. Based on a big-bang strategy (Starke 2007) with the slogan 'speed kills' as basic leitmotif of policy change, the ÖVP/FPÖ government quickly launched a series of far-reaching reforms that for the first time included third order changes in particular sectors of the welfare state.

The 'reform sequence hypothesis' (Palier 2006) emphasized in this volume is corroborated by the social policy reforms enacted by the Grand Coalition that governed between 2007 and 2008 (Obinger 2009). Even though it is impossible to speak of a new phase in social policy, given the cabinet's short term in office, this period witnessed (with some exceptions) the end of retrenchment and the return of corporatism in particular welfare state areas. Policy change was motivated by attempts to cushion the consequences of some reforms adopted by the preceding center-Right government. Further stimulated by socio-economic problems such as inflation and demographics, the measures adopted mainly focused on long-term care and poverty alleviation. However, some of the proposed measures, such as the harmonization of the territorially fragmented social assistance benefits offered by the *Länder*, could not be realized as a consequence of the breakdown of the coalition. The supply-side oriented policy course in economic and labor market policy remained unchanged, however.

If we compare the contemporary welfare system with the welfare settlement in the early 1980s (Tables 4.2 to 4.5), we can see that social policy development over the past three decades is characterized by Janus-faced reforms which have strengthened some aspects of the Bismarckian legacy enshrined in the Austrian welfare state, but have also weakened others.

Table 4.2   Institutional changes in old-age income security (changes in italics)

	ca. 1980	2008
Eligibility	Employment, invalidity and co-insurance of spouses (females only) and children; statutory retirement age: 65 (men) and 60 (women)	Employment, invalidity, *child raising,* co-insurance of spouses *(gender neutral)* and children, stepwise harmonization of retirement age until 2033 (65 years)
Benefit structure	Predominance of public pensions, status preservation, strong occupational fragmentation (benefits and contributions)	*Multi-pillarization of pension system: First tier: tighter contribution-benefit nexus, pension harmonization (federal civil servants), cutbacks of survivors' benefits, rollback of early retirement Second tier: Conversion of severance payment into occupational pensions Third tier: publicly subsidized individual saving plans*
Financing	Contributions, taxes	First tier: (*higher*) contribution rates, taxes Second tier: contributions Third tier: tax breaks
Management	Employers, employees, state supervision	Employers, employees, state supervision (first tier), *employee income provision funds (second tier), private companies/insurances (third tier)*

Table 4.3   Institutional changes in health care policy (changes in italics)

	ca. 1980	2008
Eligibility	Employment, co-insurance of spouses and children, almost universal coverage	Employment, co-insurance of spouses and children (*but not for childless couples*), de facto universal coverage
Benefit structure	In-kind benefits and (occupationally fragmented) cash benefits.	In-kind benefits and cash benefits (*differences between professions were almost leveled out), Long-term care allowance*
Financing	Contributions, taxes (hospitals), co-payments for particular professions only (civil servants, farmers)	*Higher* contribution rates, taxes (hospitals, *long-term care*), higher co-payments and deductibles for all insured
Management	Employers, employees, federal government and Länder governments	Employers, employees, federal government and Länder governments, *public control over the health care system was strengthened over time*

Table 4.4   Institutional changes in unemployment insurance (changes in italics)

	ca. 1980	2008
Eligibility	Mandatory insurance for employees, unemployment assistance for citizens only	Mandatory insurance; *tightened eligibility criteria, inclusion of quasi-freelancers (mandatory) and self-employed (on a voluntary basis)* unemployment assistance: *incorporation of foreigners*
Benefit structure	Unemployment compensation: re-placement rate based on wages scales; means-tested unemployment assistance	Unemployment compensation: *uniform but lower net replacement rate, activation (tighter regulations in terms of suitable work, stricter sanctions), efforts to create a low wage sector (e.g. subsidized employment, service check);* means-tested unemployment assistance, *minimum wage*
Financing	Contributions	*(Higher)* contribution rates *and taxes (low-income groups and older unemployed are exempted from contribution payments)*
Management	Ministry of Social Affairs	Decentralization, tripartite management (AMS), private job placement firms

Table 4.5   Institutional changes in family policy (changes in italics)

	ca.1980	2008
Eligibility	Universal coverage (family allowance) employment: parental leave allowance (females only), employment (tax breaks)	*Further universalization of benefits (child-care benefit), incentives for both parents to share family work (via enhanced benefit duration)* Employment (tax breaks)
Benefit structure	Generous cash benefits, shortcomings with regard to social services (especially for the under-3s)	*(Higher)* family allowances, *expansion of family-related tax breaks, childcare benefit (lump sum), increase in the number of childcare facilities but still low coverage (under-3s).*
Financing	Employer's contributions, taxes, user fees (childcare facilities)	Employer's contributions, taxes, user fees (childcare facilities)
Management	Federal government: cash benefits Länder and municipalities: social services	Federal government: cash benefits Länder and municipalities: social services

A first example of a path departure refers to the occupational fragmentation of the social welfare system which has to considerable extent been diminished. The prime example is the introduction of a unified pension system in 2005 which now includes (federal) civil servants. A similar development took place in health insurance, where differences between the blue- and white-collar workers in terms of cash benefits and contribution rates have been to a large extent removed. Other health care related reforms such as the introduction of long-term care allowance can be seen as more ambiguously related to the question of whether or not the Bismarckian legacy was reinforced. On the one hand, this benefit is universal and financed from the general budget, seemingly indicative of a clear departure from the traditional welfare state set-up. On the other hand, this program reinforces the role of the family in social provision, since its main objective is to compensate for (additional) care-related costs and to remunerate the efforts of caregivers, i.e. women.

The shift towards a multi-pillar pension system unambiguously marks a further path departure from the traditional way of doing things. This policy shift towards a multi-pillar system can best be described as layering (Streeck and Thelen 2005b). Two aspects are of particular relevance. One is a shift in the public private mix towards private and therefore less redistributive forms of benefit provision (Castles and Obinger 2007); the other results from the de facto departure from the idea that public pensions should secure previously achieved standards of living. Even though the statutory pension system guarantees about 80 percent of the average income earned over a 45 years period, a high replacement rate in comparative perspective (OECD 2007), it is clear that future pensions can no longer guarantee status preservation for people with atypical work careers. Pensions, for example, are henceforth calculated on the basis of an individual's lifetime contribution record, whereas benefit calculation in the early 1980s was based on the average income during the five years before retirement. The more actuarial calculation of pensions will contribute to a dualization between the insiders (i.e. the full-time employed labor force) and the outsiders (i.e. atypical workers and the long-term unemployed). Between 2000 and 2006, the number of quasi-freelancers and persons holding a marginal job increased by some 20 percent. In addition, the ratio of part-time workers went up from 14.7 percent in 1997 to 21.1 percent in 2006. The segmentation between the core labor force and the outsiders will increase in the future because the latter are neither in a position to accumulate major private savings nor to benefit from generous occupational pensions.

Recommodification by strengthening the principle of equivalence is also a major trend in labor market policy. In a manner similar to many other Western countries, and not least because of European Union stimuli, activation and active labor market policies have been strengthened, whereas passive benefits have been subject to cutbacks.

Regardless of these examples, there is also evidence that the Bismarckian roots of the Austrian welfare state have in other respects been preserved or even reinforced (Unger and Heitzmann 2003). Family policy is still very much attuned to the assumptions of the classic male breadwinner model even if the contemporary social regulations are much more gender neutral due to societal modernization and Constitutional Court rulings (e.g. uniform retirement age, widower's pension). Despite an increase in the number of childcare facilities, family policy is more than ever based on a combination of long spells of leave periods with very generous cash benefits.

Health insurance is, by and large, a further example of path dependence. Unlike Germany, there is neither the possibility for the better-off to take out private insurance nor any competition between different sickness funds. The insured are free to choose physicians, but cannot select their insurance carrier. The strong occupational fragmentation in terms of cash benefits has been removed over time, however.

The Bismarckian legacy has also been preserved in terms of welfare state financing. The three phases of social policy development distinguished in this paper are also mirrored in welfare state financing. As outlined above, government responded to the mounting economic and labor market problems by raising social security contributions until the mid-1990s. As a result, both the share of social security contributions as a percentage of total tax revenues and the contribution/GDP ratio reached an all-time high in 1995. Against the backdrop of the supply-side oriented turn in economic policy and EU accession, the stabilization of non-wage labor costs gained growing importance in the political debate. Since the mid-1990s, the relative weight of social security contributions in the tax structure has declined. Despite notable changes in the very recent past (e.g. the exemption of low-income groups and older employees from unemployment insurance contributions), social security contributions continue to represent by far the most important pillar in welfare state financing.

The strengthening of the equivalence principle makes clear that the losers of past welfare state reforms are employees whose employment record deviates from the standard employment relationship. These groups consist mainly of women, immigrants and low-skilled workers. As a consequence of the dualization between insiders (the full-time employed labor force) and the new social risk groups, a higher share of the population will be doomed to rely on means-tested benefits. For example, the number of recipients of social assistance benefits increased by 105 percent between 1996 and 2008 (Pratscher 2008: 598). However, this dualization is less pronounced compared with other Continental countries since Austria's economic performance was and still is better than in many other Bismarckian welfare states.

5 Continental Welfare at a Crossroads: The Choice between Activation and Minimum Income Protection in Belgium and the Netherlands

Anton Hemerijck and Ive Marx

5.1 Introduction

Belgium and the Netherlands represent excellent *prima facie* cases for a comparative study of social policy reform and redirection in Continental welfare systems and this is for several reasons (Hemerijck, Unger and Visser 2000). First, Belgium and the Netherlands are small, open economies that share a tradition of social partnership in the areas of wage bargaining and social insurance administration. Employers and workers are well organized, especially among large and medium-sized firms, and collective bargaining occurs predominantly at the sectoral level. At the same time, however, the two countries are distinct in terms of the institutional frameworks of the political system within which their welfare states and industrial-relations systems are embedded, suggesting possible explanatory variables for *divergent* policy outcomes. Compared to the Netherlands, Belgian federalism and linguistic regionalism have decisively constrained the scope of government intervention not only in wage bargaining but also in a host of other social and economic policy areas. Also social partnership is more fragmented, making it difficult to establish and enact broad corporatist social pacts. As a result, the mechanisms through which Belgian governments have pushed for social policy reform have tended to be more informal and subtle than in the Netherlands, although recent Belgian governments have been far from passive observers of social and economic change. During the past fifteen years, the Dutch and Belgian governments have been instrumental in promoting social reform and compensating for the policy failures of Continental policy legacies and corporatist institutions, as we shall see below. The nationally distinct trajectories of reform provide clear support for the central argument of our contribution to this volume. They demonstrate that Continental welfare systems are dynamic and evolving entities, rather than fixed institutions with a unique policy legacy producing stable and predictable path-dependent, regime-specific policy reform trajectories, even in a period of fiscal austerity, economic internationalization, slowed economic growth, demographic aging, and revolutionary family change.

In our chapter, we compare sequences of reforms in core areas of the Dutch and Belgian welfare systems, focusing on wage policy, social security 'active' and 'passive' labor market policy and pensions. We are unable to cover health insurance because of the limits with respect to the chapter length of our two country comparison. By exploring these key, functionally interdependent, policy areas, we hope to shed light on how national social policy legacies and political institutional particularities shape both the options available to state and non-state policy actors to reconfigure Continental welfare arrangements. In sections 5.2 and 5.3 respectively we present a detailed analysis of recent reforms in the Netherlands and Belgium, focusing upon the contingent dynamics and multifarious character of reform initiatives. We thus compare two trajectories of how difficult it was and still is to make a U-turn from the *cul-de-sac* of 'welfare without work' (Esping-Andersen 1996a) towards a more activating welfare state without suspending minimum income protection in Belgium and the Netherlands, from both the angle of the policy substance of the Bismarckian heritage and the angle of institutional capacities, beginning with the Dutch experience.

Whereas the Netherlands (Section 5.2) is often singled out by many as a successful example of a Continental welfare state in enacting the transition of a passive to an activating welfare state, Belgium (Section 5.3) appears to be the archetypal frozen Continental welfare state which seems to have trapped itself in a vicious circle of higher social spending, higher taxation, labor shedding, increasing public debt and deficits. This, as we will reveal below, is a misunderstanding. Also, the Belgians have experienced profound change over the past decades. Most strikingly, and in contrast to the Dutch success at 'activation', is that the Belgian social insurance state has been transformed from a traditional Bismarckian system into one with a overriding emphasis on minimum income protection and universal coverage. Moreover, in terms of its temporal dynamic, the self-transformation of the Belgian social insurance system, due to the particular institutional make-up of the Belgian polity, proceeded gradually, cumulatively and effectively by stealth, whereas the Dutch turn towards activation, has been far more 'disjointed' and 'punctuated' by more radical policy responses to successive recessions in the 1970s and 1980s and the impending disability pension crisis in the Netherlands in the 1990s. We end with assessing each country's reform experiences (Section 5.4) and the lessons that they offer about the dynamics of welfare reform in Continental welfare states (Section 5.5)

5.2 The Dutch Miracle Revisited

Until the early 2000s slowdown in the world economy, the Dutch economy had prospered almost uninterruptedly for two decades. With unprecedented job creation, sustained economic growth and low inflation concurred without sharp increases in wage dispersion and incomes, the 'Dutch model' became a catchphrase for progressive European politicians pondering the possibilities of a new model of 'third way' capitalism with a human face (Visser and Hemerijck 1997; Hartog 1999). But behind the façade of the effective 'competitive corporatism' lies a far more difficult and not nearly as successful attempt by Dutch policy-makers in bringing down the overall volume of social security claimants through structural social security reform in the 1990s.

In Dutch politics, coalition governments and corporatism delineate the institutional capacities of social and economic policy-making. The Dutch political economy is furnished with a firmly established apparatus of bi- and tripartite boards for nationwide social and economic policy-making, like the bipartite Foundation of Labor (*STAR, Stichting van de Arbeid*), the central meeting place of the social partners, and the tripartite Social-Economic Council (*Sociaal-Economische Raad, SER*), one of the most prestigious advisory councils of Dutch government in the area of social and economic policy-making. As the key financiers to the system (through premiums and contributions), the social partners have until the mid-1990s also been strongly involved in the management, administration, and implementation of social security provisions (Visser and Hemerijck 1997).

It is important at the outset to emphasize that the social security system of the Netherlands has a mixed Beveridgean cum Bismarckian design structure (Hemerijck 2003). The Bismarckian component is made up of occupational social insurance provisions, providing earnings-related benefits to workers and employees, financed through earmarked employers' and employees' contributions, insuring employees against sickness (*ZW*

– Sickness Benefits Act), disability (*WAO* – Disability Benefits Act) and unemployment (*WW* – Unemployment Insurance Act), set originally at 80 percent of last earned wages. The Beveridgean component pertains to universal people's insurance, which consists of a number of general tax-funded schemes, geared towards supporting non-working citizens, providing benefits at a uniform subsistence level for all residents. In the late 1950s, the General Old-age pension Act (*AOW*), providing universal benefits for persons over 65, was implemented. In the mid-1960s, the Public Assistance Act (*ABW)* replaced the former poor law (from 1854) and improved the general safety net for residents with insufficient means. Local authorities (the municipalities) administer social assistance. Over the course of the post-war period, the mixed Dutch pension system has come to deviate significantly from most other Continental European pension systems because of its evolving 'three-pillar' architecture. The first pillar comprises the Beveridgean basic public pension. This is a PAYG-financed lump sum benefit for all individuals, linked to the minimum wage. The second pillar includes obligatory occupational pension schemes, organized by employers and employees at the company or at the industry level. These schemes are funded and largely defined benefit. The third pillar features strictly individual retirement provisions with a favorable tax treatment.

Wage Moderation and the Disability Crisis

The depth of the 1981-82 recession in the wake of the oil crises of the 1970s catalyzed path-breaking social policy change, beginning with a government-led suspension of wage indexation, a squeezing of the minimum wage and a lowering of social benefits. The elections in 1982 brought to power an austerity coalition of the CDA (the *Christen Democratisch Appel*) and the Liberal VVD (the *Volkspartij voor Vrijheid en Democratie*), led by the Christian Democrat Ruud Lubbers. Surprisingly, after a decade of failed tripartite encounters based on Keynesian premises, the Dutch social partners crowned the new austerity coalition's entry into office with a bipartite social pact on 24 November 1982, known as the 'Wassenaar Agreement', named after the suburb of The Hague where the agreement was prepared. The agreement ushered in a period of vibrant corporatism and negotiated social reform in the 1980s and early 1990s (Visser and Hemerijck 1997). The unions accepted protracted real wage restraint in exchange for a so-called 'cost-neutral' reduction of working hours and job sharing. This new Dutch corporatism of the 1980s proved fairly robust, although it was certainly not free of conflict.

Although the social partners repaired the wage-setting system and introduced some flexibility into the labor market, they nevertheless externalized the costs of economic adjustment onto the social security system. This eventually resulted in uncontrolled growth in the volume of social security claimants. In response, the second Lubbers coalition of Christian Democrats and Conservative Liberals, in office between 1986 and 1989, enacted a package of cost-containment measures, including a reduction of the replacement rate of social security benefits from 80 to 70 percent of previous wages. Despite these cuts, the number of people receiving disability benefits continued to rise. As the number of disability claimants neared the politically sensitive figure of one million in 1989, out of an adult population of seven million, prime minister Lubbers publicly dramatized the issue by proclaiming that the country was 'sick' and required 'tough medication'. The Prime Minister recognized that he needed the Social Democrats (the PvdA), led by ex-union leader and Wassenaar negotiator Wim Kok, in the government to share responsibility for the unfinished business of welfare reform. The PvdA re-entered the government in 1989 as a partner in Lubbers' third cabinet. The new government shifted from a 'price' to a 'volume' policy, aimed to reduce the number of benefit recipients. After a great deal of agonizing, the government decided to restrict disability programs (WAO) and close off other routes to a labor market exit. The legal requirement that partially disabled WAO benefit recipients accept alternative employment was strengthened and eligibility criteria for the WAO scheme were tightened, including a reduction of replacement rates for workers under the age of 50. This episode had far-reaching political consequences, leading the unions to organize their largest post-war protest, with nearly one million participants, in The Hague, generating a profound crisis within the PvdA, nearly leading to Kok's resignation as party leader in the fall of 1991.

Hard won social security reform slowly but surely concurred with a shift in the problem definition of the alleged crisis of the Dutch welfare system. In the early 1990s policy-makers came to realize that the low level of labor market participation was the Achilles heel of the extensive but passive welfare system of the Netherlands. In 1990, the Netherlands' Scientific Council for Government Policy (WRR), an academic advisory board with a mandate to carry out future studies in areas it sees fit, proposed to break with the past and advocated a policy maximizing the rate of labor market participation as the single most important policy goal of any sustainable welfare state (WRR 1990).

In 1992, the Public Audit Office (*Algemene Rekenkamer*) published a report, suggested that the sluggish pace of social insurance reform in the Netherlands was in no small part due to the social partners' administrative authorities within the social security system. In response, Parliament decided to use its biggest weapon, an all-party parliamentary inquiry, involving testimony gathered by numerous legal authorities. In September 1993, the Buurmeijer report revealed that social security was being 'misused' by the social partners for the purpose of industrial restructuring and advocated a fundamental recasting of bipartite governance in Dutch social security administration. What is fundamental in the diagnosis of the Buurmeijer Parliamentary Inquiry is that the disability crisis was conceived of as primarily an institutional problem of failing social security administration by the social partners (Veen and Trommel 1999).

The 1994 elections took place in the shadow of popular discontent over welfare reform, and the Lubbers-Kok coalition was voted out of power. Despite being stripped of 12 of its 49 seats, the PvdA became the largest party. The progressive Liberals (the Democrats 66) persuaded the PvdA and the Conservative-Liberal VVD to form a coalition, resulting in the first government since 1917 without a confessional party. This new, so-called 'Purple' coalition placed 'jobs, jobs, jobs' at the center of its social- and economic-policy agenda. The PvdA, however, stipulated a non-negotiable condition for its cooperation, namely, that the level and duration of social benefits remain untouched. In substantive terms, the restructuring of the Dutch social security system by two successive 'Purple' governments under Wim Kok (1994-2002) entailed a partial privatization of social risks, placing a heavier financial burden for covering sickness and disability risks on employers, so as to create incentives for them to limit sickness- and disability-related absences (Hemerijck 2003). With respect to Beveridgean tier of Dutch social security, in 1996, the new National Assistance Act (*nABW*) was individualized. Single persons were to receive 50 percent of the minimum wage; single parent households were granted 70 percent of the minimum wage; married and cohabiting couples get 100 percent of the minimum wage. Participation in activation programs became obligatory for all recipients. Exemption was only granted to parents with children under the age of five.

Towards a More Robust Pension System and Activation

In May 1998, the Kok administration was re-elected, rewarded by the voters for its excellent employment record and tough stance on social security reform. The economy grew by 2.9 percent per year in the 1990s, and the rate of unemployment fell to 3 percent, the lowest in the EU after Luxembourg. With 1.4 million new jobs, labor-force participation rose from 59 percent to 67 percent of the adult population. In 2000, a budget surplus of 0.3 percent of GDP was achieved, and the public debt was reduced from 80 percent of GDP in 1994 to 54 percent in 2001.

The Purple coalition also committed itself to preserve the basic public pension (AOW) (van Riel, Hemerijck and Visser 2003). Expected increases in the public financing burden resulting from demographic aging were to be dealt with by a number of measures, including efforts to increase labor-force participation (especially by limiting early-retirement schemes), lowering interest payments through public-debt reduction, the establishment of a public pension-savings fund; and broadening the financing of the AOW. The latter goal would be achieved by fixing pension premiums at their 1997 level of 18.25 percent. Anxious to defend their authority over supplementary pensions, the social partners within the bipartite Foundation of Labor strongly opposed a forced change in the basis of benefit calculation from final salaries to average wages. They did agree, however, to increase coverage of supplementary pensions and modernize benefit rules in order to increase flexibility and individual choice. This agreement in turn led to a 'covenant' between the social partners and government at the end of 1997, which, like the 1982 wage accord, was concluded under a strong 'shadow of hierarchy.' The 'covenant' was a compromise in which the government promised not to reduce the tax deductibility of pension premiums, while the social partners agreed to modernize pension schemes by incrementally shifting the calculation of defined benefits from last-earned wages to average earning.

Like most Continental welfare states, the Dutch welfare state did not deploy active labor market policies until the early 1990s. After long preparation, in 1991, a tripartite employment service was created. As the tripartite demonopolization of placement failed to live up to political expectations, the ambitious Social Democratic minister of Social Affairs and Employment, Ad Melkert introduced special 'activation' programs, so-called 'Melkert jobs,' for low-skilled workers, women, younger workers, foreign nationals, and the long-term unemployed. Other efforts included: the introduction in 1997 of cuts in employers' social security contributions – or payroll subsidies – for the long-term unemployed and low pay workers. With the introduction of the Jobseekers Employment Act (WIW) in 1998, each new unemployment benefit claimant has to undergo an assessment interview, which is officially the responsibility of the municipalities. In this interview, a person's chances for employment or further education are assessed, after which an individual route to either work or social activation is sought. Participation is obligatory for the unemployed and a refusal can result in the withdrawal of benefits (Spies and Berkel 2000).

Since the mid-1990s, labor market flexibility has become an integral part of the new Dutch labor market policy mix. With an estimated 2.5 percent share of total volume of employment, in the EU second only to the UK, temporary agency work is a relatively widespread phenomenon in the Netherlands. In 1995 unions and employers signed the first collective agreement for temporary workers, which introduced a right of continued employment and pension insurance after four consecutive contracts or 24 months of employment. This novel collective agreement for temporary work prepared the ground for the 1996 agreement on 'Flexibility and Security' which in turn paved the way for a new Working Hours (Adjustment) Act in 2000, which gave part-time workers an explicit right to equal treatment in all areas negotiated by the social partners, including wages, basic social security, training and education, subsidized care provision, holiday pay and second tier pensions rights.

Dual earner family policy was finally recognized as of crucial importance for expanding female employment beyond part-time work. In the course of the 1990s, the Netherlands expanded parental leave at a 100 percent replacement rate from 12 to 16 weeks and introduced an optional leave right for up to 24 weeks. With respect to childcare the Netherlands remained a laggard in comparison to other Continental welfare states. This has improved, but even today many day care centers and schools offer places only on a part-time basis, requiring one or both parents to work part-time or flexible hours.

In late 1998, also the basic institutional architecture of the newly integrated organizational structure of Dutch social insurance administration was presented, based on the notion that social insurance organizations and employment boards should join forces in so-called Centers for Work and Income (CWIs). The new 'Work and Income (Implementation Structure) Act', which came into force on 1 January 2002, reduced the role of the social partners in this area and granted more responsibility to the Ministry of Social Affairs and Employment. The Work and Income Board (RWI), with representatives from employers, employees and local authorities, was set up to help formulate overall policy directions in the areas of work and income, but lacked any real executive authority (Hemerijck 2003).

The Resurgence of the Politics of Austerity

After the stock market's downward spiral and the terrorist attacks in the United States on 11 September 2001, a right-populist, Islamophobic politician, Pim Fortuyn proved able to mobilize a number of hidden anxieties and frustrations with the Purple government. When, nine days before the elections, Fortuyn was murdered by a radical environmental activist, the elections of 15 May assumed an extremely emotional character, ultimately leading to a landslide victory of the List Pim Fortuyn (LPF). In July 2002, the VVD agreed to partake in a right-wing coalition with the CDA and the LPF, led by the Christian Democrat Jan-Peter Balkenende. In office for only 87 days, the government fell as a result of a tussle within the populist LPF. After new elections, a reconstructed Balkenende coalition, with D'66 taking the place of the LPF, was very resolved to enact an austerity reform program.

Having spent the previous eight years in opposition, the Christian Democrats were especially anxious to mark a clear break with the Purple coalition's active labor market policy heritage by stopping or reducing the active employment programs initiated by minister Ad Melkert in the preceding years. The new government focused more narrowly on removing unemployment traps by lowering benefits and raising sanctions for those failing to engage in job searching. The duration of unemployment insurance benefits was cut from five years to three years and two months (after an employment record of 38 years). With the new Work and Social Assistance Act (2004), municipal authorities have been given more leeway and financial responsibility to deliver tailor-made solutions for getting social assistance clients back to work. The new Act gives municipalities their own budgets, from which they can make savings if they successfully move claimants of social assistance into jobs. The criterion of 'suitable jobs', i.e. a job with similar qualification and pay levels, has also been watered down.

As from 2004, employers are liable to pay sick leave for two years instead of one. This extension of the obligation to pay sick leave was a precursor to the new Labor Capacity Act, the WIA, which came into effect in 2006, to replace the old Disability Insurance Act. The act makes a clear distinction between people with a complete or long-term occupational disability and people who are still partially capable of doing paid work. People who are genuinely no longer capable to work will receive a permanent allowance of 75 percent of their last earnings. The new act also encourages employers to hire workers with a partial disability with lower social security premiums and contributions towards sick leave expenses if workers become ill (again).

To discourage workers from stopping work before their 65th birthday, Social Affairs minister Aart-Jan de Geus, a former Christian trade unionist, firmly committed to no longer providing tax support for collective early retirement schemes. The new life course policy (*levensloopregeling*), developed by the Christian Democrats during their years in opposition, would offer workers the opportunity to save funds, supported by tax breaks, to finance periods of leave for various purposes, such as long-term care, parental leave (with extra fiscal advantages), or education. The union vehemently opposed the new life course arrangement. In November 2004, after a half year of social unrest, triggered also by the confrontational style of the center-Right Balkenende governments, minister De Geus signed the Museum Square Pact in 2004, named after the square where the unions organized their second biggest demonstration against any post-war government. The pact combined wage restraint together with a compromise facilitating life course savings for early retirement up to three years. The tripartite SER, Social and Economic Council, however, failed to reach a consensus with respect to dismissal protection and employability, so as to inspire a shift in policy emphasis away from job security to work security. The proposal ultimately fell through in the face of tough opposition from the trade union and the Social Democrats, which returned to office in 2007, joining the Christian Democrats and a small social Christian party, again under the helm of Jan Peter Balkenende.

After a number of years of sluggish growth, the Dutch economy has again prospered. It thus seemed that the Balkenende politics of retrenchment paid off. In 2006 the average growth rate was 3 percent compared to 2.4 percent in the Euro zone. Employment also was growing at a faster pace then elsewhere in the Euro zone. In 2006, just after Denmark (3.8 percent), at 3.9 percent the rate unemployment in the Netherlands was the lowest in the Euro zone (8.2 percent). For the first time in ten years the number of people depending on social security was going down across the board. In addition, labor market participation of older workers (55-64 years) had caught up rapidly, from 29 percent in 1994 to 51 percent in 2007.

5.3 Belgium's Reluctant and Erratic Path towards Activation

The roots of the Belgian system go back to voluntary initiatives in the context of mutual societies organized along ideological lines (Deleeck 2001). A long phase of incremental, though at times still erratic expansion of various, mostly occupationally segregated social security schemes culminated in the 'Social Pact' of 1944. Born in the exceptional atmosphere of solidarity and consensualism of the final war days, it marked a consolidation of the welfare system. While extending compulsory social security coverage, the pact confirmed the subsidiary principle in that non-government organizations (i.e. unions and mutual societies) remained responsible for the administration of benefits.

While firmly Bismarckian in terms of its governance, financing and general operating principles, the equivalence principle was never as strong in the Belgian system as it was for instance in Germany. Unemployment insurance, for example, for a long time provided flat-rate benefits differentiated according to criteria unrelated to previous wages or contribution record. It was only at a relatively late stage that the system became truly Bismarckian and even then it was confined by a relatively small spread between minimum and maximum benefits.

Belgium's social protection system came to maturity just before the economic crisis struck. With the main social security pillars in place, by and large in the Bismarckian mold, all that remained was to deploy the final safety net as a statutory right ensured by law. This happened through three laws enacted in the late 1960s and early 1970s.

It was just after these final pieces had been put in place that Belgium's social protection system was challenged in a most profound way, due to a combination of economic, socio-demographic, political and budgetary pressures. In response, the Belgian welfare system underwent substantial change, contradicting its apparent corporatist immobilism. But unlike in the Netherlands, this change happened in a very gradual and almost 'stealthy' way. Yet it amounted to a fundamental transformation of Belgium's social welfare system, as we will show below.

The Crisis Years: The Initial Shift towards Minimum Income Protection

As an early industrializer, Belgium's economy was particularly hard hit by the oil price shocks and the subsequent economic downturn of the 1970s and 1980s. As elsewhere throughout the continent, Belgium resorted to an expansion of early exit routes in order to drain off excess supply and to alleviate the social consequences of structural economic adjustment and massive job shedding (Esping-Andersen 1996a).

The main exit scheme that was implemented around the late 1970s to shelter the casualties of industrial decline was an early retirement scheme consisting of unemployment insurance benefits, supplemented by an additional benefit paid out by an industry or sectoral fund. Although instituted during the late 1970s, the scheme saw its biggest expansion during the 1980s. This had a number of beneficial effects at the time (Marx 2007a). It provided adequate income protection to those (often sole breadwinners) who lost their jobs during a time when re-employment chances were extremely low. At the same time, the scheme facilitated industrial restructuring allowing Belgium to embark on a high productivity path.

In addition, there was a heavy influx into unemployment insurance. As elsewhere this had been instituted to protect against frictional unemployment in a full employment environment, at least as far as the male breadwinner was concerned. And as elsewhere, the system was confronted with a dramatic change not only in the magnitude but also in the nature of the unemployment risk: frictional unemployment increasingly became structural unemployment. In addition, socio-demographic change affected the redistributive efficiency of the system; benefits originally intended to protect sole breadwinners and their families against poverty increasingly ended up with laid-off second earners.

In response to these multiple dysfunctions, Belgium's unemployment insurance system started to undergo a radical transformation, evolving from a social insurance system in the classic Bismarckian mold into a minimum income protection system, with the financing and governance dimension of the system remaining distinctively 'Bismarckian'. That is to say, benefit levels became far more of a function of assumed need rather than past wages and contributions, but contributions remained proportionally tied to wages. This transformation happened gradually through piecemeal reforms, but the accumulated effect amounted to a fundamental transformation nonetheless, as is documented in greater detail in the literature (Andries 1996; De Lathouwer 1997; Clegg 2007; Marx 2007a).

The initial policy response in the wake of the 1970s recession was relatively successful in what it sought to achieve: providing adequate minimum income protection to those who were then still regarded as the 'victims' of the economic crisis (Marx 2007b). The alterations did not only help to alleviate poverty among the unemployed, they also served to contain the cost consequences.

What is remarkable and probably rather unique, is that in Belgium the Bismarckian insurance and equivalence principles gradually became subordinate to the need principle, and this essentially for the sake of cost containment and poverty relief. Trade unions (especially the socialist union) did at various points in time demand a restrengthening of the insurance function but they never really pushed the issue. There were plenty of other issues relating to unemployment insurance (the unlimited time duration of benefits for example) where trade unions were more ferocious in having their demands met (Kuipers 2006). In the wider political sphere, the decline of the insurance function also remained a non-issue.

It is unclear who actually initiated the shift away from insurance but the move appeared to be very much consensual at the level of the social partners and the governments of the time, which were Christian-Democrat dominated coalition governments, partnering either with the socialist or Liberal parties. But why did the unions go along? Perhaps part of the reason is that the unemployed and the early retired were and remain as much part of the core constituency of trade unions as workers. This is because the majority of trade union members get their unemployment benefit through their union. In addition, unions provide additional services, such as (advice in) dealing with the administration. Such services provide a powerful incentive to become and remain a loyal union member.

Unions, therefore, have always had a strong incentive to keep benefits, above all, widely available rather than to insist on the maintenance of the equivalence principle, which after all was less historically entrenched in the system than in other Bismarckian systems. At the same time, they had to face the reality of an out and out cost explosion of the system after the mid-1970s. The scale, severity and suddenness of the labor market crisis created inescapable pressures for change. Unions had in effect no choice but to accept the almost complete abandonment of the equivalence principle. The alternative, however, would have been a virtual bankruptcy of the UI system, which would have necessitated government intervention (i.e. third party funding) and hence more government involvement in the running of the system. Clearly, the social partners – not only the unions

– wanted to maintain their autonomy from government in the domain of collective bargaining and governance of the social security system. In short, the unions had to strike a balance between keeping the system affordable, hence maintaining their autonomy, and keeping a loyal and dependent clientele within the system.

Towards 'Activation'

The shift towards more adequate minimum income protection started to run into systemic limits during the 1980s when the turnaround in macroeconomic policy remained elusive. The strong shift towards more adequate minimum income protection grinded to a halt after the mid-1980s. Real benefit levels (i.e. adjusted for inflation) became largely stagnant, though some segments like single parents continued to experience some improvements (Cantillon et al. 2004). In addition, the late 1980s were an era of strong real wage growth, and as a consequence benefits dropped rapidly relative to wages and overall living standards.

Adding poignancy at the time was the dire state of Belgium's public finances. By the late 1980s Belgium had the highest public debt rate in the industrialized world. In an attempt first to maintain a hard currency (deemed essential for Belgium as an exporting country and also to maintain a good credit rating) and then to qualify for EMU membership, expenditure control became a major preoccupation. Also marking this turnaround was the introduction, in 1996 under the Dehaene government, of the so-called Competitiveness Law. This marked a turning point in that this was the first successful government initiative to structurally limit the bargaining freedom of the social partners in an *ex ante* way. Past state interventions had only occurred after wage growth had derailed. Specifically, the law requires wage rises to remain within the limits of wage growth in Belgium's main competitors: the Netherlands, France and Germany.

The late 1990s, then, mark a more radical shift in emphasis. The talk all across Europe became of The Third Way, the Activating Welfare State, and Belgium followed suit (Vandenbroucke 2001). The political context also changed dramatically around that time. The Verhofstadt-headed 1999 'Purple' coalition of Liberals, Socialists and Greens ended four decades of almost interrupted Christian Democrat domination.

Much effort was directed at employers in an effort to boost demand for unemployed and less skilled workers. This mainly took the form of sizeable reductions in employers' social security contributions. To compensate for lost social security contributions some alternative financing was introduced, mainly in the form of earmarked VAT levies.

Efforts at the demand side were matched, to some extent, by measures at the supply side. In 2000, a social security contribution reduction for low paid employees was introduced which increased net pay and which, consequently, made work at or around minimum wage (marginally) more attractive. The 'work bonus' of 2005 was a further expansion. In addition, there was the so-called 'activation of benefits'. People on unemployment benefits were allowed and even stimulated to take up certain activities like gardening, house cleaning and other types of personal services – jobs deemed to have been priced out of the regular labor market.

Yet the increased emphasis on active labor market policies has not as yet gone accompanied with the kind of social security reform needed to create a real pay-off. Government effort to boost work willingness has relied on 'carrot' rather than 'stick' type of measures. It has proved rather more difficult to introduce more stringency on the benefit side in a more purposeful way. Unemployment insurance benefits in Belgium remain unlimited in time as a matter of principle. Only certain categories are liable to have their benefit terminated after an 'abnormally' long spell of unemployment. During the 1990s, there was a wave of benefit suspensions but average benefit duration in Belgium nevertheless remains much higher than in other countries. Most recently, however, there have been new waves of benefit suspensions over reporting irregularities or failure to show up for job counseling or training.

The failure to scale back benefit dependency is nowhere more evident than if one looks at early retirement. At less than 40 percent, the employment rate for older workers is at one of the lowest levels in Europe. As already explained, the principal early retirement scheme in Belgium was formally instituted as an extension of the unemployment insurance system. But as the name implies, the so-called 'bridge pension' was conceived from the start as a retirement scheme and not as an unemployment scheme. It was also perceived as such. By the time that economic conditions had improved (the 1990s), a powerful coalition had formed around the main early retirement scheme. Early retirement remained after all a cheap and low-resistance way for companies to make less productive workers redundant. And many workers had come to expect to get what many of their former co-workers had obtained: the chance to leave the labor market early with an attractive financial package.

In 2005, the government tried to build a consensus around the so-called Generation Pact. The main objective of this pact was to increase the effective age of retirement; the early retirement age was increased from 58 to 60. The social partners achieved an agreement of sort but the Pact encountered strong resistance from the union base. The Generation Pact triggered a lot of posturing by the powerful sectoral organizations, outdoing each other as the 'true defenders' of acquired rights (i.e. the right to early retirement) effectively, to the embarrassment of senior trade union figures at the central level who (initially) defended the Generation Pact. Add to that the lukewarm enthusiasm for a radical scale back among employers. Despite calls for drastic reform by the representative organizations, employers remained happy users of the bridge pension as a vehicle for facilitating restructurings. As a result of all this, the Generation Pact was finally adopted in a watered down version, which went into effect in 2008.

Pensions

In line with its Bismarckian design, the first pillar system for employees is funded through social contributions and co-governed by the social partners. Pensions are also, in principle, related to past contributions and past wages. But as in other sectors of Belgium's social security system, there has been a marked shift from income insurance to minimum income provision. Maximum pension entitlements have become an increasingly smaller fraction of real past earnings for people with above average earnings. At the same time, more and more people have come to gain entitlements on the basis of activities that are deemed 'equivalent' to being an employee who actually pays for social security contributions or for whom such contributions are made by the employer. Spells in unemployment, for example, count as equivalent. Time spent in career interruption schemes do too. It has been calculated that about a third of pension entitlements are gained on other grounds than paid work and past contributions (Peeters and Larmuseau 2005).

At the same time, the withering of the equivalence principle is feeding a creeping privatization. Public pensions, as provided through social security, have become so low that average to high earners have come to rely on occupational and private schemes to obtain a pension commensurate with their past earnings. Here, a duality has emerged between people with access to such schemes and those without. The 2003 'Vandenbroucke' Law on supplementary pensions aims to contain this divide and to generalize access to such provisions but it remains to be seen what effect it is having.

Belgium has been labeled a 'Conservative welfare system' in which the Christian Democratic 'subsidiarity principle' has institutionalized familialism. It is true that the labor market and welfare system remain geared somewhat towards male breadwinners in the sense that derived social security rights remain extensive and that some elements of the tax system still support the sole breadwinner model. At the same time, however, childcare provisions for working parents have become extensive, especially in the Flemish part, making Belgium a case in point of what has been called 'optional familialism' (Leitner 2005). That is to say, the caring family is supported but at the same time families are also given the option of being (at least partially) unburdened from care responsibilities. And while the sole breadwinner household is fiscally supported, the dual earner household is clearly even more supported.

Belgium has extensive childcare provisions both in the form of institutionalized day care centers as in the form of subsidized 'substitute mothers'. Gross fees are strongly income related as well as partially tax deductible rendering childcare close to costless for those with the lowest incomes. Belgium's maternal employment rate is around 70 percent, which, at the level of Denmark, Sweden and Norway, is among the highest in Europe. Important bottlenecks remain. The main problem is localized scarcity of available childcare places. Waiting lists remain long and this seems to be a particular problem in larger cities. In addition, parents find it difficult to find institutionalized childcare outside of regular hours – that is to say for evenings, weekends, holidays etc. This is posing a particular barrier to less skilled parents taking up jobs in the services sector where hours are often irregular (Marx and Verbist 2008).

5.4 Path-Dependent Policy Divergence across Small Continental Welfare Regimes

The Continental welfare regime is historically organized around the axial principle of (male breadwinner) employment. This is often seen as a weakness, especially in combination with social insurance welfare financing. Under conditions of macroeconomic austerity, raising social contributions runs into constraints at a time when firms are particularly sensitive to increases in gross labor costs. It then becomes necessary to either reduce employment-related benefits at a time when people become more dependent on them, or to stimulate employment growth by more daring social and economic policy reforms. These two alternatives sum up the policy choices made in recent decades in Belgium and the Netherlands.

Continental welfare states may be slow reformers, but they are not immobile. For both Belgium and the Netherlands the era of permanent austerity was also a period of permanent reform and adjustment. Inferring from the comparative country experiences above, it is possible to paint a broad picture of welfare self-transformation in the Netherlands and Belgium in terms of a sequence of policy changes across a number of policy dimensions. In both Belgium and the Netherlands a successive series of incremental policy changes and more daring reforms across a number of interrelated policy areas reveal fundamental system changes in the make-up in the two neighboring welfare states. It goes almost without saying that the general direction of change can only be observed in a longer term perspective.

During the past thirty years, the transformation of the Dutch welfare state from having a heavy reliance on income maintenance towards adopting an overriding focus on maximizing labor market participation proceeded in rather 'disjointed' fashion, captured by episodic successes, like the 'Wassenaar Accord' and politically charged policy failures, like the disability pension crisis, together with the more recent overhaul of early retirement and the introduction of the new life course savings scheme. Belgian welfare state change, in contrast to the Dutch case, revolved around a transformation in social insurance from a system in the Bismarckian tradition of status maintenance into one with an overriding emphasis on minimum income protection and universal coverage. Moreover, the pace of Belgian social and economic policy change proceeded more gradually, cumulatively and effectively by 'stealth'.

Disjointed Social Policy Transformation in the Netherlands

The Dutch welfare state has certainly experienced the greatest transformation and shown considerable capacity for reform and policy innovation, marking a paradigm shift from fighting unemployment through labor supply reduction in the 1970s and 1980s, the typical Continental welfare state's response to industrial restructuring, to a deliberate policy of raising employment levels for both men and women from the 1990s onwards. The Dutch welfare transformation process was based on a sequence of four fundamental and cumulative policy reorientations, which ultimately allowed the Dutch to reverse the vicious circle of 'welfare without work'. In the first place, retrenchment and cost containment measures principally dominated the reforms in the 1980s. Levels of insurance benefits were reduced slightly and the benefit duration was shortened. In the second place, the success of sustained wage restraint, after serving to boost competitiveness in the exposed sector, helped to create more jobs in domestic services. This in turn slowed down and eventually even lowered the number of people dependent on social benefits. The reduced social wage component, subsequently, allowed Dutch governments to use improved public finances to lower the tax and contribution wedge and to expand active labor market policies in the 1990s. Third, the Dutch social reform momentum of the 1990s can be characterized by an increased emphasis on curtailing easy exit, activating labor market policies and flexicure labor markets, together with a fundamental overhaul in the administrative and incentive structures of social security. And finally since the mid-1990s, labor market flexibility has become an integral part of the new policy mix of labor market regulation and has enjoyed significant support from the social partners. Together with the incremental individualization of the tax system, 'flexicurity' legislation has contributed to the 'normalization' of part-time employment, which now encompasses nearly one-third of the workforce.

Today paid work is seen by all the relevant policy actors in the Dutch political economy as the key route for attaining personal welfare and social cohesion as well as contributing to the sustainability of a generous welfare state. The growing emphasis on the importance of paid work in promoting social inclusion was accompanied by introducing more market-oriented approaches in the management of the social security system. In the domain of social security reform, the Dutch state adopted a fairly aggressive posture, both privatizing and nationalizing portions of the welfare state, in particular the regulation of the intake of new claimants, in order to secure reforms that limit expenditures and the number of beneficiaries. The reforms in the 2000s to unemployment and social assistance programs as well as the introduction of the new disability benefit program (WIA) have profoundly reinforced the activation requirement in the Dutch welfare system. The overall trend was towards increased employment conditionality, increased activation, more stringent targeting and reduced generosity. The Continental insurance principle has on the one hand been fortified in unemployment insurance and disability benefits, with stricter coverage, increased importance of relative work history, and the linking of benefit duration to work history, considerably strengthened the insurance principle. This, in turn, resulted in a greater inflow in social assistance, which, in the meantime, was reorganized around the principle of activation. Beyond the shift from calculating defined benefits on the basis of last-earned wages to average earnings, the Dutch old-age pensions have remained robust and stable with broad coverage in the second pillar of occupational pension and its basic income floor for all residents in the first pillar.

Belgian Welfare State (Self-)Transformation by Stealth

Relative to the Netherlands, trade unions, employers and the government remained stuck in a state of corporatist quasi-immobilism. Until the mid-1990s, Belgian trade unions did not accept that wage restraint was necessary for economic recovery and job growth. In part, this reflects the continued strength of the Belgian unions compared to their Dutch counterparts. The Belgian government ultimately had to impose wage restraint from above. This not only sacrificed micro-flexibility for the purpose of macro-adjustment, it also made any form of productive issue-linkage between different areas of social and economic regulation difficult to achieve. In sharp contrast to the Dutch experience, the Belgian welfare state proved unable to reverse the cycle of 'welfare without work'. Instead, Belgian policy-makers and other social actors ultimately found each other on a course towards an overriding emphasis on minimum income protection.

Strikingly, the changes to the system did not benefit the 'insiders' – i.e. the traditional core constituency of the Bismarckian welfare state. Instead, many of the reforms have been aimed at improving the minimum income protection effectiveness of the system hence catering to what are usually considered 'outsiders' within the Bismarckian framework, for example women, youngsters and the long-term unemployed. In this respect, Belgium has proved to be all but the archetypal 'frozen' welfare state. But the changes that have happened have also been mostly defensive, in order to cope with the inescapable pressures imposed by external circumstances: first massive job loss, then the need for budgetary restraint (EMU).

The social partners have sought and largely succeeded to maintain their autonomy from government in the domains of collective bargaining and governance of the social security system. The social partners, fragmented as they are along sectoral, ideological and, increasingly, linguistic lines, and hence unable to escape the multiple negotiators dilemmas they were and remain trapped in, have time and time again sought to maximize short-term gains and minimize short-term losses on the issues of most importance to them. Successive governments, from their side, have remained reluctant to challenge the autonomy of the social partners in any real way, especially in the domains in which the social partners have sought to maintain their autonomy most ardently in: collective bargaining over wages and social security. On the contrary, governments have mostly accommodated and compensated whatever settlements the social partners reached – mostly in the name of social peace – widely seen as an essential precondition to Belgium's economic prosperity if not its endurance as a political entity. This is not to say that the government has been a passive actor. For example, Belgian governments have at various times stepped in, suspended autonomic wage bargaining and imposed wage moderation. But each time the goal has been to maintain or to restore the status quo, to keep things from worsening, but never actually to achieve positive goals like job growth. In reality, the fact that the government stepped in at various times actually accommodated the social partners in that it helped them to save face whenever they failed to reach an agreement. Suspensions of autonomous wage bargaining have arguably always happened with some degree of tacit agreement on the side of the social partners, although not always all of them. Wage moderation, therefore, has also never gone further than maintaining the status quo. Achieving redistributive outcomes through job growth has never been pursued.

One could even argue that seemingly 'offensive' initiatives on the part of the government have in fact turned out to be measures of compensation. For example, a lot of budgetary resources have been put into employers' social security reductions, ostensibly to encourage job growth. Evidence that this has happened in any real way remains elusive but the reductions have clearly accommodated wage increases and contributed to the maintenance of automatic wage indexation.

Table 5.1   Summary of reform trajectory: Belgium

Types of change	Context	Diagnosis
Augmentation and incremental expansion (1970s)	– economic downturn; – mass job loss in industry; – baby boom cohort and women entering labor market; – massive labor market imbalance	– social benefits should help the victims of the crisis
Selective augmentation as well as retrenchment: the shift towards minimum income protection (mid-1980s)	– continuing imbalance in the labor market between demand and supply	– social benefits should help the victims of the crisis, BUT cost should be contained
Selective retrenchment (1990s)	– economic conditions improve but demand/supply imbalance remains – public finance situation dismal – EMU requirements	– further cost containment essential in view of public finances and cost of labor
A hesitant shift towards activation (mid-1990s) up to the late 2000s?	– economic conditions more favorable	– activation imperative

Table 5.2   Summary of reform trajectory: Netherlands

Types of change	Context	Diagnosis
Crisis management with a benign expansion of early exit (1978-89)	– oil crisis and economic recession with mass job loss in industry and firm bankruptcies	– Dutch disease: expensive exports with high inflation: need for wage moderation

Content of the policy	Politics of the reforms	Consequences
– sharp increase in the generosity of the benefits – new benefit schemes, especially early retirement	– incremental expansion – corporatist consensus	– mass inflow in benefit dependency – sharp rise in social expenditure – growing financial imbalance
– more categorical targeting according to assumed need, insurance principle abandoned	– gradual reform bit by bit (layering) – corporatist consensus, with mainly token resistance from unions against increased targeting	– continued inflow in benefit dependency – stabilization of social expenditure, but still shrinking contribution base – welfare without work at peak, i.e. high dependency, low poverty
– still more categorical targeting – benefit levels stagnate – efforts to reduce chronic benefit dependency	– more government activism in areas of wage setting and benefits – increased tension between social partners and government – failure to achieve social pact consensually	– benefit dependency drops slightly but remains high – poverty rises – legitimacy of the system suffers
– cautious efforts to reduce benefit dependency, especially early retirement – increased spending on active labor market policies	– continued failure to achieve a real change in direction consensually – increased conflict and fragmentation in the political as well as the industrial relations field	– Belgium now mediocre performer in terms of employment and poverty outcomes – stalemate

Content of the policy	Politics of the reforms	Consequences
– Wassenaar accord: wage moderation in exchange for flexible labor time reduction with state-led mild retrenchment	– broad consensus strongly supported by the social partners (except for retrenchment)	– improved competitiveness – job creation – due to inactivity trap, mass inflow in benefit dependency – sharp rise in social expenditure – growing financial imbalance social insurance

Table 5.2 Summary of reform trajectory: Netherlands

Types of change	Context	Diagnosis
From a price- to a volume policy through institutional change (1989-95)	– improved economy, but post-German unification crisis seen as a driver of continued austerity	– disability crisis and social partners misuse of social insurance administration BUT benefit levels are contained
Towards activation and flexicurity (1995-2001)	– economic conditions improve – stable public finances – but low employment	– redefinition of crisis of the welfare state: from fighting unemployment to raising participation in the labor market
Resurgence of the politics of retrenchment (2001-7)	– end to wage moderation – falling competitiveness – low growth also due to procyclical boom and bust macro policy	– retrenchment and modernization with an eye on prolonging working life

5.5 Explaining within Regime Policy Divergence

Why is it that these two neighboring Continental welfare states embarked on such different trajectories of social policy (self-)transformation, given that there have been more convergent tendencies during the last decade? One might distinguish broadly between two explanatory categories, one emphasizing the importance of broad material and substantive differences and policy contingencies, the other underlining the importance of political institutional differences between the Belgian and Dutch political economies.

From a material perspective, the Belgian economy was arguably harder hit by the oil price shocks and the subsequent economic downturn of the 1970s and 1980s. It must also be noted that Belgium never had the gas revenues which provided much needed budgetary relief in the Netherlands during the 1970s and 1980s. The inflow into benefit dependency (especially disability) never affected Dutch public finances in the way it did in Belgium, where, as indicated, things were much exacerbated by costly settlements of interregional conflict.

Content of the policy	Politics of the reforms	Consequences
– selective retrenchment (eligibility and targeting) – institutional overhaul; – managed competition in sickness and disability insurance	– broad and strong political consensus, with token resistance from unions against selective retrenchment and institutional change.	-improved cost containment on social expenditures; – inactivity problems remain in passive social insurance
– activation in social insurance and social assistance – active labor market policy – (female) part-time revolution – pension modernization – flexicurity agreement and legislation	– broad political consensus with token support of the social partners (employers more responsible with tougher activation for workers)	– Dutch miracle of unprecedented job creation, sustained economic growth, low inflation without large increases in incomes and wage inequality
– new conditions for disability, – cuts in unemployment insurance; – phasing out pre-retirement; life course policy	– after serious confrontation between trade unions and the government, – two social pacts (2003;2004) – strained relations social partners	– successful recovery in terms of growth, jobs and public finances – stalemate over dismissal protection

In the Dutch case, when path-breaking reforms were undertaken, the premise was that there had to be 'light at the end of the tunnel' for reasons of political legitimacy. This was vital to the 'jobs, jobs and more jobs' strategy. The promise of these jobs had to be realistic when social insurance programs and employment protection regulation were drastically recast and curtailed. The Wassenaar Agreement, in retrospect, generated a benevolent positive feedback dynamic of enhanced trust and policy learning, which over time allowed for more path-breaking social policy innovation and experimentation. Due to the depth of the initial crisis and failed policy responses in encouraging wage restraint, positive feedback effects remained absent in Belgium. Hence, one could argue that the Belgian context was an unlikely one for a Wassenaar-style pact ever to emerge. And in effect, in Belgium the social partners never came close to such a pact. It was left to the government to take up responsibility for restoring economic competitiveness which it did by resorting to a major currency devaluation in 1981. Whereas wage moderation required sustained discipline on the part of the social partners, the devaluation effectively offered a bail-out to the social partners to continue in their old ways, i.e. seeking short-term (wage) gains for their membership.

Institutionally, beyond the general image of Belgium and the Netherlands as coalition polities and corporatist political economies, Belgium and the Netherlands are worlds apart. Belgium, unlike the Netherlands, is characterized by major and deep-cutting internal divisions along ethnic/linguistic and religious/ideological lines. These multiple, intersecting divisions have resulted in a far more fragmented, complex and conflict-ridden political system than the Netherlands. Linguistic conflict took up and effectively depleted political time and energy in Belgium at a time when economic and social policy took center stage in the Netherlands. The unions have remained unitary in name, but in reality major divisions have always existed between the Flemish and French-speaking wings. Whereas successive social conflicts in the Netherlands have brought the secular and Christian trade union movements more together, the Belgian generation pact, for example, have left the unions more divided than ever, also internally.

A second important institutional difference between the two neighboring polities concerns the role of the state. In the Netherlands, where the state is unitary but decentralized rather than federal, authorities have at times been able to intervene more directly than their Belgian counterparts. That said, both Belgium and the Netherlands have witnessed greater assertiveness on the part of state actors relative to earlier periods. In the Netherlands, the government has had the power to secure moderate wage agreements, increase labor market flexibility, curtail moral hazard in the social security system, redirect pension modernization, by way of a 'shadow of hierarchy', involving the state's implicit or explicit threats to intervene in the event of the social partners' failure to act. While the Dutch story reflects possibilities for corporatist renewal, then, it also demonstrates that such an outcome can, and often is, dependent upon a significant degree of state intervention within the policy-making process. The initiative for welfare and labor market reform in the 1990s in the Netherlands was political. It is not insignificant that in the past twenty years all major political parties, from Left to Right, in various grand coalitions, have participated in welfare retrenchment, often involving significant departures from the traditional paradigms of policy-making. Belgian policy-makers, by contrast, have had to work within an institutional context marked by both a less capacious state and greater institutional, legal and political impediments to unilateral state action due to their federal, regional and linguistic, institutional structure. With federalization, successive governments were not in a strong position to legislate path-breaking social policy reforms. The lack of a broad political compromise on domestic social and economic policy, thwarted by a federal division of authority, also negatively affect the construction of an imperative for change in Belgian political and policy discourse. In the Dutch context, important reports of the tripartite Social Economic Council, and other expert committees like the Buurmeijer Parliamentary Inquiry and 'think tanks' like the Scientific Council for Government Policy (WRR), have since the mid-1980s prepared the mindset for the radical reorientation in social and economic policy in the Netherlands.

While the Dutch social partners have seen their involvement in social insurance administration being severely restricted, the trade unions in Belgium continue to co-administer unemployment benefits and get substantial finances for doing so. As we argued in section 5.3 this has created specific incentives, which probably account in some measure for why Belgium's social security system evolved the way it did, most notably why the equivalence principle was abandoned for minimum protection and widened access to benefits. That said, the fact that the equivalence principle was historically not as strongly entrenched probably also accounts for this peculiarity of the Belgian trajectory.

Based on the welfare reform experience over the past three decades in Belgium and the Netherlands highlighted in this chapter, the image of Continental welfare inertia and political immobilism surely cannot be corroborated. The precise policy mixes that have ensued from these reform experiences have not only been critically shaped by past policy legacies and institutional structures of decision-making, but also and more in particular by policy-makers' capacity for *innovation*, intelligently using the institutional constraints and policy resources at their disposal in the face of new external and internal challenges.

6   Italy: An Uncompleted Departure from Bismarck

Matteo Jessoula and Tiziana Alti[1]

6.1   Introduction

The Italian welfare system emerged under two different political regimes: the competitive, Liberal regime from the country unification (1861) to 1922, and the Fascist regime (1922-1943). The profound variation of the political background, however, did not have a decisive impact on the institutional traits of social protection schemes that from its inception displayed a Bismarckian imprint. They were in fact built along occupational lines – aiming to protect dependent workers primarily – and financed through social contributions paid by employers and employees (though the state contributed with a share of the total cost, i.e. *tripartite financing*); benefits were broadly contributions related and differentiated among occupational groups and categories (private/public employees, blue/white collars).

After World War II the bulk of the system was managed by a public institution[2] – the national institute for social insurance *Inps (Istituto nazionale della previdenza sociale)* – which was structured on several funds (*casse* or *fondi*) for different risks (old-age, survivors, disability, unemployment, family and sickness) and professional categories – i.e. initially dependent workers in the private sector as the self-employed were covered in the 1950s-1960s (see below). *Inps* was originally administered by civil servants, while the social partners would be formally involved in the management at the end of the 1960s. This change was important because it granted the social partners (especially the unions) formal legitimacy to participate in the social protection policy-making, but it should not be overestimated. In fact, on the one hand the unions had until then relied on a more direct channel for interest representation, as the parliamentary groups of the major parties – the Christian Democrats (DC), the Communist Party (PCI) and the Socialist Party (PSI) – had a 'union component' which included some unions' leaders. On the other hand, major decisions in the field of welfare policies were in the hands of political and institutional actors, such as the government and the Parliament.

Section 2 briefly sketches the development of the Italian welfare system during the so-called golden age (1945-1975). Section 3 constitutes the core of our analysis, dealing with four different sequences of welfare reform: a) the ambivalent interventions of the 1980s; b) the first retrenchment reforms in the period of fiscal emergency (1992-93); c) the path-breaking reforms of the mid- to late 1990s; d) the growing tension between these modernizing interventions and more conservative measures in the recent years (2000-2008). Finally, in section 4 we propose an evaluation of the trajectory of reform of the Italian welfare system.

Against this background, in the following paragraphs we do not pretend to provide an encompassing analysis of welfare and labor market developments in Italy.[3] We rather aim to interpret the trajectory of development and reform of the Italian social protection system by focusing on four different factors. First, *sequencing*, as we argue that major departures from the institutional path have been triggered by a stepwise process of reform. Second, we analyze how *Bismarckian institutions* have contributed to mold both the policy-making and the outcomes of reform. Third, we evaluate the *influence of Europe* on the reform trajectory, also aiming (fourth) to shed a light on likely processes of (policy and social) *learning* that might facilitate change.

6.2 A Bismarckian Route... With a First Departure

A System of Social Solidarity for Workers and their Families

After World War II and the foundation of the Republican regime the Italian welfare system underwent three decades of major expansion. As occurred in other Continental European countries in the same period, a 'system of social solidarity for workers and their family' (CRPS 1948) was set up in order to achieve (quasi)Beveridgean goals – i.e. to free all citizens from need, alleviate poverty and protect against major social risks – through Bismarckian means. This meant extending coverage to those professional categories not yet protected and to workers' dependents, therefore confirming the original Bismarckian (and fragmented) institutional design of the system. In fact, during the 1950s and the 1960s piecemeal reforms repeatedly extended compulsory sickness insurance, family allowances were introduced also for public sector employees, the retirees and the unemployed, while the self-employed were compulsorily insured against old age and disability with the creation of three new funds within *Inps* (farmers 1957, artisans 1959, merchants/shopkeepers 1966). Moreover, in the field of pensions the 'typical' PAYG earnings-related system was adopted (1968-69) and eligibility conditions were loosened with the introduction of seniority pensions in the public (1956) and the private sector (1965). Public employees were thus allowed to retire after only 20 years of regular work (reduced to 15 for married women and mothers), while private employees and the self-employed were required to have 35 years of contributions.

After these reforms, the public pension system covered roughly 100 percent of those in employment through a number of occupational schemes and started to provide generous benefits – often with loose eligibility conditions – also presenting some schemes which were 'structurally underfinanced'. In fact, since the establishment of the new schemes for the self-employed (see above), the contribution rates for these categories were set at a very low level and the equilibrium between revenues and expenditure was guaranteed by the transfers either from other funds (especially dependent workers') or the public budget. This structural deficit together with the extremely favorable rules for seniority pensions would become critical issues in the 1980s-1990s (see below).

The Italian welfare system was thus built upon the assumption that (quasi-)universal coverage could be achieved through work-based social insurance schemes in a condition of high economic growth and full-employment, at least for the (typically) male employed family member – the well-known 'male breadwinner model'. Sustained growth and full (male) employment were thus both preconditions for effective social protection and the major aims of the governments in the phase of Keynesian welfare capitalism. Therefore, between the end of World War II and the early 1990s the state was deeply involved in the economy – not only as a regulator, but also through controlled enterprises – and in the labor market. Employment grew in the public sector as well as in publicly-controlled firms; the public monopoly of employment services was introduced (1949) and the possibility of individual firing was drastically limited in 1966 and 1970.[4] The strong protection of those in employment (job-security) and the low investment in ALMPs generated a rigid labor market, with a high level of job stability on the one hand, and already in the 1970s a high share of long-term unemployed (especially the young and women) on the other hand.

Such a profound gap between the 'insiders' (i.e. people that had access to employment and, through this, to social insurance) and the 'outsiders' was also reinforced by the peculiar features of the unemployment protection system, social assistance and family policies. As to the protection of unemployment, the system was based on 'first pillar' contributory schemes which displayed a great variation in coverage and benefits generosity along occupational lines. In fact, the protection was generally stronger in the industrial sector and in medium and large-sized firms, where employees were not only entitled to ordinary unemployment benefits but also to very generous programs for wage replacement in case of (partial or total) working-time reduction without definitive dismissal. By contrast workers employed in micro and small firms had access to ordinary benefits only, which were not related to previous wages and of a very modest amount. Any other pillar – unemployment assistance or a last resort safety net for those not employed – was lacking (Ferrera 2006; Alti 2003). The absence of a tax-financed, non-contributory minimum income scheme for all the people in need was in fact one of the peculiar features of the underdeveloped Italian social assistance, which was also characterized by the lack of a national regulatory framework and, as a consequence, by a high territorial variation in terms of benefits, beneficiaries and generosity. Family policies also lagged behind and displayed some peculiarities: first, they mostly relied on cash transfers, with very few in-kind benefits; second, most benefits were contributory and only workers were entitled. In particular family allowances were not conceived as universalistic, tax-financed benefits related to children, being considered rather as wage supplements, financed through social contributions, for (employed, unemployed and retired) dependent workers only.

Yet, during the 'golden age' these gaps in coverage and risks protection did not generate intense political debate, and they were mostly compensated by: a) the persistence of the traditional family patterns – that guaranteed access to welfare benefits through the secure job of the male breadwinner and operated as a redistributive agency for its members; b) the distortion and abuses in the provision of certain benefits – e.g. disability pensions – that especially in southern regions performed social assistance functions as unemployment subsidies in disguise.

A Partial Hybridization of the Model

If, as illustrated, the Bismarckian institutional design of income maintenance schemes (pensions, unemployment insurance, family allowances)
was repeatedly confirmed in the post-war decades, this did not rule out
the introduction of alternative goals, principles and instruments that
partly hybridized the Italian welfare state. The major change was the transition from an insurance-based to a universal health care system with the
establishment of the National Health System in 1978.[5] This represented a
clear path-shift in the field of health care and also led to the replacement
of contributory financing with tax financing.

But old-age protection schemes were also somewhat 'contaminated'. If
the bulk of the system remained fully Bismarckian, the goal of poverty
prevention was introduced next to the traditional income maintenance
one: a social assistance supplement for contributory pensions under a
certain threshold (*minimum pension*) and, above all, a *social pension* – i.e.
a tax-financed means-tested flat-rate benefit – for all the people in need
over 65 were introduced in 1952 and 1969 respectively.

6.3 Departing from the Bismarckian Compromise: A Stepwise Process of Reform

The Early Creaks in the Welfare Edifice and Contradictory Reforms (1975-
1990)

The first oil shock of 1973-74, which is usually considered a turning point
in the studies on welfare state development, had only a limited effect on
the Italian economy (apart from spiraling inflation rates).

Things worsened after the second oil shock (1979), when the national
economy entered a prolonged phase of stagflation: four years of recession
coupled with very high inflation rates (around 20 percent in 1980-81) and
the continuous growth of unemployment (7.6 percent in 1980, 10.4 percent in 1985, *OECD*) – due to the progression of the deindustrialization
process. Furthermore, public finance presented annual deficits around 10
percent.

Nevertheless, in the early 1980s, financial issues were not at the top
of the political agenda, nor was the impact of social expenditure on the
public budget. The period was in fact characterized by the first attempts
to move from Keynesianism to liberalism, though these attempts were
often timid and, above all, encountered harsh opposition by the unions

and the Communist Party. Even if some measures were taken in order to introduce a greater discipline in the parliamentary budget session, the priorities were the reduction of inflation and the struggle against unemployment.

In spite of some analyses that pointed at the burden posed by the welfare system on public finances (Ferrera 1984) and field specific studies about future fiscal and economic compatibilities with particular reference to old-age[6] and health care expenditure, the welfare state continued to be (generally) considered a useful, effective and efficient institution. Moreover, politicians did not have enough incentives to embark on retrenchment policies. Two factors, in particular, hampered the shift from the distributive, 'credit claiming' (Weaver and Pierson 1993) policies of the golden age to cost containment interventions. On the one hand, such interventions were very risky in political terms as the Bismarckian imprint of income maintenance schemes induced the perception of social benefits as 'quasi-property rights' (Myles and Pierson 2001) and legitimized union actions in defense of the status quo. On the other hand, the peculiar features of the Italian political system – a 'polarized' (Sartori 1966) democracy characterized by a high cabinet instability and a low autonomy of the latter from both political parties and a 'turbulent' Parliament – made it very difficult for the various governments to adopt retrenchment measures. The clash between the alarming projections envisaging future problems of financial and economic sustainability and the 'short-term horizon' of policy-makers (Pierson 1997) was then resolved in favor of the latter.

Therefore during the 1980s the governments followed a strategy based on four cornerstones. First, fighting against unemployment by undertaking the well-known 'labor reduction route'. Thus, labor shedding strategies were pursued and the traditional reliance on passive policies was reinforced by introducing the possibility of early retirement (1981), exploiting pre-existing rules for seniority pensions (see previous section) and increasing the (still very low) ordinary unemployment benefits (1988). Second, pressure from (micro)categories forced governments to adopt some further incremental expansionary measures – i.e. increase of benefits – especially in old-age insurance schemes. Third, such interventions were counterbalanced by raising social contributions (five times between 1980 and 1990, from 23.9 percent to 25.9 percent), and in order to offset the consequent increase of labor cost – that might have a negative effect on the economic competitiveness of the country – the national currency was frequently devalued (twice in 1981 and once in 1982, 1983 and 1985).

In contrast with these expansionary interventions aimed at strengthening social protection, the fourth strategy consisted of the adoption of a few cost containment measures and the revision labor market rules. The frauds, waste and inefficiencies in the management of certain welfare programs were tackled by both introducing a means-test to get entitled to minimum pensions (1983), and tightening eligibility conditions and reinforcing control mechanisms in the schemes for contributory disability pensions.[7] As for labor policy, the priority goals of the period – i.e. inflation control and unemployment reduction – were pursued. In 1983, a 'tripartite social pact' led to a revision of the automatic indexation mechanism for wages, making it less generous in order to put a brake on spiraling inflation, and a similar measure was adopted by decree one year later, in a situation of harsh social conflict between the leftist union (Cgil) and the government/employers. These interventions were somewhat 'compensated' (in 1984 and 1986-7) by the introduction of a few innovative 'activation' measures aimed at fostering employment growth.

At the end of the 1980s the Italian welfare system was still strongly Bismarckian – apart from, as already noted, the health care sector – and much geared towards the protection of the so-called 'insiders'. Moreover, the implementation of the new 'active' labor market policies was often not effectively pursued and these measures did not prove very successful in tackling unemployment and creating new jobs. The employment rate was 1.9 point below the level of the early 1980s and, even more important, long-term unemployment (i.e. one year and over) had grown significantly, from 51.2 percent of total unemployment in 1980 to 70.4 percent in 1989 (OECD 1991).

In the early 1990s, two further interventions confirmed the ambivalent nature – partly expansionary, partly cost containment – of the Italian social policy since the late 1970s. In the field of old-age protection, despite increasing expenditure (around 12 percent of GDP) and growing transfers from the public budget to fill the gap between contributions and revenues, the earnings-related system was extended to the self-employed (1990), also setting the contribution rate for this category at a very low level (ca. 12 percent in contrast with ca. 26 percent for private employees). This represented an expansionary change which dramatically worsened the financial situation of the three schemes affected by the reform (Franco 2002) and increased the unfairness of the system – as the return on contributions for the self-employed was higher than for private employees. As we shall see, both these factors would play a role in the reform of old-age pensions in the following years. Secondly, in order to tackle mounting unemployment (11.5 percent in 1990, OECD) a new unemployment protection scheme was set up – so-called 'mobility allowance' (1991) – providing generous benefits (replacement rate: 80 percent) for 12 months, with a possible extension to 48 months with a lower replacement rate. This measure reinforced the traditional reliance on passive policies and aimed to reduce the job offer on the labor market as the new scheme was often employed as an instrument for early retirement (Geroldi 2005). Moreover, as the mobility allowance was only introduced for workers of big firms mainly in the industrial sector (coverage was in fact limited to ca. 32 percent of dependent workers) it further increased the segmentation of the unemployment protection system.

To conclude, we may say that the modest interventions adopted in the first sequence of reforms, though introducing some innovative measures (mainly in employment policy), did not alter the nature of Italian social protection schemes, which were still mostly directed to workers, earnings-related and contributory-financed (social contributions represented roughly 70 percent of social protection receipts in 1990, Eurostat), and they presented problems of fairness that resulted from the high heterogeneity of rules. The policy-making had in fact remained insulated from external pressures and domestic actors did not have enough incentives to radically modify both the existing welfare architecture and the underlying (re)distributive compromises.

Pressures from 'Beyond': Path-Dependent Change in Emergency (1992-1993)

By the early 1990s, Italy had mostly closed the gap with most Continental countries in terms of 'welfare effort' and expenditure for social protection (23.7 percent of GDP in 1980) was just slightly below the EU15 average (24.4 percent, Eurostat). Furthermore, the expansionary reforms of the golden age and the maturation of some social protection schemes – namely, pension schemes – had entailed a realignment of goals and means: the post-war objective of *poverty alleviation* had in fact been replaced by the goal of *income maintenance*, which was pursued through typically Bismarckian, contributory schemes providing earnings-related benefits.

The social and economic background differed slightly from the previous decade, as most problems were still on the ground though with varying intensity. Inflation was still rather high but more under control (6.4 percent in 1990, 5 percent two years later, IMF), while the increase of unemployment (11.7 percent in 1992, OECD) and the alarming decrease of the employment rate (from 52.6 percent to 51.5 percent between 1990 and 1994, OECD) were signs of an acute 'welfare without work' syndrome. Meanwhile, the good economic performance of the late 1980s had come to an end and financial problems had become extremely acute – the public debt reaching ca. 100 percent of GDP and annual deficits over 10 percent.

1992 represented the turning point for both government priorities and the content of public discourse: attention and actions rapidly turned from the struggle against inflation to financial recovery. Pressures from the international and supranational (i.e. EU) arena were crucial for this u-turn of the Italian macroeconomic policy, that soon affected welfare institutions too.

In July 1992 – in the midst of the political turmoil provoked by the corruption scandal that would soon remove all traditional parties from the political stage (*Tangentopoli*, i.e. bribe-city) – the partly technocratic cabinet led by the socialist Amato revived the season of tripartite agreements (Regini and Regalia 1997) signing an important social pact on labor cost: the automatic indexation of wages to prices was eliminated, and this represented an important step that would contribute to reduce inflation rates in the following years (from 5 percent to 1.9 percent between 1992 and 1997). This agreement was also decisive as it allowed the government to focus on fiscal recovery and consolidation that, after the inclusion of the convergence criteria in the Maastricht Treaty and the definition of the path towards the monetary union, could no longer be avoided. In order to reduce public deficits – the priority goal at that time – a decrease of interest rates was vital, though it seemed to be out of reach when speculative attacks on the Lira were launched in September 1992. The Italian government thus faced a tremendous challenge stemming from the interplay between the process of European integration and financial markets. On the one hand, in order to prove their commitment to the construction of the monetary union, Italian policy-makers could not resort to the 'same old route' of currency devaluation, on the other hand, persistent speculative attacks pushed the Bank of Italy to raise interest rates (Barucci 1995). In the end, a few days before the French referendum the Lira was devalued – and pulled out the EMS – but the government opted to accompany this intervention with a plan (presented by mid-September) aimed at improving public finances. This plan included a pension reform that was much more incisive than the interventions proposed in the early summer, and some guidelines for the revision of the National health care system.

But, why precisely did external pressures induce the government to reform pension as the first, and most important step, of the process of fiscal consolidation? Considering that Bismarckian schemes are financed through social contributions, the link between pension reform and financial consolidation is not that straightforward, and it requires closer investigation. Indeed there were at least three reasons that pushed the Italian government to adopt a pension reform in order to 'restore-to-health' the public finance. First, both pensions and contributions for public employees and civil servants were paid directly from the Treasury Ministry, thus contributing to the general state outlay (just as the wages of public employees). Second, the likely gaps between revenues and expenditures for contributory pensions were to be filled, ultimately, by the state budget. Though estimates vary (due to the fuzzy accounting relationship between *Inps* and the state budget), the deficit for private sector schemes (dependent and self-employed workers) was around 2 percent of GDP in 1988 (Castellino 1988), and increases were forecast for the future. Third, it is necessary to consider a sort of 'demonstrative effect' of pension reforms: in a nutshell, pension reforms may reassure financial markets – as they are taken as evidences of the commitment to financial rigor – and this facilitates the reduction of interest rates and, finally, the decrease of both debt service and deficit.

The Amato pension reform relied on two components: the revision of the public PAYG pillar and the introduction of a regulatory framework for supplementary DC (defined contributions) funded pensions, which were to be financed primarily via the voluntary transfer of the *Tfr*.[8] Though the second component represented the first step for the structural transformation of the pension system into a multi-pillar model, the reform mostly entailed a path-dependent, incremental change. Some cost containment measures were introduced, but the first PAYG pillar maintained its primary role and the earnings-related method for benefits calculation was preserved together with its traditional income maintenance function.

Even path-dependent changes and marginal cuts, however, might have been risky in political terms and, due to the traditional involvement of workers organization in pension policy-making, (at least) the acquiescence of the unions was a fundamental precondition for a successful reform (Bonoli and Palier 2007). Therefore the Amato cabinet followed two strategies. On the one hand, long transition periods and key exemptions were introduced in order to protect the core members of the trade unions, i.e. older workers and pensioners. On the other hand, the Bismarckian connotation of the system – characterized by a high institutional frag-mentation and regulatory variation along professional lines – and its un-justified redistributive consequences were exploited by pushing the lever of fairness in order to introduce cost containment measures that might have triggered the reaction by the unions (Levy 1999).

Therefore, if the joint pressures from the international arena were cru-cial to push policy-makers on the retrenchment path, the resistance to change that had appeared during the 1980s was overcome by a) the use of 'tactical devices' in the design of the reform and, b) the exploitation of the fragmented institutional architecture of the Italian pension system. Though carefully calibrated and gradually implemented, however, the re-form not only contributed to tackle some typical problems of Bismarckian schemes – namely, the above mentioned welfare-without-work syndrome – but it also 'lightened' the fragmentation of the system by reducing the great variation of rules between professional categories.

The Path-Breaking Reforms under European Influence (1995-2000)

In the mid-1990s the run-up to EMU continued in a climate of financial emergency and there was a large consensus among the Italian decision-makers on the need for a second pension reform in order to reduce public expenditure and deficit. The Amato reform had in fact left some prob-lems on the ground. First, the comparatively short minimum contribu-tory period to be entitled to seniority pensions (35 years), which was the major cause of the low average age of exit from the labor market (58.4 years); second, if the rules had been thoroughly harmonized between public and private employees, the favorable treatment for the self-em-ployed persisted; finally, further massive increases of both contribution rates and transfers from the public budget would be necessary in the near future in order to keep the balance between revenues and expenditure (Inps 1993).

The Watershed Pension Reform: Beyond Income Maintenance through Public Benefits

The years 1994-5 were crucial for the evolution of the national pension system. In September 1994 the center-Right cabinet led by Berlusconi presented a plan to reform pensions, which mostly pursued financial sus-tainability in the short term through some interventions on seniority pen-sions, the reference earnings and the indexation mechanism. The unions harshly reacted because these measures would affect the pension entitlement of their core constituencies. A vast national demonstration and a general strike were organized, and a further strike was planned for early December when the government had to retreat and the original proposal was drastically watered down.[9]

The failure in the field of pensions contributed to the resignation of the Berlusconi government (December 1994), which was followed by the technocratic Dini cabinet. This was expected to remain in place for a limited time in order to implement a few crucial reforms that might contribute to tackle the fiscal crises and smoothen external pressures coming from financial markets (cfr. Ferrera and Gualmini 2004). As Treasury Minister of the former Berlusconi government, Dini had been a major actor in the policy-making on pension reform and, consequently, he had 'learned' that unions' consent was a fundamental prerequisite for successful reforms. The social partners were thus involved in a concerted effort to draft the new reform proposal. The final agreement (May 1995) – which was not signed by employers' representative (Confindustria) – was transposed into law 335/1995 that represented a critical watershed for the Italian pension system.

The Dini reform was in fact based on two cornerstones. The first was the replacement of the earnings-related system in the first pillar with a 'notional defined contribution' system (NDC) – where benefits are no longer linked to previous earnings – but depend on the amount of contributions actually paid, the age of retirement as well as economic and demographic trends. The second consisted of more generous tax incentives and a more effective exploitation of the Tfr in order to support the take-off of supplementary funded pensions based on voluntary membership.

Such developments testify a greater reliance on individualized insurance and market mechanisms that represents at least a partial (as schemes are still occupational and contributory financed) 'retreat from Bismarck'. Moreover, the reform included some provisions aimed to tackle some typical problems of Bismarckian systems: the low age of retirement and the 'welfare without work' syndrome. In fact, the implementation of the NDC system with a new flexible retirement age (57-65 years) would provide strong incentives to postpone retirement because of the links between retirement age and pension value, while the gradual increase of the contributory requirement for seniority pensions (from 35 to 40 years) would pose a brake on early retirement.

What is worthy to note is that – as in 1992 – the departure from the traditional Bismarckian route was accomplished by exploiting two typical features of Bismarckian welfare systems: fragmentation and the earnings-related method to calculate pensions. In fact, the final agreement on the introduction of the NDC system for all categories (private/public employees and the self-employed) was found because, on the one hand, it would improve financial sustainability – which pleased the cabinet – and, on the other, it phased-out the favorable treatment for both the self-employed and those workers with the most dynamic careers (namely, medium-high income workers), thus matching unions' requests for greater harmonization and (actuarial) fairness (Jessoula 2009).

However, such a concerted reform protected the pension rights of the unions core constituencies to an even greater extent than the Amato reform: extremely long transition periods[10] for the implementation of the new NDC system – that fully applies to new entrants in the labor market after 1996 only – and for the phasing-in of the new contributions requirement for seniority pensions were introduced in order to safeguard the 'acquired rights' of older workers, and retirees were not affected. Once again, key exemptions were provided in order to forestall union opposition.

Learning from Europe to Go Beyond Bismarck

After the adoption of the Dini reform, and the 1996 elections that registered the victory of the center-Left coalition led by Romano Prodi, economic recovery and (relative) political stability slightly allayed financial worries, thus allowing a partial reorientation of both the public discourse and the policy-making on welfare reform. Arguments about fiscal rigor were still present – especially because of the 1998 deadline for the verification of the convergence process across EC member states – and they would stimulate a further incremental revision of the pension system in 1997 (*Prodi reform*), mostly directed at achieving (modest) cost reductions in the short run. Nevertheless, a wider debate on the shortcomings of the national system of social protection and the need of a deep 're-calibration' (Ferrera and Hemerijck 2003) aroused. An experts commission – so called *Commissione Onofri*, also including the leading scholar in welfare studies Maurizio Ferrera – pointed at the weaknesses of the national welfare system by stressing its very acute 'double distortion'. The first ('functional distortion') was related to the overprotection of old age at the expenses of other risks/sectors like unemployment, family and social exclusion/assistance; the second ('distributive') had to do with the wide security gap between the insiders and the outsiders and, as such, it was due to the interaction between the Bismarckian imprint of the welfare system – according to which eligibility to social benefits is based on work and employment – and the rigidity of labor market rules.

This diagnosis and the policy solutions proposed by the commission were deeply influenced by the inputs coming from the supranational, European arena, which channeled innovative ideas into the national debate, thus reorienting the attention of domestic actors towards the so-called 'new social risks' – e.g. lone parenthood, longer life expectancy, need for care activities, interrupted careers and precarious jobs. Such issues – that posed a serious challenge to the national Bismarckian welfare edifice and the underlying 'male breadwinner model' – came to the top of the government's agenda in the late 1990s. This happened especially with the Prodi cabinet, which aimed to represent a modernizing coalition committed to bring Italy – with all its vices and few virtues – closer to Europe and its social model.

Privatization, Flexibilization and Activation in the Labor Market

In the field of labor policy, the persistent problems of low employment and high unemployment were tackled by acknowledging the shortcomings of the strongly regulated labor market and prompting a radical, 'paradigmatic' change.

Building on the social pacts of the early 1990s, the 1997 'Treu reform' (from the name of the Ministry of Labor and Social Protection) triggered a shift towards a more flexible and deregulated labor market. The public monopoly on placement services was abolished and so called 'atypical', flexible job contracts, like temporary and part-time jobs were either introduced or relaunched after the failure of the late 1980s. Moreover the traditional predominance of passive policies was limited, moving towards a more equilibrated 'policy mix' (Graziano 2007) with the development of ALMPs to facilitate insertion, especially for the most disadvantaged groups (younger and older workers, women).

For the adoption of these measures, supranational influence was indeed crucial, as the strengthened competition in an open Continental economy made the long-lasting shortcomings of the Italian labor market no longer tolerable. But EC influence was also more straightforward. On the one hand, the then-in-the-making European Employment Strategy channeled into the domestic policy arena detailed principles (i.e. adaptability, employability, modernization of the labor market) and guidelines for employment policy reform that induced a *learning process* by national actors. On the other hand, the liberalization of employment services was implemented under the pressure of an impending sentence by the ECJ which was about to sanction Italy for the public monopoly of placement services.

As illustrated in details by Graziano (2004) these developments facili-tated the emergence of a pro-reform *'advocacy coalition'* (Sabatier 1998) that acted to modernize, and to a certain extent 'europeanize', the Ital-ian labor market. Such a coalition, which managed to overcome (at least partly) the traditional policy network oriented at the maintenance of the status quo, was formed by a part of the trade unions movement (especially the moderate unions, Cisl and Uil), some members of the government (above all, the Ministry for Labor and Social Protection) and a portion of the central bureaucracy. Within this new coalition a prominent role was played by some experts (especially those involved in the *Onofri commis-sion*) and by the external advisers of the Ministry that aimed to reshape national policies in accordance with the goals, the principles and the pol-icy instruments elaborated at the European level.

It is worthy to note, however, that labor market flexibilization was not accompanied by adequate investments on the security side: in fact, the reform of unemployment insurance was not included in such a major re-vision of Italian employment policy.

Bridging the Insiders/Outsiders Divide

A similar and, to some extent, interconnected process unfolded in the fields of social assistance and family policies that – as noted above – were both underdeveloped and (especially the latter) geared towards the pro-tection of the insiders due to work-based eligibility.

Since the beginning of the 1990s community institutions – e.g. the European Observatory on National Policies for Combating Social Exclu-sion – had addressed the issue of social exclusion and in 1992 the Council Recommendation 92/441/EEC had stressed the relevance of anti-poverty policies for both the integration process and the construction of the Euro-pean citizenship. Finally in 1997 the fight against poverty and social exclu-sion had been included in the Treaty of Amsterdam. This attention to the issue of social exclusion/inclusion went in parallel with the proliferation of field specific technical committees such as the European Anti-Poverty Network. These contributed to the formation of supranational 'epistemic communities' that socialized national experts and bureaucrats on the sub-ject, thus stimulating a process of *policy learning* and *diffusion* in a two-level policy and political arena (Alti 2003).

The transposition of ideas emerged at the community level into the Italian policy-making on the reform of social assistance was mainly ac-complished by two groups of experts: the committee on poverty and so-cial exclusion (*Commissione di indagine sulla povertà e l'esclusione so-*

ciale) and the above mentioned *Commissione Onofri* appointed in 1997. Both committees played a crucial role in the formulation of the major reform proposals in line with the EC approach, which aimed to reinforce social assistance and family policies, but also to overcome the traditional work-based approach through much more inclusive and comprehensive universalistic programs. This matched the modernizing aspirations of the Prodi cabinet (and subsequent center-Left governments) which prompted a recalibration of the national welfare system in order to bridge the insiders/outsiders gap. A number of measures were therefore adopted in the period 1998-2000 that mostly relied on the innovative principle of *selective universalism* (Ferrera 1998), according to which eligibility to social assistance benefits had to be conditional on *citizenship* and *need* only. In other words, the introduction of new policy instruments for all people (universalism) in need (selectivity) was considered to be crucial in order to strengthen social assistance and overcome the traditional work-based approach in family policies.

The budget law adopted in 1998 set up a 'Fund for social policies', reinforced means-testing through the implementation of an 'indicator of socio-economic conditions' for those applying for social benefits/services and introduced three innovative, non-contributory, means-tested benefits aimed at alleviating poverty. These benefits were: 1) the allowance to families with more than three children, 2) the maternity allowance and, above all, 3) a 'Minimum insertion income' (Mii) pilot scheme, which was designed as a non-categorical, means-tested, tax-financed measure, addressed to all the people under a predefined poverty threshold. The innovative character of the latter was also related to its 'activation' component, since the monetary transfer was accompanied by integration programs in order to tackle social exclusion and stimulate recipients' autonomy. The establishment of a last resort safety net, as well as its characteristics, were perfectly in line with the indications of the European Commission, that in the communication COM(98)774 strongly advocated the reinforcement and, eventually, the harmonization of minimum income schemes across member states.

The budget law for 2000 provided for a two-year extension of the experimentation of the 'Mii', and in the same year the Italian social assistance seemed to take another big step forward with the approval of a national regulatory framework. Law 328/00 established that social assistance would be based on an integrated system of services and benefits, with the reinforcement of the former in order to reduce the Bismarckian 'cash-transfer bias'.

If fully accomplished, the plan could have led the Italian welfare state and labor market clearly beyond Bismarck. However the early 2000s saw contradictory developments.

Steps Back and Forth between Modernization and Conservatism (2000-2008)

In the early years of the new millennium Italy entered a four year recession – with GDP growth between 0 percent and 1.1 percent in 2001-05 (*IMF*), that is much lower than most Western countries – and, above all, a continuous loss of competitiveness of the national economy during a decade. By contrast, the public finances gradually improved, with low deficits (generally below 3 percent of GDP) and a (slowly) declining public debt. Therefore, if during the previous decade the 'keyword' in the public discourse had been fiscal consolidation, in the early 2000s it turned to be 'competitiveness' (Radaelli 2002).

The debate on welfare reform was affected by the new context and framed by the effects of the reforms adopted in the 1990s, but it also registered the change of government majorities: the center-Left cabinets of the late 1990s were followed by the new center-Right government led by Berlusconi (2001-2006), while the coalition led by Prodi won the 2006 elections before Berlusconi came back to power in 2008.

The discourse therefore focused on four issues. First, in the field of pensions the issue of benefits adequacy (especially for younger cohorts) became more relevant next to 'traditional' arguments on economic and financial sustainability. This was the result of the 'generational break' provoked by the Dini reform, as the long-transition period for the implementation of the NDC system and the increase of contribution rates (33 percent of gross wages since 1995) overburdened younger generations, who will bear most of the costs of reforming pensions and fiscal recovery. Second, the interplay between the cost of social protection (especially pension) and labor market performance became a major concern in light of the above mentioned competitiveness deficit of the country. Third, in the short-medium term the compatibility between public expenditure for welfare programs and the equilibrium of public finance was at risk, particularly in light of the projected tax cuts that represented a top priority for the Berlusconi government. Fourth, the latter's vision of the welfare system stressed the role of the family more as a redistributive/caring agency than a recipient of social provisions.

Against this background, the early steps of the new cabinet aimed to find a way out from employment, economic and fiscal problems that still affected the country and two proposals for reforming pensions and the labor market were prepared in 2001.

Doing and Undoing in the Field of Pension

The first draft of the plan to reform public pension had two major goals: 1) containing pension deficits in the short-medium term and, 2) supporting employment via an increase of the actual average age of retirement and a reduction of labor cost. The first objective was pursued through stricter requirements for seniority pensions – which might also contribute to raise the average retirement age – while a cut of contributions for workers hired with open-ended, permanent contracts was directed to promote employment. Next to these interventions, the reform plan also contained a provision for the definitive transition to a multi-pillar system: the compulsory transfer of the *Tfr* to supplementary pension funds – a measure that would have made available for funded schemes roughly 13 billion euros per year (around 1 percent of GDP). The reconfiguration of the system on different pillars was justified by the projected sharp reduction of replacement rates for first pillar pensions – ca. 55 percent of last wage around 2030 according to the Ministry of Welfare (Ministero del Welfare 2002). But the transition was also 'pulled' by financial actors (bank, insurance companies), that had entered the pension policy arena after the reforms of the 1990s and then met the benevolent attitude of the center-Right cabinet (Jessoula 2009, 2010). The unions strongly opposed the reform and mobilized their members against the government proposal. This time, however, the government – learning from the 1994 defeat on pension reform (Natali and Rhodes 2005) – adopted a wiser tactic aimed to smoothen the unions' protest. A few times, the policy-making was suspended, various rounds of negotiations with the social partners followed and, finally, the cabinet withdrew the most controversial measures from the plan – i.e. the reduction of contributions and the compulsory transfer of the *Tfr*.

The final version of the reform was adopted in 2004. A compromise was found for supplementary pensions with the introduction of the so-called 'silent-consent' formula for the transfer of the *Tfr* to pension funds.[11] As for the first pillar, the interventions mostly followed the EU recommendations on the promotion of employment of older workers: a) incentives for later retirement in the period 2004-2007 were introduced and, b) the age requirements for seniority pensions were tightened (three-year increase by January 2008). On the other hand Law 243/04 replaced a key element

of modernization introduced by the Dini reform – the flexible age of retirement – reintroducing a rigid (and differentiated according to gender)
retirement age (65 for men, 60 for women).

It is worthy to note, however, that the three-year increase of the age requirement to be entitled to seniority pensions was repealed by the center-
Left government (2007), which introduced a more gradual tightening of
eligibility conditions, together with other incremental adjustments.

Flexibility without Security

As for employment policy, the learning process that had started during
the 1990s continued in the early 2000s, regardless of the political orientation of the cabinets. Once again, experts played a major role in the
elaboration of both the diagnosis and reform proposals, and the White
Book (Ministero del Welfare 2001) inspired by Marco Biagi suggested a
move towards a more 'flexible and secure' labor market in accordance
with EU recommendations (especially from the EES). The government interpreted these guidelines in the light of its policy and political priorities
and drafted a reform proposal which for the first time included a measure
that, if adopted, would undermine the long lasting pattern of job security
for the *insiders*. In fact the government's bill aimed to modify Article 18
of the Workers' Statute on the compulsory reintegration of workers in
case of unmotivated dismissal, by allowing employers to choose between
reintegration and monetary compensation. In contrast to what happened
in the field of pensions, however, in this case the unions front split, and
only the major workers organization (Cgil) strongly opposed the reform
– in particular the intervention on Article 18 which was seen as a deliberate attack to workers. Once again the rank and files were mobilized and
a vast demonstration was organized in March 2002. Despite such strong
resistance, in the following months a pro-reform coalition emerged and
a new social pact was signed (Pact for Italy) by the government, the employers' association and two unions (Cisl and Uil), while Cgil continued
its opposition. The agreement drew the guidelines for the following 2003
employment policy reform.

Law 30/03 contained measures which were much more tuned towards
flexibility than *security*, though the revision of Article 18 was ultimately withdrawn. Flexibilization was relaunched with the introduction of a
number of new 'atypical' contracts, mainly directed at those entering the
labor market, and placement services were strengthened. However, the
comprehensive reconfiguration of the unemployment protection system
was not included in the reform. This absence is particularly striking for

at least two reasons. First, because the Pact for Italy had already pointed at the need to increase the replacement rate of ordinary unemployment benefits (from 40 percent to 60 percent, more in line with European standards). Second, and even more important, as the growing share of 'atypical workers' on total employment (16.2 percent in 2003 from 9.3 percent 10 years before) and the spread of flexible contracts amongst the new entrants the labor market indicated that: a) at least for the younger generations the traditional pattern of job security had been abandoned, and consequently, b) the system to tackle unemployment should be radically revised in order to protect atypical workers that could hardly get entitled to ordinary unemployment benefits.

Moreover, the missed reform of unemployment compensation went parallel to the developments in the social assistance sector where the minimum income safety net – aimed to protect from lack/loss of income – was all but reinforced. Privileging a welfare model based on family and community networks (Ministero del Welfare 2003), the center-Right government drastically cut the fund for social policies and put an end to the experimentation of the Minimum insertion income.

More recent developments have not modified the situation either. In the short period of the center-Left Prodi cabinet (2006-8) the issue of setting up a safety net for those in need has disappeared from both the political agenda and the public discourse, while the plan to expand childcare services had just been started when the government resigned. By contrast, resources have been directed to strengthen ordinary unemployment benefit – by extending duration to eight months and increasing replacement rate to 60 percent for the first six months: as employees on open-ended contracts in small/medium firms mostly benefit from this improvement, it represents another case in which available resources have been 'captured' by the insiders at the expenses of both the atypical, temporary workers and the outsiders. As a consequence, even taking into account the whole range of ordinary and special benefits, ca. 69 percent of the unemployed was not covered in case of unemployment at the end of 2006.

Finally, the measures aiming to tackle poverty which have been adopted during the early months of the new Berlusconi government seem too timid (if not completely inadequate). A lump sum benefit for low-income households ('family bonus') and a so called 'social card' – i.e. an income-tested benefit targeted to persons over 65 and to families with children below three years old – have been introduced, but they are extremely low: between 200 euros (single person) and 1,000 euros (family with three children) the former, 40 euros/month the latter.

6.4   Towards the End of the Bismarckian Compromise

Over the last three decades the fundamental components of the 'Bismarckian compromise' aimed at securing income protection both in employment and retirement for workers and their families have been substantially modified. The major changes have been adopted in the fields of employment policy and old-age protection.

Firstly, though a high level of job protection (and stability) has been maintained for the 'insiders' – due to the strong resistance by the major union on this issue – the pattern of employment based on full-time permanent contracts has been overcome, at least for the new entrants in the labor market, and flexibilization has rapidly increased.

As for pensions, first, incremental adjustments have managed to tackle some shortcomings of the Bismarckian model by pursuing a thorough harmonization of pension rules across the major occupational categories and foreclosing the gateways to early retirement; second, structural reforms have entailed a major shift from the typical Bismarckian configuration, characterized by the predominance of first pillar, public, compulsory insurance schemes providing earnings-related benefits to a multi-pillar model. This is based on the combination of public Notional Defined Contribution and supplementary Defined Contribution schemes, which implies a deep modification of the Italian model of old-age protection, and particularly of its underlying logic. In fact, if the NDC system will be decisive for containing old-age expenditure and reducing deficits in future decades, fiscal and economic sustainability is likely to be attained by abandoning the traditional goal of *income maintenance through public pensions*. The new system is built on the idea that in the future income maintenance after retirement will have to be achieved via a much more complex interplay between mandatory and voluntary insurance, first and second/third pillar schemes, state and market, PAYG and funding. Within this new arrangement the income maintenance function is not guaranteed as, first, it depends on workers' voluntary affiliation to supplementary funds (members are currently 5 million out of 23 million employed) and, second, it is not an explicit objective of both NDC and DC schemes. In fact, these are informed by the principles of *'individual saving'* and *actuarial fairness* and, consequently, they do not provide any predetermined level of benefits – as only the contribution rates are fixed and pensions vary according to different parameters – thus shifting on insured workers the risk associated with old-age insurance.

In the late 1990s, these far-reaching changes seemed likely to be accompanied by the introduction of innovative goals (poverty prevention), principles (selective universalism) and policy instruments (minimum insertion income, means-tested family benefits, development of social services) that, if fully institutionalized, might have helped to bridge the traditional insiders/outsiders gap. However, more recently a growing tension between these modernizing developments and more conservative measures has been registered. Attempts to overcome the traditional work based approach – or, in other words, to go 'beyond Bismarck' – in the fields of unemployment protection and family policies have been rare, the path towards the institutionalization of the new goal of combating poverty/social exclusion has been barred – thus letting Italy without a minimum income safety net – the provision of in-kind benefits (e.g. childcare facilities) has not caught up with European standards, and a comprehensive income protection system for the growing share of atypical workers is still a far prospect.

In the previous sections we have illustrated how innovative reforms have been propelled by external pressures. EU budget constraints, the road to EMU and financial markets stimuli have jointly represented *indirect pressures* for the adoption of retrenchment measures in pension and employment policy, whereas labor market, social assistance and family policy reforms were *directly influenced* by the ideas and the policy solutions elaborated within supranational and cross-national 'epistemic communities.' However, the close investigation of both adopted and failed reforms and the recent cases of policy reversal suggests that European influence has been *mediated* by: a) the domestic *institutional (policy) settings* and their links with *interest groups*, b) the *political priorities and strategies* of national actors. On the one hand, retrenchment interventions – especially in the pension sector – have in fact been successful when governments have been willing (and able) to exploit the fragmented Bismarckian institutional structure (and regulatory variation) and craft package deals that were acceptable by the unions (the actual veto players in this field). On the other hand, the 'politics matter' argument holds particularly true when looking at the path-breaking, and mostly expansionary, reforms in the field of unemployment protection, social assistance and family policy, but also at the more recent policy reversal. In fact the learning process has fully occurred when the innovative policy recipes from the European level have matched the political and policy priorities of the center-Left Prodi government – that aimed to represent a modernizing coalition open to Europe and its social model – thus empowering the pro-reform national coalition. By contrast, the center-Right Berlusconi cabinet has referred to Europe in order to adopt retrenchment measures while mostly disregarding the stances in favor of the consolidation/expansion of innovative welfare programs like the 'Mii' (selective learning). Finally the (indeed very weak) center-Left Prodi government has been more committed to repeal some of the measures introduced by the previous cabinet than to significantly modify the longstanding pattern of relations between the welfare system, the family and the individuals/workers.

6.5 Conclusions

What are therefore the prospects for the Italian welfare system after the partial departure from the Bismarckian arrangement illustrated above? In order to answer this question two final considerations should be put forward.

Firstly, it must be acknowledged that the peculiar mix of modernizing interventions and conservatism has led to the accomplishment of the retrenchment component of the reform process whereas the introduction of innovative instruments that should constitute the compensatory component has lagged behind. The consequence is that the Italian welfare state currently adds to the traditional gaps in terms of protected risks and social groups, new gaps – which mostly affect younger generations – stemming from the end of the 'Bismarckian compromise' in employment and pension policies. There is, thus, urgent need for a further revision of the welfare architecture in order to make it more respondent to the new risk profiles. This would very likely require a greater reliance on new principles and policy instruments, such as citizenship/need-based programs and the loosening of the equivalence principle in contributory schemes.

And here comes the second consideration. Is this revision of welfare arrangements probable, or possible, in the near future? The analysis of the trajectory of reform has shown that Italy has long been unable to revise the national welfare system endogenously and, in accordance with neo-institutionalist arguments about the relevance of exogenous shocks for policy change, innovative reforms have been adopted due to external pressures/influences. The current financial and economic crisis seems therefore to be a good testing ground to see if national policy-makers will be willing to exploit once more exogenous shocks in order to complete the departure from Bismarck.

Table 6.1 – Summary of reform trajectory: Italy

Sequence	Contest	Diagnosis
Contradictory reforms in the 1980s	– Stagflation; – Slower economic growth; – Budget deficits	*Priorities*: fight inflation and unemployment – Welfare still a useful institution; – Welfare laggard: expansion needed; – Waste/frauds and inefficiencies in some welfare sectors
1992-93: First retrenchment measures in emergency	– Soaring public debt/deficits; – Employment crisis; – External constraints on the public budget and speculative attacks on national currency	*Priorities*: Fiscal /economic/ employment crisis – Pension system not unsustainable and unfair (Health care expenditure)
1995-2000 The path-breaking reforms under European influence	– Still employment crisis; high public debt/deficits; – Slight economic recovery; – Run-up to EMU jointly with financial speculative attacks, though less intense after 1995	*Priorities*: – Fiscal and employment crisis; – Cut pension expenditure; – Overcome the double distortion of national welfare system
2000-08: Steps back and forth between modernization and conservatism	– Recession; – Rising deficits but looser budget constraints; – Loss of competitiveness	*Priorities*: – Tax cuts; – Welfare cause of loss of competitiveness and labor market distortions; – Pension adequacy problem

Content of the policy	Politics	Consequences
Ambivalent: – Labor reduction route; – New benefits/ more generosity; – Higher contribution rates; – A few cost containment measures: more targeting	– Still 'insulated' domestic policy-making: higher contributions and transfer for public budget allowed; – Resistance to retrenchment: unions struggle to maintain status quo; – 'Short-term horizon' of policy-makers prevails	– More welfare expenditure: closing the gap with Europe; – More intercategorical unfairness; – Acute welfare without work syndrome
– Moderate retrenchment; – Pension reform: path-dependent, incremental change; – Higher contribution; – Framework for supplementary funded pensions	– Domestic policy-making porous to external pressures: indirect EU influence; – Short-term and long-term interests merge: policy-makers forced to take actions; – Social pacts: technocratic cabinets and social partners	– Cost containment and (partial) harmonization in the field of pensions (and health care); – Measures to reduce labor cost
– Deep retrenchment; – Path-breaking reforms: new principles and goals (market, poverty alleviation, selective universalism, actuarial fairness); – New policy instruments; – Higher contributions	– Domestic policy-making porous to external pressures: direct & indirect EU influence; – Corporatist concertation to overcome veto players; – Social pacts; – Policy learning	– Fiscal consolidation; – Pension sustainable and actuarially fair; – Retirement income depends on the combination of public and supplementary schemes; – Labor market: flexibilization, privatization and activation; – Safety net and activation for the outsiders
– Pensions: contradictory incremental reforms; fostering multi-pillarization; – Labor Market: more flexibility and activation; – Conservative familialism	– Confrontation with political learning; – Social pacts: center-Right cabinet; – Concertation: center-Left and unions; – Selective learning	– More flexibility; – New security gaps; – Intergenerational issues

7 Defrosting the Spanish Welfare State: The Weight of Conservative Components

Ana Guillén

7.1 Introduction

The transformation of the Spanish political system as well as the Spanish economy and welfare state has been dramatic since the advent of democracy 30 years ago. Because of the process of democratization, changes in the political domain have been the most salient.

Spain has been a parliamentary monarchy for the last 30 years. This is the longest historical experience of consolidated democracy. Since 1982, the party system is dominated by two major parties: the Social Democratic PSOE (*Partido Socialista Obrero Español*) and the Conservative PP (*Partido Popular*, called *Alianza Popular* before 1989). As Chuliá (2006) notes, due to the key roles of the government and the Congress in the Spanish political system, during the periods in which a party enjoys an absolute majority, both institutions emerge as one and the same veto player; hence there is no veto to government proposals. Conversely, minority governments are very vulnerable to the veto power of the minor parties supporting them. Supporting parties to the central government have usually been 'nationalist' ones, that is, regional parties.

Since 1978, Spain has become a strongly decentralized country. The territory is split in 17 autonomous regions enjoying political and administrative powers. Therefore Spain has three levels of government, namely central, regional and local. The relations between the regions and the central state depend on the identities of the parties in power. Spanish autonomous regions enjoy responsibility over many social policies including education, health care, social services and social assistance. Autonomous regions spend one third of total public expenditure nowadays and around 60 percent of their budget on health care, social care services and education. The income-maintenance system remains in the hands of the central state.

The social partners enjoy high levels of representativeness in Spain. As regards unions, two big confederations, namely the socialist UGT (*Unión General de Trabajadores*), and the communist CCOO (*Comisiones Obreras*) have come to represent the interests of virtually all workers. Although unions have not reached high levels of affiliation (15 percent of salaried workers), this dual repartition of representation was consolidated through the results of elections of workers' committees.[1] Employers have gathered around one single organization, CEOE (*Confederación Española de Organizaciones Empresariales*), integrating the firms of all territories and economic sectors. The CEOE later incorporated the association of medium size and small firms (CEPYME).

Like France, Spain is not a veto-heavy political system. Vetoes can and have been exercised by unions through strikes and demonstrations, and employers' associations are also very capable of exercising pressure. Obviously, regions have become very salient political actors, especially regarding the negotiation of financial flows from the central state. Political pressure can be exercised much less intensely by consumers' associations, some professional associations (medical doctors' associations do not enjoy much power in comparison to the situation in other countries), and by the Catholic Church, the latter regarding issues dealing with the teaching of religion in primary and secondary education and ethical issues (abortion, homosexual rights, genetic engineering).[2]

For its part, the Spanish economy has experienced a deep transformation in the last three decades, and it has done so in at least three aspects, namely the relative share of productive sectors, the degree of openness of the economy and the activity of the public sector.

Regarding the first aspect, the relative share of productive sectors has varied, as in many other advanced economies, towards a reduction of the primary and secondary sectors and an intense growth of the tertiary one. From 1980 to 2000, the primary sector was reduced to half its size, while the secondary sector lost 5 percentage points and the tertiary sector gained 10 points. In 2000, the split was of 3.63 percent for the primary sector, 30.52 percent for the secondary sector, and 65.85 percent for the services sector (Fundación BBVA 2005). This split has remained stable until the present.

In the second place, the Spanish economy has undergone a deep process of opening. Trade fluxes, i.e. exports plus imports, hardly reaching 31 percent of GDP in 1985, went up to 43 percent in 2003. This constitutes an openness coefficient which is comparable, and even superior, to that of other European countries of similar size. If we take into account that the point of departure was of much more severe economic isolation, these data reflect an intense effort of international projection (Alonso 2005: 481).

The third salient transformation of the Spanish economy was experienced by the public sector. Fiscal reform was carried out starting in 1979 and has led to the modernization of the Spanish fiscal system on the one hand, and to a significant growth of fiscal pressure on the other. Fiscal pressure has increased from 25.7 percent in 1980 to 35.6 percent in 2005, with a maximum of 36.8 percent in 1992.[3] The composition of state revenues has changed as well. While the percentage of social contributions over GDP at current prices has remained fairly stable, direct and indirect taxes have almost doubled their rates, but growth of indirect taxation has been more intense. As a result, in 2005, state revenues amounted to 13.1 percent of GDP collected through social contributions, 12.1 percent collected through indirect taxes and 10.4 percent through direct taxes.[4]

Finally, the entrance of Spain into the EC (1986) and then the EMU have also significantly conditioned the activities of the public administration in a twofold way. In the first place, social expenditure growth in the 1980s was also possible thanks to the arrival of structural and cohesion funds, which served the purpose of financing productive investments. In the second place, the requirements to join the EMU have deeply conditioned budgetary policies from 1996 onwards, by obliging the state to contain public expenditure in order to maintain deficits at the levels required by the Maastricht Treaty and the Stability Pact.

7.2   The Point of Departure: The Spanish Welfare State in the Late 1970s

When Franco died in 1975 and Spain began its transition to democracy, a social protection system was already in place. Many Spanish scholars refuse to refer to social policy under the dictatorship as the building of a 'welfare state', given the non-democratic context in which it was constructed and also its underdevelopment in comparative terms with other European countries.[5] However, whatever social policy existed (and it can hardly be labeled as either 'residual' à la Titmuss or 'rudimentary' à la Leibfried) it was clearly organized mirroring the Bismarckian tradition. Franco's admiration for Nazi Germany and fascist Italy explains the emulation of the Bismarckian model when the social protection system started to be built in the 1940s.

The principles on which the authoritarian welfare system was based are not easy to spell out, for Franco and his ministers did not have a clear-cut ideology. However, one can easily deduct from the declaration of motives preceding legal texts (especially the Basic Law of Social Security of 1963), and also from outcomes, that the Spanish welfare system did not share all the main normative/ideational elements common to all Bismarckian welfare systems. The Spanish *Seguridad Social* did share the emphasis on security, i.e. job and income security for male workers. The social protection system was in charge of income maintenance and one of the most rigid labor markets in West Europe was responsible for job security. It also shared the importance of professional identities: curiously enough Spaniards paid social contributions according to their professional sector and the amount of social contributions was quite detached from the amount of their salary. Furthermore, the orientation towards the support of traditional family roles was crystal clear even in the public discourse. The Spanish welfare system also favored subsidiarity. But it is here where shared principles come to an end. Collectively negotiated rights were impossible in the absence of free unions. Proportionality does not apply when social contributions (and, derived from it, benefits) are not proportional to salaries. By 1980, these two latter principles had been included in the system, the first thanks to democratization and legalization of the unions and the second thanks to the legal reform of social security in 1975 and the outstanding fiscal reform of 1979.

Institutional arrangements meant that social protection policies were aimed at workers and their dependants. The rest of the population was either referred to Poor Relief (*Beneficencia*) if their income was very low or to the private market if their income was high. The Basic Law establishing social security had been passed in 1963 and implemented from 1967 onwards. In 1975, the *Seguridad Social* comprised a general scheme for salaried workers and a good number of special regimes for other categories of workers (Velarde Fuertes 1990). The so-called *mutualidades laborales* (social protection associations rooted in big firms or industrial/ services branches) remained in place with the 1963 reform, but withered away in subsequent years.

Benefits came to be earnings-related by 1980. The system was financed entirely by social contributions paid by workers and employers; the proportion of state revenues was negligible. Franco's dislike for taxes was notorious, despite the insistence of his finance ministers on the need to introduce a broader and progressive tax on income. The mid-1970s were still a time of large surpluses in social accounts but they were not to last, as soon as the economic crises struck the Spanish economy.

Management and administration were centralized, both from a political and economic point of view. As a consequence the Spanish system was not split in social funds (*Kassen, caisses,* etc) right from its establishment.

It should also be recalled that the role played by unions and employers' associations in the management and administration of the system was non-existent under an authoritarian regime.

In 1975, the Spanish social protection system was comparatively less developed than other Bismarckian systems. Nonetheless, it comprised several public programs: income maintenance (retirement, unemployment and sickness allowances), health care, social care services, family policies, housing policies and education, having attained different levels of development. Especially family and care policies for children, the disabled and the elderly were underdeveloped since the authoritarian regime deeply believed in the different social roles of men and women, the latter having to stay at home and provide care. The Francoist regime always made intense propaganda about its pro-natalist family policies, but by the mid-1970s the amount of family transfers had become very modest.

Retirement pensions were organized along professional lines. As already noted, a general regime for salaried workers existed and several others, but financing, management and administration were centralized in a single institution, i.e. the *Seguridad Social*. Since the advent of democracy, though, the vocation expressed in the legal texts was to reduce the number of professional regimes gradually and equalize the conditions of access and benefits. Retired workers could all count on a pension. A small program for those people having failed to gather contributory pension rights was also in place, namely that of *pensiones asistenciales*. Even at this early stage some internal redistribution within the social security system could be ascertained; the agrarian regime always suffered from deficits, so transfers from the general regime were done in order to be able to pay for agrarian pensions.

Health care services were grouped under the *Asistencia Sanitaria de la Seguridad Social* (ASSS) also created by the Basic Law of 1963. The ASSS was in charge of providing health services for all insured workers and their dependants. The proportion of the population covered by the ASSS in 1975 was of 80.9 percent (Fundación FOESSA 1983: 809). The ASSS owned its own network of public health institutions, consisting mainly of primary and specialized care providers (*ambulatorios*) and hospitals (*residencias sanitarias de la Seguridad Social*). However, other public networks of health institutions existed, as for example, health care services for the military or the network established before social insurance began, which was administered and managed by the Home Office and owned the so-called 'provincial hospitals' (one in the capital of each province). Doctors were salaried employees beginning with the establishment of health care insurance in 1943, a condition that was maintained by the Basic Law of Social

Security in 1963. Furthermore, the system was organized so that primary doctors acted as the doorkeepers, referring patients to higher levels of care.

Unemployment protection had a very limited scope in the mid-1970s, A program started in 1963. However, male full employment was the norm at that point in time and only a few workers benefited from it before the impact of the crises of the 1970s was felt in the economy. Two peculiarities of Spain should be noted in this respect. First, full employment was attained under the dictatorship not only by insertion in the Spanish labor market but also by emigration to other more developed European countries. Second, the Spanish labor market under Franco's regime was one of the most rigid and overprotected in Europe with very costly firings and stringent legislation on permanent contracts.

The Spanish social protection system was deeply predicated on the principles of the breadwinner model. Because on the one hand, women were expected to stay home and look after children, the disabled and the elderly and, on the other hand, female access to education and the labor market lagged well behind other European countries, social care services remained very underdeveloped in the mid-1970s.

In sum, the Spanish welfare state of the mid- to late 1970s was an underdeveloped version of the Bismarckian model. In 1980, roughly half of the financing was done out of social contributions (12.6 percent of GDP), and the other half was split on similar proportions between direct taxes (6.7 percent) and indirect taxes (6.4 percent).[6] Public expenditure on social protection amounted to 17.1 percent of GDP, while the average for the EU15 was of 21.9 percent (OECD, several years). As already noted, management was centralized in a single institution and in the hands of public authorities. Finally, population coverage was broad (around 80-85 percent for pensions and health) but not universal. Family and care policies were severely underdeveloped, while voluntary associations played a prominent role regarding the protection of the poor and socially excluded.

But there is another way of assessing the character of a Bismarckian system. According to the re-examination of welfare regimes carried out by Esping-Andersen (1999: 81), 'the essence of a Conservative regime lies in its blend of status segmentation and familialism'. The Spanish system of the mid-1970s was Bismarckian but not quite. It was markedly based on 'Conservative familialist' principles, that is, a biased male breadwinner model where the family becomes central as a caregiver and responsible for the welfare of its members. Still, some of the corporatist institutional arrangements were missing, especially those related to the existence of independent professional funds and those concerned with the management and administration of the system and the role played by the social partners. As a working hypothesis, it is my contention that it is precisely this lack of intense corporatist traits that eased the way for the paradigmatic reforms of the 1980s and the recalibration of the 1990s. Conversely, the 'Conservative familialist' character of the Spanish welfare state has proved more difficult to overcome.

7.3 Reforming Social Protection in the Last Three Decades

Transition to Democracy: Expansion without Institutional Change (1975-1982)

As I have argued elsewhere (Guillén 1996), expansion in terms of coverage and expenditure rather than structural reform took place from the beginning of the transition to democracy in 1975 to the victory of the Socialist Party (PSOE) in 1982. In fact, expenditure on social protection was one and a half times higher in 1982 than in 1975, due especially to the increasing role of taxation in the financing of social protection. The reasons for expansion without organizational change in the social protection system previous to 1982 were related to the need to stabilize the new political regime, the concurrence of the economic shocks of the 1970s and the pressures to alleviate social needs caused by massive unemployment and inflation. In a few words, two goals had to be reached in parallel. The first goal consisted of meeting the population's needs and aspirations. The second goal was to achieve broad consensus for political reform. In this context, the reform of social protection institutions was postponed, the stabilization of the new democratic political institutions was much more pressing. This is in sharp contrast with the Portuguese transition to democracy, which was more of a 'rupture' in character, and more similar to the Greek one, which also chose a 'reformist' and consensual path to transition to democracy (Maravall 1995).

But deep reform after 1982 was also possible thanks to certain developments taking place in the first few years of the transition to democracy. These developments eased the way for paradigmatic changes thereafter. Among them are:

a) The separation of health services from the Ministry of Labor and Social Security and the creation of an independent Ministry of Health.
b) The approval of a democratic constitution, allowing for devolution of powers to the regions.

c) The general trend towards increased democratization and participation of social partners in the decision-making process, in particular within the social security governing bodies.

d) Full development of public preferences in favor of both enlarging social protection and of basing entitlements to welfare *services* (not to income maintenance transfers) on citizenship rights.

Towards Universal Coverage (1982-1992)

The problem to be dealt with in this sequence of reforms was bringing the Spanish social protection system closer to that of its European counterparts. Upgrading of protection and closing protection gaps was the landmark in both the public discourse and public preferences, which shared an acute conscience of backwardness. The absolute majority of the Socialist Party in the 1982 elections raised big hopes among the population. However, the poor state of the economy and the need to restructure industry delayed reforms. Things began to change rapidly and deeply in the second half of the 1980s, thanks to the positive economic cycle on the one side and to pressures exercised by the unions on the other.

Growth in expenditure and coverage was spectacular from 1982 to 1992 (Rodríguez Cabrero 1994). Social contributions became insufficient to finance the system and the state had to start using more resources from general taxation. Unemployment protection was expanded in 1983/4 and health care provision in 1984/1986 and 1999. Contrarily, public retirement pensions were reformed in 1985 in a restrictive way.

Pensions: Rationalization

The pension reform of 1985 initiated a series of rationalizing measures that were to be continued during the 1990s. In 1985, the minimum contributory period was enlarged from 10 to 15 years, while the formula to calculate the benefits came to include the salaries of the last eight years instead of the two previously required. It is important to highlight that cost-control reforms were not introduced in most other Bismarckian welfare states until much later. Still, retirement pensions remained in the hands of the central state and organized along professional lines.

The 1985 reform was imposed by the socialist government, even at the cost of breaking their historical brotherhood with the socialist union (UGT), because of clear domestic reasons. At that point Spain was undergoing severe economic difficulties and previous reforms enacted under the late authoritarian regime had rendered the cost of pensions unbearable. Conversely, after the successful 1988 general strike, unions were able to press the socialist government into expansionary measures, such as the creation of a non-contributory pension scheme and the indexation of pensions to past inflation. The introduction of non-contributory pensions can be considered a major shift in the trajectory of pension provision.

The creation of flat-rate non-contributory pensions for the elderly and the disabled in 1991 meant that all citizens and not only workers were entitled to pensions; it resulted in a universal coverage in terms of income maintenance for all people over 65. Another salient departure from the path also took place in 1989, when private pension plans were allowed for the first time. The creation of private plans was fostered by the introduction of fiscal exemptions. Both reforms were in line with EC recommendations to lower poverty among the elderly and to complement public pension systems.

Furthermore, the restrictive reform of 1985 did not impede the internal redistributory measures initiated in the early 1980s, namely the continuity of the so-called minimum pension supplements (*complementos a mínimos*). The Spanish system counts on a minimum and a maximum retirement pension. The minimum pension is granted to all beneficiaries (having contributed for a minimum period) irrespective of whether their contributory career allows them to reach the minimum pension or not. This measure became more and more costly over the 1980s and 1990s. Furthermore, a strategy was also initiated in order to narrow the gap between the average retirement pension and the minimum salary. This was done by raising the minimum pension, by indexing pensions to the cost of living, and also by ameliorating the lowest pensions, mainly those of survivors. The objective of equalizing the average pension to the minimum salary was attained in 1995 (Guillén 1999).

Employment Policies: A Typical Bismarckian Trajectory
Early retirement and disability pensions were used broadly in the early 1980s with the aim of covering situations of need among the unemployed. The situation began to be reversed towards the end of the decade through the fight against fraud and abuses.

Passive unemployment protection was reduced in 1980 because of the poor condition of the economy and expanded in 1984. Coverage rates grew from 43.4 percent in 1986 to a peak of 80.3 percent of the unemployed in 1992, when they reached the maximum during the democratic period (Cruz Roche 1994). However, the number of contributory beneficiaries lost ground and that of non-contributory ones kept increasing, a measure clearly in favor of the long-term unemployed but also meaning an assistentialization of the system. Investment in active measures began to take off in the second half of the 1980s (Toharia 1997; Gutiérrez and Guillén 2000).

Also in 1984, the first wave of labor market liberalization took place. It introduced fixed-term contracts while leaving the ordinary framework of contracting untouched. This move had a decisive influence on the configuration of the Spanish labor market. Temporary contracts facilitated the adaptation of staffing to cyclical conditions and stimulated the creation of employment. Still, fixed-term contracts quickly reached 30 percent of all salaried workers (the highest rate in the EU up to the present), produced a dualization of the labor market structure and were not able to drastically reduce unemployment (15 percent at the end of the 1980s).

Health Care: Universalization

Health care suffered the most dramatic change towards universalization, which has of course to be considered a paradigmatic change. The very important reform of primary care in 1984 and the General Health Law of 1986 constituted a major departure point from the Bismarckian path. A public national health system (*Sistema Nacional de Salud*) was created comprising all pre-existing public networks of providers. At the same time the new legislation allowed for the devolution of powers over health care to the autonomous regions, as already sanctioned by the 1978 democratic constitution. The reform was carried out gradually. Devolution took place in several stages, each autonomous region negotiating individually with the central state. The process of decentralization began in 1982 in Spain with the devolution of health care powers to Catalonia and was only completed in December 2002, 20 years later. In Spain, there were no health funds, so they did not have to be suppressed. Coverage of the population was already almost universal (over 90 percent), a circumstance that was possible, on the one hand, because of the previous inclusion of more and more categories of workers into the system of social security and, on the other, by the loosening of the rules on access for dependants (Guillén 2002).[7] Thus, the economic effort to turn a social insurance health system into a national health service covering 100 percent of the population was not too demanding. It was not until 1989 that a royal decree allowed for the incorporation of previous beneficiaries of poor relief into the Spanish NHS. However, access to the system was not turned into a citizenship right and the professional principle (with several corrections to allow for universal coverage) has remained in place.[8] Hence universalization in Spain could be said to have happened *de facto* rather than *de jure*. The composition of financing was gradually modified to become increasingly dependant on general revenues.

The shift from health care insurance to a national health service was possible thanks to the formation of a broad coalition in support of such a change. The coalition included the central government, leftist parties, regional governments and the unions. Public opinion was also very clearly in favor of it. The Conservative Party in the opposition, employers associations and medical associations were not able to impede it.

Family Policies: Nothing Much New Under the Sun

Family policies remained untouched until 1990 when a universal means-tested scheme substituted the almost negligible economic transfers inherited from the previous regime. Transfers were ameliorated for those families with disabled kin, but the amount of the economic support remained low (Cruz Roche 1994). The postponement of the reform of family policies can be explained, among other reasons, by the reluctance of the socialist governments (1982-1994) to be identified with the natalist orientation of the Francoist dictatorship (see Valiente 1995 for a detailed analysis). Care policies were expanded and ameliorated, especially for children between three and five years of age, for whom places at pre-schooling were provided. Expansion of care policies for the disabled and the elderly was also notorious and the creation of a Ministry of Social Services in 1988 helped to improve this area (Ministerio de Asuntos Sociales 1993). Nonetheless, these policies departed from extremely low levels of provision and the intense ageing of the population did not help. Thus, at the beginning of the 1990s, care was still massively in the hands of families.

Social care services were devolved to the autonomous regions in the late 1980s and early 1990s. Given the small development of this policy and its low economic weight, it was easy for the central government to please the regions by devolving responsibility to them. This move enhanced the introduction of innovative solutions, but provision started to show geographical heterogeneity not only among regions but even between different localities.

Social Assistance: Introducing Minimum Income Schemes

Social assistance made an important move ahead as well in the late 1980s. Faced with a refusal on the part of the central state, the unions began bargaining with regional governments in order to introduce minimum income schemes. By the early 1990s, all Spanish autonomous regions used either social salaries or social insertion salaries. In this way, Spain was the first Southern European country to introduce minimum income policies. Their generosity also varies with the region and, in general, the intensity of protection is modest (Aguilar et al. 1994; Arriba 2001).

In sum, the 1980s witnessed major changes in Spain. As a consequence of those changes a new, mixed way of understanding welfare provision was born: corporatist in income maintenance and social-democratic as regards health (and education), overriding the Bismarckian path clearly in the latter case. Furthermore, what is peculiar of the Spanish case is the early rationalizing reform (1985) of the pension system comparatively with other Bismarckian welfare states. In addition, some moves can be ascertained in the direction of narrowing protection gaps in the realms of family and care policies, protection of the disabled and non-contributory income maintenance policies. The introduction of minimum income policies at the regional level also meant a substantial departure from the path. The expansionary and path-deviant trend lasted until 1992-1993, when a significantly different sequence of reforms started.

In Search of Efficiency (1992-2004)

The early 1990s, and especially the 1992 Maastricht Treaty initiated a totally different context from that of the 1980s for all EU member states. The problem now became how to rationalize expenditure and gain efficiency. In Spain, austerity challenges became even more acute because of the economic recession and the public economic effort undertaken to finance the Universal Exhibition of Seville and the Olympic Games in Barcelona. As already noted, public expenditure peaked in 1993 (47.6 percent).[9] It is hardly news that Spain did its homework properly and was able to put in place a smooth and well organized process of convergence to access the EMU, especially after 1996. However, cost-control and austerity measures left a clear mark on social policy developments.

Unemployment Protection: Drastic Cuts
Unemployment protection policies were the first to be reformed in 1992, this time in a restrictive way. The minimum period of contribution required for access was expanded from 6 to 12 months. The payment period was reduced from one half of the period contributed to one third. Replacement rates of previous salaries also decreased. Coverage rates fell dramatically from 80.3 percent in 1992 to 50.7 percent in 1995 (Ministerio de Trabajo 1996: 803). The reasons for this move were as much the need to reach the convergence criteria imposed externally as internal politics. As noted above, the introduction of fixed-term contracts by the 1983/84 labor reform resulted in a share of over one third of all contracts being temporary in the Spanish labor market. Such a situation meant continuous

entries to and exits from the labor market and peaking costs in terms of passive unemployment protection. As a consequence, the National Institute for Unemployment (INEM) went almost bankrupt and retrenchment was necessary. Expenditure growth on activation policies also slowed down for the rest of the decade (Gutiérrez and Guillén 2000). In 2000, an active integration subsidy was created for aged long-term unemployed. Two years later, a softened version of a most controversial reform was passed, aiming at enhancing geographical mobility of workers and avoiding rejection of jobs (CES 2001 and 2003).

The 1990s also witnessed two further waves of labor market flexibilization. The first took place in 1993-1994. Among other measures, these reforms included promoting job creation through new tax and social contribution exemptions for employers contracting young people, the long-term unemployed, people aged 45 and over, and the disabled. The measures also fostered work-experience and job-training contracts and the reduction of barriers for certain kinds of redundancies. On this occasion, and in contrast to the 1984 reform, part-time contracts were more vigorously promoted by providing them with more public subsidies (CES 1994). The 1993 reform also included the legalization of non-profit private employment agencies; thus, the National Institute of Employment lost its monopoly as a job placement agency. The unions agreed on this reform because they were weakened by corruption scandals and because they were compensated mainly in terms of union electoral regulations and in the devolution of the historical patrimony lost during the dictatorship.

The second reform of the labor market of the 1990s took place in 1996, under the recently elected government of the Partido Popular (PP, of Conservative orientation). It was the first consensual reform, achieved through a social pact, in comparison to the previous ones which had been imposed on the social partners. The 1996 reform promoted the creation of open-ended contracts, modified part-time contracts and reduced the cost of redundancies. In this case, the social agreement was reached because the unions feared the possibility of the Popular Party reforming by decree without consulting them. All in all, after three flexibilizing reforms, the rigid labor market of Francoist times had become only a vague memory at the end of the 1990s.

Pensions: Rationalization and Redistribution

Retirement pensions also underwent cost-control reforms. In 1994, pensions were indexed to the estimated inflation rate for the next year, instead of remaining tied to past inflation as had been the norm from 1989. By the mid-1990s, worries about future sustainability of the public pension system in a context of austerity and rapid population ageing had grown so much that a parliamentary commission was appointed. After a year of activity, the commission decided that the existing system, based on intergenerational solidarity, should be kept but forwarded 15 recommendations for reform in order to secure future viability. This commission came to be known as the 1995 Toledo Pact, to which both the unions and employers' associations quickly adhered. The Toledo Pact has guided the reform of pensions until the present, since it was renewed and readapted to the socio-economic context in 2003.

The second major reform of the pension system was agreed on in 1996 via social pact and turned into law in 1997. Once again, the rule of the Conservative Party raised fears of privatization and unions 'swallowed' another restrictive reform in order to ensure future viability of the public pension system. The main reforms of this law followed part of the Toledo Pact recommendations. Among many other measures, the rules to calculate contributory pensions were tightened again so the last 15 salaried years were to be included incrementally in the formula to calculate the initial pension. As a counterpart, widows' and orphan's pensions were ameliorated (Chulià 2006). Furthermore, short and/or discontinued contributory careers were allowed to have a non-proportional positive impact in the calculation of the initial pension, a measure favoring workers with a high record of temporary contracts. What we can see here is a reduction of core workers' rights and a (modest) amelioration of the conditions for non-core ones.

More recent reform in the realm of pensions has followed the same strategy. In 1999, the 'Agreement on the Amelioration of Pensions' dealt with contributory pension increases. In 2001, the 'Agreement for the Amelioration and Development of the Social Security System' insisted again on an increase of widows' pensions, longer protection periods for orphans, and the convergence among the different social security professional schemes in terms of access and the calculation of benefits (in this latter case, attention was focused on autonomous workers) (CES 2000 and 2002).

Last but not least, the recommendations of the Toledo Pact included the split of financing sources so that contributory benefits were to be financed out of social contributions and taxes were to be used to finance non-contributory transfers and welfare services. Reform in this direction was initiated in 1998.

Protecting Labor Market Outsiders

Other social pacts have resulted in increased protection of non-core labor workers in the late 1990s. First, the 'Agreement on Employment and Social Protection of Agrarian Workers' of 1996 meant a step forward in the conditions of protection of peasants of southern Spanish regions, by including previous unemployment subsidies into the general scheme of social security (enacted in 2000). The 'Interconfederal Agreement for Stability in Employment' of 1997 also fostered improvements in the protection of non-core workers, namely part-time and temporary workers. A specific agreement on part-time workers was reached in 1998, resulting in the passing of two royal decrees in the same year. In particular, conditions for access to social security were conflated with those of core-workers in terms of the relation between time worked and benefits, and in terms of sickness allowances and maternity benefits. As regards fixed-term workers, employers' social contributions for unemployment were raised by a royal decree in 1998 both for fulltime and part-time temporary workers, with the aim of increasing their unemployment subsidies. A law on the amelioration of social protection of autonomous workers was also passed.

Health Care: In Search for Enhanced Efficiency without Compromising Equality

Health care services were also affected by rationalization. Worries about increasing expenditure were also present already from the late 1980s (we should note that expenditure on health care in Spain grew most among EU members in the second half of the 1980s). Such worries were conducive to the establishment of a parliamentary commission (Abril Committee AC) in charge of producing recommendations for rationalization of health care expenditure and the introduction of cost control measures. The AC did produce a whole set of reform proposals but it was frontally rejected by the unions and the population. Thus rationalization had to be put in place in a low-visibility way (Cabiedes and Guillén 2001). Reform can be summarized by saying that rationalizing measures affected the supply side rather than the demand side, thus not affecting the existing level of equity so much as if the contrary had occurred.

The process of health care decentralization came to an end in late 2001, so that all 17 Spanish autonomous regions enjoy their own health care system today. This was coupled with a new agreement on regional financing and a new statute for health professionals. In 2003, a law on Cohesion and Quality was passed aiming at securing territorial equity and quality levels in the provision of health care.

Family Policies: Towards Reconciliation

Family care policies did not undergo major change during the 1990s, but rather modest expansion. Two exceptions should be mentioned, though, that of the amelioration of income maintenance for maternal leave in 1995 and the approval of a law on reconciliation of work and family life in 1999 (Flaquer 2000). Also, the number of offspring necessary to gain access to large families discounts was first reduced to four kids and later to three kids. Monoparental, separated or divorced families enjoy large families protection since 2005 (the law was passed in 2003).

To sum up, the 1990s were a period revolving around contention, rationalization and cost-control needed in order to join the EMU. The Popular Party government even passed a law on zero public deficit in 2000. Still, some redistributive or even expansionary measures may be signaled in almost all policy areas.

Recent Developments: Enhancing Equity and Protecting Dependency (2004 onwards)

As soon as the socialist party (PSOE) gained office in 2004, expansionary social protection reforms intensified. Two laws have been passed in the realm of family policies. The first allows marriages and the adoption of children by gay people with the same rights as any other marriage. The second deals with enhanced protection for battered women (passed in 2005). Furthermore, in January 2006, paternity leave was introduced for workers of the central public administration and some regions have since done the same for their employees.

A new major reform of the labor market has been agreed on with the social partners in May 2006 and turned into law in June 2006. The main aim of the reform is to reduce temporality in the labor market and to gain in 'flexicurity'. The reform has already rendered positive results in the reduction of fixed-term contracts. Also in 2006, another significant social pact has been reached on the reform of pensions, focused on an amelioration of both contributory and non-contributory benefits. The reform includes an expansion from 13 to 15 years of the minimum period of contribution to gain access to the system. Also, it introduces incentives to continue work after the legal retirement age and measures oriented at further equalization of special (professional) schemes.

Last but not least, other legal reforms are of importance. The 2007 Law on Gender Equality follows EU legislation and aims at establishing public and private equality measures for women in the employment and social security spheres, and in access to goods and services. Nonetheless, perhaps the most salient achievement of the recent phase of social dialogue has been the tripartite Agreement on Protection of Dependent People of late 2005, turned into law in December 2006. The aim of the law on dependency is the creation of a National System of Dependency of public character and of universal coverage for all people in need of care, financed out of public funds and of the user's out-of-pocket payments (these latter dependent on income). It will affect 1.1 million people, the majority being the elderly. The reform started to be implemented in the Spring of 2007 and should be fully developed by 2014. It is of the utmost importance for the evolution of the Spanish welfare state from the point of view of establishing the third pillar (clearly non-Bismarckian) of any well developed social protection system at the national level.

Main Traits of the Reform Trajectory in Spain

All in all, the Spanish welfare state has undergone major expansion and change. Such change is clear in the realm of health care, provided its departure from the health insurance model and its conversion into a national health service. It can be added that the process of devolution of health care has been completed. It is also clear in the introduction of new social programs, such as minimum income schemes, non-contributory pensions for the elderly and the disabled, and reconciliation of family and working life (even if modest). Private pension plans introduced in the late 1980s have also grown steadily. The recent creation of a National System of Dependency means another significant turning point in the realm of social care. The Spanish labor market has also become much more flexible and active labor market policies have been introduced.

The change may not be so apparent in the field of pensions. Most international organizations reports issued by the OECD, the IMF or even the EU on the evolution of pensions in Spain talk about mere path dependency with cost-control adjustments. Yet, the present Spanish pension system can hardly be compared to the one existing in the late 1970s. As shown above, changes aimed at lowering the amount of the initial pension have indeed taken place on two occasions; important changes have also occurred through the introduction of non-contributory pensions and private pension plans. The lowering of the replacement rate has not impeded an amelioration of the amounts of pensions compared to the minimum salary. In 1995 the average retirement pension had surpassed the level of the minimum salary; nowadays, it is the minimum pension which has reached the level of the minimum salary. Furthermore, reforms initiated in the 1980s and continued to the present clearly show a vocation of internal redistribution within the system. An amelioration of widows' and orphans' pensions and those of workers with short-contributory careers has taken place. In 2004, 28.34 percent of all pensioners enjoyed supplements in order to reach the minimum pension (CES 1995). Almost half a million pensioners received a non-contributory pension. Also, the Reserve Fund of the

Table 7.1   Summary of reform trajectory: Spain

Types of change	Context	Diagnosis
Expansion without departure from the path 1975-1982	– economic downturn (mid-1970's onwards) – rise in unemployment and inflation	– social benefits should help the victims of the crisis, provided democracy is superior to dictatorship
Paradigmatic changes 1982-1992	– positive economic cycle (mid-1980s onwards) – peaking unemployment still present	– Spanish welfare state is underdeveloped – gaps in social protection have to be closed – universal access to health care should be provided
In search of efficiency (1992-2003)	– economic recession (early 1990s), then quick and intense recovery – single market – preparation of the single currency	– the system has to be consolidated, but efficiency is a must in order to join the EMU
Rounding up 2004-	– employment grows steadily – immigration comes to the rescue	– search for enhanced gender equity and better protection of dependent people

pension system amounted to 40,334 million euros in March 2007, which is equivalent to the cost of pensions over a period of eight months.[10] Moreover, another trend was initiated in the mid-1990s towards enhancing the protection of non-core workers. This trend, even if incipient, should not be overlooked. Last but not least, the private pillar has expanded significantly so that 40 percent of all workers counted on a private pension plan in 2006 and 10 percent counted on an occupational pension (CES 2006: 611). Big reforms may be attained through piecemeal partial ones.

Content of the policy	Politics of the reforms	Consequences
– raise in taxes – increase in the generosity of the benefits, with the exception of unemployment – welfare without work	– broad consensus	– no big changes of the welfare state institutions, but expansion of existing policies
– change of model in welfare services, towards universalization of health care and education – rationalizing pensions and expanding unemployment protection	– broad coalitions – strikes by unions – regional governments take the lead	– huge expansion in expenditure and coverage – creation of an NHS – minimum income schemes introduced at regional level – non-contributory policies initiated (financed through taxes and means-tested: non-contributory pensions for the elderly and the disabled, family allowances, minimum income schemes)
– rationalizing, fight against fraud and abuses – tax financing of all non-contributory policies (Toledo Pact) – 'quid pro quo'	– negotiated on the bases of social pacts aimed at ensuring future viability – negotiation involves an exchange where the state accepts to pay for non-contributory benefits and upgrading of the lowest pensions in exchange of the social partners accepting some cuts in social insurances	– greater efficiency in expenditure and management – slow down of social protection expenditure growth
– enhancing gender equity and paying attention to dependants outside the family	– social pacts still base of reform	– developing care policies at last? – but the family remains severely underprotected

7.4 Explaining the Spanish Trajectory of Reform

The previous analysis has shown that Spain hardly looked like a frozen landscape in social protection reform during the last 30 years. When explaining the Spanish case, the coincidence in time of a process of transition to democracy, deep political decentralization, and joining the European Community becomes crucial. One could easily argue that windows for reform were opened precisely due to such overarching political and social transformations, which tended to foster the diffusion of ideas and learning processes. Indeed, Spain has tried to behave as a deserving (and always very enthusiastic) member of the EU and to comply with any recommendations or policy orientations of the European Social Model.[11] Decentralization has brought about an intense process of innovation in social protection. Novelties introduced in one region have quickly expanded to other regions in a sort of domino mechanism, so that very frequently the central state has had to deal with situations in which innovations had become a fact for the whole territory and act accordingly.

Comparative immaturity of the social protection system at the point of departure of the present analysis may have also helped the 'defrosting' process, for the legitimization of the system was not as entrenched as in other national cases. There is little doubt also that other aspects of domestic politics, such as the permanence in office of the Socialist Party for 14 years, have helped reform in a social-democratic direction (health care and education, expansion of social care and social assistance). Nonetheless, in my view, and without denying the salience of such factors, the peculiar inherited Bismarckian institutional design of the Spanish social protection system can provide part of the explanation for the present mixture of principles in social provision, that is, why income maintenance has remained corporatist, health care (and education) has become Social Democratic, and social services and social assistance have become Liberal/means-tested.

The reform of the pension system shows a good number of parallels with other Bismarckian systems (Bonoli and Palier 2007), such as reductions in the replacement rate through changes in the formula to calculate the initial pension and the fostering of second and third pillar pensions. In general, one could claim that the Spanish pension system has been changed as a result of internal politics and, in some instances, of external influences. Regional governments were not a relevant actor in this domain for pensions remained centralized. The reason for this has been that devolution would make crystal clear which regions contribute more than they spend or vice versa, which would surely become a source of conflict, given deep regionalist feelings. Unions were very relevant actors. The attainment of the Toledo Pact and a great number of social pacts since the mid-1990s had both guided and eased reform. EU recommendations in the late 1980s in the direction of reducing poverty rates among the elderly had a positive impact on the introduction of non-contributory pensions in 1990. Also, the blame-avoidance opportunities provided by the Maastricht criteria and the need to comply with the conditions to enter the EMU eased restrictive reforms. There are also possible explanations related to the institutional design of the Spanish pension system and the role played by the unions within it. In short, one could say that Spanish unions, as is well known, are weak in terms of direct representation (15 percent of affiliation at present) but strong in terms of representativeness (the main unions, UGT and CCOO represent all workers in tripartite and collective agreements). Thus, they follow an inclusive (in favor of all workers and the unemployed) rather than exclusive (in favor of special categories of workers) strategy. If we add that to the fact that there have never been social funds run by the social partners and the state, it becomes clear that their opportunities to fight for the interests of particular productive sectors or categories of workers are diminished. Under such conditions, it is easier for the central state to negotiate encompassing reforms, even if it remains true that the bases of affiliation of the unions still lie mainly in large and public enterprises.

A similar argument could be put forth in the case of unemployment protection, which has followed a pendulum trajectory in the Spanish case. The 1983-84 reform was expansionary and led to significant increases in unemployment coverage. In this case, the unions were successful in their claims but only in exchange for agreeing on the first wave of labor market flexibilization, introducing fixed-term contracts. The 1992 restrictive reform was triggered precisely by the costs impinged on the unemployment system by the growth of fixed-term contracts and the continuous entries to and exits from the labor market. Obviously Maastricht, on one side, and the new emphasis on activation policies on the other, also eased reform. In this latter case, the unions were undergoing a period of weakness due to corruption scandals and other factors, but their inclusive strategy did not allow them to fight for the main clients of unemployment passive protection: the industrial and hard core services. Instead, the compensation for their agreement was the amelioration of non-contributory unemployment schemes and the creation of job-experience and job-training contracts.

In the domain of health care services, changes in the Spanish case have comprised a jump from health insurance to the establishment of a (decentralized) national health service in the 1980s and the introduction of rationalizing and cost-control policies in the 1990s. Explanations of such policy changes in terms of internal politics and processes of learning and diffusion among regions have been analyzed in depth (Rico 1997). However, what we are looking for here are institutional constraints, challenges and opportunities. From this latter point of view, the creation of a national health service was eased in Spain because of the existence of several institutional features, namely the fact that the health care system was not split in independent funds right from its creation and was managed and administered by a centralized institution. It also helped greatly that doctors were salaried employees from the beginning and doorkeepers of the system. When doctors are paid on a fee-for-service basis and users can access higher levels of care at wish, doctors have a much more powerful position vis-à-vis public decision-makers and administrators. Thus, it becomes much more complicated to negotiate with them the change of role needed to create a national health service. The administrative separation of income maintenance from health care in two different ministerial bodies was also important, for it allowed health care to be detached from the occupational principle of access to the system. Centralized financing also helped in making the shift from a financing system based on social contributions to one based on taxes. This is not to deny the centrality of other explanations related to internal politics, such as the formation of a broad and strong coalition reform, the salience of the devolution process and the diffusion of new policies it entailed, or the formation of clear public preferences in favor of the change towards universalism. However, it can also be argued that the peculiar institutional design of the Spanish health care system also had something to do with policy developments.

In the 1990s, the Spanish health care service reacted as most other national health services by introducing cost-control measures based on the managed competition paradigm (see Cabiedes and Guillén 2001). The Spanish state was more able to rationalize the system because a central budget was in place. This was due to a clear reluctance of the population to admit new measures challenging or reducing the only recently acquired high level of equity of the system.

The explanation for the less intense development of family, social care, social assistance and inclusion policies and their Liberal/means-tested design lies first in the fact of their major comparative underdevelopment at the point of departure of this analysis (mid-late 1970s). Spain had to wait until rapid and intense incorporation of women to the labor market took place and until dramatically low fertility rates led to a most adverse demographic situation to start changing wide socially shared values about the excellence of the family as the preferred carer. It is no news that social values are hard to change, even when a society becomes as secular as the Spanish one.

7.5   Conclusions

The result of the Spanish trajectory of reform constitutes a very interesting mix of traditional models à la Esping-Andersen. The principles and normative/ideational elements of the Spanish welfare state have changed accordingly. In the realm of income maintenance, 'job and income security for male workers' has lost its central importance as has the orientation towards the support of traditional family roles. Conversely, collectively negotiated rights for all workers (not only hard core ones) on the one hand, and enhanced proportionality of benefits to contributions, on the other, have been adopted as principles. The Social Democratic principle of universal access as a citizenship right reigns now in the health care and education domains and will do so in the social care area when the legal reforms of 2006 become fully implemented.

Access also follows, at present, the three-fold nature of the Spanish welfare state: workers' rights, citizens' rights, and low income, depending on the policy area. Benefits are earnings-related in pensions and unemployment, and flat-rate in social assistance (with corrections depending on the family situation). A homogeneous and broad package of health care services is common for all Spaniards and legal immigrants, and also for illegal immigrants under 18 years and pregnant women. Means-tested programs, such as family allowances and social assistance economic transfers, have very limited access because of the existence of a very low-income threshold to enter the programs. In the social care services domain, again the income threshold is very low.

Financing mechanisms tend to be used also according to the principles of the policy area. Such a move was agreed in the Toledo Pact of 1995. Pensions and unemployment remain financed out of social contributions and so is the new Pension Fund. All non-contributory and social assistance benefits, together with the main bulk of health care services are financed out of taxes (the transformation for health care is still under way but almost completed). As was the case in other Bismarckian countries, this was part of the negotiation, political exchange between government and social partners (particularly unions). In general, the reliance on taxes for the financing of social protection has grown dramatically from the late 1970s. However, the growth of indirect taxation as a proportion of total financing is hardly good news, for it implies regressive effects on equity. The major shift in management and administrative structures has been brought about by political devolution, which has endorsed the social partners and civil associations with new opportunities to participate in the policy-making process.

In sum, if we compare the four dimensions characterizing the Spanish welfare state today with that of the late 1970s, the difference is stunning. Expenditure over GDP has not grown dramatically but it has kept its level despite the EMU (around 20 percent of GDP, see Eurostat, SEESPROS). Population coverage has expanded significantly to reach universal coverage in pensions and health care, and many protection gaps have been closed. Efficiency gains in management can also be ascertained. Most unfortunately, one cannot say some crucial policy areas have undergone major change. The expenditure levels of Spain on family, housing and inclusion policies are still very low and have not shown any tendency to grow significantly in the past decades (see again Eurostat, SEESPROS). Furthermore, the deep fragmentation of the Spanish labor market, the still soaring proportion of fixed-term jobs, and the fact that it is young people and women who are the losers is hardly a reason for rejoicing. Hence, the changes in the system of social protection have both assets and liabilities. The system is successful in dealing with pensions and health care problems. Social security balances and dependency ratios have ameliorated significantly from 2000 thanks to massive immigration and outstanding employment growth up to 2007. Although advancements have taken place in the rest of social policy domains and there is room for hope, the rapid and acute ageing of the Spanish society and a still too high reliance on family provision may be the cause of severe difficulties in the near future. Finally, despite insistent government declarations reassuring Spaniards that social protection will not suffer from the economic negative cycle started in 2008, it is yet to be seen how hard the crisis will strike the Spanish economy and how it will affect the evolution of social protection policies.

8 Reform Opportunities in a Bismarckian Latecomer: Restructuring the Swiss Welfare State

Silja Häusermann

8.1 Introduction

With the transition to post-industrialism and financial austerity, most Bismarckian welfare systems have started to face similar structural challenges for reforms since the 1970s: budgetary pressures for retrenchment contrast sharply with new demands for social protection, resulting from the failure of both labor markets and traditional family structures (Esping-Andersen 1999). Hence, welfare policies have shifted from a dynamic of steady growth to a period of restructuring and redefinition of social rights. Even though the precise content and timing of the reforms varies across countries, similarities in the new politics and social policies of Bismarckian welfare systems are striking: retrenchment of existing benefits, increasingly means-tested benefit entitlements and a stronger emphasis on activation and social investment, notably with regard to former welfare state outsiders.

Accounting for similarities and differences in this common trend is, however, all but obvious, since a plurality of factors may have influenced the content and timing of this process of restructuring. While many studies refer to the explanatory power of the macroinstitutional context of decision-making, notably the number of veto points in an electoral system (Immergut 1992; Swank 2002), more recent studies also point to the micro-institutions of the Bismarckian welfare system as variables shaping the dynamics of reform endogenously (Bonoli and Palier 2000). These micro-institutions comprise mainly the rules of eligibility and the type of benefits and financing, as well as the actual organization of policy-management. In addition, business cycles and/or the color of the party in government are supposed to influence the dynamics of reform or stability (Huber and Stephens 2001; Korpi and Palme 2003); and last but not least, the emergence of the EMU may have triggered common dynamics of reform, as well (Palier and Manning 2003; Ferrera and Gualmini 2004).

In testing how this plurality of 'usual suspects' explains Bismarckian welfare system reforms across countries, Switzerland is particularly promising for at least two reasons. Firstly, the oversized Swiss coalition government has been composed of the same major four political parties for over fifty years. National elections may shift the power balance in the national Parliament to some extent, but overall, it remains stable. All parties have to negotiate constantly over reform and there are no sharp ideological changes in power relations or business cycle effects. The color of the government as an independent variable is therefore constant: this allows us to exclude party competition and power relations as explanations of *similarities* in the pace and content of the Swiss reform trajectory with reforms in other Bismarckian welfare systems. Secondly, Switzerland is not a member of the EU. Therefore, it provides a rare and interesting comparative test case for the direct impact of binding EU and EMU regulations on welfare state development. Given these two characteristics, the Swiss case is beneficial for the comparison, because it raises the variance on two crucial independent variables: electoral dynamics and the EU. Cross-nationally, similarities between the Swiss and other cases should be attributed to common structural and institutional features, rather than power resources or the EU. In addition, with electoral dynamics being constant, Switzerland is *also* particularly well suited for a longitudinal study of the interplay of micro- and macroinstitutional factors in reform dynamics.

The main arguments of this chapter are as follows: the *macro-institutions* of federalism and direct democracy led to a very slow and incremental development of the Swiss welfare system in the industrial era. Social protection in Switzerland was never the result of a 'Bismarckian master plan', but grew incrementally out of and alongside pre-existing, private or sub-national policies. Hence, at the end of the 1970s, the Swiss welfare system, even though increasingly Bismarckian in its overall structure, was still of a rather modest size and consisted of a pragmatic bricolage of juxtaposed insurance and protection schemes.

In line with the overall argument of this book, I will show in this chapter that this *micro-institutional structure* of the Swiss welfare system itself became an important explanatory variable for the content of the subsequent reforms after the 1970s in two ways. On the one hand, the Swiss welfare system displayed the typical social protection loopholes of a Bismarckian male breadwinner regime in a post-industrial structural context. Therefore, new social needs and demands of labor market outsiders became prominent on the reform agenda, creating leeway for modernizing reforms. On the other hand, the multi-layered structure of the most developed parts of the welfare system has become important for subsequent reforms, because it serves as a blueprint for pragmatic restructuring in various other social policies.

Hence, the *interaction* of structural developments and the micro-institutional welfare state arrangements prove to be the most important variables to explain the *content* of post-industrial reform policies. By contrast, the dynamics of the post-industrial reform politics cannot be explained by micro-institutional factors alone. The consensual macroinstitutional framework and the looming threat of direct democratic referenda largely account for the fact that negotiation and compensation remained the main mechanisms of reform.

A last argument concerns the question of *regime change*, i.e. the issue whether the recent reforms change the Bismarckian characteristics and if yes, in what direction. The Swiss welfare system has rightly been described as a 'latecomer' (Obinger 1998; Armingeon 2001). This is why it entered the era of austerity at a somehow less developed stage than most other Bismarckian welfare systems. Therefore, financial consolidation and retrenchment of the Swiss welfare system has indeed taken place since the 1970s, but it has remained more of a gradual and continuous first and second order adaptation, than a radical third order paradigm shift (Hall 1993). Hence, the restrictive reforms have certainly not changed the overall Bismarckian regime characteristics of the Swiss welfare system, i.e. insider orientation and an accent on stratification. More systemic changes, however, can be observed since the late 1980s in modernizing reforms that tend to drive the Swiss welfare system away from a typical male breadwinner Bismarckian model, towards a pragmatic hybrid of typically Bismarckian, targeted and universalistic policies. Social insurance schemes have become more gender egalitarian, focused on activation rather than income compensation, and the minimum income protection has gradually been expanded in pension, health and unemployment insurance. In Switzerland, these modernizing reforms tend to benefit the former 'losers' of Bismarckian welfare systems, i.e. labor market outsiders, atypically employed and women.

By introducing both restrictive reforms in terms of insurance eligibility, and expansive reforms in terms of a new means- and income-tested basic benefit level, the Swiss welfare system has both become more egalitarian at the bottom of the income distribution and remained equally or even more stratifying for the middle and higher income-classes.

The chapter is structured as follows. In a first part, I will review the development of the Swiss welfare system in the 'golden age' of European capitalism until the 1970s and assess its characterization in regime-terms. I will then lay out the way in which the micro-institutions of the Swiss welfare system endogenously shaped the challenges to the welfare system, before turning to an account and interpretation of the two main strands of policy reform since the 1980s, i.e. retrenchment and modernization. A final section assesses the explanatory power of structural, institutional and actor-specific variables that drive the development of the Swiss welfare system and points to the importance of negotiation and learning as mechanisms of change.

8.2 Welfare State Growth in a Context of Institutional Power Fragmentation

In Switzerland, welfare state growth was heavily influenced by the macroinstitutional context of power fragmentation, i.e. direct democracy, federalism, the grand coalition and corporatism. Many authors, such as Immergut (1992), Obinger (1998) and Armingeon (2001) have presented striking evidence that these institutions have slowed down the growth of the welfare system by several mechanisms: first of all, the federal government can only legislate on a social policy once the authority to do so is transferred from the sub-national to the federal level by a popular vote.[1] Once this popular vote legally attributes the legislative competence to the national government, the actual decision-making process can start. However, the new nation-wide legislation must then take into account not only the pre-existing cantonal (or private) policies, but also the main interests of all major parties, labor and capital, because any bill proposal can subsequently again be challenged in a popular vote, if an actor succeeds to collect 50,000 signatures against the bill.

The legislative authority for most social policies was transferred in the late 19th or early to mid-20th century, but in some fields, such as unemployment insurance or occupational pensions, this happened only in the 1970s, because the social problems were already at least partly addressed by voluntary, private and cantonal laws. The time lag, which often occurred between the constitutional amendment and the adoption of a national bill is even more impressive (see table 8.1 below). In most cases, it results from lengthy negotiations and failures in popular referenda.

Table 8.1   The slow growth of the Swiss welfare state

Policy field	Constitutional amendment	Coming into effect of the national law	Time lag (years)
Health insurance	1890	1914	24
Mandatory health insurance	1890	1996	106
Accident insurance	1890	1918	28
Old-age insurance	1925	1948	23
Disability insurance	1925	1960	35
Family benefits	1945	1953*	8
Maternity insurance	1945	2005	60
Occupational pensions	1972	1985	13
Mandatory unemployment insurance	1976	1984	8

* only in agriculture (most family allowances remain cantonal)
Source: adapted from Bonoli 2006, Armingeon 2001

This *institutionally induced delay* in welfare state growth had two main consequences: Firstly, the welfare system was still of a rather modest size in the late 1970s, when the economic context began to turn from prosperous to financially constraining. Pension levels were still below the level prescribed in the constitution, no maternity insurance existed, health insurance was voluntary and in 1975, only 22 percent of the people were insured against unemployment (Armingeon 2001). It was widely acknowledged that several social problems, such as mandatory health, unemployment insurance or maternity protection, were still unsolved and that some expansive reforms needed to remain on the agenda, despite the financial difficulties. Therefore, the context of austerity after the 1970s did *not* trigger overall radical retrenchment, but slower growth, selective cost containment and a targeted, often means-tested expansion instead of overall growth.

The second consequence of the institutionally hampered growth was that the welfare system developed in an incremental and layered (Streeck and Thelen 2005a) fashion. When strong cantonal and private regimes existed, they were (at first) often only harmonized or complemented with a national policy that alleviated the most important shortcomings of the pre-existing policies. The multi-pillar old-age protection scheme illustrates this most clearly: The universal basic pension scheme of 1948 provides only flat-rate 'Beveridgean' benefits, which remain below the target level required by the Constitution. As a temporary solution to old-age poverty, means-tested and tax-financed supplementary benefits were therefore introduced in 1972. In addition, private occupational pension funds had been flourishing notably in high-skill sectors since the early 20th century and voluntary private savings plans became fiscally encouraged in the 1970s. Hence, when occupational pensions became mandatory in the early 1980s, they built on a strong pre-existing structure of highly diversified private funds. Therefore, Swiss old-age security, even though Bismarckian in its overall organization and effect, relies on a set of very diversely structured social policy schemes (Nova and Häusermann 2005; BSV 1995). A similar diversity of welfare providers and policies can be observed in other fields such as health care and family policy, where various cantonal, national and private providers and regulations coexist.

This 'layered' micro-institutional structure had an important effect on the subsequent reform trajectory after the 1980s: In Switzerland, as compared to other countries, there was always little fundamental and categorical opposition to any specific type of welfare policy design. Whereas in countries such as France, the introduction of capitalized pension funds or means-testing *as such* became a huge political controversy in itself, the policy repertoire in Switzerland was always large and reforms rather pragmatic. Hence, for the early period of policy development in Switzerland, it is important to note that the macroinstitutional context influenced the pace and design of micro-institutions, which in turn influenced the policy and politics of reform further down the road.

Given the fragmented and underdeveloped character of the Swiss welfare state, its *classification* in terms of regimes has been difficult and highly debated until recently. The comparatively modest level of benefits made some authors classify it as a Liberal regime until the 1970s (Esping-Andersen 1990) or advocate a separate classification of each policy field instead of the whole national regime (Obinger 1998). Today, however, a consensus has emerged that the Swiss regime is mostly Bismarckian or Conservative, with some Liberal traits (Armingeon 2001; Bonoli et al. 2005; Bonoli 2006). An assessment of Swiss social policies of the early 1980s in terms of the main Bismarckian characteristics confirms this verdict:

- Bismarckian welfare schemes typically implement *work-based eligibility* to benefits. This rule applied in Swiss unemployment and accident insurance, mandatory occupational pension funds, family allowances, and disability pensions at the beginning of the 1980s. In some of these schemes, the work-related characteristics were particularly strong, such as for occupational pensions, which only include employees with an income over a certain threshold (of about 16,000 euros per year in 1982). Exceptions from the rule of work-based eligibility are the basic pension scheme (AIIV) and health insurance (voluntary until 1994 and universal from then onwards), as well as – of course – social assistance.

– Benefits in Bismarckian welfare systems tend to be *earnings-related*, because the main goal of these welfare systems is *not* redistribution, but status protection and income replacement. This characteristic applies most clearly in the Swiss case. A recent study financed by the National Science Foundation and based on data from the 1990s comes to the striking conclusion that the Swiss welfare system is particularly status-preserving (Künzi and Schärrer 2004): if you compare what different income strata of the society pay to social policy schemes in terms of contributions and premiums, and what they receive on average from the welfare system, there is hardly any redistributive effect (except for pensioners who benefit markedly from the welfare system). Overall, the Gini-coefficient across the whole income distribution remains constant before and after taxes and transfers.[2] This is because some social policy schemes are strictly contribution related, such as unemployment, accident, disability and – more recently – maternity insurance. Other schemes, mostly occupational and private pensions, as well as health insurance are even degressive in character, i.e. they benefit over-proportionally to higher income classes, because high incomes have better insurance conditions (in pensions) and because some premiums and contributions (in pensions and health insurance) can be deducted from taxes, which results in higher tax savings, the higher the tax rate. This anti-redistributive character of the Swiss welfare system was probably somewhat weaker at the beginning of the 1980s, because the degressive health insurance and occupational pension schemes were less developed, but structurally, the system was then equally axed on stratification as it is today.

– The typical Bismarckian mechanism of financing is through *contributions*, rather than taxes. This also applies to a large extent to the Swiss case. In 1980, about 77 percent of the revenues of the welfare system came from contribution-payments (BSV 2003). Basic pensions, occupational pensions, unemployment insurance, accident insurance and family allowances are mostly or almost exclusively financed through payroll-taxes, which are shared equally between employers and employees (except for family allowances, which are financed exclusively by employer-contributions). The most redistributive parts of social policy, however, i.e. supplementary pension benefits and social assistance, are tax-financed.

–   The fourth main characteristic of Bismarckianism, i.e. *devolved and decentralized policy management,* has always been almost exemplified by the Swiss case. Trade unions and business organizations participate in the legislation and management of basic and occupational pensions, unemployment, accident and disability insurance. Power fragmentation, however, goes even further. Social assistance is entirely regulated at the sub-state level, and even private welfare plays a powerful role in the fields of health care and occupational pensions. Basic health insurance is mandatory, but the insurance plans are provided by around 100 private insurance companies, which define both contributions and benefits. The law states that everybody is entitled to basic insurance, irrespective of age and health status, but additional services and benefits must be purchased on a private basis. In the field of occupational pensions, the importance and variety of private providers is even bigger. Several hundred private and semi-private insurance companies and foundations provide second pillar pension plans for employers. Regulation and control of these pension funds is relatively strong – and has become stronger in the last years after a series of problems of regulatory capture – but the pension funds still differ strongly in terms of their insurance conditions, additional benefits and their investment strategies. The large variety of actors in the Swiss welfare regime is both a determinant and a consequence of its decentralized structure.

Finally, the Swiss welfare system as it had developed until the early 1980s also shares the typical characteristic of Bismarckian welfare systems to be *strongly gendered,* i.e. a male breadwinner system. Maternity insurance, maternal leave and care infrastructure were non-existent at that time. Entitlements being heavily employment and contribution-related, women received much lower benefits throughout the pension, unemployment, accident and disability insurances. The occupational pension scheme was particularly exclusionary for women, since it was accessible only for employees with a certain minimum income per year, excluding de facto most women for whom discontinuous part-time work is the standard form of employment in Switzerland (Wanner and Ferrari 2001).

Tables 8.2 to 8.5 below (section 8.4) summarize the micro-institutional characteristics of the main policy schemes of the Swiss welfare system in the early 1980s. This Swiss welfare system became confronted with financial austerity and societal modernization from the 1970s onwards, which led to both exogenous and endogenous challenges for reform.

8.3 Endogenous and Exogenous Challenges to the Swiss Welfare System

This section singles out the factors supposed to explain the restructuring of the Swiss welfare system since the 1980s.

Structurally, the changes confronting the Swiss welfare system are similar to those challenging its Bismarckian neighbors: a) a *context of austerity* triggering claims for financial consolidation and b) *post-industrialization*, i.e. new social risks. In both cases, the clash of exogenous structural change with the existing welfare architecture fosters an endogenous need for reform.

With regard to the first pressure, Switzerland is no exception among the Continental countries: a downturn in economic growth and productivity since the 1970s and looming demographic changes tend to undermine the financial stability of public households, because they lead to both rising demands for welfare benefits and lower contributions. It is true that the 'welfare without work'-problem (Esping-Andersen 1996b) has always been less severe in Switzerland than in other countries. Because of a very flexible labor market and selective immigration policies, Switzerland had secured nearly full employment until the 1990s. Still now, the unemployment rate has remained below 5 percent and labor market participation rates are high. However, between 1990 and 1997, the number of unemployed people grew from 18,000 to 190,000, i.e. from 0.5 percent to more than 5 percent (see figure 8.1).[3] Even though these numbers might seem low in international comparison, the sudden appearance of (long-term) unemployment came as a major shock in Switzerland.

Figure 8.1 Development of unemployment rates in Switzerland and in its Continental neighbor countries over time

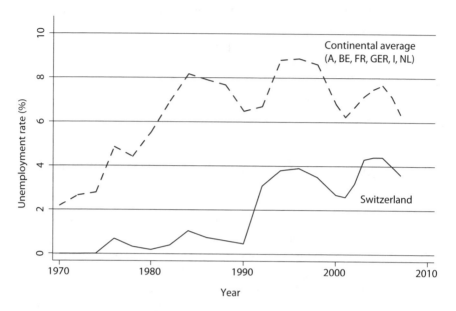

Figure 8.2 Development of economic growth rates in Switzerland and its Continental neighbor countries over time

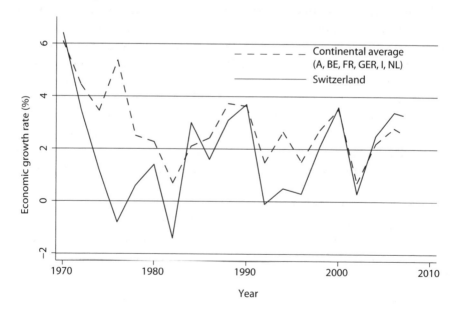

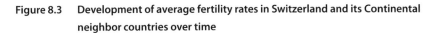

Figure 8.3   Development of average fertility rates in Switzerland and its Continental
              neighbor countries over time

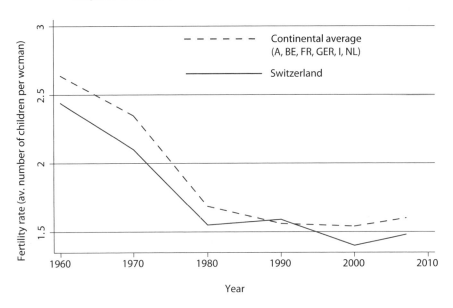

In addition, growth has been almost absent for the last decade (see figure 8.2), productivity is low and the rates of long-term unemployment, disability benefits and social assistance dependencies[4] tend to rise. Together with the negative demographic developments – see the comparatively very low fertility rate in figure 8.3 – this creates a *context of austerity*.

Hence, political demands for cost containment became increasingly prominent on the reform agenda, already in the early 1980s, when major social insurance schemes were not even fully developed. Retrenchment claims grew constantly, and in the mid-1990s, the government appointed a commission of experts, representatives from labor and capital and civil servants, who developed an encompassing overview of the financial threats and problems of social insurance in Switzerland (IDA Fiso I 1996; IDA Fiso II 1997). Hence, a debate on cost containment and policy priorities started *even before* the welfare system had reached its full development. Therefore, the pressure for retrenchment was present, but less severe than in other countries.

The second structural change to which social policy-makers became confronted was *post-industrialization*. The spread of atypical, mobile and unstable work relations, changing skill requirements on the labor market, rising divorce rates and the massive entry of women into paid employment have changed the social risk structure in the Continental welfare systems and created new challenges to these industrial male breadwinner regimes (Bonoli et al. 2005; Bonoli 2005; Bonoli 2006). As with austerity, the new social risks are not an entirely exogenous pressure for change, but they result also from the institutional characteristics of Continental regimes: being concerned primarily with the protection of standard, male industrial employment, trade unions and employers had over time created a male breadwinner model, which presented many loopholes with regard to the coverage of the above mentioned new social needs and demands. Hence, this structure of the welfare system reflected the primary concerns of the constituencies of trade unions and employers organizations. Labor market outsiders and women never belonged to labor and capital's core constituency. Hence, the post-industrial loopholes in social insurance protection are to some extent also a rather direct consequence of Bismarckian insider-focus. These loopholes in social protection became increasingly visible from the 1970s onwards. As a consequence, some agreement mainly across Left and value-libertarian political parties emerged with regard to the need for modernization of policies such as maternity protection, women's pension rights and the protection of atypical employment (Bonoli 2006: 7; Häusermann 2006, 2010b; Häusermann et al. 2004). Hence, the very structure of the Bismarckian welfare system produced insider-outsider conflicts, some leeway for expansive reforms and an opportunity for new actors, mainly the political parties instead of trade unions, to play a decisive role in welfare system restructuring.

8.4   Reform Dynamics since the 1980s along Two Dimensions

The reforms restructuring the Swiss welfare system since the 1980s can be divided into *two categories*: Firstly, path-dependent changes aimed at *cost containment*. None of the reforms in this category entailed fundamental cutbacks of the existing welfare system. Rather, they consisted in a gradual scaling back of eligibility conditions, contribution- and benefit levels in the fields of unemployment benefits, the basic and second pillar pension schemes and disability pensions. In terms of Hall's categorization of change (1993), these reforms must thus be seen as first and second order changes. The losers of these reforms are the formerly privileged insiders, i.e. the standard insured whose benefit rights have been somewhat lowered. However, none of these reforms modified the overall goal of the existing regime, which is to provide encompassing income replacement to standard insured workers. Eligibility remained work-related, benefit levels contribution-related and the whole schemes contribution-financed.

The second type of changes, however, is systemic and more far-reaching, because these reforms tend to reorient the Swiss welfare system away from its Bismarckian profile in two directions. Firstly, these recent reforms have started to shift the focus of the policies from standard insider workers, male breadwinners and families, to individuals and less privileged groups. Thereby, they opened insurance benefits to former outsiders and improved the minimum-coverage of low-income groups (e.g. by introducing maternity insurance, by opening occupational pensions for part-time workers, by improving the level of supplementary means-tested basic pension benefits and by reinforcing public subsidies for health care insurance). Secondly, the focus of social security on income replacement is being replaced by a focus on activation (e.g. by active labor market policies and by the improvement of external childcare facilities). These two sets of changes must be seen as more structural second and third order changes. Both categories of reforms entail new beneficiaries among the labor market outsiders and both can be subsumed in the category of *modernizing reforms*.

Retrenchment and Financial Consolidation

Attempts at financial consolidation started as early as the late 1970s. The economic crisis of this decade abruptly interrupted the linear process of growth, and raised concerns about cost containment. The widespread new perception – mostly held within right-wing parties and employers' organizations – was that expenditure levels needed to be limited in order to preserve the viability of the welfare system. The relatively low levels of consumption taxes (7.6 percent VAT) and non-wage labor costs[5] (below 20 percent, except for the oldest age group of labor market participants) in the Swiss system were viewed as a comparative advantage of the Swiss economy that had to be preserved. In spite of these concerns, considerable expansion of the Swiss welfare system continued, since many social insurance schemes remained clearly underdeveloped in the 1970s. However, the further expansion became more modest, means-tested and overshadowed by the concerns for cost containment. In addition, several schemes actually did undergo retrenchment. The following sections provide an overview of these reforms.

In *pension policy*, the restrictive dynamic started already in 1976, almost two decades before the *basic pension scheme* (first pillar AHV) actually entered a structural financial deficit. In this early reform, the contribution levels of self-employed were raised and the indexation of pensions was limited. Financial consolidation continued in the 1990s with the increase of women's retirement age from 62 to 64 and the rise of an additional per-centage-point of the value added tax on consumption. Indeed, since the VAT level in Switzerland is still only at about 7.6 percent, consolidation through shifts to this consumption tax are an important issue. However, the most recent attempt at retrenchment was rejected in a popular vote in 2003. In this reform, the Parliament had not only decided retrenchment of widows' pensions, a further rise in women's age of retirement and – again – an additional percentage-point of VAT for pension insurance, but had also denied any financial support for the flexibilization of the retirement age.[6] In the mandatory *occupational pension scheme* (second pillar BVG), how-ever, cost containing reform were successfully adopted by the Parliament in 2003, when the level of benefits was lowered, women's age of retirement was raised to 65 and the legally required level of interest rate on individual pension savings was lowered. In addition, and somewhat paradoxically, the rise of the level of *means-tested supplementary pension benefits* in 1985 and 1996 also contributed to financial consolidation in the basic universal pension scheme.[7] Indeed, the Swiss Constitution states that basic pensions must be high enough to allow for a decent existence. However, pension lev-els still have not and probably will never reach this goal (BSV 1995). Hence, the strengthening of supplementary pensions contributes to legitimize the low level of first pillar pensions (Nova and Häusermann 2005). The heavier accent on means-tested supplementary pensions also implies a shift of fi-nancing mechanisms from contributions to general taxes.

Cost containment also became an important issue in the mandatory *unemployment insurance* only a decade after its introduction in 1982. With the economic downturn in the beginning of the 1990s, massive un-employment appeared in Switzerland for the first time. Therefore, the government by decree extended the benefit period to a maximum of two years and temporarily lowered the replacement rate from 80 to 70 percent in 1993. This lowering of the level of benefits was then permanently con-firmed in 1995. In addition, the 2002 reform enacted a longer minimum contribution period and cut back the duration of benefit entitlements from two years to one (Berclaz and Füglister 2003).

Similar cutbacks have been adopted with regard to *disability insurance*. With the appearance of unemployment, more and more labor was shed into disability insurance. Therefore, this scheme accumulated a huge deficit of almost a billion Swiss francs per year by the end of the 1990s (Künzi and Schärer 2004: 44). As a consequence, various cost containing measures were adopted in 2007: access to disability benefits was restricted, the definition of 'reasonable' work enlarged and a waiting period for benefits was introduced.

Finally, costs have most dramatically risen in *health care*. Basic health care insurance became mandatory in 1994 only, but this scheme had to deal with cost containment right from the start. Since health care is financed mainly (by about 2/3) through individual premiums, which are not set by law, but by private insurance companies, the disastrous financial development manifests itself so far mainly through premium increases of 5-10 percent year after year. The average basic insurance premium for an individual person has been no less than between 150 and 250 euros per month since the early 2000s. In addition, all insured have an annual franchise of between 200 and 1500 Euros. Given these very high costs (which do not depend on income-levels, at all), the financial burden health care imposes especially on middle class families, who are not eligible for income-tested premium subsidies, is very heavy and continues to rise each year. Thus, the reform initiated in the early 2000s was concerned with limiting costs by – among others – lowering the catalogue of treatments included in basic insurance and limiting the free choice of medical doctors for patients (European Observatory on Health Care Systems 2000). This reform was rejected in Parliament in 2003 and since then, several less encompassing reforms have been adopted, such as an increase in income-tested premium subsidies for families in 2005.[8] However, proponents and opponents of the main points of the reform (notably cutbacks and the limitation of free choice ['Vertragsfreiheit']) are very polarized and therefore, the reform process proceeds only very slowly.

In sum, consolidation and cost containment have been constant topics in Swiss welfare system reforms over the last twenty years. Benefits were lowered in the fields of unemployment insurance, basic and occupational old-age pensions and disability pensions. In addition, premiums and contributions were raised in the field of health insurance and – by means of an increase of the VAT – old-age and disability insurance. However, retrenchment remains highly *controversial* in the policy-making arena. In pension policy, unemployment insurance or family policy, there is no agreement on the actual problem pressure facing the Swiss welfare system, because the assumptions on future economic and demographic development diverge considerably (Nova and Häusermann 2005). Given the macroinstitutional context of welfare policy-making, cost-containing reform must be negotiated, and since the positions diverge so massively, they remain limited so far. Too drastic cuts in benefit levels can be challenged by a popular referendum and several attempts at cuts in pension and unemployment insurance have been rejected in popular votes throughout the recent years. Therefore, retrenchment in Switzerland is limited and incremental (Bonoli et al. 2005).

Recalibrating the Swiss Welfare System

The second strand of reforms is a more substantial change in systemic terms, because it tackles the inherent weaknesses of the Bismarckian welfare system. These reforms can be described as *recalibration* (Pierson 2001a) or *modernization* (Bonoli 2005; Häusermann 2010a) of the welfare system, because they adapt it to specific post-industrial social needs and demands of mostly labor market outsiders and women. In analyzing these reforms, one needs to distinguish between a set of second order reforms, which open the access to existing insurance schemes for former outsiders, and a set of third order changes shifting the goal of income compensation to activation, social investment and tax-financed minimum protection.

The main thrust of the first set of modernizing reforms consists in granting benefit entitlements to categories of the population who had none before. The proportion of systemic *outsiders* grew from the 1970s onwards, because more and more people did not correspond to the profile of the standard insured anymore (Wanner and Ferrari 2001). By 2000, the proportion of part-time employees in the Swiss labor market had reached 30 percent, almost 80 percent of which being female. About 5 percent of the workforce holds employment contracts of less than two years duration and self-employment has increased over the 1990s from about 15 to almost 20 percent (Rechsteiner 2002). Hence, when labor markets became more precarious, gender roles changed and divorce rates rose after the 1970s, new social needs and demands of these former welfare 'losers' appeared more prominently on the reform agenda. Parties of the new Left, the Greens and women's organizations were the most important advocates of these new social needs and demands. A series of reforms started to address them from the late 1980s onwards.

Most prominently, in the field of *pensions*, the 1995 reform introduced equal splitting of contributions and benefits between spouses and pension credits for mothers. Both changes drastically improved the pension rights for non-working women (Nova and Häusermann 2005; CONSOC 2003). Similarly, the second pillar occupational pensions were extended to more low-income earners in 2003 (by means of a lowering of the access threshold). Even though this expansion remained clearly below the demands of the Left and of women's organizations, it was an important signal for the recognition of part-time work (Häusermann 2002). Still in the field of occupational pensions, the law on 'free movement' of 1994 enacted the rights of workers to job mobility. Furthermore, the reforms of the unemployment insurance in the 1990s extended the benefit period and thus improved coverage of long-term unemployed. All these reforms were recalibrating, insofar as they extended Bismarckian income protection to people who are not in standard employment.

The second set of recalibrating changes is focused on enhancing standard employment through *activation* policies. These reforms are again more important for outsiders who struggle to 'earn' sufficient social rights through labor market participation. This new trend is most visible with regard to the *active labor market policies*, which were introduced in 1995 for the first time. This reform forced the cantons to create 25,000 places of training for unemployed and these measures were continuously reinforced over the following years (Berclaz and Füglister 2000). Within a decade, the expenditures for active labor market policies in Switzerland have been multiplied by six (Bonoli et al. 2005).[9] The 2007 reform of disability insurance shows a rather similar thrust, with a strengthened commitment to the reintegration of disabled and the early detection of employees at risk.

Recent developments in *family and care policy* also go in the direction of enhancing labor market participation: maternity insurance for working mothers was introduced in 2004 and in 2003, the national Parliament voted a four-year credit of 200 million Swiss francs encouraging the development of a – so far almost completely lacking – infrastructure for external childcare. The most important developments in the reconciliation of work and care, however, are currently taking place at the level of the cantons and communes (Bonoli et al. 2005; Dafflon 2003). Several cantons are implementing financial care infrastructure, in order to improve the possibilities for the reconciliation of work and care.

This account of activation policies should not obscure the fact that the modernization of the Swiss welfare system has remained rather limited and far below the criteria that characterize a 'social investment state' (Lister 2004). A social investment state focuses on investment in human capital in order to create opportunities for people to earn their own living.

The above reforms do indeed go in this direction, but important problems of care infrastructure scarcity or inefficient active labor market policies still persist, and the adoption of these reforms often depends on a series of conjunctural conditions (Bonoli et al. 2005). It can be hypothesized that in this specific field of reform, EU membership would indeed have contributed to a more rapid and comprehensive reorientation of policies (Daly 2004; Bonoli et al. 2005; Morel 2007).

A third and last set of modernizing reforms concerns the increasing importance of tax-financed minimum protection schemes in various fields of social policy-making. The supplementary means-tested pension benefits, which are granted to particularly underprivileged pensioners, have been expanded continuously since the 1980s. This scheme also serves as a functional equivalent to long-term care insurance, because most pensioners in homes and care centers rely on these supplementary benefits. Similarly, the tax-financed subsidies for low-income earners in health care insurance have also been expanded several times. Today, no less than a third of the population receives such subsidies for health insurance premiums (Künzi and Schärrer 2004). Finally, the contributions of the central governments to the basic pension scheme, to the unemployment insurance and to the disability insurance have also increased over time, strengthening the proportion of tax financing of the welfare system as compared to contribution financing (see tables 8.2 to 8.5 for a summary of these changes).

The modernization of the Swiss welfare system as I have described it in the above sections, should, however, not be considered as a radical upheaval. Rather, in a pragmatic and incremental fashion, new recalibrating elements were either added to the existing Bismarckian insurance policies or these latter insurance policies were used to cover new risk profiles.

New Winners, New Losers

In section 8.1 of this chapter, I have shown that the micro-institutions of the Swiss welfare system were indeed Bismarckian at the beginning of the 1980s (see table 8.2). After discussing the record of reforms of the last 20 years in the above two sections, we can now assess the extent of change and the winners and losers of this restructuring.

Tables 8.2 to 8.5 summarize the main changes for the four major social policy fields, i.e. pensions, health care, unemployment and family policy.[10]

Table 8.2   Institutional changes in old-age income security (changes in italics)

	Early 1980s	*Mid-2000s*
Eligibility	Universal access to basic pensions (first tier); selective access to private occupational pensions	Universal and *individualized basic pension insurance for men and women*; *mandatory* occupational pension insurance (*extended to lower income-earners and part-time workers in 2003); increased fiscal privileges for private pension savings*
Benefit structure	Flat-rate benefits (first tier); moderate supplementary pensions	Flat-rate benefits (first tier); *increased* supplementary pension benefits; *earnings-related occupational pensions;*
Financing	Contributions and taxes (first tier); supplementary pensions are entirely tax-financed; private occupational pensions are entirely contribution-financed	Contributions (70%), *VAT* and taxes (26%) (first tier); taxes (supplementary pensions); contributions (60%) and interests in capital (36%) (occupational pensions)
Manage-ment	Tripartite (first tier), central govern-ment and substate entities (supple-mentary benefits); private companies (occupational pensions)	Tripartite (first tier), central govern-ment and substate entities (supple-mentary pensions); *central government* and private companies (occupational pensions)

Table 8.3   Institutional changes in health care policy (changes in italics)

	Early 1980s	*Mid-2000s*
Eligibility	Voluntary insurance; basic regulatory framework for insurance conditions	Mandatory universal basic insurance; voluntary supplementary insurance schemes
Benefit structure	Depending on the benefit-catalogue of the private insurance companies	Regulated catalogue of guaranteed basic treatments and benefits;
Financing	Private insurance contributions	Premiums (not earnings-related) (ca 80%); private franchise and tax-subsi-dies (ca 20%);
Manage-ment	Private companies and weak central state control	*Central government* and private insu-rance companies

Table 8.4   Institutional changes in unemployment insurance (changes in italics)

	Early 1980s	Mid-2000s
Eligibility	Mandatory insurance for employees from 1982 onwards	Mandatory insurance; *tightened eligibility (longer contribution period)*
Benefit structure	Income replacement (about 80%)	*Lowered* income replacement (about 70%); *activation policies*
Financing	Contribution payments (90%) and interests on capital (10%)	Contribution payments (95%), *tax-financed subsidies (6%)*
Management	Tripartite	Tripartite; *central government control on activation measures;*

Table 8.5   Institutional changes in family policy (changes in italics)

	Early 1980s	Mid-2000s
Eligibility	Family allowances for parents in standard employment (strong differences between cantons); voluntary maternity insurance in some companies	Universal family allowances (harmonized across cantons); mandatory maternity insurance;
Benefit structure	Financial transfers (family allowances); strong variation in benefit-levels between the cantons;	*Harmonized* financial transfers (family allowances); *maternity insurance benefits (80% of the income for 12 weeks); state subsidies for external childcare infrastructure*
Financing	Employer contributions	Contributions (family allowances and *maternity insurance*); taxes *(care subsidies)*
Management	Cantons and employers	Cantons, employers *and central government*

On each of the four micro-institutional characteristics, changes can be observed, even though none of them has become completely transformed. With regard to *eligibility*, social rights have generally been *extended* to new groups of beneficiaries (women and part-timers in pensions, universal access to health care, mandatory unemployment insurance, universalization and harmonization of family allowances, mandatory maternity insurance). Hence, the scope of beneficiaries has become larger, which benefits most clearly those groups, who were excluded from the purely Bismarckian schemes.

The changes in *benefit structures* are more complex: on the one hand, the benefits for low-income groups and outsiders have been improved in pension insurance, health care and family policy. But on the other hand, the general insurance conditions have even been tightened with regard to pension insurance rights in the first and second insurance tier, and in unemployment insurance. In addition, the degressive aspects of the Swiss welfare system, i.e. the occupational and private pension tiers and the premium-financed health insurance scheme, have even been reinforced over the last 10 years, strengthening the inegalitarian and anti-redistributive character of the Swiss welfare system. The bottom line of these changes is that the standard insured of the middle class tend to be the main losers of the recent reforms, because they are clearly hit by retrenchment, but they are also 'too well-off' to benefit from the expanded minimum protection. The lowest-income groups, however, tend to benefit from the recent expansion of the basic protection scheme. Finally, the most privileged income strata have become even more privileged, since they benefit from fiscal subsidies for occupational and private pensions, and they have access to voluntary health insurance.

The structure of *financing* tends to shift away from contributions to other sources of revenue, such as general taxation, VAT and interests from capitalized savings. Overall, 77 percent of the Swiss welfare system was financed through contributions in 1980, as compared to 70 percent in 1990 and only 65 percent in 2002. By contrast, the proportion of tax-financing amounts to 14 percent in 2002 (as compared to 11 percent in 1990) and 16 percent of the financing in 2002 came from interests on capitalized funds. Hence, the financing structure has become more diversified.

Finally, *management* remains largely decentralized, but – not least with the stronger role of general taxation – the central government has become more important, especially in unemployment insurance (where the central government supervises the cantonal activation policies) and in family policy (harmonization of family allowances, national maternity insurance and subsidies for childcare infrastructure).

The changes are most marked with regard to eligibility criteria and benefit structures, with simultaneous trends of a) cost containment, and b) the expansion of minimum protection and private insurance. Now who are the winners and losers of this recent neo-Bismarckian restructuring in the Swiss welfare state? It seems like the distributional impact is highly differential. At the bottom of the income distribution, the welfare system is getting more universal: the recent reforms have introduced a range of means- or income-tested minimum subsidies and benefits that are not dependent on previous contribution-records or earnings. With regard to the middle class and the more privileged strata, however, the Swiss welfare state tends to become even more stratifying, because benefits are linked even more tightly to previous contribution-records and the partly private system reduces redistribution and accentuates income inequality. Overall, the old core constituency of the welfare system – namely male middle class labor market insiders – seem to be the main losers of the recent Swiss welfare system restructuring. For outsiders, by contrast, the expansion of universal minimum benefits has extended social rights. The extent to which the recent restructuring has improved benefits for outsiders varies, however, from country to country. While this seems to be the case in Switzerland and the Netherlands, the welfare state remains more insider-focused in countries such as France or Italy (see the other country chapters in this volume).

In terms of the development of the Bismarckian welfare systems, this welfare state restructuring since the 1970s has also been marked by an interesting *procedural change*. Indeed, in the past, most reforms were designed in specialized extra-parliamentary committees composed of civil servants, trade union and business representatives, before they were handed over to Parliament, where they were hardly modified (Kriesi 1980; Sciarini 1999). Most of the recent modernizing reform elements, however, have not been introduced by trade unions and employer organizations, but only at a later stage of the reform process, i.e. by the political parties in Parliament. In virtually all the important reforms of the 1990s – the pension reforms of 1995 and 2003, the unemployment reform of 1995 and the current disability insurance reform – it was only in Parliament that the modernizing elements of reform were added (Bonoli 1999; Häusermann et al. 2004).

Among other reasons, this can be explained precisely by the changing configuration of winners and losers of welfare system reforms: recalibration benefits mainly outsiders – women, unemployed, young families, atypical workers – who do not belong to the main constituency of labor and capital (Häusermann et al. 2004). Hence, trade unions and employers proved unable to draw a compromise on these policies in the pre-parliamentary arena. The political parties, by contrast, proved to be more sensitive to the claims of the new risk groups, because of the higher proportion of women in Parliament as compared to corporatist decision-making arenas (Bonoli 2006), and because political parties are more responsive to value issues such as gender equality (Häusermann et al 2004). Therefore, the political parties have become the main drivers of Swiss welfare system restructuring.

8.5 Conclusion: The Politics Linking Modernization and Cost Containment

For the sake of comparison and synthesis, the following table summarizes the three broad stages of Swiss welfare system development in a synthetic manner. The Swiss reform trajectory comprises an early period of expansion and two parallel periods of restructuring – both restrictive and expansive – from the late 1980s and early 1990s onwards.

Table 8.6   Summary of reform trajectory: Switzerland

Type of change	Context and diagnosis	Content of policy changes	Politics and conflict lines	Reform output and consequences
Growth until the late 1980s	Full employment; industrialism; economic growth; Diagnosis: 'The Swiss welfare system must be extended to provide sufficient insurance to all employees'	Development of mandatory insurance schemes; increase of benefit levels; development of basic minimum benefits	Negotiated compromises between labor and capital; low level of class conflict	*1st order changes*: Slow development of the Swiss welfare system as a bismarckian latecomer; *main winners*: male labor market insiders and their families
Cost containment and consolidation since the 1980s	Economic downturn; demographic changes; rising expenditure levels; Diagnosis: 'Expenditures need to be limited: cost containment and retrenchment'	Selective retrenchment of benefits in pension and unemployment insurance; further welfare system expansion is only limited and increasingly means-tested	Highly controversial negotiations between capital, labor and political parties; no agreement on the diagnostic; Strong class-polarization	*1st order changes*: parametric retrenchment in the major insurance schemes; *2nd order changes*: shift to increased tax-financing; *main losers*: middle class insiders
Modernization since the 1990s	Postindustrialism; unstable labor markets and family structures; Diagnosis: 'The welfare system needs to be adapted to new risk profiles; activation is more economical than income compensation'	Inclusion of welfare system outsiders in the insurance schemes; Activation of unemployed, disabled and mothers; minimum support for low-income classes	Negotiated compromises between political parties (less so labor and capital); insider-outsider conflicts; value-conflicts on gender equality	*2nd order changes*: coverage of new risk groups by existing insurance schemes; *3rd order change*: shift of policy goals from compensation to activation; *main winners*: outsiders and women;

It is important to note the *striking parallels between the mechanisms of welfare system retrenchment and modernization in Switzerland and in many other Bismarckian countries*. Cost containment in pensions and unemployment insurance has occurred in most of these countries in a very similar fashion (see the other country chapters in this volume). Similarly, almost all of these countries have simultaneously reinforced tax-financed minimum protection schemes, and they have all developed a stronger focus on activation, family policy and female labor market participation during the recent years (except for Austria, which still seems to pursue a Conservative family policy; see Obinger and Tálos, this volume).

How can we explain these changes? It appears clearly that we need to attribute them to factors that are equally similar across these countries: structural pressure and the common micro-institutional characteristics of the Bismarckian welfare systems.

Indeed, in Switzerland as in all the other countries, the Bismarckian *micro-institutions* have clashed with the *structural developments* of austerity and post-industrialism. This clash has led to a redefinition of the reform agenda. The actual reform output in each and every country does, however, depend on national factors.

In this respect, the *macroinstitutional context* has definitely been the single most important factor explaining the *mechanisms and pace* of reforms. The fragmented institutional structure of the Swiss consensus democracy accounts for the fact that the Swiss welfare system developed so slowly and in a very modest and fragmented manner, combining different logics of welfare system policy (insurance, capitalization, means-testing, private health care etc.) from the very start. This macroinstitutional context also continued to shape the reform trajectory later on in both an indirect and a direct way: indirectly, the micro-institutional diversity of the Swiss welfare system widened the repertoire of available '*policy instruments*', thereby facilitating the pragmatic 'modernization' of the typically Bismarckian weaknesses after the 1980s.

But the Swiss reform pragmatism is also linked more directly to the macroinstitutional context: political decision-making power is spread across a wide range of actors. Not only are all relevant actors involved in decision making, but every reform in Switzerland can be challenged in a popular referendum. Hence, reforms must be carefully balanced in order to gather sufficient support. Therefore, *negotiation* is the main mechanism of reform in Switzerland. I would even go further and argue that the simultaneous emergence of cost containment *and* modernization on the Swiss reform agenda since the 1980s enabled precisely the required compromise. Hence, the modernizing reforms often benefit from rather unexpected cross-class coalitions between leftist and socially Liberal actors, because they combine retrenchment of existing benefits with expansive elements in favor of former outsiders. This pattern of reform could for example be observed in the 1995 pension reform and the 1995 unemployment insurance reform (Bonoli 1999; Hausermann et al. 2004; Häusermann 2010b), but also in the 2003 reform of occupational pensions (Häusermann 2002).

Finally, layering has also become an important mechanism of reform. As I have outlined at the beginning of the chapter, the Swiss welfare system grew in a layered fashion. Slowly growing insurance schemes were gradually complemented by additional policies, designed to alleviate the most important loopholes. The system of old-age protection exemplifies this logic, since it relies on a 'multi-pillar' logic, which has incrementally developed over time: flat-rate universal PAYG-pensions are complemented by means-tested and tax-financed supplementary benefits, capitalized occupational pensions and voluntary, fiscally encouraged private pension savings plans. This system, combining different logics of benefits and financing, proves to be more resilient to structural and demographic challenges than purely Bismarckian regimes and has recently become a model for reform in other policy fields. Recent reform propositions (e.g. Bauer et al. 2004) call for the *emulation* of this design in the fields of family and health policy. Hence, the micro-institutional design of the existing welfare system itself feeds back into the dynamics of reform.

In conclusion, let me come back to the *regime classification* of the Swiss welfare system? Is it still Bismarckian? In this chapter, I have shown that the Swiss welfare system tends to become both less Bismarckian at the bottom of the income distribution (means-tested minima, outsiders policies, universal health care etc.) and more Bismarckian – i.e. stratifying and inegalitarian – with regard to the middle and higher income classes. Hence, it is crucial to acknowledge that the 'modernized' Swiss welfare system is neither becoming universalistic (i.e. Scandinavian), nor residual or Liberal (i.e. Anglo-Saxon). Rather we may be witnessing the start of a genuinely Continental 'way out' of the post-industrial challenges: the inegalitarian and insurance-related aspects are reinforced with the reduction of replacement rates, the lengthening of contribution periods and the inclusion of former outsiders in the insurance schemes. At the same time, however, a basic minimum protection allows for this reform-strategy by easing the most pressing poverty risks, and by providing the reforms with the necessary political legitimacy.

9 The Politics of Social Security Reforms in the Czech Republic, Hungary, Poland and Slovakia

Alfio Cerami

9.1 Introduction[1]

In 1989 Central and Eastern European policy-makers were suddenly confronted with the difficult task of restructuring a welfare system under a completely different economic and political system. The restructuring of welfare institutions accompanied the emergence of new and serious societal problems. More and more people were hit by unemployment and poverty, the family pattern in force during communism had to be re-discussed, and also protection during old age and sickness had to be renegotiated. Reforms started immediately and involved important structural changes. The four Visegrad[2] countries (Czech Republic, Hungary, Poland and Slovakia) raised retirement age and pension insurance contributions while reducing the pay-as-you-go principle, introduced health insurance while guaranteeing the access to health care through the obligation of the state to ensure unprotected citizens, implemented a German-like unemployment insurance consisting usually of three pillars (unemployment benefits, unemployment assistance and social assistance), reduced the family benefits heritage of the communist system while continuing to pursue pro-natalist policy and extensive childcare provisions (very often until the child is enrolled in university education), as well as establishing a basic safety net for those citizens at persistent risk of poverty (Cerami 2006).

Despite the fact that great attention has recently been given to the role played by institutions and path-dependent mechanisms in the development of European welfare systems (see, for instance, Bonoli and Palier 2000; Pierson 2004; Ebbinghaus 2005; Streeck and Thelen 2005b), the possible outcome of such institutional transformations is still the object of a controversial debate. Here, the main problem is to characterize the new internal configuration, which results from a continuous process of structuring, destructuring and restructuring of existent welfare institutions. The literature usually addresses Central and Eastern European welfare systems as extremely diverse and doomed to follow, on a country basis, one of the Esping-Andersen's (1990) three-fold typology. For Bob Deacon (1992), Poland should have become a good example of a 'post-communist Conservative corporatist' welfare state, Czechoslovakia of a Social Democratic model, while Hungary of a Liberal welfare regime. More recently, Zsuzsa Ferge (2001) and Erzsébet Szalai (E. Szalai 2005) have expressed their worries that Hungary might be on the move towards the Liberal welfare regime, whereas other political scientists have argued that a mixture of corporatism and liberalism (see J. Szalai 2005; Fuchs and Offe 2008; Gans-Morse and Orenstein 2006; Bohle and Greskovits 2007) or of corporatism and social democracy (Fenger 2007) was, in reality, the main characteristic of the new welfare state. Despite undisputable merits, these authors have paid only limited attention to the commonalities that the four Visegrad countries shared, even though it would have been interesting to explore more in detail how Bismarckian institutions in force before Word War II were adapted to the universal communist principles and then eventually recombined in the new post-communist environment (for recent exceptions, see Bakken 2008; Sirovátka and Saxonberg 2008).

This chapter aims to further investigate this issue by asking how and to what extent Bismarckian institutions survived the communist and post-communist social policy reorganization, as well as what the new internal structure of these welfare systems in transition is. Here, four distinct types of politics of social security reforms are identified and discussed: the *politics of expansion for legitimization* implemented during the communist period of transformation, followed by the *politics of expansion for compensation, politics of retrenchment through privatization* and *politics of recalibration* in the post-communist transitions.

Contrary to common assumptions that look at the establishment of welfare institutions as being implemented by design or as the result of an aseptic *policy transfer*, this chapter will argue that the four Visegrad countries have built their contemporary welfare system on the ruins, and with the ruins, of the welfare institutions they had previously introduced in the pre-communist and communist period. The reason for the inclusion of these countries in the family of Bismarckian welfare systems lies, therefore, not only in the fact that they have a long tradition of Bismarckian social insurance and are usually considered the front-runners of reforms that might be implemented elsewhere, but also in the fact that Bismarckian institutions, established before World War II, lived, adapted and evolved during the communist social policy reorganization from 1945 to 1989, and also succeeded in surviving the, perhaps, even more rapid structural transformation following the dissolution of the central planned economy.

Compared to other contributions in this volume, this chapter goes back further in the history of social protection by including the soviet and pre-soviet social policy organization. As will be shown, this analysis is crucial to understanding the real path of development in countries that have witnessed several phases of economic, political and social transformation. In the conclusion, it will be affirmed that Central and Eastern European countries develop around a new welfare logic, which combines, in a path-dependent and innovative way components of Bismarckian social insurance, communist egalitarianism and Liberal market orientation (see also Cerami 2006). In short, it includes elements of each of the Esping-Andersen's three-fold classification.

The chapter is structured as follows. Section One describes the system of social protection established in the period antecedent World War II, while Section Two provides an overview of communist social policy with the associated politics of social security reforms. Section Three then goes on describing the period 1989 onwards. It highlights the main welfare reform trajectories after communism, but also their main politics of social security reforms, as well as the role that international organizations have played in the transformation of post-communist welfare states.

9.2 The Period before 1945

Historical Background

As recently highlighted by Inglot (2003, 2008), Szikra (2004), Tomka (2004a, 2004b), Cerami (2006), Haggard and Kaufman (2008), and Sirovátka and Saxonberg (2008) the four Visegrad countries have a long tradition of social insurance that dates back to the Austro-Hungarian Empire. This can be seen if we look in turn to eligibility criteria, type of benefits, financing and management of the early social protection schemes in these countries.

A brief overview of pre-communist pension systems shows, for example, that these countries had already established some form of Bismarck-style pension insurance, which linked access to benefits to professional status. This link was particularly strong in the Czech Republic and in the Slovak Republic, in Hungary and in Poland. In the years 1906 to 1933, the numerous funded pension schemes established were based on a corporatist vision of social solidarity, primarily aiming to secure occupational standards. Health care was also provided on the basis of professional activity and financed primarily through social insurance contributions. In the Czech Republic and Slovakia, the first health policy was introduced in 1918, when the Czech Lands declared their independence from the Austro-Hungarian Empire. The first fully functional health insurance system, however, came into force in 1924 with the adoption of the Health Insurance Act, which provided coverage for employees, approximately one third of the total population. Hungary enacted the first act on public health in 1876 (Act XIV of 1876). According to the law, the eligible poor obtained free health care at special surgeries. Corporatist social insurance was the foundation of the system. Health care was delivered through the private sector and in some state hospitals. Poland, which has a long tradition of Bismarckian social insurance, dates the first legislation back to 1918. This system provided, however, very limited coverage with only 7 percent of the population insured.

The benefit structure also clearly reflected a Bismarckian orientation. As mentioned, pension and health care benefits were associated with the employees' insurance records and aimed at reproducing professional achievements. Pension benefits were earnings-related, while the access to health care services, obtainable in public as well as in private practices, depended on the payment of health insurance premiums or, when not available, by payments in cash. This system was highly non-egalitarian and a significant segment of the population remained uninsured. As highlighted by Dorottya Szikra (2004: Table 1, p. 267), while in 1900 approximately 9 percent of the total population was insured in the compulsory sickness insurance in Western Europe, this percentage was only 3.5 percent in Hungary. Forty years later, in 1940, the gap was even higher with 31 percent of total population insured in Western Europe against 10 percent in Hungary.

The main financing mechanism was social insurance contributions, which aimed at covering individuals primarily against the risks associated with old age and health. There was a basic social safety net for the poor, sponsored by the state or by charity organizations; this net did not aim at guaranteeing minimum living standards, but rather aimed to alleviate extreme poverty temporarily.

The management of the social security system was fairly decentralized. The responsibility for old-age and health care protection was primarily given to local communities or workers' associations, which had the duty to ensure a minimum level of subsistence (rather than a minimum living standard) for their members. State intervention in workers' life was minimal and primarily relegated to resolve workers' disputes. The increasing internal tensions, caused by the very low living standards of factory workers and agrarians associated with the possible spread of socialist ideals, lead the governments of these countries to adopt the strategy developed by Bismarck. The maintenance of social peace was then linked to the introduction of occupationally based schemes, in which central authorities had only limited regulatory powers (primarily legislative rather than that of supervision).

9.3   The Period from 1945 to 1989

The Bismarckian Characteristics of the Communist Welfare System

Following the Soviet occupation after World War II, the dominant Bismarckian mode of access to benefits was not completely abolished by the communist regime, but rather it was expanded in order to bring it in line with the egalitarian aspirations of the Bolshevik revolution. Here, it is important to point out that the communist understanding of citizenship coincided with the idea of the perfect communist worker (such as Stakhanov). Every citizen had the right and obligation to work not only for the sustenance of his or her family, but also for the economic development of the country. As a consequence, welfare rights and entitlements continued to be based on professional activity, but the corporatist orientation was covered by egalitarian communist propaganda and by the fact that there was practically no unemployment. Clearly, things were different for those minorities, who were, for some reason, outside of the labor market (such as Roma, pensioners, handicapped). In this case, the universal and egalitarian aspirations of the communist regime faced a drastic slowdown. Poverty and what we would call social exclusion were associated with an implicit social stigma. In the eyes of the many citizens that regularly took part in the economic, social and political life, being the beneficiary of some form of social assistance benefit (in-kind or in-cash) was inevitably the result of a reactionary or, in the worst case, of counter-revolutionary behavior (Milanovic 1998; Cerami 2006).

With the introduction of the central planned economy, the benefit structure was equalized. Flat-rate rather than contributory benefits became the new characteristics of the pension system, while universal and standardized treatments were the norm in public, state-run hospitals. Unfortunately, the egalitarian aspirations of the communist nomenclature did not coincide with a positive performance of welfare institutions. A poor working life was usually followed by a poor retirement (Connor

1997), while health care services were highly inefficient and characterized by high morbidity rates (Deacon 2000).

The extremely differentiated schemes established during the Bismarckian period in Eastern Europe were put under the control of central authorities, with social insurance revenues and expenditures becoming an integral part of the central planned economy. Social insurance contributions, which persisted in these countries even during the 1970s, were transferred to the state budget (or in funds within the state budget) and, subsequently, redistributed to the entire population. The management of the social protection system was highly hierarchical and based on a top-down approach. The Ministry of Social Affairs (or Health) planned the relative policies. These were then implemented by local authorities on the basis of the decisions and the national priorities taken at the central level, often with little or no knowledge of real local needs. Trade unions were also in charge of social insurance administration, but since only the official communist trade union was allowed, the independence from state authority was extremely limited. The access to welfare benefits, by contrast, followed a bottom-up direction and was characterized by a high degree of discretion of those officials who were responsible to grant the benefits.

Although state participation in the financing of the communist welfare system was greatly enlarged, social insurance contributions did not completely disappear from the scene. While in Czechoslovakia, social insurance premiums were automatically included in the state budget[3], in Hungary and Poland they were still considered to be a separate part of social security receipts. As Table 9.1 shows, during the period from the 1960s to the end of the 1980s, the receipts from employers' contributions in Hungary were equal or higher than state participation receipts, while the contributions paid by the insured corresponded to approximately one-fifth (slightly below 20 percent) of total social security revenues. In Poland, the largest part of total social security receipts was paid through employers' contributions, which remained constantly higher than the receipt coming from state participation, and that covered the low revenues of insured premiums.

As Manow (this volume) has demonstrated, the ways in which a welfare system expands may depend on the existing financing structure of welfare institutions (tax vs. social insurance contributions), but also on the degree of freedom of the institutions responsible for monetary policies. In economies based on central planning, the main characteristic was an ambiguous, contributions-oriented system that equally redistributed the resources collected, while the institutions responsible for monetary poli-

Table 9.1   Social security receipts: Percentage of contributions paid by insured person, employers and state intervention

CZECHOSLOVAKIA			
Year	Insured	Employers	State intervention
1963	2	33	65
1966	0	35	65
1971	0	3	97
1974	0	3	97
1977	0	3	97
1980	0	4	96
1983	0	4	96
1986	0	4	96
1990	0	4	96

HUNGARY			
Year	Insured	Employers	State Intervention
1963	12	47	42
1966	14	40	46
1971	17	52	31
1974	17	43	40
1977	16	46	38
1980	14	40	46
1983	15	47	38
1986	21	79	0
1991	25*	75	0

POLAND			
Year	Insured	Employers	State intervention
1963	0	63	37
1966	1	61	38
1971	10	54	36
1974	4	59	37
1977	1	57	42*
1980	2	52	46
1986	3	61	36*
1989	2	70	28*
1990	3	68	29*

*Estimated

Source: ILO/MZES 2001. Author's calculations.

cies were fully subjected to state authority. It comes then as no surprise that rising contributions also coincided with an increase in an external debt as it happened in countries with a low degree of central bank independence and Bismarckian welfare systems such as Belgium, France, Italy, Portugal and Spain. The increase in external debt could, however, not last forever, and ultimately it undermined the stability of the same system it was maintaining (see below).

Expansion for Legitimization

During the period of the communist social policy reorganization, governments increased benefits in order to buy social peace and avoid political contestation. This *divide and pacify strategy* so brilliantly identified by Pieter Vanhuysse (2006) for the first years of post-communist transformation took place, in reality, before the fall of communism. A *politics of expansion for legitimization* took place in the early 1960s accentuating, in the late 1970s and 1980s, the pressures on the communist economic system, ultimately unmasking the persistent economic and social crisis. The process of modernization in Central and Eastern Europe, started, in fact, with the development of heavy industry in the second half of the 1950s, which resulted in an extraordinary increase in living standards. These, however, were maintained artificially high, for political and propaganda purposes, beyond the real possibilities of the central planned economy. The artificial rise in living conditions through various state subsidies, coupled with a constant increase in military expenses, put the productive and distributive capacities of the central planned economy under great financial pressure. Constructing an always larger number of nuclear missiles, submarines, or engaging in the 'space race' with the United States were extremely expensive political exercises that, in some way, had to be financed. Funds could only be raised at this point either from a reduction in expenditures for those policies indirectly aimed at subsidizing the economy and, hence, at raising living standards (such as price subsidies or subvention to modernize the firms) or, as last resort, from an increase in external debt. The latter option was the one preferred by almost all countries. By 1989, for example, the gross convertible external debt reached 7.9 thousand million US dollars in Czechoslovakia, 19.2 thousand million US dollars in Hungary and 40.8 thousand million US dollars in Poland (E. Szalai 2005: 32).

During the 1970s and 1980s, social expenditures thus continuously expanded[4], financed through external debt, in order to ensure the social stability, especially after the attempts of revolt in Budapest in 1956, after the

Prague Spring in 1968 and in Poland in the early 1980s. In front of mass demonstrations, political leaders tried to consolidate their power through an expansion in welfare provisions (E. Szalai 2005). The establishment of an extensive welfare system was, thus, the compensation that Eastern European citizens received in exchange for their liberty. However, despite numerous attempts to increase the distributive possibilities of the central planned economy, by the end of the 1980s the welfare system had grown to its limits with external funding, and the dissatisfaction among citizens, already high, grew, leading to the collapse of the system on 9 November 1989, the day of the fall of the Berlin Wall.

9.4 The Period from 1989 onwards

Welfare Reform Trajectories after Communism

At the beginning of the 1990s, structural reforms were implemented that remained under the dominant Bismarckian logic, that had been introduced in the pre-soviet period and continued even during communism. Welfare benefits granted on the basis of professional activity and according to the work record of individuals continued to be financed through the payment of social insurance contributions, which this time, however, were redistributed to a lesser extent among the population in the absence of a centrally planned economic mechanism. Professional diversity, differentiation of provisions and privatization of schemes soon became the keywords of the new post-communist consensus. In short, three sequences of reforms can be identified since the collapse of communism: 1) compensation for the transition, 2) retrenchment through privatization; and 3) rebalancing. These phases corresponded to a peculiar politics of social security reforms. *Politics of expansion for compensation* for the first phase, *politics of retrenchment through privatization* for the second phase and *politics of recalibration* for the third one.

Table 9.2   Parliamentary elections 1989-2007

Czech Republic	Hungary
1990: center-Right coalition (Czechoslovakia)	1990: center-Right coalition
1992: center-Right coalition (Czechoslovakia)	1994: center-Left coalition (ex-communists)
1996: center-Right coalition	1998: center-Right coalition
1998: center-Left coalition	2002: center-Left coalition
2002: center-Left coalition	2006: center-Left coalition
2006: center-Right coalition	

Table 9.2   Parliamentary elections 1989-2007

Poland	Slovak Republic
1991: center-Right coalition	1990: center-Right coalition (Czechoslovakia)
1993: center-Left coalition	1992: center-Right coalition (Czechoslovakia)
1997: center-Right coalition	1994: center-Left coalition
2001: center-Right coalition	1998: center-Left coalition
2005: center-Right coalition	2002: center-Right coalition
2007: center-Right coalition	2006: center-Right coalition

Source: Cerami 2006, pp. 17-29; Parties and elections in Europe 2008

Compensating for the Transition

The first sequence coincided with the temporary growth of welfare provisions called to aid the democratic transition of Eastern Europe. The new problem of mass unemployment resulting from the dismissal of workers of state-owned enterprises was first tackled by the introduction of extensive early retirement policies, followed by the establishment of relatively far-reaching unemployment and social assistance programs, which should have had the important function of social pacification (Standing 1996; Milanovic 1998; Vanhuysse 2006). Vanhuysse (2006) has defined this as a *divide and pacify* strategy aimed at reducing workers' mobilization capacity through access to relatively generous welfare benefits (generous if compared to the real possibilities of these transition economies). This phase is parallel to the 'labor shedding' strategy (Esping-Andersen 1996b) implemented earlier in Western Bismarckian welfare systems.

During this phase of *compensation for the transition*, not only temporary emergency policies were implemented (see Inglot 2008), but also the first steps for future, long-lasting reforms were taken (a *politics of expansion for compensation*). In pension, the governments of the Czech Republic, Hungary, Poland and Slovakia started the first attempts to move away from the old pay-as-go-system, by creating the basis for the future adoption of the three-pillar schemes (or private funds in the case of the Czech Republic). This also included the reinforcement of principles based on pension insurance, as well as a slow raise in retirement and contribution rates, which remained set at an extremely low level during the entire communist period. In the health care sector, the main characteristics of reforms were the reintroduction of health insurance, a clearer separation in the management and financing the system (from taxation to contributions and from the state budget to separate funds), as well as the establishment of private practice. With unemployment and social assistance, this involved the introduction of unemployment insurance, as well as the establishment of a basic social safety net. Finally, concerning family benefits, the temporary maintenance of extensive family policies had the aim of cushioning some of the costs of transition, since policy-makers in the region saw family protection as the most effective way to target poor people.

Retrenchment through Privatization

Of course, the early generosity soon became unsustainable, especially due to the escalating number of unemployed. In the second sequence of reforms, *retrenchment through privatization*, new policies were introduced in order to reduce the expansion of the welfare system. The measures, used to prevent such uncontrollable extension of rights and claims, involved the privatization of provisions, as sponsored by the most influential international financial institutions, and also, perhaps more importantly, the reinforcement of principles based on professional diversity. A process of *monetization[5] and individualization of risks and responsibilities* was then enclosed in a Bismarckian welfare logic, resulting in the (re-)establishment of insurance-related pension, health care and unemployment schemes. This *politics of retrenchment through privatization* seemed the best way to cut expenditures, while, at the same time, ensuring professional diversity and market orientation. In Hungary, attempts at retrenchments were carried out by finance minister Lajos Bokros in 1995, who unsuccessfully tried to introduce a set of austerity measures (the so-called *Bokros package*) with the aim of making family allowance no longer universal and automatic, of conducting a shift from flat-rate to means-tested benefits, of reducing childcare assistance and of introducing the tuition fees for universities. In the Czech Republic, the Klaus governments pushed for a drastic reduction in protection against unemployment policies, especially during the second half of the 1990s. Fascinatingly, the policy discourse during these years reached a peak in neoliberal orientations with some Czech officials affirming that unemployment was something natural and beneficial for the country. If no unemployment had existed, then something would have been wrong with the country (Consensus II 1999: Czech Republic, Part IV, p. 150). In the mid-1990s, a report called *Security through Diversity* also opened a tempestuous debate in Poland between the Ministry of Finance and the Ministry of Social Affairs on the incontrovertible necessity of drastic social security reforms. Similarly in Slovakia, violent discussions on the necessity of privatizing health and pensions also took place at about the same time. Most pension and health care reforms (notably the full introduction of the three-pillar scheme in Hungary and Poland, and the reinforcement of health insurance principles in Czech and Slovak Republic) took place towards the end of the 1990s. These were, undoubtedly, the years where endogenous and exogenous economic vulnerabilities became stronger and actions were addressed as urgent by the national, as well as by the international, community.

Interestingly, the Left/Right divide was not a determinant factor for party preferences towards neoliberal or Social Democratic reforms. Not only center-Right parties, like the ODS of Vaclav Klaus in Czech Republic, but also left-wing governments, like the MSZP of Gyula Horn in Hungary, or the catholic *Solidarity* coalitions in Poland, opted for welfare cuts. One plausible explanation for the rather unusual behavior of left-wing parties is provided by Müller (2004), who sees such reform attempts as being driven by the necessity of Left governments, on the one hand, to increase their international legitimacy after 40 years of communism, while, on the other, to let the population digest more easily the absolutely necessary reforms. Right-wing parties would not have had the same moral authority. The *Nixon goes to China Syndrome* (Müller 2004) seems, as a consequence, to have characterized the politics of social security reforms of the left-wing parties in these years of transition, even though this does not seem to be the case anymore.

Rebalancing: The Return to Bismarck?

Owing to problems connected with the growing number of unprotected citizens attempting to claim from the already indebted social insurance funds, the excessively optimistic expectations for *market-driven change* did not survive its arrival. The third sequence of reforms characterized by a *politics of recalibration*, and by policy learning dynamics (see Pierson 2001b; Hemerijck 2008), was that of *rebalancing* the neoliberal approach introduced by most Central and Eastern European governments. In the Czech Republic, numerous private health insurance funds deemed unable to provide minimum standards for their clients have been abolished, while in Hungary the compulsory affiliation with the second private pillar of pension, once mandatory for younger generations, has been eliminated. In Poland, unemployment benefits still financed by employers' contributions are granted on a flat-rate rather than on an occupational basis so as to reduce the financial pressure caused by raising unemployment, whereas in Slovakia the full implementation of a strong market-oriented health insurance is facing increasing policy resistance because of the universal requirements expressed by the Slovak Constitution.

How can such a change in orientation be explained? Undoubtedly, *blame avoidance* (Weaver 1986; Pierson 2001b) and *credit claiming* (Mayhew 1974) strategies in these countries play a greater role now than in the past. Politicians are increasingly searching for ambiguous political and policy agreements in order to see their economic and social policy goals implemented, while, at the same time, trying to ensure the continuation of their own political career.[6] Political leaders who stay in the government are also more often claiming responsibility for the 'missed disaster', which would have followed the non-implementation of reforms. Also parties in opposition affirm with more determination responsibility for having avoided an even more painful economic transformation through their blockades in the Parliament.

Despite the importance of these actor-centered explanations, the political behavior of citizens and politicians is still not sufficient to fully understand the path of social security reforms in the Visegrad countries. The role played by already existing institutions must also be seriously taken into account. As the next paragraph will summarize, reforms in the mode of access, benefit structure, management and financing of the new welfare system were carried out according to two main principles, which were deeply rooted in the communist and pre-communist past. The first principle was driven by the experience of the excessive standardization of economic and social life caused by the regulatory mechanisms of the central planned economy, which produced the undesired effects of limiting work performance in the absence of incentives, stagnation, and even regression of modernization. As a result, the aim of politicians and policy-makers was to provide a differentiated socio-economic system in which the personal aspirations of citizens could be better realized. In the areas of social policy, this coincided with the reintroduction of provisions based on occupational diversity, which also had a long tradition in these countries. At the same time, 40 years of communism had produced a system of formal and informal norms that made an extremely reduced and difficult access to welfare provisions not a viable political decision. The paternalist welfare system established during communism could not simply be dismantled overnight, especially in times where the costs of the economic transition would primarily lay with the poorer social classes. The reinforcement of Bismarckian institutions, never completely dismantled during communism, was then the most obvious option.

The Current State of Welfare Systems in Visegrad Countries

In 2008, the mode of access to benefits in the four Visegrad countries is based on the Bismarckian model, but significant universal aspirations still exist (Cerami 2006; Bakken 2008; Sirovátka and Saxonberg 2008). In the Czech Republic, Hungary, Poland and Slovakia, the access to pensions is regulated by the payment of social insurance contributions, but a strong link to social assistance provisions (the so-called fourth pillar) ensures coverage for those people who, otherwise, would remain uninsured (Wagener 2002; Tomka 2004a; MISSOC 2008). The same applies with regards to health care protection. All these countries grant health services upon the payment of health insurance premiums, but the state is often called to cover the deficit of the newly established health funds and to ensure that numerous unprotected citizens, such as the unemployed, students, children, pensioners, and persons in need are covered.

Though primarily Bismarckian in its character (in the four Visegrad countries, welfare benefits are: a) primarily financed by social insurance contributions; b) earnings-related; and c) granted on the basis of the professional record), the benefit structure of current Central and Eastern European welfare institutions can be described as an ambiguous mix of differentiation and equalization of provisions. Just to quote a few examples, in the Czech Republic, pensions are financed by social insurance contributions and are calculated on the basis of two amounts: 1) a basic flat-rate based on citizenship and 2) an additional earnings-related component based on professional status. The flat-rate component of pensions plays the role of equalization at the expense of the middle and upper classes (Consensus Program II 1999; Tomeš 2003; MISSOC 2008). In Hungary, most health services are included in the mandatory health package, which is covered by the compulsory insurance scheme. As a consequence, there is little space for additional private health care services and because of this the majority of citizens have access to the same provisions (Gál et al. 2003: 78; MISSOC 2008). For Kornai (2001) the current Hungarian health care system still displays some characteristics of 'market socialism'. In Poland, unemployment benefits are financed by social insurance contributions, but their amount is granted on a flat-rate basis. A differentiated welfare system also exists for farmers, who are insured by KRUS (Social Insurance Fund for Farmers) in contrast to ZUS (Social Insurance Institution), which is responsible for employees. Differently from ZUS, in KRUS, pensions are still based on a first pay-as-you-go component (1st pillar), while health insurance has higher universal aspirations. In Slovakia the aim of the new pension formula is clearly that of encouraging professional diversity, but the system, work-related in scope, still has universal aspirations. Article 39 of the Slovak Constitution affirms the right to adequate material provisions for pensioners establishing a strong linkage with the minimum guaranteed income (MISSOC 2008).

In Central and Eastern Europe, decentralization and devolution of responsibilities to regional and local authorities and to funds has been the main characteristic of reforms, although some form of re-centralization is observable. Devolution can be explained as a reaction to the communist over-centralization, which had neglected local requests in order to meet national priorities. As can be seen by the administrative organization, the system is far more differentiated. In the Czech Republic, Hungary, Poland and Slovakia, the Ministries of Labor and Social Affairs are responsible for planning policies and drawing up legislation for the overall social security system, with the exception of health care, which is, usually, under the control of the Ministry of Health. Distinct and autonomous bodies (such as the Czech Administration of Social Security, the Hungarian Central Administration of National Pension Insurance, KRUS and ZUS in Poland, or the Slovak Social Insurance Agency) administer the new social insurance system and pay the benefits through their district and local offices.

Also the role of trade unions, usually addressed as the *weakest link* in the reforms process, has drastically increased. Despite common assumptions, tripartite consultations have played a crucial role in the first stage of reforms by helping the introduction of a new welfare system, in the second stage by facilitating the continuation of reforms mediating different interests and needs, and in the third stage of reforms, by calling attention to the necessity to include a social dimension of transformation (Ladó 2003: 258). In this context, it can be affirmed that not the absence of corporatism, but rather a form of *state-led corporatism*, to use Schmidt's description (Schmidt 2006), is the main characteristic of the transition towards a market economy. If Ebbinghaus' classification is applied (Ebbinghaus, this volume), then *state-led corporatism* would come very close to the *consultation* type as the state may consult the social partners but not seriously negotiate with them (in this case it would be *concertation*). Moreover, actors in the four Visegrad countries seem to lack the capacity of being true corporatist actors in both policy formation and implementation, since priority was very often given to macroeconomic stabilization measures.

Finally, as far as the financing mechanism is concerned, the general trend occurring in the four Visegrad countries seems to be a rapid devolution of state responsibility in financing the system of social protection through an increase in social insurance contributions and a gradual equalization of employers' and employees' participation rates. With respect to the important issue of how, and how much, taxes are levied on citizens, while during communism the system was distributive in scope, since 1989 taxation tends to produce a diversified impact on individuals. In Slovakia the revenues from all taxes, as percentage of GDP, are the lowest (30.6 percent), followed by Poland (35.8 percent), the Czech Republic (36.2 percent) and Hungary (39.1 percent, which is the only country close to the EU15 average of 40.6 percent). Looking at the structure of taxation it is clear that social insurance contributions, as a percentage of total taxation, in Hungary are equal to the contribution rates in the EU 15, but substantially higher in the Czech Republic, Poland and Slovakia. The structure of taxation in the four Visegrad countries is, for the most part, based on social insurance contributions and indirect taxes, while direct taxes remain significantly below the EU15 average, both as a percentage of total taxation and as a percentage of GDP (see Table 9.3). This implies that taxation continues to have a dual orientation: an employment-related character due to the payment of social insurance contributions, and a collective character due to the revenues raised by indirect taxes, such as VAT and taxes on products, which tend to be accumulated more independently of individual's own income.

Table 9.3   The structure of taxation (2003)

	Total taxes % of GDP	Indirect taxes % of total taxation	Direct taxes % of total taxation	Social security contributions % of total taxations	Indirect taxes % of GDP	Direct taxes % of GDP	Social security contributions % of GDP
Czech Republic	36.2	31.4	27.1	41.5	11.4	9.8	15.0
Hungary	39.1	42.4	25.0	32.5	16.6	9.8	12.7
Poland	35.8	42.8	20.1	39.4	15.3	7.2	14.1
Slovakia	30.6	37.6	23.6	40.2	11.5	7.2	12.3
EU15	40.6	34.6	33.1	32.5	13.6	13.7	13.2

Source: Eurostat 2005

9.5   Policy Discourses and International Organizations

Numerous studies have often emphasized the crucial role played by international organizations in influencing the post-communist social policy reform process (Deacon et al. 1997; Cerami 2006; Deacon 2007; Orenstein 2008; Orenstein et al. 2008). The most common approach to welfare state transformation in the region sees international organizations as being extremely successful in influencing the policy direction through *binding directives* or through forms of *moral suasion* (see McBride and Williams 2001). Examples of binding directives can be found in the World Bank and the IMF's conditionality strategy for granting access to loans (or in the case of the *Accession Agreements* during the EU Enlargement process), while an example of *moral suasion* can be found in the OECD's *Economic Surveys* (McBride and Williams 2001) or in the EU policy evaluation reviews with their attempt to show governments what good policy-making should look like.

Policy discourses (see Schmidt 2002, 2008), promoted by international organizations have, undoubtedly, influenced national policy-making by increasing transnational communication and thus convergence to already identified policy priorities. In the case of the World Bank and the IMF, the policy discourse has primarily focused on the need for a market-oriented, financially stable and residual welfare state. The EU, on the other hand, has been influential not only in cognitive terms (Guillén and Palier 2004; Lendvai 2004), increasing, for example, transnational solidarity and mutual learning, but it has also been a vital actor in facilitating the introduction of new social policy ideas, interests and institutions (Cerami 2008).

Here, it should be remembered, however, that even the most convincing discourses tend to be mediated in their acceptance by the individual's own preferences. Transformation in Central and Eastern Europe has not been simply the result of a silent, or semi-silent, acceptance of prescriptions, through *policy transfer* or *policy diffusion* respectively, but rather as a result of a *recombinant policy implementation*, in which existing institutional structures have constrained and/or fostered the full completion of reforms.

The introduction of a welfare system based on professional diversity and private arrangements was not only the most suitable scheme, if the historical background of these countries is taken into account, but it also corresponded to the functional necessity of occupational and market diversification, which stemmed from the excessive centralized and homogenized economic system in force during communism. In this context, it is not surprising that more than 10 years after the first attempts of the World Bank to see its policy prescriptions fully and successfully implemented, its Operations Evaluation Department (OED) desolately concluded that more attention to the existing institutional and administrative capabilities of the countries should have been given in order to ensure a more consistent policy execution (World Bank OED 2004).

In attempting to assess their real impact on national policy-making, it must certainly be remembered that international organizations have been important *facilitators* (Inglot 2003: 242) in the social policy reform process, but this is still not sufficient to address them as the only causes responsible for specific outcomes. The presence of social insurance institutions still based on professional activity, even though encapsulated in the central planned economy, inevitably influenced the reform options of the Visegrad countries. As will be shown in the following sections, the reinforcement of such schemes, based on the payment of contributions and on the professional record of workers, was the option of a system which previously worked on full-employment, as well as the establishment of social insurance funds being the natural option on the side of the management and financing mechanism, which, in reality, never disappeared from the scene but continued within the state budget. Once the communist state collapsed and with it, numerous enterprises, the organs responsible for managing the benefits had to be replaced in order to ensure the survival of welfare institutions. The market was the only available option and with that the strengthening of independent social insurance funds became unavoidable.

In addition, despite strong pressures from international financial institutions, policy recommendations have tended to be mediated and negotiated in the political arena, according to clear institutional rules, instead of having been implemented by design. Just to quote a few notable examples: the introduction of the three-pillar scheme in Poland, proposed by the minister of Finance Grzegorz Kołodko, was blocked for two years by the opposition from the minister of Labor and Social Policy Leszek Miller. The decision of Miller was reinforced by his commitment to the PAYG principle and by his personal rivalry with Kołodko (quoted in Nelson 2001: 244). In Hungary and Slovakia, the introduction of the three-pillar scheme was also subjected to several discussions among politicians and social policy experts and only at the end of a difficult process of political bargaining was finally introduced. In the Czech Republic, by contrast, no agreement on the three-pillar scheme could be found, primarily as a result of the strong opposition by the trade unions (Fultz 2002).

9.6   Conclusion

If one looks at the reform trajectories prior to the fall of the Berlin Wall, similarities with the reform trajectories in other Bismarckian countries (such as France) can be found. These similarities can partly be explained by similar external economic shocks that the countries of Central and Eastern Europe were facing (such as the oil crisis of the 1970s), but also by the existence of similar Bismarck-oriented welfare institutions. A *politics of expansion for legitimization* characterized the 1960s, 1970s and early 1980s and was largely associated with an increase in external debt and in social insurance contributions. Modifications in social policy remained under the dominant communist logic, but Bismarckian features, already present, became more preponderant. After a brief period, where a *poli-*

tics of expansion for compensation resulted in an abnormal increase in welfare efforts called to amortize the costs of economic transition, attempts towards welfare retrenchment characterized the policy trends in these countries in the 1990s. In comparison to other Western democracies, the political discourse in these years focused on the necessity to ensure system and financial stability. In the Central and Eastern European case, a *politics of retrenchment through privatization* was also linked to the future consolidation of democratic institutions. More recently, alteration and amendments in the national legislation are taking place in almost all welfare system sectors, involving the reduction, but also, in some cases, the expansion of the level of benefits, as well as the introduction of new calculation rules and new kinds of entitlements and benefits. These changes tended to go beyond simple 'retrenchment' policies, since they aimed to recalibrate the system to the new emerging social problems, which differed from the early days of post-communist transition. This last trend can be defined in terms of a *politics of recalibration*.

The role that the preparation for EU membership played in this process of welfare state restructuring has been far from limited, as common wisdom would suggest. As highlighted in the previous sections, the EU not only drew the attention of the candidate countries to the social dimension of reform (though rarely in an unambiguous manner), but it has also promoted through cognitive processes (see Guillén and Palier 2004) the introduction of new social policy ideas, interests and institutions (Cerami 2008) fairly distant from the classical neoliberal values of the Washington Consensus promoted by the World Bank, IMF and OECD.

Central and Eastern European countries have, thus, developed a new welfare logic, which has both path-dependent and innovative components. These have been identified in: a) the re-enforcement of Bismarckian-oriented policies as a heritage of the Austro-Hungarian Empire (path-dependent); b) the maintenance of egalitarian and universal aspirations as fostered during the communist period (path-dependent); and c) the introduction of market-friendly welfare provisions (innovative). If analyzed in their global context, the abovementioned characteristics are evidence for a significant degree of cohesion among these welfare systems in transition and may allow for the emergence of a new and unique welfare regime (Cerami 2006), in which different *worlds of welfare* coexist and are recombined together. To use a definition recently provided by Lamping and Rüb (2004) for Germany, the welfare regime in Central and Eastern Europe can, therefore, be described in terms of a 'recombinant welfare system'[7], where Bismarckian features remain preponderant.

Table 9.4   Summary of reform trajectories: Czech Republic, Hungary, Poland and Slovakia

Types of change	Context	Diagnosis
Expansion for legitimization	– Economic downturn (1960s, 1970s and early 1980s); – Social budget deficits	– Social benefits can help the system and (un)democratic stability
Compensating for the Transition NOTE: Temporary and due to exceptional circumstances	– Economic collapse following the dissolution of communism; – Introduction of market economy; – Preparation to a new economic mechanism; – Massive socio, political, economic and demographic changes	-The democratic transition has to be rescued, maintained and consolidated
Retrenchment through privatization	– Severe economic deterioration; – End of what remained of Keynesianism; -Neoliberal policy ideas and discourses promoted by international organizations	– Welfare systems are seen as partly the cause of the crisis: excessive state involvement reinforce social exclusion; – Income maintenance is disincentive to work; – State involvement damages competitivity and creates unemployment; – State management rules hinder reform capacities
Re-balancing: The return to Bismarck?	– Global and European orientation/ coordination of economic and social policies; – EU pre-accession and enlargement	– Welfare systems need a profound adaptation to the new EU based socio-economic context; – Recombinant implementation of EU, OECD, World Bank and IMF ideas in the light of the EU enlargement

Content of the policy	Politics of the reforms	Consequences
– Preservation of full employment; – Raise in social contribution; – Change in the generosity of the benefits (upwards); – Additional financing necessary raised through external debt	Politics of expansion for legitimization	– Continuous welfare expansion beyond the possibility of the central planned economy; – Increasing inefficiencies of such policies (impossibility to cope with Western achievements in living standards); – Re-enforcement of Bismarck features as existing before communism – Increase in external debt
– Increase in the contributions to social insurance benefits; – Introduction of generous early retirement, protection against unemployment and establishment of basic safety net	Politics of expansion for compensation	– From social to more individual insurance; – Anomalies of the new system covered under state responsibility; – Reinforcement of Bismarckian features; – Negotiated, but based on TINA (There Is No Alternative)
– Increasing importance of targeted and market-based benefits; – Expansion of private provisions; – New mode of management (private); – Reinforcement of main international organizations' policy ideas and discourses	Politics of retrenchment through privatization	– Weakening of state responsibility, while increasing social insurances mechanisms and actors; – Negotiated, but STRONGLY based on TINA (There Is No Alternative)
-Reconsideration of neoliberal approach (private pillars in pension, and health insurance are recalibrated); – Activation of unemployed; – Competition in health; – Emphasis on social inclusion due to Lisbon European Council	Politics of recalibration	– Recalibration of previous reforms; – Hybridization of the system; – Negotiated, but based on a new, more socially-aware approach

10   Reforming Bismarckian Corporatism: The Changing Role of Social Partnership in Continental Europe

Bernhard Ebbinghaus

10.1   Introduction

In most Continental European welfare systems the state 'shares public space' (Crouch 1986) with the social partners, employers and trade unions, over such public policy areas as employment regulation and social protection. Corporatist participation of social interest groups in public policy-making has a long tradition in Continental Europe. Since the first Bismarckian reforms in response to the 'workers question' by mandating social insurance in the late 19th century, employers and workers received representation in the self-administration in return for their contributions to these parafiscal funds. The Bismarckian social insurance principle with strong reliance on co-financing through social contribution and bipartite self-administrative governance became also the dominant model for and distinct feature of Continental welfare systems. Esping-Andersen's typology (1990) acknowledges this 'corporatist' legacy of Conservative welfare (state) regimes.

Given participation in Bismarckian self-administration, the social partners can play an important role in coordinating policy initiatives and implementing welfare reforms. However, these organized interests can also provide obstacles to reform as they defend vested interests and block changes in the status quo (Ebbinghaus and Hassel 2000). Even when co-operating and negotiating reforms, the social partners can still pursue rather narrow self-interests, externalizing the costs of their actions onto non-participating third parties or the public at large. However, unilateral action by the state without the social partners' consent often meets their resistance, which can lead to large-scale mobilization against government reforms. Despite long-term losses in union membership and estrangement between unions and allied political parties (Ebbinghaus and Visser

2000), trade unions remain important political and social actors in most Continental European countries (Scarbrough 2000). In fact, public status through *erga omnes* extension of collective bargaining and self-administration of social insurance give an institutionalized role to the social partners.

When the state shares public space, it usually lacks the legitimacy, competencies, and implementation capacity to single-handedly carry out desired reforms of social and employment policy. Therefore, formal or informal forums for tripartite social dialogue between the government and the social partners facilitate the development of a shared understanding of problems, the discussion of policy alternatives and their implications, and the negotiations of a consensual response (Ebbinghaus 2001). Consensual reforms not only have the advantage of common political support and legitimacy, but also societal coordination may facilitate policy implementation. Involving the social partners in the day-to-day administration of social protection and employment services enhances not only the legitimation but also the in-depth knowledge of actors. However, much depends on how inclusive social partnerships are; that is, whether they include only the interests of the 'insiders' or not. Continental European trade union movements tend to represent more the old than the new social risk groups, such as women, young jobseekers and the lower educated (Ebbinghaus 2006b). Increasingly, it is of relevance whether the social partners engage in social responsibility, i.e. whether they pursue public-regarding and long-term perspectives instead of defending the status quo (Brugiavini et al. 2001).

To fully understand the roles of social partners in current reform processes in Continental European welfare systems, we thus need to examine the historical modes of social governance and its evolution (Berger and Compston 2002). The industrial relations literature has tended to ignore the role social partners play in the social policy area, leaving the matter to their colleagues in comparative welfare analysis (Crouch 2001). The 'new politics' thesis has often either belittled the role of social partners (Pierson 1996) or assumed institutional veto points for the social partners (Pierson 2001b) without analyzing its real veto power. As shown in this chapter, we need to look at social governance more closely to ascertain such claims' validity and reliability for Bismarckian welfare systems. Far from confirming path-dependent inertia, the recent developments show considerable changes despite potential veto power of social partners. These developments call into question the assumption of path dependence common to much of the new politics thesis.

My comparative analysis will focus on the post-war development of social governance in four Continental European countries: Germany, the Netherlands, France and Italy. Not only the overall role of social partners in corporatist institutions will be reviewed, but also two specific policy fields, in particular old-age (and disability) pensions and labor market policies (unemployment insurance and employment services). Both policy areas touch on fundamental interests of the social partners. Other policy areas, such as health care, long-term care and family also represent interesting cases to study the influence and impact of social partners on Bismarckian welfare systems, though such analysis is beyond the scope of this chapter (see Palier and Martin 2007b).

In this chapter, I first discuss the different approaches to studying the role of social partners from power resource theory to the new politics thesis and beyond. Second, I review the different governance modes that involve the social partners and the importance of consultative advisory bodies. Next, I look at the social partners' involvement – either through delegated self-administration or through self-regulation – and the actual impact of social partners, in particular trade unions, in pension policy (see Bonoli and Palier 2007). As the second policy field, the social governance and reform processes will be analyzed for unemployment insurance and public employment agencies (see also Clegg 2007). Finally, the recent changes in social governance and the reform dynamic will be discussed in the light of path dependency and path departure. Increasingly, governments and employers sought to alter long established social governance in order to instill more social responsibility and 'reformability' in social partnerships.

10.2 The Role of Social Partners in Welfare System Theories

Different theoretical approaches were advanced to explain the development of welfare systems, in particular the origins and expansion of social security across Continental Europe. The role of social partners is central to the power resource theory, but in the case of Continental Europe also authoritarian state traditions and corporatist legacies have to be considered. Yet these past theories of the 'old politics' are seen as inappropriate to explain the new politics of current reform processes in times of permanent austerity and weakened labor movements. The new politics thesis stresses the path dependency of welfare state development, given the popularity of welfare states and the blame avoidance of politicians. But social partners (and their political allies) still play a role in more recent reforms efforts, either by blocking or facilitating change. Some observers point to the veto power of social partners given their institutional involvement, but this requires more in-depth empirical analysis.

The 'Old' Politics Thesis and the Corporatist Legacy

Comparative studies of welfare state development emphasize the importance of the power of organized labor, the state traditions and political economy factors. The power resource thesis postulates the importance of the labor movements' strength, often measured by union membership and centralization as well as the electoral and governmental success of Left parties, especially those allied with trade unions (Esping-Andersen 1990; Korpi 1983). While this approach can explain the rise of universalist welfare states in Scandinavia with the power of the labor movement, the electoral success of social democracy and the strong allied trade unions, it also claims that in countries with less powerful organized labor more residual welfare states would persist. However, the Continental European countries do not easily fit into such a monocausal view.

Esping-Andersen's threefold regime typology acknowledged that Conservative welfare states were neither residual nor universalist, but welfare regimes of their own type. Societies with social-Christian orientation and *worker wings* of Christian-Democratic parties provided a favorable political context for the expansion of social transfers (van Kersbergen 1995). Esping-Andersen and Korpi argued that the weaker and fragmented labor movements in Continental Europe went together with Conservative occupationalist welfare regimes (Esping-Andersen and Korpi 1984), this legacy derived from a divide and rule strategy of authoritarian states.

State-centered approaches had stressed that the Conservative regimes have their origin in authoritarian state traditions and Conservative elite policies that introduced welfare 'reforms from above' to legitimate the national state (Flora and Alber 1981). Using a carrot-and-stick strategy, Bismarck enacted the first social insurances and the anti-socialist laws in order to integrate the working class into the paternalist nation-state, while unsuccessfully stemming the tide of the labor movement. However, as Bismarckian welfare systems granted workers self-administrative representation rights on social insurance boards, this allowed their organizations to receive indirect institutional and financial support (Manow 1997). These authoritarian corporatist legacies survived the reform of Bismarckian welfare systems in the post-war Liberal democracies of Continental Europe.

Neo-corporatist theory saw the post-war expansion of Continental welfare systems as part of an implicit social pact: social protection was expanded in exchange for the acceptance of the uncertainties of social market economies (Crouch 1993). In export-oriented economies, social protection became an important buffer against the cyclical proclivity of the international market, thereby helping to maintain the social consensus typical in corporatist, small European states such as Austria, the Netherlands and Switzerland (Katzenstein 1985). More recently, the 'varieties of capitalism' approach (Hall and Soskice 2001) linked the development of *coordinated* market economies in Germany and its neighbors to the emergence of social welfare institutions that were beneficial to maintain a skilled labor force (Estevez-Abe et al. 2001). Recent historical research rediscovered the role of employers in providing corporate welfare and suggests that it was not always against the interests of firms to support public social policies (Mares 2003).

The New Politics Thesis and Bismarckian Welfare Systems

Prominently, Paul Pierson (2001b) argued that the 'new politics' of welfare state reform under austerity conditions does not mirror the 'old politics' of welfare state expansion. Despite the weakening of trade unions and political shifts towards the right, Pierson observed that welfare state reforms under Reagan and Thatcher in the 1980s were not able to retrench as much as ideologically claimed (Pierson 1994). But he claims that this surprising inertia was not due to the traditional interest groups (such as the weakened trade unions) but the result of 'path dependency' (or policy feedback). Past welfare policies led to vested interests among those profiting from these programs both the public in general and the welfare clientele in particular. The new politics thesis assumes that it was not organized interest groups but the blame avoidance of politicians who were afraid of electoral backlash that would maintain popular welfare programs. Studies on public attitudes to welfare states show widespread popularity of current welfare systems (Bonoli 2000; Brooks and Manza 2007); indicating limited support for retrenchment and a majority in favor of the status quo.

However, in Bismarckian welfare systems the insured who paid into social insurance and are represented by trade unions in self-administrative bodies tend to defend the contributory earnings-related benefits as 'deferred wages' and earned social rights (Myles 1989), this holds for contributory old-age and disability pensions as well as unemployment insurance benefits. 'Unlike generic schemes for those in "need" or for "citizens", each individual has his or her own contract with the government with specific benefits attached to his or her specific work record, years of contribution, and earnings history' (Myles and Pierson 2001: 321). Particularly in Continental Europe, given the shared public space, trade unions have been active in voicing protest and blocking reform.

The new politics thesis also assumes that politicians are 'vote maximizers', worried about the political costs of welfare retrenchment. Thus they are reluctant to retrench benefits in pay-as-you-go systems: 'The politics of retrenchment is typically treacherous, because it imposes tangible losses on concentrated groups of voters in return for diffuse and uncertain gains' (Pierson 1996: 145). One political strategy has been to exempt current retirees or obfuscate through invisible technical changes (Myles and Pierson 2001). In Bismarckian pension systems, for example, reforms increased retirement age only slowly, if at all, affecting mainly younger cohorts, while current retirees are spared. These concessions are more palatable to trade unions that represent the more senior workers (Ebbinghaus 2006b). Or in the employment policy area the pressure on long-term unemployed is increased in assistance schemes, while contributory unemployment insurance remains untouched. The policy case studies will show how reforms, particularly in France and Italy, have been influenced by trade unions defense of their core constituency.

The Veto Power Thesis Revisited

Bismarckian welfare systems are often seen as 'frozen' not only due to strong public support but also due to institutionalized *veto points* (Immergut 1991) that provide particularistic interests groups, that is *veto players* (Tsebelis 2000) with potential 'veto power'. However, we need to consider more carefully the veto points in the political decision-making process as well as in social policy implementation in Bismarckian welfare systems. Do the social partners, in particular trade unions, have an effective veto power? Continental European political systems provide numerous veto points for interest groups to influence policy-making, if not to block major changes detrimental to their own interests. According to Ellen Immergut and Karen Anderson, a veto can be of significance for two reasons: 'First, it indicates how difficult it is to pass legislation – and hence to introduce policy change. Second, the more difficult it is to change existing policy, the more opportunities there are for interest groups opposed to particular legislation to demand concessions' (2007: 7). Thus veto points provide an opportunity to veto players to block or negotiate changes.

Particular institutional arrangements account for cross-national variations in the political capacity of governments to unilaterally intervene in welfare state arrangements. In Continental Europe, institutional veto points (Bonoli 2001) include the federalist second chambers (Germany, Switzerland), presidential cohabitation (France), coalition governments that rely on small parties opposed to a reform (Continental Europe), popular referenda (Switzerland) and Constitutional Courts (Germany). These political institutions allow interest groups that do not represent the majority (i.e. the median voter) to block reforms that affect their interests, provided that these veto points can be used in social policy-making either indirectly through political parties or directly by mobilizing or advocating for intervention on their behalf. Whether interest groups, here trade unions or employer organizations, actually use institutional veto points to pursue their interests depends on the strategy of these veto players vis-à-vis their contenders but also on the particular opportunity structure in a given policy area.

In the non-political realm, it is more difficult to assess institutionalized veto points. This depends often on more informal channels of influence to political decision-making as well as the more occasional threat or use of protest power (political or economic strikes, mass scale demonstrations). It was less union membership strength than the institutionalized role unions play in corporatist industrial relations and participatory social insurance that led to the expansion of Conservative welfare states in Continental Europe (Brugiavini et al. 2001). Moreover, today trade unions (and to a lesser degree employer associations) have lost membership compared to the period of expansion, yet collective bargaining coverage and institutionalized corporatist participation has been less affected. Since it is often more assumed than shown that the social partners have 'veto power' through their self-administrative role in the governance of welfare systems, the subsequent sections will compare the influence social partners have in two policy fields (pension policy, labor market policy) and four selected countries (France, Germany, Italy and the Netherlands).

10.3 Social Governance in Bismarckian Welfare Systems

Social Governance Forms

In Continental European countries, the social partners' involvement ranges from institutionalized consultation of interest groups by policy-makers to 'concertation' between the government and social partners on economic and social policy goals. We should further distinguish whether the state delegates' self-administrative functions in a semi-public agency to the social groups affected or whether the social partners have assumed self-regulatory functions without state interference. In the case of self-administration, legitimacy derives from delegation of public authority by the state to an agency, whereas in the case of self-regulation, the state abstains from intervening into the self-help of the social actors according to the principle of subsidiarity. One can thus distinguish four social governance modes for sharing responsibilities between the state and social partners: institutionalized *consultation*, voluntary social *concertation*, delegated *self-administration* and autonomous *self-regulation*.

The state's influence varies, often considerably, according to the mode of social governance. Consultation preserves the most authority for the state. The government (or Parliament) may wish to confer with the social partners or it may be legally obligated to consult an institutionalized advisory council, but the policy-makers are free to diverge from the given opinions and recommendations. In contrast, concertation entails an agreement ('social pact') between the government and the social partners, involving some concessions by the government in order to reach a compromise. These social pacts also bind the state to the terms of the agreement unless they are renegotiated. While consultation is legally prescribed or informal but routinely practiced, concertation occurs primarily on an ad hoc basis and depends on the voluntary agreement of all sides.

In the case of self-administration, the 'principal' *delegates* some (though not all) decision-making authority and implementation power to an 'agent' – an independent self-administered agency (Mabbett and Bolderson 1999). Depending on the authority delegated and resources provided, the self-administrated agency may be more or less autonomous of the state. Moreover, the social partners' influence depends on the rules of representation (nominated or elected), the composition (bipartite or tripartite), and the decision-making rules (qualified or simple majority). We would expect their influence to be small when self-administration is decentralized, representatives are elected from open lists, composition is tripartite (with independent experts), and no minority veto exists. In contrast, the social partners' power would be highest when self-administration is centralized, social partners can nominate representatives, composition is bipartite (without state involvement), and each side has a veto right.

In contrast to delegated self-administration, *self-regulation* results from voluntary agreement between the collective bargaining partners without state interference. The state can only indirectly influence the outcome of the 'autonomous' decision of the social partners by refusing *erga omnes* extension of collective agreements, by making state subsidies or tax concessions conditional on particular policies, or by intervening as an exceptional measure (but thereby damaging the principle of subsidiaristic self-regulation). Although free collective bargaining is an example of such self-regulation, the social partners may also negotiate occupational welfare outside the public welfare system.

Bismarckian Corporatism

At the pinnacle of Bismarckian corporatism stand statutory advisory bodies consulted in public policy-making either by legal mandate or informal convention. Dating back to pre-modern *Ständestaat* and feudal guild traditions (Crouch 1993), local chambers of commerce were installed at the end of the 19th century in Continental Europe, some of which assumed self-regulatory functions. Countries like the Netherlands 'embodied complex and contrasting mixes of liberal and old-corporate institutions' (Crouch 1993: 319). Following the discrediting experience of state-authoritarian corporatism during the interwar and German occupation period, post-war consultative institutions were remodeled to bring them in line with Liberal parliamentary democracy.

The Netherlands has two post-war corporatist forums (Cox 1993): the Dutch Social and Economic Council (SER), a tripartite consultation forum on social and economic policies since 1950, and the Foundation of Labor (STAR), formed by social partners in 1945. As SER failed to facilitate reforms and was widely criticized in the 1990s (Visser and Hemerijck 1997), the Left-Liberal government abolished the obligation to consult SER in 1994. While SER subsequently often became bypassed, STAR became a more important informal forum for social partner consensus-building (Hemerijck et al. 2000).

Despite its corporatist tradition, no general advisory body was established in the post-war Federal Republic of Germany (Berger 2002), while in neighboring Austria a Social and Economic Council was established for policy-making consultation. Instead, 'social partnership' was institutionalized throughout (West-)Germany's 'social market' economy through autonomous collective bargaining, co-determination by works councils and parity representation on supervisory board, consultative ministry councils and social self-administration. Efforts to tripartite concertation were undertaken in the economic crisis of the 1970s, the transition of Eastern Germany after unification in 1990, and in the late 1990s in the Alliance for Jobs, though remained rather limited instances.

The dualism of polarized labor relations and institutionalized tripartite consultation remains a paradox of Latin Europe. The French Economic and Social Council (CES), set up after the war (1946) and reaffirmed with the Fifth Republic, suffers from heterogeneous interests, ranging from the 'most representative' unions and employer associations to farmers and many other social groupings. Similarly, the Italian National and Economic Labor Council (CNEL, 1957) is a statutory advisory body that remained rather unimportant, while direct government negotiations with the social partners have become more important with the rise of social concertation in the 1990s (Haddock 2002).

Statutory consultative councils are not sufficient to provide enough 'veto power' for the social partners because their advisory role remains rather limited and they are often consulted at a late stage in policy-making. The French and Italian advisory councils remain rather symbolic but fragmented institutions, while governments seek either unilateral action or direct negotiations with the social partners. In the Netherlands, government initiative, bipartite consensus building, and ad hoc tripartite concertation increasingly substituted the institutionalized consultation via SER. In Germany, interparty consensus has often played a surrogate role for social consensus in a federalist system with coalition governments, though it often increased reform blockages (Lehmbruch 1999). In general, the traditional statutory advisory forums seem too cumbersome, whereas more informal institutions appear to be more flexible. The most important function of consultation institutions is to develop a shared understanding of policy problems and deliberate on joint solutions with long-term returns for all sides (Streeck 1999; Visser 2001).

10.4 Social Governance in Bismarckian Pension Systems

Self-Administration in Pension Insurance

The social partners may find more opportunities to influence pension policy through their role in the self-administration of social insurance (Reynaud 2000). In contrast to Beveridge-type basic pensions for all citizens (Marshall 1950) in Britain or Scandinavia, which are financed by general (or payroll) taxes and publicly administered, Bismarckian old-age pension insurances are financed and self-administered by both the employer and the insured (Flora and Heidenheimer 1981; Palier and Bonoli 1995). In addition, social partners perform self-regulatory functions in (private) occupational pensions (Rein and Wadensjö 1997), involving not only employers, but also unions through collective bargaining, most notably in France and the Netherlands. Although these main differences in pension systems still hold, there have been some path departures under demographic and financial pressures (Bonoli and Palier 2007; Hinrichs 2000; Korpi 2001; Schludi 2005).

Since Bismarck's pension reform in 1889, German trade union officials and employer representatives were elected into self-administration (Manow 1997), although the social insurance funds were fragmented along occupational lines until 2005. However, union and employer representatives have rather limited influence since the main parameters (contributions, benefits and eligibility rules) are set by legislation. Until recently, additional occupational pensions have played a limited role because they were provided on employer initiative only (except for a collective agreement in the public sector), with little say by unions and limited consultative rights for works councils. Nevertheless, the recent pension reforms of 2001 and 2004 introduced a new precedent of collectively negotiated pensions that provide unions the opportunity to develop a new self-regulatory role at the collective bargaining table (Schludi 2005).

Following the Bismarckian example, Italy introduced with considerable delay pension insurance schemes for blue-collar workers (1919) and white-collar employees (1939), as well as separate schemes for self-employed and public sector employees. The National Institute (INPS) is governed by a bipartite board including unions vis-à-vis employers (and the self-employed) (Klammer 1997). However, the government uses parliamentary acts or administrative decrees to define and change pension policies, often after budget law negotiations with the trade unions. More recently, Italian unions and employers have begun to negotiate collective agreements on occupational pensions, which have first been limited to few sectors but 'took off' since 1998 due to the transfer of end-of-service-pay (*Tfr*, see Jessoula, this volume) at firm level into occupational pensions (Ferrera and Jessoula 2007: 442).

In contrast, the French and Dutch social partners play a more direct role in social insurance – at least in their self-regulatory function outside the basic public schemes. French unions and employer representatives sit on hundreds of social insurance funds at different national, regional and local levels. Under supervision of the social affairs ministry, these self-administered funds include health insurance funds, family allowances funds, disability insurance as well as the first tier public pension. A year after the contentious Juppé plan, a reform of the self-administration of sickness and pension funds occurred in 1996, introducing full parity of social partners and state appointees, additional power to the state-nominated directors, new supervisory councils, and parliamentary approval of the annual budget. In 1999, employers chose to leave these social insurance funds, provoking a consequential debate on the governance of social insurance in France, and making it an object of reforms which lead to the weakening role of social partners in the main sickness and old-age insurance funds (see Palier, chapter 3 in this volume). The French old-age insurance system includes two tiers: contributory public social security, providing basic state benefits (except for public employees), and mandatory complementary regimes run by the social partners (Palier 2005a). State influence is more limited in the second tier supplementary pension funds, set up by collective agreements and made compulsory in 1972, though the employers press for reforms. The introduction of voluntary private funded pensions has been only of minor importance thus far.

In the Netherlands, the post-war pension system is similarly divided into two tiers: tax-financed basic state pension and (quasi-)mandatory occupational pensions negotiated by the collective bargaining partners. Although the social partners are involved in the tripartite administration of the state pension, the second tier (private) occupational pensions are either employer-led or industry-wide funds run by the social partners based on collective agreement that can be extended by the Labor Ministry. Following a public debate on the collusion of the social partners in using disability pensions for labor shedding the bipartite self-administration of sector-wide insurance boards was radically remodeled in 1995/1997 (Visser and Hemerijck 1997: 140-150). An independent public supervisory agency and the new National Institute for Social Insurance (LISV) were introduced to replace all bipartite sectoral funds. However, the occupational pension funds and early retirement schemes (VUT) that were set up by collective agreements are not affected, though there have been calls to reform these to funded defined contribution schemes (Ebbinghaus 2006a). Under pressure from the government to withdraw tax benefits, the social partners agreed on a 'covenant' to reform their occupational pension schemes by controlling costs, increase coverage and mobility, and reduce gender biases. A 2004 reform only changed the oversight body (pension chamber), while 'the social partners have considerable freedom to negotiate the details of their pension arrangements, and they are negotiated as part of collective agreements' (Anderson 2007: 728). Thus the social partners lost influence in public schemes but were able to maintain their self-regulatory leeway in the occupational pension funds.

In Dutch and French pension insurance, the social partners have traditionally had the most say, particularly in the negotiated supplementary funds, while self-administration is more symbolic in Germany and Italy given government responsibility for setting financial and regulatory parameters. Following recent reforms that foster a 'second pillar' of private pensions, German and Italian unions could enhance their bargaining role in negotiating occupational pensions. The state can use regulatory power and 'incentives' through taxation policy to influence private pensions and encroach into social partner self-regulation. Thus, while shared responsibilities in the social policy arena have made reforms more difficult, particularly in implementation, the state still has considerable authority over important parameters with respect to the public pension system, and it can influence occupational pension development by using regulatory frameworks.

The Social Partners' Role in Pension Reforms

In Bismarckian pension systems, the social partners can play an important role in pension reforms because of their role in self-administration of social insurance (in all four countries) and self-regulation in occupational pensions (particularly in France and the Netherlands). The reform pressures are particularly severe in Bismarckian systems with pay-as-you-go financing (Bonoli and Palier 2007): the German and Italian old-age and disability pensions, the French dual tier basic and supplementary pensions, and the Dutch disability pension (not the public basic pension). At the same time, in these countries pension policy is traditionally shared between governments and social partners, therefore the government has very limited capacity to push through unilateral reforms against the opposition of the social partners, in particular trade unions. Governments may therefore seek to engage in concertation with the social partners on pension reform to overcome reform blockage.

Traditionally, pension reform in Germany was consensual between the main political parties and social partners until the 1992 pension reform that phased out early retirement based on unemployment, occupational disability, seniority, and career interruptions for women (Ebbinghaus 2006a). Since unification in 1990, East Germans' pension rights are being paid out of current contributions, putting additional pressure on pension sustainability. Facing increasing social costs and the Maastricht deficit criteria, the Conservative-Liberal government decided to phase in the planned measures more rapidly and introduce a 'demographic factor' that would cut benefits in line with increasing life expectancy. The new reform was opposed by the social democrats, who undid it after winning the 1998 election. But the new Red-Green government soon innovated with the Riester Reform (2001), introducing further cuts in public pensions combined with a new voluntary privately funded pension (with tax incentives for lower income groups) to fill the future gap in old-age income. The unions' influence was rather limited, circumvented by an independent commission and only indirectly through left-wing back benchers in Parliament. Moreover, despite union protests, the incoming grand coalition passed a reform in 2007 to increase retirement age from 65 to 67 between 2012 and 2029. With the exception of the new collective bargaining route for collectively negotiated occupational pensions, German trade unions have lost much of their influence in affecting pension policy-making, increasingly circumvented by governments of all colors.

Despite the 'polder model' of concertation, the Dutch welfare reforms proved very difficult given the social partners' externalization of social costs (Hemerijck and Manow 2001). While tax-financed basic pension remained less contentious, contributory early retirement and disability pension benefits had become major pathways to facilitating the restructuring and reduction of the labor supply since the late 1970s. After some benefit cuts in the 1980s, the government pushed ahead further retrenchment in 1991, despite massive protests by trade unions (and suffering severe electoral losses in 1994) but without a substantial turnaround (Aarts and de Jong 1996). As long as the social partners were in control of the self-administration of social insurance and voluntary schemes, and counteracted the *public-regarding* intention of welfare reform policies by *rent-seeking* externalization strategies, no solution to the crisis could be expected (Visser and Hemerijck 1997). Only after a report on mismanagement by the social partners, the new Left-Liberal government imposed a radical governance reform (1995/1997) in order to enforce public responsibility and faithful implementation. Instead of concertation, the government thus had used the reform of governance to achieve the needed policy reversal.

The most prominent example of social concertation is the Italian pension pact negotiated in 1995 by the center-Left government with the major three union confederations, but without employer participation (Regini and Regalia 1997). The Italian pensions were among the most expensive and generous in Europe, having contributed substantially to Italy's huge public debt (Ferrera and Gualmini 2000). Facing the severe Maastricht criteria, the Italian government attempted to reform pensions in the early 1990s. In 1994, welfare retrenchment plans by the Berlusconi government led to widespread strikes called by the Italian unions (which also had substantial membership among pensioners), ultimately causing the Conservative coalition to break apart. The incoming center-Left government was then willing to negotiate with the unions because it needed both political and social consensus on pension reform in 1995. The negotiated reform was a compromise that brought some limited immediate relief and phased-in long-term cuts and systemic changes. In the 1995 pension reform, the role of trade unions was considerable, while the social partners' influence was also present in the 1997 pension reform. The Prodi government and social partners signed a tripartite agreement on welfare, labor market and pension reforms in 2007, but the subsequent Berlusconi government has been more ambivalent between unilateral action and consulting with the social partners.

Pension reforms in France have been a rather contentious issue, given the unions' stake in social administration and the tradition of political strike mobilization. However, the 1993 Balladur-Veil reform that extended the necessary contribution period for private sector pensions did not cause widespread protest. The Conservative government under Balladur had consulted the social partners informally and included *quid pro quo* concessions to the unions, guaranteeing their role in social administration (Bonoli 1997). In November 1995, when the Conservatives proposed the Juppé plan that applied similar changes in public sector pensions and a governance reform, the unions were largely opposed and led a wave of mass strikes, forcing the government to partially backtrack (Béland 2001; Vail 1999). Moreover, the socialists won the next election and did not attempt a new reform despite recommendations by expert reports (Vail 1999). With the 2003 Raffarin Reform, the Conservatives were able to divide the union protest over pension reform for public employees, as it entered dialogue with two moderate unions (Conceição-Heldt 2007).

Concertation on pension reform in Bismarckian systems does not necessarily follow corporatist traditions. In fact, concertation *and* social conflict have been present since the 1990s. The strikes against the pension reform in Italy 1994 and in France in 1995 indicate that at least in countries with contentious labor relations, unions remain able to muster a political strike. Mass protest depends on the seriousness of welfare retrenchment and the unions' mobilization capacity. In most cases, governments had good reasons to opt for consensual reform. Concerted reforms were undertaken in Italy in 1995 and 1997, an all-party consensus led to the German 1992 reform, and the Balladur government made concessions in 1993 that prevented such mobilization. Bringing the trade unions into reform coalitions entails phased-in reforms and quid pro quo side-payments.

However, if negotiated reforms were not possible due to protracted re-form blockage by interest groups or if such reforms remained too slow and costly, governments decided to reform the conditions for reform, that is, to alter the social governance structure. In addition to cutting benefits and restricting eligibility, governments aimed at changing social governance, through limiting self-administration and by exerting pressure through public financing. The Dutch government shifted from self-administration to reliance on private actors. Similarly, the French government increasingly assumed financial responsibility. The new governance in pension policy often includes not only cutting back benefits but also increased state control over publicly financed (means-tested) benefits. But the trend towards privatization may increase social partners' self-regulation, and indeed in France and the Netherlands, there is a long tradition of negotiated supplementary benefits. Similarly, when private pensions gain in importance, such as in Germany and Italy, the social partners may utilize the opportunity to negotiate private pension improvements in exchange for wage moderation. Hence, there is a double trend in Bismarckian pension systems: governments weaken the role of the social partners in public self-administration, while potentially re-enforcing their role in self-regulation thereby bringing social policy issues into the collective bargaining game.

10.5 Social Governance in Bismarckian Labor Market Policies

Self-Administration in Labor Market Policy

Labor market policies affect the interests of both social partners more directly than in the case of old-age (and disability) pensions. Unemployment benefits set the reservation wage (or 'disincentive to work'), the level at which social benefits are more attractive than earnings from work. Conditions of eligibility and benefit duration also directly alter the willingness of unemployed persons to accept jobs at market wages. Among the Continental European countries, France (1905) and the Netherlands (1916) were early in nationally subsidizing voluntary unemployment insurance like the Belgian Ghent-system. After Britain's pioneering role in introducing a national unemployment insurance (1911), on the Continent, Germany (1927) and the Netherlands (1949) made unemployment insurance mandatory much later, while the French scheme was negotiated by the social partners in 1958 (made compulsory in 1967) and Italy did not even develop a full unemployment insurance.

In addition, employment services were introduced by the state or the social partners, often with different modes of governance. Since they match labor demand and supply, and administer active labor market policies, all three main actors have an interest in administering it. Trade unions sought to control the placement of jobseekers to prevent wage competition, while employers were concerned about collusion by labor. The central state had an interest in controlling active labor market policies, and local governments sought it as relief for communal obligations to provide social assistance. Public employment offices exist in all Continental European countries, but they differ in functional scope – whether they include unemployment insurance or not, offer placement services and training, and whether they involve the social partners more or less directly (Mosley et al. 1998). The role of the social partners in Bismarckian unemployment insurance and employment services has been relatively well institutionalized in tripartite self-administration (or bipartite self-regulation).

German unemployment insurance is integrated with active labor market policies in one tripartite federal employment agency (BA) since 1952. Self-administration remains limited since the government stipulates contributions, sets benefit levels, and approves BA's budget and the state subsidy. Following a reporting scandal, the Hartz Commission recommended in 2002 a new BA governance structure with three directors nominated by the state, employers and unions, while self-administrative bodies have a more remote supervisory position. The Hartz reforms also integrated BA's unemployment assistance and social assistance by the communes in a new means-tested scheme with activation measures (Ebbinghaus and Eichhorst 2007).

In the Netherlands, the central government assumed responsibility for the national employment service (CBA) and unemployment assistance in 1944, while mandatory unemployment insurance (WW) was administered by bipartite sectoral insurance boards until the 1990s. Corporatist councils to coordinate ALMP at national and regional level were introduced in 1969, while the communes in charge of social assistance extended their own ALMP since the mid-1980s, partly circumventing CBA. In 1991, following the recommendation of SER, the government introduced tripartite self-administration and regionalization of public employment services to enhance coordination between social partners and communes (Mosley et al. 1998: 47). Increasingly, the social partners grew critical of the government's interventions, while the unanimity requirement made decision-making inefficient and particularistic. In 1994, the government imposed simple majority voting and appointed tripartite members in the 'public interest', and decentralized and further privatized employment services. Several governance reforms in the mid-1990s ended the bipartite administration of unemployment benefits, the long-term unemployed (and disability benefit claimants) are now administered by new private agencies supervised by a tripartite institution. The Dutch social partners have lost in influence due to government driven governance reform in order to facilitate activation measures (Hemerijck and Manow 2001).

French employment policy is even more fragmented: an unemployment insurance run by the social partners (UNEDIC, 1958), a public employment agency (ANPE, 1967); and national public fund for labor market policy (FNE, 1963). Although the state has limited influence on UNEDIC, the government negotiated its subsidies with the social partners and installed a tripartite supervisory council. ANPE is a public agency under the Labor Ministry governed by tripartite boards at national, regional and local levels, but their decisions require ministerial approval (Mosley et al. 1998: 29-30). Similarly, the government controls ANPE's budget as well as the public FNE fund. Despite the tripartite advisory council of ANPE, 'most measures of active policy are decided by the French state without consultation with the social partners' (Mosley et al. 1998: 12). French employment policy thus oscillates between state imposed solutions and negotiated deals. The employer-initiated 'social refoundation', which led to a bipartite agreement in 2000, did not alter the bipartite self-regulation of UNEDIC although it did introduce further steps towards activation (Palier 2005a: 407). In 2008, the French government imposed the merger of both ANPE and UNEDIC into a single 'pôle emploi', to be implemented in 2010, which will most likely bring a loss of power for the social partners.

Italy's labor market policies are less comprehensive and more fragmented (Gualmini 1998). The bipartite INPS administers the comparatively low unemployment benefits and the wage-compensation fund (CIG), a wage subsidy for industrial workers threatened with redundancy. The public employment offices at national and lower levels have adjunct tripartite committees, separate from the benefit administration. Overall, the social partners exert considerable influence in the political realm since 'they have often served to block the introduction of urgently required and fundamental reforms of labor market policy' (Höcker 1998: 202), in particular the highly regulated dismissal law is defended by unions for lack of sufficient unemployment benefits.

In Continental Europe social partners traditionally are involved in unemployment insurance and employment services, either via tripartite public administration or bipartite self-regulation. Only Germany has fully integrated both active and passive labor market policies in one central organization; all others have divided these functions. Unemployment insurance is self-administered in Germany, France and Italy, while it has been curtailed in the Netherlands. The more the state subsidizes or exclusively finances unemployment insurance, the more influence it assumes. Although tripartite self-administration is common for public employment services, here the state also assumes a more dominant role through its increased financial involvement and the shift from passive towards active labor market policies. With respect to governance structures, quite contradictory moves have occurred in Europe. In most countries, we see a trend towards decentralizing active labor market policy and its administration, seeking new cooperation between communal assistance and employment services. In the Netherlands, after a short experiment in tripartism, and more recently in Germany, the social partners' involvement has been criticized and the government pushed through governance reforms. In France, the government has taken responsibility for active labor market policy, while the employers have pressed the unions to accept a reform of the costly unemployment insurance scheme, while the flexibilization of Italian labor markets remains a contentious issue.

Social Partners and Labor Market Policy Reforms

Continental European labor market policy has been criticized for its passive orientation and rigid employment regulation. A policy shift towards activation and flexiblization had been advocated by international organizations (OECD, EU) as well as by national governments and policy experts (Casey 2004). However, labor market policy is a field in which responsibility tends to be shared in Bismarckian welfare systems. Although tripartite employment services provide a forum for exchange, substantial labor market reforms are more likely to be negotiated by ad hoc concertation. Since labor market reforms, in particular introducing flexibility in employment regulation, depend partially on supporting collective bargaining practices, governments need to take the social partners on board. Coordination also involves lower levels, including local 'partnerships' between local government, employers and workplace representatives. While we would expect social concertation to be more likely in countries with traditions of tripartite social governance, the veto power of the social partners in these organizations may also provide an obstacle to change. Nevertheless, we can observe in Continental European countries considerable changes in labor market policies towards more activation and administrative reforms (Clegg 2007; see Hemerijck and Eichhorst, this volume).

In Germany, relative passive labor market policies were applied after unification as before, despite the severe employment problems in the East. As the BA pays for both passive benefits and active policies, while communes were responsible for social assistance, the financial burden was shifted back and forth between contribution- and tax-financed benefits as well as between federal and local level (Widmaier and Blancke 1997). Moreover, active labor market policy created a secondary labor market, while unions aimed at working time reductions and early retirement to better 'share' employment, both increasing labor costs. The tripartite talks in an 'Alliance for Jobs' under the Conservative and later new red-green government did not result in negotiated labor market reforms in the late 1990s, instead the main reform initiatives were largely advanced by the government (Bispinck and Schulten 2000). Following a scandal at BA, the independent Hartz commission proposed improvements in the employment service and several labor market reforms in 2002. These were implemented in four legislative packages (2003-2004) with only minor concessions to the unions and Left party fractions, although some adjustments (postponing reforms for older workers) followed later. Most importantly these reforms merged tax-financed and means-tested unemployment assistance with social assistance, making these benefits more conditional on activation policies.

The Dutch social partners played a more constructive role in employment policy, though the main activation policies came from government initiatives, including subsidized jobs (Hemerijck et al. 2000). The Dutch social partners assumed a more active role in negotiating flexibility, facilitating employment growth through temporary and part-time jobs. They negotiated a SAR agreement on 'flexicurity' in 1996, enacted by Parliament without alteration, entailing a compromise between the 'flexibility' interests of employers in minimizing regulation and the employment protection ('security') interest of atypical workers (Wilthagen 1998). Likewise, the social partners agreed on the inclusion of ethnic minorities and the enhanced 'employability' of less skilled workers, while implementation remains a matter for partnerships at company or local level.

Also in France, passive and active labor market policy measures were used to combat mass unemployment, yet in an uncoordinated manner. For financial reasons, unemployment benefits were cut back and made more stringent by a tripartite agreement in 1993, leading to a shift in the new minimum income scheme (RMI since 1989) financed by the state (Malo et al. 2000: 257-258). Except for the Conservative Chirac government in 1986, which abolished the authorization of redundancies and lowered entry wages for young workers, French governments have rarely pursued labor market deregulation. In order to boost employment, French governments used special general taxes to finance social inclusion measures, such as reduced payroll taxes for low-wage workers. Labor market policy was largely government driven, causing opposition by the employers, and defense of the status quo by trade unions. Nevertheless, the government and the social partners needed to come to terms on pressing financial issues, leading to some ad hoc agreements between government and the unemployment funds. The shift in political power to the Conservatives in 2002 added more weight to the employers' push to force harsher reinsertion measures on long-term and youth unemployed. In 2008, under the pressure of the government, the social partners signed a series of agreements on new labor contracts increasing flexibility while increasing partial security for redundant workers.

Italy's labor market remains highly regulated, while unemployment benefits and active labor market policies are relatively underdeveloped. Reforms in the 1990s were often contradictory, retrenchment and expansion of CIG wage supplementation fund. The tripartite Pact for Employment (1996) and subsequent legislation liberalized fixed-term and part-time contracts. Yet, many issues remained contentious, such as reducing working time. The December Pact of 1998 aimed to increase public investment, foster training, and reduce labor costs to boost employment. Plans of the Berlusconi government to reform the Workers Statute of 1970, which would flexibilize the rigid employment protection law, caused major conflicts with the social partners. But Italian government and two union centers signed a 'Pact for Italy' in 2002, which led to the end the public monopoly in employment service and more flexiblization. Although social concertation occurred, the negotiations were often difficult and slow, the defense of employment protection remained important to unions, leading them to call for large scale demonstrations such as against the removal of the article 18 of the labor code (see Jessoula, this volume). The 2007 tripartite agreement under the Prodi government engaged in concerted reforms to improve the social 'shock absorbers' in case of mass dismissal and to introduce flexicurity measures. However, the political change to the Berlusconi government made the social concertation road less likely, in particular in the contentious area of labor market deregulation.

Developments in social concertation in the case of labor market reforms have been contradictory. Tripartite social pacts remain more limited than one would expect (only the Netherlands and to a lesser degree Italy show some positive results), given the necessity of coordinating labor market policies. By comparison with pension reform, the stakes are higher for labor market reform as it affects more immediately union members' interests and unions' bargaining power, while employers support governments in retrenchment and activation policies. To the degree that the social partners represent the 'insider' interests, the state, as the third partner, has to bring in the interest of the 'outsiders'. Indeed, the efforts by governments to surpass established tripartite social governance, in particular the Dutch and German governance reforms have been important in facilitating subsequent government-driven reforms.

10.6 Conclusion: Towards Reforming Governance

In this chapter, I discussed the modes of *social governance* in Bismarckian welfare systems that involve the social partners in pension and labor market policies. In most Continental European countries, instead of unilateral state intervention against the social partners' will, the state shares public space with the social partners in these policy fields. Traditionally, these Bismarckian welfare systems have a high degree of institutionalized consultation, delegated self-administration and some scope for self-regulation in pension and labor market policies. The influence of social partners in self-administration is lowest in Germany and Italy, while the self-regulatory role is considerable in France and the Netherlands. Concertation efforts have not had much impact in France and Germany, whereas particularly in Italy and partially in the Netherlands, concerted reforms have been negotiated. Moreover, the Dutch government and the French government and employers (with partial success) advanced major governance reforms; similarly the German government reformed the employment agency. The rather unimportant Italian and German self-administration of the pension systems remained unaltered but self-regulation in occupational pension has gained in importance.

The comparative overview on institutional consultation and ad hoc concertation in both pension policy and labor market policy areas indicates that social partners have had some influence in social policy-making when governments sought to circumvent reform blockage by negotiating with them. The success of social concertation was however dependent on the credible threat of state intervention, compelling the social partners to find a common solution. When state intervention is unlikely, the social partners might not even be willing to enter a political exchange. Similarly in social policy matters, governments do not always have the means to intervene, especially in the case of voluntary occupational welfare schemes. But frequent and substantial state intervention may also have negative effects on the social partners' capacity to develop consensual partnership in both the wage bargaining and social policy areas.

However, when governments were unable (or unwilling) to negotiate changes in consensual ways, they aimed at changing social governance to limit the influence of social partners to block reforms. Such significant state intervention into the procedural aspect of social governance, however, required enough political force and opportunity. This was provided in the German and Dutch cases through reports about mismanagement by self-administered agencies and a weakened influence of the social partners. Hence, the past institutions seem not to be written in stone and there is scope for path departure from the 'frozen landscape' of Continental welfare systems described by Esping-Andersen (1996a).

Three main developments have the potential to reshape social governance in the long run:

1) Continued *privatization* trends in pension policy increase opportunities for the social partners to assume a larger role in negotiating occupational pensions. This has implications and promises repercussions for the linkages between wage and pension development as the social partners internalize portions of the social security costs into wage bargaining. The retreat of the state from its responsibility can lead to an increased scope for the two collective bargaining partners, provided they are willing to and capable of assuming such self-regulatory responsibility.

2) Further *decentralization* in labor market policy will also lead to changes in social governance in this policy area, shifting power from tripartite national institutions to new devolved public-private partnerships. Here it will be critical whether firms and workplace representatives can be convinced to cooperate in activation and social inclusion policies that take into account the plight of labor market outsiders. Moreover, in times of economic downturn, the workplace representatives will gain an important role in negotiating employment security and social plans.

3) Finally, *social governance reforms*, advanced by governments or employer organizations (as in the Netherlands and France, respectively)

will gain in importance in the future. These governance reforms seek to readjust social partnership in the social policy area to overcome reform blockages, limit the social partners' externalization strategies, and reinstill social responsibility.

In this respect, the most important transformation of current Bismarckian welfare systems may very well be the reforms of governance structures: these alter the conditions under which the social partners will be able to influence future reforms and whether they will share responsibility for a new balance of welfare rights and employment goals. In this way, these institutional changes may lead to a long goodbye to traditional Bismarckian self-administration by the social partners and a renewed lease for the self-regulation via collective bargaining by the social partners.

11 Trajectories of Fiscal Adjustment in Bismarckian Welfare Systems

Philip Manow

11.1 Introduction[1]

The comparative literature which analyzes the fate of the welfare state in our economically 'dire times' started with the assumption that an increasingly internationalized market will force the generous welfare states of the Western world in a common, downward direction. Yet, today it seems that the advanced OECD economies have maintained their ability to 'tax and spend' to a surprising degree. What is most remarkable from the viewpoint of the early pessimistic predictions is that the welfare state has basically survived (Kuhnle 2001) rather than outlived itself.

One of the most prominent explanations for the resilience of the welfare state in our times of austerity has been put forward by Paul Pierson (Pierson 1994; 1998; 2001b). For Pierson, welfare states are by and large 'immovable objects' due to electoral 'short-termism' combined with the political support that social spending programs generate among those that benefit from them – an argument that follows the Olsonian diffuse costs/visible gains logic. If we were to follow Pierson's arguments, however, we would *generally* expect welfare retrenchment to be unlikely given that cuts in spending programs are always very unpopular. Yet, in the wake of the economic pressures and challenges of the 1980s and 1990s we *did* observe instances of substantial welfare retrenchment that – from time to time – even saw impressive electoral approval (Häusermann 2010b). To put it bluntly: while welfare retrenchment may be unpopular, the ever increasing tax- or debt-burdens caused by uncontrolled spending dynamics may be just as unpopular. It seems that we need much more fine grained 'blame avoidance' arguments if we want to account for the varying reform trajectories in the OECD since the mid-1970s.

Since it is *variance,* not overall downward *convergence* or general *inertia,* which calls for an explanation, I propose to look at different political opportunity structures that have made retrenchment in some places more likely than in others. This, as we will see, helps us to better understand the specific reform trajectory of Bismarckian welfare systems. I follow Paul Pierson in counting the welfare state itself among the dominant features of advanced democracies and industrialized countries so that the 'new politics of the welfare state' are strongly determined by the political options that the welfare state itself provides. I will focus on welfare state finances, which is in my view one of the most important, yet most under-studied elements of this new political opportunity structure. In particular I claim that whether a welfare state is financed through taxes or through social insurance contributions had a crucial impact on how the welfare state adjusted to the dire economic environment since the end of the golden age in the mid-1970s. Welfare state finances were also key in triggering the reform of the Bismarckian welfare states, as the chapters in this volume demonstrate with rich detail.

My argument starts from simple assumptions. Governments essentially could respond in three ways to the fiscal stress caused by diminished growth combined with increased welfare spending demands: they could cut costs, run a higher debt, or increase revenue. I argue that these basic strategies were associated with varying political costs depending on how the welfare state is financed in a given country and depending on how easy it was to run a higher public debt, specifically whether an independent central bank could make the 'run a higher debt'-option less attractive via interest rate hikes (for the details of the argument see the subsequent section). Given these varying costs, national adjustment strategies differed. In this chapter I will focus in particular on Bismarckian welfare systems, characterized notably by the dominant role of social insurance contributions in financing social protection. I argue that for a variety of reasons it proved to be much easier to increase social insurance contributions than to increase taxes, which is why Bismarckian welfare systems for such a long time have followed the strategy of boosting revenue through contribution hikes rather than cutting benefits or running a higher public debt – with all the problems associated with this raise-revenue strategy like ever higher non-wage labor costs, low employment rates, sluggish job growth especially in the less productive service sector and – therefore – high and persistent unemployment. When the high level of social contributions became perceived as an economic problem in the new European context, it became one of the main reasons for reforming and restructuring welfare systems.

The chapter is structured as follows: In section 11.2 I will briefly sketch my argument. In particular, I will highlight the political attractiveness of social insurance contributions as a means of welfare state funding and the adverse long-term effects of ever rising non-wage labor costs. In section 11.3 I will present empirical evidence in support of my hypothesis that specific institutional combinations of modern welfare states go a long way in explaining their different reform trajectories. In section 11.4, I will specifically focus on the French and German cases. These two countries are typical examples of Bismarckian welfare systems; for a long time they followed a similar path of steadily increasing social insurance contributions until they both recognized the detrimental effects of high non-wage labor costs. More recently, however, they have been variously successful in substituting taxation for social insurance contributions. In the conclusion I will discuss some of the implications of my argument.

11.2 Revenue, Debt, Expenditures

The starting assumption of my analysis is that politicians will reform the welfare state only in the case that this promises to be less damaging for their re-election prospects than any other coping strategy would be. True, politicians will be reluctant to engage in profound welfare retrenchment (cf. Pierson 1994; 1996; 1998), given that cuts in social benefits do not make for a very popular policy. Yet, welfare retrenchment is only one among several political options. Politicians can react to economic slumps or to sustained periods of low growth by either cutting (social) spending, raising taxes (including increasing social insurance contributions), or by running a higher public debt. Since at least the late 1980s, simple legislative inactivity has no longer been an option since it would lead unavoidably to either higher taxes or higher debt. *All* of these measures are unpopular, so that simple 'blame avoidance' arguments (Weaver 1986; 1988; Pierson 1994) are not very helpful analytically. Should we then expect that politicians would employ a random policy mix among more or less equally unattractive alternatives? I argue that different political opportunity structures have rendered the one or the other choice out of the basic option set (cut costs, raise taxes, run a higher debt) more or less costly in political (but sometimes also in economic) terms.

In this respect I first of all want to highlight the fiscal structure of the welfare state as a particularly crucial dimension of variation among the

OECD countries, which in my view has been – at least partially – responsible for the marked differences in the response of these countries towards the new situation of diminished growth and high unemployment. A basic distinction is whether the welfare state is financed predominantly by contributions or by taxes.[2] The welfare state's fiscal dimension has as of yet failed to attract sufficient scholarly attention in the analyses of the OECD-countries' economic response patterns since the 'end of the golden age'.[3]

The prominence of social insurance contribution in financing social expenditure is one of the specific traits that distinguish Continental European welfare systems from their Nordic or Anglo-Saxon counterparts. Yet, it has attracted relatively little scholarly attention in studies of welfare state development and reform (see however Bonoli and Palier 2000). The studies gathered in this volume are the exception that proves the rule: they all highlight the centrality of social contribution in explaining the trajectory of Continental European, Bismarckian welfare regimes, both as a means to finance their labor shedding strategy, and, once they had become an economic problem in the new European context, as one of the main reasons for reforming and restructuring welfare systems.

In typical Bismarckian welfare systems, social contributions not only finance social protection, they also provide the insured with entitlements. Actually, social contributions play a role in connection with all four dimensions that characterize a Bismarckian welfare system (see Palier, chapter 1, this volume): eligibility, benefits, finance and governance. Entitlements are conditioned upon the previous payment of social contribution and benefit levels and the 'drawing period' depends mainly on the previous contribution record (especially in old-age and unemployment insurance and sick pay). Finally, the role assigned to the social partners within the system (as members of the board of the *Kassen, caisses* etc.) is mainly justified by the fact that they represent those who pay social contributions, i.e. employers and employees. The role of social contributions in Bismarckian regimes both as a fiscal instrument as well as a central concept that defines eligibility, benefits and governance contrasts with the minor role they play in the two other 'worlds of welfare' (Esping-Andersen 1990).

What is the specific political attractiveness of social insurance contributions? Basically I claim that the 'increase revenue'-response in times of fiscal stress has been politically less problematic in contribution financed welfare states as compared to tax-financed regimes of either the generous or residual variant. There are several reasons for this. The first refers to differences in political visibility. Most tax increases have to be legislated, while social insurance contributions often rise automatically whenever revenue falls short of expenses ('automatic government'; Weaver 1988). Moreover, such automatic increases can be attributed to 'secular' trends like demographic aging or costly medical progress, which dilutes direct political responsibility for tax increases, and thus makes them much less attributable, and therefore less political dangerous. Increases in contribution rates can also be better legitimized due to their strong nexus with entitlements – more revenue promises higher expenses *from which the contributing person himself expects to benefit* (Hibbs and Madsen 1981: 418-423). Harold Wilensky speaks of the 'illusion that social security taxes (...) are paid for benefits duly and directly received, while an income tax is lost to the winds' (Wilensky 1975: 61; see on fiscal illusion Oates 1991). As a consequence, contributors tend to defend social benefits as 'deferred wages' and earned social rights. 'Unlike generic schemes for those in "need" or for "citizens", each individual [seems to have] his or her own contract with the government with specific benefits attached to his or her specific work record, years of contribution, and earnings history' (Myles and Pierson 2001: 321).

Yet, a much less often noted but at least as important difference in the political incentive structure provided by the welfare state's funding mode pertains to the budget process. Financial questions in tax-financed welfare states are dealt with in the annual budget process, decided by the cabinet and with a more or less influential role of the minister of Finance (Hagen 2006; Hallerberg and Hagen 1999; Hallerberg, Strauch and Hagen 2001; Hallerberg 2004). By contrast, in contribution-financed welfare states, the minister of Finance usually not only has no formal right to be heard in questions concerning welfare state finance, but – more importantly – also has no immediate fiscal interest in the 'social budget'. Earmarked social insurance contributions are not formally part of the government's budget but go into the 'parafiscal' budgets of the social insurance schemes. But if the government budget is not directly affected, a finance Minister develops no political interest in preventing contribution hikes. Instead, most often a minister of Labor and/or Social Affairs is responsible – and (s)he is usually a minister with a pro-spending bias.[4] Moreover, fiscal autonomy secures political autonomy – another reason why a minister of Labor is often willing to disregard the unfavorable economic consequences of high non-wage labor costs – and, if confronted with the choice, would be more likely to increase revenue than to cut costs.[5]

In other words, a government's *political capacity* to cut costs as well as its *political interest* to do so are generally much less developed in Bismarckian welfare states. The flipside of the politically important separation between the welfare state budget and the general budget in Bismarckian-type welfare states is that the government is also continuously tempted to shift spending out of the public budget (financed by taxes) and into the special budgets of the social insurance schemes (financed by contributions). In other words, if the finance Minister in countries with Bismarckian welfare states should develop any interest in welfare state finance, it is one *to increase* (labor) taxes in order to bring fiscal relief to the government budget (see Trampusch 2003). The long-lasting debates on '*versicherungsfremde Leistungen*' in Germany (Hinrichs, this volume) and on '*charges indues*' in France (Palier, chapter 3, this volume), which revolve around expenditures with which politicians have inappropriately burdened the social insurance schemes, proves that separate budgets of the social insurance schemes present a strong temptation for any government under fiscal stress. In this context one would also need to mention the fact that German unification was largely paid out of the social insurance funds (cf. Manow and Seils 2000 and Hinrichs, this volume).

The fiscal temptation is even stronger if an independent central bank exerts strong pressures on a government to observe strict budget discipline. A central bank committed to a non-accommodating monetary policy responds to an increase in the public debt and to its inflationary impulse with retaliatory interest rate hikes. This makes the 'debt-option' as compared to the other two options – raise taxes or cut costs – more expensive (Masciandaro and Tabellini 1988; Eijffinger and de Haan 1996). It is therefore no surprise that the literature regularly finds a 'fairly strong negative relationship of CBI to debt' (Franzese 2002: 146-147). This also means that countries with a strong independent central bank cannot respond flexibly with a loose fiscal or monetary policy to economic shocks. Because of these costs of 'monetarist credibility' (cf. Ball 1993; Jordan 1997) the welfare state as an economic shock absorber grows in importance in these countries. But in Bismarckian welfare systems the costs of 'social credibility' complement those of monetarist credibility because contribution finance narrows the government's room for maneuver in a crisis. If welfare state revenue comes from contributions rather than from taxes, expenditures are quasi-earmarked to honor the entitlements 'earned' by these contributions. Such a welfare system is much less free to put its revenue to use and it is much less flexible to target its resources according to need or criteria of maximal efficiency. Instead, the welfare system is far more inclined to follow a reactive, post-factum approach with a heavier reliance on compensation of income loss than, for instance, labor market activation policies and with a stronger emphasis on transfers than on welfare services (Scharpf 1997; Boix 1998; Garrett 1998; Huber and Stephens 2000; 2001). In times of crisis the necessity to honor the entitlements earned by previous contributions crowds out all measures (like active labor market policies) that cannot legitimate themselves with a tight contribution-benefit nexus – despite the fact that these are often the very measures that would be particularly needed in times of economic shocks. Thus, the responses of Bismarckian welfare systems to economic crises reveal a typical pattern: governments face systemic incentives to cover the increasing revenue/spending gap in times of sluggish growth via contribution rate hikes, especially if an independent central bank prevents an increase in public debt. With increased contribution rates, the budgets of the social insurance schemes turn into surplus once the economy recovers. Now politicians have the incentive to use this 'surplus'-money to introduce new entitlements or expand existing ones. This results in a fiscal ratchet effect in Bismarckian welfare systems leading to higher levels of social insurance contributions with each economic crisis, while contribution rates are prevented from decreasing in the subsequent boom.

From the above we can derive a few expectations about the paths of fiscal adjustment in Bismarckian welfare systems in the post-'golden age' era. First of all, I expect to observe that the OECD countries headed into very different directions after they woke up from the 'dream of permanent prosperity' in the mid-1970s. More specifically, I expect those countries with welfare systems primarily financed by contributions (i.e. predominantly Bismarckian ones) to have covered their rising welfare bills mainly from increased contributions and, depending on the degree of central bank independence, also from the public debt. A second expectation pertains to the reform sequences of Bismarckian welfare reforms trajectory (see Palier, chapter 1 and 13, this volume), since nothing suggests that their typical policy mix will remain stable over time. Given that each of the three basic responses to fiscal strain comes at increasing political costs, we would rather expect that over time the relative weights given to certain policies shift and that initially 'dominant strategies' may later become 'dominated strategies'. It is therefore much more plausible that – in a longer perspective – countries do not differ so much with respect to their policy mix but with respect to the *order* in which they ruin their basic policy options. In this respect we would predict that the Bismarckian welfare systems were those that followed the 'raise revenue/increase social insurance contributions'-path first and for the longest before the adverse effects of this strategy forced them to switch.

In absolute terms, almost all OECD countries since 1970 have increased spending, debt and revenue at the same time (Franzese 2002). Welfare state regimes differed profoundly, however, with respect to the weights with which they employed these strategies. And we need to keep in mind that the long-term relationship between the three options is not simply one of substitution. In relative terms the basic policy options – while being substitutes for each other in the short run (e.g. if you can run a higher debt, you feel less pressured to raise taxes) – are complements to each other in the long run (e.g. increasing the debt now may force you to raise revenue later in order to finance debt service). Finally, we have to take into account that countries may also change strategy because the institutional matrix that attaches costs to different responses has not remained stable over time. In the time period under inspection central bank independence has significantly increased in almost all OECD-countries, in particular for countries joining the euro, which was associated with giving up sovereignty in monetary policy and also with accepting severe restrictions on fiscal policy autonomy – namely the Maastricht-criteria and their limits on deficits and debt. Yet, all this apparently has not led to one common 'mixture of malaise' in all European welfare states. Obviously, some sequences were more (economically and politically) advantageous than others.

The following section will provide some empirical evidence in support of my argument. First, I give a descriptive overview of the development of revenue, expenditures and debt in the OECD in the three decades since the early 1970s. The chosen time period begins with the onset of the first oil crisis, which introduced the next thirty years of sluggish growth, and it ends with the latest available data around 2005. The period of investigation therefore also covers the effects of the establishment of the European Monetary Union, which quite profoundly altered the parameters of monetary and fiscal policy for an important subset of the OECD-countries. Subsequently, I will ask whether the basic assumptions of my argument are corroborated by two brief case studies. I will focus on the sequence of fiscal policies in two prototypical Bismarckian welfare systems, i.e. where the expenses are mainly financed through social insurance contributions, namely France and Germany.

11.3 Dilemmatic Policy Choices

Let us start with a brief descriptive overview of the development of government receipts and expenditures, debt and social insurance contributions for 15 OECD countries over the last 30 to 35 post-'golden age' years (see figures 11.1 to 11.3). I distinguish the three 'classical' welfare state regimes, but in addition analyze separately a Continental and southern Bismarckian regime type according to the other important dimension of institutional variation that I have highlighted above, namely central bank independence. It is striking that the frequently made distinction between a Continental and a southern variant of the Conservative regime type (cf. Ferrera 1996; 1997) is fully congruent with my distinction between political economies with and without independent central banks. I therefore base my analysis on the following country clusters: *Scandinavian regime* – Sweden, Denmark, Finland, Norway; *Liberal regime* – US, UK and Ireland; *Conservative-Continental regime* – Austria, Belgium, Germany, Netherlands; *southern Conservative regime* – France, Italy, Spain, Portugal. The following figures show that these regimes do indeed stand for rather different 'mixtures of malaise' and display profoundly different patterns of adjustment and reform.

Figure 11.1   Debt as a percentage of GDP, 1970-2005

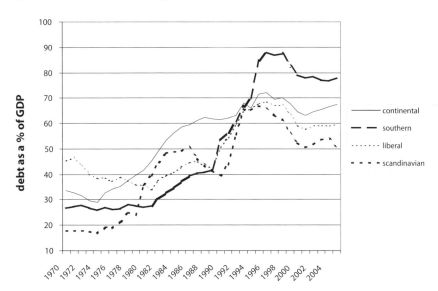

Figure 11.2   Government receipts from taxes and social insurance contributions as a % of GDP, 1970 – 2005

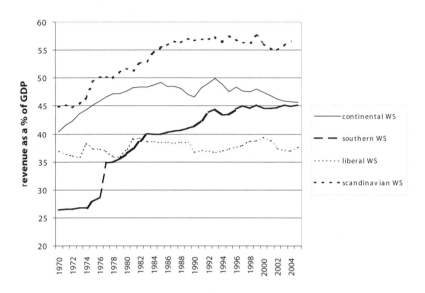

Figure 11.3   Government expenditures as a % of GDP, 1980 – 2003

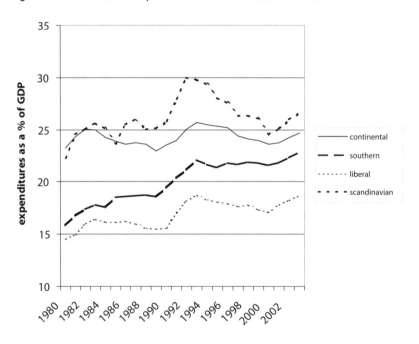

Figures 11.2 and 11.3 clearly reveal that the Continental and southern variants of the Bismarckian model have become very similar in their revenue and spending patterns. That the southern welfare state has caught-up with the high tax-and-spend levels of the Continental welfare states only in the mid-1990s is due to the two late-comers, Spain and Portugal. The only – in the light of my argument non-surprising – difference between both the Continental and southern variants of 'welfare Bismarckianism' is in respect to public debt. Clearly, the southern welfare states Italy, Spain, France and Portugal were much less disciplined in their fiscal policy, and although both the disciplinary effects of the Stability and Growth Pact as well as the 'windfall profits' due to lower interest rates in the wake of the European Monetary Union are very visible in figure 11.1, the southern welfare states continue to run a much higher public debt. The Liberal and Scandinavian welfare states, however, show the well-known pattern of persistent lower and higher revenue- and spending levels, respectively. Since I could not collect data for enough countries to allow for a meaningful comparison of social contribution levels between southern and Continental Bismarckian welfare states, Figure 11.4 reports social insurance

Figure 11.4   Social Insurance Contributions as a % of GDP, 1970-2003

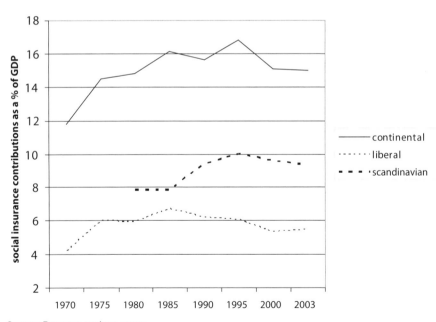

Source: Eurostat, various years

contributions for the three main regime types only – Scandinavian (Denmark, Finland, Sweden), Anglo-Saxon (Ireland and UK) and Continental regimes (Austria, Belgium, France, Germany, Netherlands, Italy) – with no further 'within-type' differentiation for the Bismarckian regime.

The following ternary diagrams visualize the systematic variation among our group of welfare states with respect to their responses to the end of the golden age (see figures 11.5 to 11.8). The diagrams portray the relative weight of either tax-, contribution- or debt-financing of public expenditures in the four different regime types. The fiscal profiles of the countries are reported against the background of the OECD-mean. In other words, a position in the ternary's center would represent a welfare state's fiscal mixture of tax-, contribution- and debt financing exactly at the OECD-average. Any move-

Figure 11.5 Anglo-Saxon countries

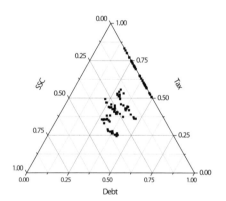

Figure 11.6 Continental European countries

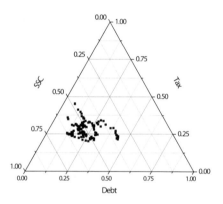

Figure 11.7 Scandinavian countries

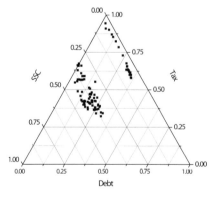

Figure 11.8 Southern Europe

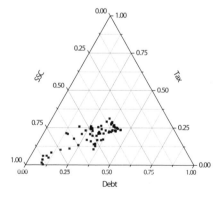

ment into one of the three corners indicates an above-average weight of the respective fiscal source, taxes, public debt or social security contributions (SSC), respectively. Points represent country-years. Data come from the IMF financial yearbook statistics (IMF, various years), but due to limited data availability only cover the period 1970-1995.

From figures 11.5 to 11.8 it is obvious that Anglo-Saxon countries typically hold a very central position, indicating that their strategy mix is very close to the 'average' strategy mix in the OECD. However, while in 1973 the USA was most central in this respect, in 1995 Sweden's strategy mix came closest to the OECD average. On the other side of the spectrum, Denmark maintained its position as the most atypical OECD country, with very few social security contributions and a small share of the public debt. The diagrams once more highlight the importance of debt financing for the Southern European welfare states.

However, a closer inspection of the fiscal profile of two proto-typical Bismarckian welfare systems, France and Germany, reveals a strikingly different success in reversing the trend towards ever increasing contribution rates. As figure 11.9 shows, since the mid-1990s French governments have succeeded in significantly reducing the revenue share of social insurance contributions. This trend reversal is primarily due to the introduction of a special earmarked tax, the *contribution sociale généralisée* (CSG), introduced in 1990 (after some experiments with a similar tax in the late 1980s). The CSG at first generated little revenue, but subsequent rate hikes from 1.1 percent (1990) to 2.4 percent (1993), then to 3.5 percent (1995) and finally to 7.5 percent of income (1998) turned the tax into a major revenue source for the French welfare state. In the 2000s the CSG has provided more than 20 percent of all social protection resources and covers around 35 percent of health care expenditures (see Palier, chapter 3, this volume). Social contributions in France have remained at high levels, since the extra revenue generated by the *contribution sociale généralisée* has primarily been used to cover cost increases and thereby to avoid benefit cuts rather than to substitute contributions with taxes. Still, the example of the CSG shows that a fiscal turnaround in Bismarckian welfare systems is possible under favorable conditions. What exactly these conditions might be and why the substitution of contributions by taxes has proved to be much more complicated in the German than in the French case will be addressed in the following section.

**Figure 11.9   Social insurance contributions as a percentage of total taxation in France and
Germany, 1970-2004**

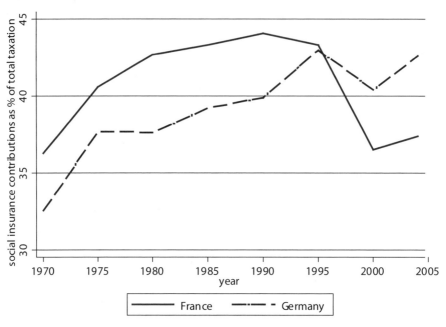

Source: Eurostat, various years

11.4   Taxes versus Social Insurance Contributions – French and German Experiences

The following two brief case studies are meant to shed light first on the fact that both in France and in Germany over the course of the 1980s and 1990s, the important role played by social contribution has become perceived as a problem, and that both have tried to substitute parts of them with taxation. I will ask why the French and the German welfare state differ so much with respect to the extent with which taxes have been substituted for social insurance contributions. Why is it that several French governments were more successful in reversing the trend to ever higher social insurance contributions, whereas German governments, despite their officially pronounced commitment, failed to bring substantial relief to German contribution payers? I will start with a brief account of the French story.[6]

After long and protracted debates about mass unemployment and France's loss of economic competitiveness, it was primarily employers who spread the idea that French non-wage labor costs, i.e. social contributions, were far too high. In 1982, Yvon Gattaz (then President of the CNPF – the French employers' organization) launched the 'battle over contributions' in order to reduce employers' fiscal burden. In France, contributions levied from employees and employers financed a larger share of social expenditure than in other European countries. In 1992, social security contributions represented 79.9 percent of total revenue of the French social security budget, in contrast with 10.8 percent in Denmark, 34.5 percent in Ireland, 41.9 percent in the United Kingdom, 52.3 percent in Luxembourg, between 60 and 68 percent in the Netherlands, Italy, Portugal, Spain, Greece and Belgium, and 69.9 percent in Germany.[7] The 'battle over contributions' debate linked the French high non-wage labor costs with France's poor labor market performance. Between 1983 and 1991, French job growth was only at 0.5 percent annually, whereas it rose by 1.7 percent within the European Community, by 1.3 percent in Japan and by 1.7 percent in the United States.

As shown in chapter 3, from the late 1980s, and even more so once the single market was put in place and intra-European competition intensified, one of the main employment policies in France was to reduce the cost of labor by exempting low wages from social contribution. This of course led to decreasing revenue and faced governments with a choice between cutting benefits, increasing the debt, or tapping into new fiscal resources other than social contributions. Increasing the role of taxation in financing social expenditure required overcoming serious political obstacles, in particular the resistance of the unions who did not wish to see their role within the social insurance system endangered by a change in the method of funding. But retrenchment was also politically problematic, since the French electorate preferred to pay higher contributions rather than see their level of social protection decline. Running a high public debt became less and less attractive in a period in which France prepared for the single currency and aimed at meeting the Maastricht criteria. Things moved very slowly, and a political compromise to use taxation to offset the revenue loss due to reduced contributions aimed only at financing 'non-contributory' benefits (i.e. to finance the 'undue charges' weighting on social insurances). This compromise led to the increased use of new forms of taxation (in particular, consumption taxes levied on tobacco and alcohol), but above all to a new form of social deduction, the 'generalized social contribution' (*Contribution sociale généralisée*, CSG).

In 1983 a proportional contribution of 1 percent on all taxable earnings was introduced; in 1985 it was abolished for earned income but was retained for income from social insurances. It was re-imposed on earned income in 1986, but at a rate of 0.4 percent. In 1989 these two contributions accounted for 0.9 percent of the revenue of the main (general) social security scheme. Once the strategy of removing the income ceiling on social contributions was exhausted in 1989, the government had to seek alternatives. At the same time, the trade unions became less unanimous in their opposition to a special, earmarked social tax when one confederation, the CFDT, altered its stance and came out in favor of levying a contribution on all income. The 'generalized social contribution' was framed so that it promised to be advantageous for all the welfare state stake holders:

- a deduction levied on all sorts of income (equity included) promised to be fairer than social contributions (which are based solely on wages);
- levying the generalized social contribution on all households would make it much more efficient than the French income tax (from which almost 50 percent of households are exempt);
- its tax source would be a household's (total) earnings and no longer wages only. As stated in 1987 by a Committee calling for new forms of revenue for the welfare system: 'The new deductions which may prove necessary should be imposed on all individuals and all forms of income, without the business community having to foot an additional bill'[8];
- the CSG promised to solve the problem of 'non-contributory benefits', since all the reports endorsed the argument advanced regularly since the 1950s about the need for consistency between the nature of funding and the purpose of a benefit: 'the principle of solidarity across occupations must be matched by funding that is not occupationally related' (Dupuis 1989: 29).

The new formula was attractive both to the Left (more fairness) and the Right (more efficiency). Nevertheless, due in particular to the trade unions' opposition, it was first implemented only on a small scale. The new source of revenue for social security saw the light of day at the end of 1990, when on 3 October the Cabinet adopted the blueprint for the generalized social contribution. The tax applied to all French residents and covered earned income, inherited wealth or income from investments. The right-wing opposition, the Communist Party and most of the trade unions, except the CFDT, opposed these plans with varying degrees of intensity. But the CSG was adopted in November 1990 and implemented in February 1991. At the outset the CSG was deducted at a rate of 1.1 percent.

Subsequently, various governments used the new tax to bolster welfare resources. The CSG levied 65.5 billion francs in 1994, 94 billion in 1995 and 97.4 billion in 1996. In the following year, the CSG brought in 148.3 billion francs. After a further increase in 1998, (up to 7.5 percent of wage or equity income, and 6.6 percent of indirect income such as pension or unemployment allowance), CSG brought in 330 billion francs in 1998 and became the most important direct tax, given that the income tax yield was only a total of 290 billion in 1998. The resources collected through the CSG rose eleven-fold in only eight years. The sum for 1998 (330 billion francs) corresponds to almost 20 percent of social security revenue for that year (1,731 billion) and since then it has remained at this level.

The German reform trajectory is one in which we find multiple policy instruments applied, among them prominently welfare cutbacks as well as attempts to increase tax financing (see Hinrichs, this volume). Retrenchment has been continuously on the agenda since the second oil crisis, but has been particularly marked since the late 1990s. The health reform of 2003 alone introduced cutbacks of over 10 billion euros in the form of higher patient co-payments and the exclusion of certain services and treatments. The various pension reforms since the mid-1990s realized significant reductions in pension benefits (Schulze and Jochem 2007). At the same time, like in France, the insight that high non-wage labor costs may explain Germany's sluggish job growth plus high structural unemployment gained ground in public debate. This motivated politicians to propose an increase of the tax-financed share of welfare state funding. Yet, the combined application of benefit cutbacks and tax transfers earmarked for social spending remained insufficient to bring fiscal relief to contributions payers, both because of adverse economic circumstances and because of the continued political temptation to bring fiscal relief to the public budget by imposing additional costs on the specific budgets of social insurance schemes (see Trampusch 2003).

The tendency to burden the 'contribution payer' with expenses for which the 'tax payer' is responsible sheds light on the importance of the political opportunity structures inherent in Bismarckian parafiscalism (see above, Section 11.2): the automatic adjustment of contribution rates is politically attractive because it is a less visible mode of generating revenue. Moreover, labor ministers are foremost spending ministers, whereas finance ministers gain their reputation by guarding fiscal discipline and by reducing taxes instead of increasing tax-transfers into the budgets of the social insurance schemes (cf. Schulze and Jochem 2007). Despite an overall increase in tax money funneled into the welfare budgets (see table

11.1 below), in 2005 the scientific council of the Ministry of Economics still estimated that the volume of all 'undue charges' not covered by tax-based transfers out of the public budget but financed by insurance contributions amounted to 65 billion euros (SVR 2005: 331). For instance, despite a public transfer to the pension insurance of almost 54 billion euros in 2003, this still left 'undue pension charges' of almost 20 billion – to be covered by contributions. According to a projection from 2005, fully covering all expenses of the social insurance schemes that are not immediately risk- and insurance-related with tax payers' money would allow a reduction of contribution rates by about 7 percent (4 percent in the health insurance, 2 percent in the unemployment insurance and 0.7 in the pension insurance; cf. SVR 2005: 378 and 387). This would significantly lower non-wage labor costs (which are at around 40 percent of gross wages). According to various studies, estimated employment effects range between -17,000 and +129,000 jobs per each percentage point reduction in social insurance contributions, with higher effects if social insurance contributions are reduced especially in the low-wage segments of the labor market. Therefore, in the most optimistic scenario, paying all undue charges out of the public budget would reduce unemployment by almost one million.

It is important to stress that substituting social insurance contributions with taxes is fully cost-neutral; it would not add a single euro to total government expenditures but simply reallocate the welfare state's fiscal burden from the insured only to all tax payers. Given its positive employment effects (whereas the effect strength remains debated), and in light of the French example, we might ask why we have not seen anything like the French CSG in Germany, where social insurance contributions continue to be high in spite of the fact that public debate has identified high non-wage labor costs as the most detrimental factor inhibiting employment growth and competitiveness. A look at the taxes that became earmarked to lower the burden on social insurance contributions helps explaining the German welfare state's specific fiscal trajectory (see table 11.1). This pattern is due to Germany's multi veto-point polity. The government uses primarily those taxes for which it can legislate an increase without the agreement of the second chamber; that is, purely federal taxes like consumption taxes (e.g. tobacco tax or energy tax [Ökosteuer]; see table 11.1). In the frequent situation of a 'divided government' with the opposition in government in the majority of state governments and therefore commanding a majority in the second chamber, any government proposal to increase joint taxes is vulnerable to an opposition veto – and the opposition will be very willing to exert its veto since tax increases are highly unpopular with voters. However, in Germany all major revenue generating taxes are joint taxes (in particular VAT, income and corporate tax) for which the government needs the consent of the second chamber, whereas consumption taxes generate only moderate revenue. Not surprisingly, it was not before a grand Christian and social Democratic coalition formed in 2005 that a significant VAT hike brought the government closer to its long declared goal of holding social insurance contributions below 40 percent of gross wages. But even under the favorable economic conditions of 2007 and 2008 and even with the broad majority over which the coalition between Social and Christian Democrats has command, the contributions rates could not be brought below this limit (see Hinrichs, this volume).

Table 11.1   Revenue transfer to the social insurance schemes in Germany

Year	Eco tax plus VAT – transfer to the pension insurance (billion euro)	Tobacco tax – transfer to the health insurance (billion euro)	VAT – transfer to the unemployment insurance (billion euro)
1998	5.6		
1999	9.1		
2000	10.5		
2001	14.0		
2002	16.7		
2003	20.3		
2004	19.8	1.0	
2005	19.9	2.5	
2006	19.9	4.2	
2007	20.5	1.5	6.5
2008	18.2	2.5	7.6

Source: SVR, various years

11.5   Conclusion

I proposed analyzing the economic adjustments of the OECD countries in response to the much more unfavorable economic environment since the mid-1970s in light of the three basic options that a government has when confronted with an increasing revenue/expenditure-gap: increase taxes, cut spending or run a higher public debt. I have suggested that these basic options possess varying degrees of political attractiveness depending on the institutional context in which a government has to employ the one or the other policy. I have emphasized the importance of two variables – in particular, 1) the financing structure of the welfare state, and 2) the level of central bank independence. A political strategy that combines fiscal conservatism with passive welfare state policies is a 'natural outcome' within a setting comprising a welfare state financed by contributions instead of taxes and an independent central bank – a combination classically represented by the German political economy and her 'Continental/ Conservative' (but not southern) homologues. It is an institutional constellation that has been prolonged in Europe under the independent European central bank. I finally showed that a reform of the fiscal basis of the Bismarckian welfare systems is possible, but depends on favorable political conditions. Whereas the French case exemplifies a successful process of increasing the share of tax-finances in the welfare budget, the German case highlights the adverse effects of Germany's multi-veto point polity. With joint taxation but diverging political majorities, the opposition with its dominance in the *Bundesrat* can block tax increases that are meant to increase the tax-share in welfare state finance. German governments were therefore constrained in using those purely federal taxes for which they do not need consent of the second chamber. But this has proved insufficient to significantly lower the contribution payers' burden.

In my view my argument has several merits. First, it allows going beyond the simple insight that welfare retrenchment might be unpopular. By analyzing welfare retrenchment in connection with the other basic policy options, we can formulate more precise, institutionally informed 'blame avoidance' arguments. In this respect I suggest not to base the analysis of welfare retrenchment exclusively on expenditure data, as many contributions to the literature still do. Instead, it seems more appropriate to look simultaneously at expenditure, tax and debt-data. Secondly, I suggested that the marked differences in distributive outcomes between the OECD-countries are not primarily or only caused by differences in voters' political preferences about these outcomes (Esping-Andersen 1990; Iversen and Wren 1998). Rather, I have argued that different political opportunity costs attached to different political strategies must be held responsible for the observable pattern of systematic variation within the OECD-world. This would explain why a measurable, political, partisan influence on welfare state development vanished in most of the econometric analyses over the 1980s and 1990s, whereas the countries largely remained on their distinct adjustment paths. With governments of different colors pursuing similar, institutionally supported strategies, a discernible partisan-political impact on welfare state development evaporated. This interpretation follows an important argument put forward by Herbert Kitschelt (1999). He proposed to treat parties' positions and programs not as given, but to posit them in a political economy perspective, i.e. to view a party as itself influenced by the broader political economy of a country. I argued here that the institutional set-up of the welfare state is an important part of this political economy.

12 Whatever Happened to the Bismarckian Welfare State? From Labor Shedding to Employment-Friendly Reforms

Anton Hemerijck and Werner Eichhorst

12.1 The Adaptive Capacity of the Continental Welfare State

Is the welfare state fit for the 21st century? This question has haunted European policy-makers and researchers for over a decade. Sluggish growth and weak job creation around the turn of the new millennium has not only given way to a fierce ideological battle between different socio-economic 'models', triggering political strife and separating antagonistic advocacy coalitions – but also contributed to a strand of analytical literature pointing out the structural impediments to 'modernize' Continental European and Mediterranean welfare states and make them both more employment friendly and sustainable (see e.g. Scharpf and Schmidt 2000). The Bismarckian version of the European social model was pitted against a false stereotype of the 'Anglo-Saxon' model of capitalism, allegedly a 'free market without a safety net', producing high levels of poverty and inequality, but also against Scandinavian welfare states with universal benefits and strong public services in education, childcare and active labor market policies.

Rather than extrapolating policy recipes from recent economic performance, urging European OECD members to recast their social market economies along the lines of American capitalism, a more illuminating way to understand recent reform dynamics is to contextualize existing social policy repertoires and reform dynamics in the face of the changing economic and technological challenges and evolving social and demographic structures. As shown in the various chapters of this book, the striking intensity and the comprehensive character of social and economic policy reform across the majority of the so-called Bismarckian welfare regimes, including the six founding EU member states of Germany, France, Italy and the Benelux countries, together with the later entrants Spain and Austria as well as the Visegrad countries (the Czech Republic, Slovakia, Hungary and Poland) and Switzerland, since the mid-1990s, is very much at odds with a prevalent image of a 'frozen welfare landscape' in the academic literature. Most important, the substantive extent of welfare re-direction across a large number of member states of the European Union (EU) adds up to the momentum of substantive policy change and goes far beyond the popular concepts of 'retrenchment' and 'roll-back'. But to say that the Bismarckian welfare states, as compared to the Anglo-Irish and Scandinavian welfare regimes, are far from sclerotic is not to say that they are in good shape.

Today four sets of challenges confront policy-makers with the impera-tive to redirect the welfare effort, to redesign institutions and to elaborate on new principles of social justice. *From outside*, in the first place, inter-national competition is challenging the redistributive scope and decom-modifying power of the national welfare state. Many academic observers believe that the increase in cross-border competition in the markets for money, goods and services has substantially reduced the room for ma-neuver of national welfare states (Scharpf 1999). Economic internation-alization constrains countercyclical macroeconomic management, while increased openness exposes generous welfare states to trade competition and permits capital to move to the lowest-cost producer countries. Fi-nally, there is the danger that tax competition will result in the under-provision of public goods.

Second, *from within*, ageing populations, declining birth rates, chang-ing gender roles in households as a result of the mass entry of women to the labor market, the shift from an industrial to the service economy, new technologies in the organization of work, engender sub-optimal employ-ment levels, new inequalities and human capital-biased patterns of social exclusion. Skill-biased technological change, the feminization of the labor market, and demographic ageing, as a result of rising life expectancy and rapidly falling birth rates, are the most important drivers of the new post-industrial risk profile. While the boundaries between being 'in' and 'out' of work have been blurred by increases in atypical work, low-wages, sub-sidized jobs, and training programs, one job is no longer enough to keep low-income families out of poverty. According to Gøsta Esping-Andersen et al. (2002), the most important reason why the existing systems of social care have become overstretched stems from the weakening of labor mar-kets and family households as traditional providers of welfare. In addi-tion, new sources of immigration and segregation, especially in the hous-ing market in metropolitan areas, pose a challenge to social cohesion. The present economic crisis is likely to pose new forms of segmentation on the labor markets to the detriment of the most vulnerable groups such as agency workers, fixed-term employees and the unemployed while labor market insiders have less to fear. Hence, risks and capacities to adapt are distributed unequally across the labor force.

And while policy-makers must find new ways to manage the adverse consequences of economic internationalization and post-industrial differentiation, their endeavor to recast the welfare state is severely constrained by long-standing social policy commitments in the areas of unemployment and pensions, which have ushered in a period of *permanent austerity* (Pierson 1998; 2001b). The maturation of welfare commitments, policies put in place to cater after the social risks associated with the post-war industrial era now seem to crowd out and overload the available policy space for effective policy responses in especially public services under conditions of low economic growth. This specter of permanent austerity is likely to intensify in the face of population ageing. Although in the current downturn many governments switch to public spending in order to reflate the economy, this may generate additional fiscal pressures in the foreseeable future.

Finally, as an intervening variable in the process, issues of work and welfare have become ever more intertwined with processes of European political and economic integration since the 1980s. It is fair to say that in the EU we have entered an era of *semi-sovereign welfare states* (Leibfried and Pierson 2000). European economic integration has fundamentally recast the boundaries of national systems of employment regulation and social protection, by constraining autonomy for domestic policy options, but also by opening opportunities for EU-led social and employment coordination and agenda setting (Ferrera 2005; Zeitlin 2005). The introduction of the internal market and the introduction of the EMU, and Stability and Growth Pact, have added a new economic supranational layer to domestic social and economic policy repertoires of individual member states. Since the mid-1990s, the EU has taken on a far more pro-active role as a central social policy agenda setter. The European Employment Strategy, based on the new Employment Title of the Amsterdam Treaty, launched in 1997, is exemplary of the EU's new role of agenda-setting policy coordination, designed to catalyze rather than steer domestic social policy reform.

Although all European welfare states face the challenges of economic internationalization, post-industrial societal change and intensified European integration under conditions of relative macroeconomic austerity, comparative research reveals how internal and external challenges confront different clusters of welfare regimes with a distinct constellation of adjustment problems and reform agendas. It has often been argued that the institutional configuration of Continental welfare states, with their traditional Bismarckian labor market and social policy legacies, with its strong bias towards the protection of the steady employment of male breadwinners, are, in comparison to the Anglo-Saxon social model and the Scandinavian worlds of welfare, the most difficult to reform. In spite of the obvious 'irresistible forces' urging for reform, the Continental welfare model has remained an 'unmovable object' (Pierson 1998). Especially the larger political economies of France, Germany and Italy, are often mocked for their 'frozen fordism', 'inactivity traps', 'welfare without work' conundrum and 'insider-outsider' segmentation, 'perverse familialism' and 'permanent pension crises' (Palier and Martin 2007a). With the Bismarckian regime type covering a large majority of EU member states, this is all the more problematic for the EU aspiring to become – following the Lisbon agenda – the most competitive knowledge-based economy in the world.

As the series of fresh and detailed analyses of reforms implemented in Bismarckian welfare systems published in this volume show, the pace and scope of Continental welfare reform is more profound, even if incomplete, than is suggested in the literature on the 'new politics of the welfare state'. To be sure, the Continental reform momentum is very rooted in the incongruence between new economic and social contexts and institutional resilience of Bismarckian male-breadwinner social policy provisions, based on occupationally distinct, employment-related social insurance principles, underpinned by traditional (single-breadwinner) family values (Esping-Andersen 1990; Ferrera 1998; Scharpf and Schmidt 2000; Ferrera, Hemerijck and Rhodes 2000; Palier 2006). Catching up with the more employment and family-friendly Scandinavian and Anglo-Saxon welfare state has been particularly difficult for Continental welfare states, as will be surveyed below. The slow but fundamental departure from the 'welfare without work' strategy in Continental welfare systems since the mid-1990s is best understood as a profound transformative process of policy change across a number of intimately related policy domains. Through a more or less protracted sequence of reforms, Bismarckian welfare states shifted from labor shedding to policies that aim at mobilizing labor supply as well as labor demand. Employment-friendly policies replaced mainly social policy approaches to unemployment. By deliberately begging the question of *Continental welfare inertia*, this contribution focuses on the *adaptive capacity* of Europe's Bismarckian welfare states to the challenges of economic internationalization and post-industrial differentiation, and permanent austerity in the shadow of intensified European (economic) integration.

The argument is constructed as follows. First, Section 2 renders an inventory of comparative employment performance so as to highlight the particular weaknesses of the Bismarck-type welfare regime, together with its recent improvements, in comparison to other European welfare state families. Next, section 3 turns a diachronic qualitative analysis of the sequence and scope of employment friendly reforms in different policy areas within and across different Bismarckian welfare systems. This overview will reveal how much the 1990s and early 2000s has been an epoch of intense policy change in the make-up of Europe's Bismarckian welfare states. To say that the Continental welfare state has been far from sclerotic is not to say that they are now fit for the 21st century. In conclusion, Section 4 highlights, by employing a life course perspective, what we think is the unfinished social reform agenda for most Continental welfare states today.

12.2 The Continental Employment Dilemma

Employment is the most important measure for judging the sustainability of the Continental welfare state and the success of social and economic policy reform. The reason for this is simple: benefits and social services have to be paid by the taxes and social security contributions from those in work. The more working people there are, the broader this funding base is. In the event of long-term unemployment, incapacity to work and early retirement, spending on social security goes up while at the same time revenues fall. From a sociological perspective, having a job also benefits people by giving them enhanced opportunities for self-actualization and self-esteem. Participating in the labor market today is the most important form of social interaction and, as such, is an indispensable element in achieving social cohesion.

The response of the Continental and Mediterranean welfare states to the process of economic restructuring in the 1970s and 1980s, but also the policy applied by the transition countries in the early 1990s was aimed at keeping open unemployment low by limiting labor supply. Most Continental welfare states began using disability pensions, early retirement and long-term unemployment schemes to remove older and less productive workers from the labor market. Luring people out of the labor market by facilitating early retirement, increasing benefits for the long-term unemployed, lifting the obligation of job search for older workers, discouraging mothers from job search, favoring long periods of leave, easing the access to disability pensions and reducing working hours, all contributed to the characteristically Continental 'welfare without work' policy strategy that became popular in the 1980s and for most of the 1990s (Esping-Andersen 1996a). Growing demands on social security led to burgeoning costs to be borne by the labor market. From the middle of the 1980s onwards, employers in Continental welfare states increasingly began using labor-saving technology and shedding less productive employees via the social security system. This turned the Continental productivity squeeze into an inactivity trap. A vicious cycle arose of high gross wage costs, low net wages, the exit of less productive workers and rising social costs, creating a spiral of falling employment and rising economic inactivity. This also undermined the financial basis of the social security system. In addition, strict employment regulation, including minimum wages and hiring and firing restrictions, protected the insiders in key industries, while harming the participation of outsiders, youngsters, women, older workers, low-skill groups and ethnic minorities (Hemerijck, van Kersbergen and Manow 2000).

From the 1990s onward the policy of labor supply reduction came to be brandished as a policy failure and, if continued uncorrected, as a threat to the survival of the welfare state. Towards the mid-1990s, the Continental or Bismarckian employment deficit triggered an important shift in the definition of the crisis of the Continental welfare state away from early exit adjustment strategies. Policy-makers came to realize that the low level of labor market participation was the Achilles heel of the Continental welfare state. This diagnosis initiated a series of reforms intended to overcome male-breadwinner policy provisions and to correct for past early exit policy mistakes in many areas of social and economic regulation, including collective bargaining, social security, labor market policy and regulation, pensions and social services, including health and education. To be sure, at times these reforms met with stiff resistance from the social partners, especially the trade unions, defending their privileged position in Bismarckian social insurance administration with its tradition of associational self-regulation by the social partners, as a corollary of the payroll financing of the Continental welfare state.

In part as a result of these reforms, since the mid-1990s, there has been a significant increase in employment across virtually all mature European welfare states over the last decade (Eichhorst and Hemerijck 2008). Figure 12.1 shows the employment/population ratios among people in the working age population (15-64 years).[1] What is striking is, first, the long-term increase in employment in most countries and, second, some persistent differences in the overall share of people in gainful employment across countries and families of welfare states. We can see substantial gains over the last decade, in particular in traditional low and medium employment

Figure 12.1   Employment/working-age population ratios 1997 and 2007

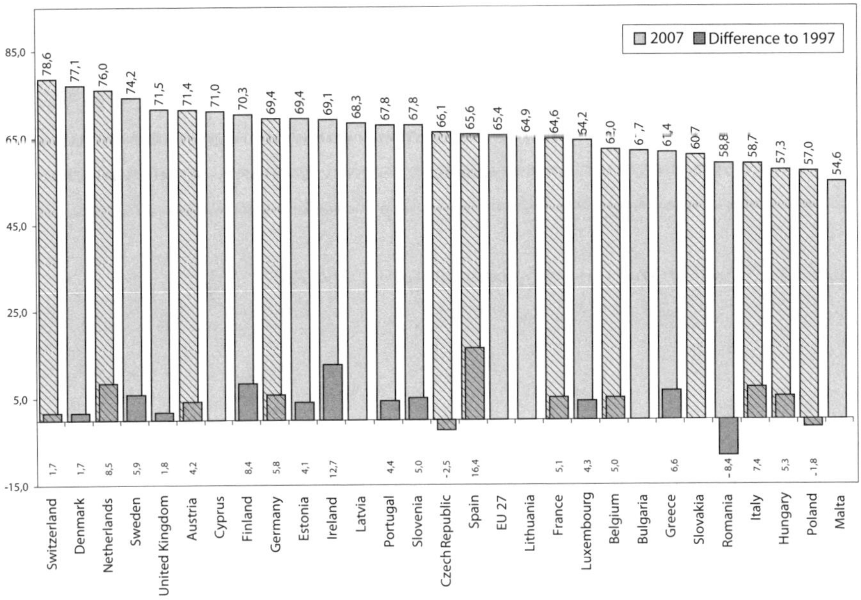

Source: Eurostat

countries. Except for three transition countries, all Bismarckian welfare states experienced job growth. It was most pronounced in the Netherlands and Spain, but also Austria, France, Belgium, Italy and Hungary saw notable increases in the employment/population ratio so that employment rates across Europe converged to a certain extent. The Bismarckian cluster can no longer be described as a group of countries with a low employment level. In fact, Switzerland and the Netherlands join Sweden and Denmark as the group with the highest employment rates whereas Austria, the Czech Republic and Germany are above the EU-27 average and France, Belgium, Italy and Hungary approached this value considerably.

Mirroring the improvement in employment performance, standardized unemployment rates declined in most European countries over the last decade as figure 12.2 shows. Unemployment continued to decline in terms of annual data in 2008, but due to the current crisis the most recent months saw some increase in unemployment again. However, the employment performance is still much better than some years ago. What is most remarkable is the strong decline in unemployment in some Southern and Continental European countries such as Spain, France and Italy while Slovakia and Poland still suffer the highest unemployment rates in the EU. The Netherlands, Switzerland, and Austria, continue to have very low levels of unemployment. In contrast to the 1970s and 1980s, however, decreases of open unemployment are no longer associated with declines of employment and inflows into inactivity, but mirror positive employment dynamics. Nevertheless, open unemployment is still the highest in some Bismarckian countries such as Slovakia, Poland, Germany, Spain and France.

Figure 12.2   Standardized unemployment rates, 1997 and 2007

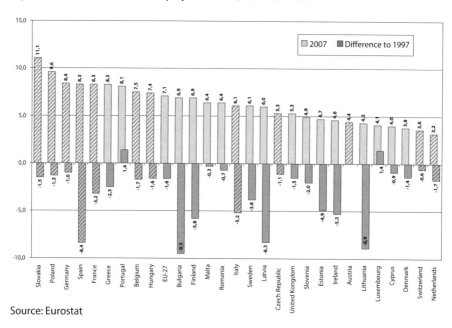

Source: Eurostat

It was not until the second half of the 1990s that there was a limited increase in the employment rate in the Mediterranean welfare states, which, in fact, have seen some of the biggest employment gains in the EU over the last decade. The Netherlands occupies a special place comparatively because it was the first Continental welfare state with a historically low female employment rate to improve its performance, trending towards Scandinavian levels. In the age group aged 25-54 years (*prime age*), a strong convergence can be observed since the middle of the 1990s (figure 12.3). Over the last decade we can observe substantial recovery in the Scandinavian countries after the crisis in the early 1990s, but also considerable improvement in the Netherlands, Spain and Italy.

Figure 12.3 Prime age employment rate, both sexes (25-54), 1997 and 2007

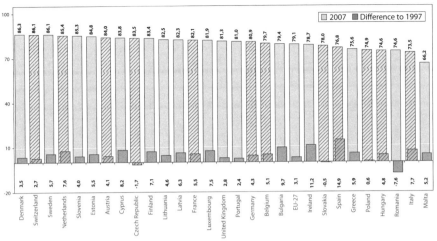

Source: Eurostat

There is much more regime-specific variation regarding the employment rates of older workers, women and the low-skilled. Differences in the extent to which these three groups are integrated into the labor market basically determine differences in the overall employment rate. With respect to the 55-64 age cohort (see figure 12.4), one can clearly identify some legacy of early retirement policies in Continental and southern welfare states, but also in the transition countries. The Continental and Mediterranean welfare states and most of the new EU member states saw a dramatic fall of more than 30 percent in the employment rate of older workers from the 1980s due to early retirement, particularly among men. Since the end of the 1990s, the employment rate among older workers has been increasing strongly in Finland, but also in some Continental welfare states, with the Netherlands taking the lead. Switzerland, which did not use early retirement massively, is close to Sweden in this dimension. Other Bismarckian countries are reversing historically low employment levels of older workers. Germany and the Netherlands are now above the 50 percent EU target employment rate for older workers while the Czech Republic and Spain are approaching this value. Austria, France, the Slovak Republic, Belgium, Italy and Hungary have also improved while Poland is lagging behind with less than 30 percent.

Figure 12.4 Employment rates of older workers (55-64), 1997 and 2007

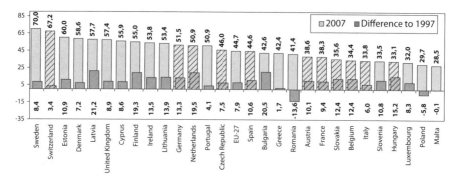

Source: Eurostat

Looking at gender, we see some cross-country convergence in the employment rate of men between 70 and 80 percent with Switzerland and the Netherlands at the top. Male employment grew slightly in most EU countries. Again, there is a structural gap in male employment in three of the Visegrad countries and the western Bismarckian countries which relied most on early retirement (Belgium, France and Italy).

Figure 12.5 Employment rate of men, 1997 and 2007

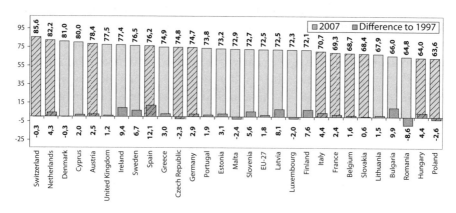

Source: Eurostat

The labor market entry of women is the most striking recent development in European welfare states (see figure 12.6). In the early 1970s, the Netherlands had the lowest female employment rate in the OECD, at 29 percent. This was lower than the figures in Ireland, Greece, Spain and Italy, where the rates were just above 30 percent. Since then the employment rate of women has grown strongly across all EU member states except for some of the transformation countries. From 1997 until 2007, the rate in the Netherlands has increased by more than 12 percentage points to almost 70 percent and even stronger in Ireland and Spain, but Germany, France, Belgium and other Bismarckian countries also experienced increases between 5 and 9 percentage points so that female employment rates in Austria and Germany are also around 64 percent nowadays while France reaches 60 percent. The female employment rate in the Netherlands is currently still lower than in the Scandinavian welfare states and Switzerland, but here as elsewhere younger cohorts are undergoing a notable convergence in the direction of stronger labor force participation. For younger cohorts, female employment in Southern and Continental Europe is rapidly catching up to Northern European averages.

Figure 12.6 Female employment, 1997 and 2007

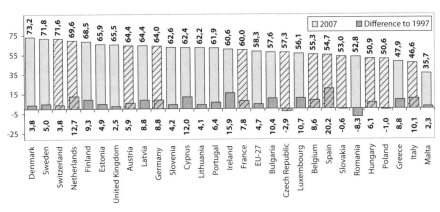

Source: Eurostat

In the Continental welfare states, the ability to work part-time has created an important means of entry to the labor market for women, in particular in the Netherlands. In countries with a long-standing tradition of female employment, such as the Scandinavian countries, part-time employment is less common. This means that the significant increases in female employment counted per heads is related to persistent, but decreasing gaps in fulltime equivalent employment between the sexes as figure 12.7 shows. This gap is smaller than 10 or 15 percentage points in the Scandinavian countries and some of the new EU member states while the difference between men and women in terms of fulltime equivalents is larger than 20 percentage points in Belgium, Germany and Austria and between 27 and 29 percentage points in Spain, Italy and the Netherlands.

Figure 12.7   Gap in fulltime equivalent employment rates between men and women, 2000 and 2007

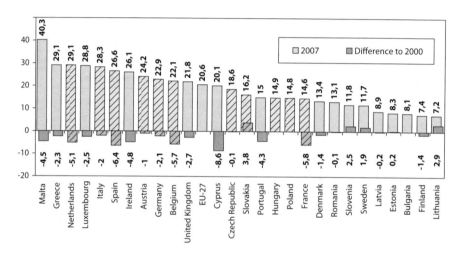

Source: Eurostat

Employment rates by skill levels differ mostly for the labor force with less than upper secondary schooling or vocational training, less so for the high-skilled. Figure 12.8 shows marked differences in low-skill employment across countries and families of welfare states. The Netherlands, Switzerland and – notably – Spain are among the countries with the highest low-skilled employment rate. Particular deficits are found in the new member states, but also in some Continental European countries such as France, Italy, Germany and Belgium where only about half of the low skilled or even less are integrated into the labor market. Given the strong pressures of technological progress and globalization it is interesting to see that there is no general decline in the employment rates of the low-skilled.

Figure 12.8   Employment rates of the low-skilled, 1997 and 2007

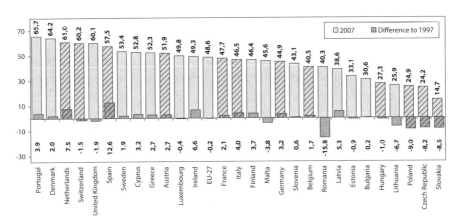

Source: Eurostat

Summarizing the overview on employment performance, we can see, first and foremost, a significant improvement in employment performance and a significant decline in unemployment across most Bismarckian welfare systems over the last 10 years. However, in terms of labor market performance, the Bismarckian countries do not form a consistent cluster. While Switzerland has always had a good labor market record and is now joined by the Netherlands, the other Continental European countries as well as the Mediterranean welfare states caught up significantly although there is still some gap in comparison to the Scandinavian and the Anglo-Saxon countries with respect to most of the labor market parameters.

12.3   Reconciling Welfare with Work: A Sequence of Intense Reforms

As this book shows, Bismarckian welfare states are not what they used to be – and they are now in a fundamentally different shape than in the late 1990s when they were described as 'frozen landscapes'. The Bismarckian countries have undergone a sequence of reforms that started in the 1970s which led to more institutional and structural changes in the following decades. Hence, the overall improvement in employment performance is related to groundbreaking social policy changes which were enacted in the majority of the European welfare states. Since the late 1970s, consecutive changes in the world economy, European politics (most spectacularly the demise of communism in Eastern Europe), labor markets, and family structures, have disturbed the once sovereign and stable social and economic policy repertoires. As a consequence, all developed welfare states of the European Union have been recasting the basic policy mix upon which their national systems of social protection were built after 1945. Below we render a stylized sketch of the employment-related reform agendas across Bismarckian welfare states since the 1970s by policy area and country cluster. If we interpret the welfare state more broadly than social protection narrowly understood, it is possible to paint a broad, cumulatively transformative process of policy change across the majority of Continental welfare states in a number of intimately related policy areas so that in the end a turn towards employment-friendly reforms can be identified (Eichhorst and Hemerijck 2008).

With some stylization of national reform trajectories, we can identify four basic stages of welfare state and labor market reform in Bismarckian countries (see the introductory chapter by Palier):
1) the phase before retrenchment from the mid-1970s onwards until the late 1980s;
2) a first wave of retrenchment in the early 1990s;
3) more far-reaching institutional reforms in the second half of the 1990s;
4) a second wave of more path-breaking changes in the 2000s.

Of course, not all national reform trajectories fit perfectly in these four phases, but overall the broad transformation of Bismarckian welfare states can be analyzed in terms of a stepwise and increasingly fundamental, i.e. progressive modification of established social and labor market policies, in order to reconcile welfare and work and overcome the 'welfare without work' syndrome.

The First Phase: The Good, Old Recipe of Labor Shedding

The first stage of transforming Bismarckian welfare states set in with the economic shocks of the mid-1970s. The macroeconomic downturn in the aftermath of the steep increase in oil prices pushed unemployment to levels unknown in the after-war period in most European countries.

To counter what was first perceived as a cyclical crisis, most Bismarckian welfare states used unemployment benefits as an automatic stabilizer and implemented some Keynesian policies basically by allowing the public and the social budget to run into deficits. As part of the social approach to unemployment and to support the victims of the economic crisis, most Bismarckian countries opened up exit routes from the labor market, actually in particular for workers made redundant in manufacturing which was most severely hit by adverse economic conditions. In the labor market, in the 1970s, most Bismarckian welfare states started using the social security system to remove older and less productive workers from the labor market, through disability pensions, early retirement, and long-term unemployment schemes. Core groups of the Bismarckian welfare state and employment model, i.e. male breadwinners in standard employment relationships, got privileged access to more generous benefits which were seen as a short-time stabilization tool in order to prevent losses in human capital first but eventually turned into pathways to long-term inactivity. Though producing short-term gains, and backed by unions as a solution to unemployment among young people, this strategy would eventually entail considerable costs in terms of job creation and fiscal pressure on the welfare state. Generous early retirement or disability benefits, but also heavy reliance on regular unemployment benefits and active labor market policy schemes, in turn, had medium-run consequences in terms of higher social insurance contribution rates for both employers and employees. But at that point in time policy-makers preferred increasing contribution rates to cutting social insurance benefits although there were some marginal attempts at budgetary consolidation such as the introduction of higher user fees in health care and smaller changes in unemployment benefits. Most notably, however, in particular the southern countries Spain (Guillén, this volume) and Italy (Jessoula and Alti, this volume) implemented some consolidation programs in pension and disability already in the 1980s ahead of other Bismarckian countries.

Overall, the welfare state arrangement itself was hardly changed in the mature Bismarckian systems where there was tendency to apply 'good old recipes'. Regarding employment, this was later seen as the root cause of the Bismarckian 'welfare without work' syndrome associated with high non-wage labor costs and a heavy reliance on non-employment benefits. In terms of welfare state change, initial responses to the crisis of the 1970s can be seen as a routine relying on existing benefit schemes and labor market policies. Labor shedding indicated a regime consistent reaction to the economic shocks of the 1970s. The policy response came from within the

Bismarckian regime. Outside alternatives, following the Scandinavian activation or Anglo-Saxon retrenchment, were not yet taken seriously. Labor supply reduction was seen as the only way to cope with rising unemployment. The regime was unchanged. To revive the Bismarckian regime, adherence to labor supply reduction made sense to the relevant policy actors.

While the mature welfare states of that period have later been described as a 'frozen' welfare states landscape, there were some notable institutional changes – not only with respect to increasing the generosity of existing benefits but also in terms of some steps to reinforce minimum income protection. This can be illustrated by the Belgian minimum income policies (see Hemerijck and Marx, this volume), but also by the introduction of the French RMI in 1988 (see Palier, chapter 3 in this volume) and the more universal access to health care (see Italy, Spain and France) as well as to family benefits and the creation of mandatory unemployment insurance in Switzerland as late as in 1984 (Häusermann, this volume). These reforms were the first, albeit partial steps to establish a general minimum support framework, which had been absent in Bismarckian welfare states thus far. Hence, in many Bismarckian countries, the phase of defensive adjustment via passive social policies was also a phase of expansion of more universal social policy coverage – in particular in those countries with less mature policy arrangements and in those areas and for those target groups typically neglected in a Bismarckian setting. This was often associated with a purification of social insurance in terms of a more direct link between contributions and benefits and a removal of redistributional elements in social insurance. This gradual shift towards tax-funded social policies gained in importance over the years to come.

While employment security for labor market insiders remained unchanged, most Bismarckian countries started liberalizing the use of more flexible jobs in the 1980s in order to allow for some additional job creation without endangering the core of the labor market. Fixed-term jobs, but also part-time employment became an increasingly prominent secondary segment in otherwise rather rigid labor markets (see the Spanish, the French or the Dutch experience). The Netherlands, however, was the first to adopt a more strategic approach to welfare state restructuring and employment creation with the renewal of corporatist negotiations in the shadow of hierarchy. In fact, the Netherlands combined wage restraint, cuts in social benefits and first steps towards activation with an expansion of flexible jobs, in particular part-time work while tolerating access to disability benefits as the Dutch exit route from the labor market (Hemerijck and Marx, this volume).

The passive labor shedding approach to unemployment led to a situation of low employment and increasing non-wage labor costs in Bismarckian welfare states.

Second Phase: Cost Containment and Retrenchment in the Name of Competitiveness and Job Creation

A first wave of more stringent retrenchment began in the 1990s in order to stabilize public budgets, limit public debts and improve international competitiveness in a situation of accelerated international and European integration. Employers in Bismarckian countries increasingly complained about high non-wage labor costs which hampered their competitive position on world markets. Therefore, cost containment on the side of social insurance contributions, which had been increased considerably in the past, and eventually welfare state retrenchment became high political priorities. However, it was only as a result of the constraints imposed by the Maastricht criteria that, in most Bismarckian countries, a change occurred in the policies implemented: instead of increasing social contributions, governments started to try to reduce the level of social benefits. The welfare state was not seen as a beneficial arrangement to help the victims of economic restructuring anymore, but was increasingly perceived as a potential source of problems and disincentives. To consolidate the social policy budget, most Bismarckian countries increased the contributive character of social insurance benefits while giving a larger role to tax-funding of welfare state provisions, in particular non-contributory benefits, i.e. universal and means-tested assistance schemes, but also cross-subsidizing social insurance. The stronger differentiation between insurance and assistance also meant a clearer dualization of welfare state programs. At the same time, however, stronger minimum income elements addressed new social risks such as poverty and exclusion that resulted from insufficient access to insurance benefits. Slowly but surely mature Bismarckian welfare systems started to converge on the mixed Dutch welfare system, combining Beveridgean social assistance and minimum state pensions with more traditional vestiges of Bismarckian social insurance for core workers.

The attempt to re-establish the Bismarckian regime through labor supply reduction created tensions within the regime when long-term inactivity turned out to be permanent. Not only were the labor shedding strategies ineffective in mitigating the economic downturn; they almost killed the Bismarckian welfare state patient. The burden of labor shedding became too great to bear in the context of the mid-1990s. The Continental model was saved, but the conditions that had sustained it before the onslaught of the 1980s recession no longer existed. The persistent 'welfare without work' syndrome generated a complex reform agenda aimed at rationalizing spending by curtailing pension commitments and 'passive' benefits, improving family policy, introducing 'active' incentives into short-term cash benefits, reforming labor markets to overcome insider/outsider cleavages, and reducing the incidence of social charges. These systems, though, are especially 'veto-heavy' and any reform must be negotiated with or around entrenched vested interests. The spur to reform in this group was the deep recession of European economies in the early 1990s, which produced a sharp rise in unemployment and ballooning public debt. From the early 1990s on, a new consensus on employment promotion spread across these countries, though the extent of reform and success in promoting new employment creation has varied.

But at the same time many Bismarckian countries continued with early retirement and disability schemes as major schemes to reduce labor supply (see the Austrian experience, Obinger and Tálos, this volume), whereas others tackled the issue of inactivity by restricting access to non-employment benefits. In the Netherlands, from 1994 onwards, the government, committed to a 'jobs, jobs and more jobs' strategy, sought greater efficiencies in social security, including partial re-privatization of social risks, managed liberalization of administration, reducing social partner involvement, and introduced and intensified activation obligations for the long-term unemployed.

Some countries such as Italy were the first to start building a second pillar in pensions while consolidating the public first pillar pension regime (Amato and Dini reforms). Parallel to this, Bismarckian countries such as France or Switzerland streamlined the unemployment benefit system, further 'purified' the insurance schemes while strengthening assistance and minimum income protection. Activation policies were expanded and started to limit the realm of unconditional receipt of unemployment benefits more effectively. The tax share in social policy was increased to stabilize or reduce the burden of non-wage labor costs (see the CSG in France). In contrast to more ambitious reform sequences, post-unification Germany expanded its established repertoire of rising social insurance contributions to fund heavy spending on passive non-employment benefits and labor market policies to accommodate the job losses in Eastern Germany in a 'smooth' and 'social' way (Hinrichs, this volume). This, however, resulted in stronger concerns regarding the fiscal sustainability of the welfare state and international competitiveness.

In terms of the political economy, the 1990s saw a major revival of negotiated welfare state reform via social pacts (see the Netherlands, Austria, but also Spain and Italy) and stronger state intervention, e.g. by introducing a parliamentary vote on the social budget (France). Reform capacities of Bismarckian welfare states were improved by a wave of successful tripartite agreements and a stronger role of governments. Social partnership also contributed to reforms narrowing the divide in labor market regulation and job protection between permanent and temporary employees after a period of strong growth in the flexible segment of the labor market (see in particular the reform sequence in Spain in the mid-1990s).

Third Phase: Mobilizing the Labor Force

The reforms of the early 1990s paved the way for institutional change beyond retrenchment. In an increasingly globalized and Europeanized economic context, welfare systems were partly seen as a cause for crisis in terms of social exclusion brought about by work disincentives and higher unemployment driven by structural weaknesses such as rigid labor market regulation and a heavy burden of taxes, and even worse, social insurance contributions. Corporatist settings were seen as somewhat detrimental to more far-reaching labor market and welfare state reforms. Building upon earlier reforms, new universal or targeted benefits beyond Bismarckian social insurance became increasingly important. The same held for the share of taxes in welfare state funding and state-driven governance as opposed to administration by the social partners. This was also associated with new modes of governance including a more prominent role of private providers of public/private partnership. This broader process of 'defrosting' spread across Bismarckian welfare states.

It is not an easy task to change policy direction, as policy actors are locked into the short-term bargains of dominant policy legacies. They need to be convinced, often by dramatic and highly visible events, that the regime has to change. Central to the 'defrosting' of the Bismarckian welfare system was a change in the problem definition of the crisis of the Bismarckian welfare state in the late 1990s, away from fighting unemployment through early exit. Instead, the Scandinavian preoccupation with maximizing the rate of labor force participation became the number one priority. The commitment to high levels of employment, 'jobs, jobs and more jobs', became the core social and economic policy objective of the Dutch governments led by Wim Kok in the 1990s.

Regarding activation, Germany, in contrast to early stages of the reform trajectory, shifted from a passive to a more active social policy by phasing out early retirement and increasing the individual's burden of proof with respect to suitable job offers, withdrawing human capital safeguard provisions as well as stabilizing non-wage labor costs by way of higher tax funding, e.g. green taxes. In many Bismarckian countries, earlier reforms towards the activation of benefit recipients and the liberalization of flexible jobs continued, but also triggered some more restrictive counter action (see France or Germany). To foster efficiency in labor market policies, public employment service monopolies were removed (e.g. in Germany or Italy) to allow for private agencies to enter this market. In reaction to the purification of contributory social insurance and the limitations to social insurance coverage, countries such as France strengthened minimal social guarantees by creating non-contributory means-tested benefits for income (RMI) and health (CMU) protection. The Netherlands probably pursued the most ambitious strategy to raise labor force participation in a low unemployment situation. This involved tackling the disability issue by tightening access to benefits, as well as using new modes of governance. In order to activate social assistance claimants a contractual approach and stronger municipal responsibility in terms of measures and resources was implemented. Performance-oriented management was also a core element of Swiss activation policies implemented after 1995. In the late 1990s, the Netherlands also managed to negotiate better employment protection for flexible jobs in exchange for some changes in dismissal protection for employees on permanent contracts ('flexicurity' legislation).

Fourth Phase: A more Fundamental Transformation towards Employment-Friendly Social Protection

Given the increasingly intensive reform dynamics spreading across countries and policy areas, the fourth phase of reforms in the 2000s can be described as path-breaking change recalibrating the welfare state to bring it in line with the reformed labor market institutions in the Bismarckian countries. By layering, i.e. adding non-traditional and non-Bismarckian elements to established arrangements of social and labor market policies, the overall character of the institutional edifice was modified and eventually allowed for more transformative reforms. Given European and global economic integration as well as the relevance of new social risks, Bismarckian countries changed their basic institutional settings and are fundamentally different from the arrangements found in the 1970s. This was not a swift and coherent change but rather the result of long and more or less protracted sequences of partial reforms. At least in some crucial situations some of the Bismarckian countries could rely on negotiated and more strategic institutional reforms while others mostly started reforming the margins of the labor market and the welfare state so that new provisions could grow in importance and pave the way for more far-reaching reforms affecting core elements.

The 2000s were characterized by increasingly generalized activation policies and the prominent role of employment incentives and employment-friendly benefits as stronger work incentives have become a major policy orientation since the late 1990s in countries which used to pursue a social approach to unemployment. As shown by Palier (2006), the growth of minimum income protection as well as the establishment of second, occupational or third, private pillars in the pension system imply a certain dualization of social protection between social insurance and social assistance programs and between public and private regimes. Both the subsidization of private social policies and the growing importance of means-tested minimum provisions bring about a higher share of tax-funding in Bismarckian welfare states. The Bismarckian regime entered a phase of more fundamental change.

Reforms in the most recent phase were not heavily driven by the momentum of EMU but rather followed from earlier steps towards flexibility and activation. The major objective of social security now changed from passive compensation of social risks to setting individual behavioral incentives for both employers and benefit claimants to achieve labor market integration: out-of work benefits were complemented by in-work benefits, human capital safeguard clauses in activation were replaced by strict suitability criteria. Activation was dominated for some years at least by a work-first orientation, but more recently preventative social investment in human capital through early childhood education, schooling, training and lifelong learning moved up the public policy agenda (especially in Spain, Switzerland or Germany). However, activation policies not only stressed labor market (re)integration of virtually all working-age benefit recipients but also meant a generalization of minimum income support for the population (Eichhorst and Konle-Seidl 2008). Exit routes such as disability and early retirement are being closed in those Bismarckian countries that had continued those schemes over the 1990s (see the Netherlands or Austria), whereas Belgium has been more reluctant when it comes to curtailing early retirement and activating unemployment benefits.

Activation is now a general objective implying intensified active labor market policy and new modes of governance such as target-oriented management of public agencies, which have become more autonomous from social partner influence over time, and contractual relationships between the state and the individual as well as between government and private providers (see e.g. in the Netherlands, Switzerland or Austria). This, in fact, is associated with a dual social protection model, combining Bismarckian social insurance, which is still in place for core workers, with Beveridgean minimum income protection systems. Both Belgium and France also targeted stricter activation at recipients of minimum income support and implemented stronger in-work benefits for low-wage earners (e.g. the French *'prime pour l'emploi'*) or their employers via exemptions from social insurance contributions. With the 2005 Hartz IV reform, Germany implemented a similar general assistance scheme for all working-age inactives who were capable of working by merging former unemployment assistance and social assistance. This was complemented with tight suitability criteria and sanctioning provisions so that strong activation requirements concerned all long-term unemployed. Germany shifted from a passive welfare state accommodating economic restructuring through long-term benefit receipts to one of the most ambitious and universal activation regimes. However, most countries aim at a more unified mode of governance and administrative streamlining of benefit payments, activation and service provision for all jobseekers, in particular the long-term unemployed. This leads to new cooperation arrangements or mergers between municipal welfare offices, public employment services and/or unemployment insurance (see the German ARGE for long-term unemployed or the most recent French *'pôle emploi'* bringing together unemployment insurance and public labor market policies).

Parallel to further benefit recalibration in public pension schemes and the introduction of minimum pension provisions, a new wave of pension reforms introduced or strengthened employer-based supplementary pensions and the fully-funded, private, but subsidized pillar of old-age pension, e.g. the Riester reform in Germany or PERP and PERCO in France. A similar objective lies behind the new severance pay funds in Austria (*'Abfertigung neu'*). Finally, the growing role of flexible employment paved the way to further flexicurity legislation in highly regulated labor markets such as Spain, while in other countries such as Germany temporary work agencies, self-employment and also part-time jobs provide for alternative flexibility channels so that dismissal protection is less under pressure than a decade ago. The Visegrad countries, which had implemented passive social policies to cope with the transition crisis in the 1990s – similar to what the other Bismarckian countries had done in the 1970s and 1980s – embarked on a trend towards retrenchment, recalibration and activation in the current decade (Cerami, this volume).

12.4 An Unfinished Social Reform Agenda for Bismarckian Countries

Neither the doomsday scenario of the demise of the Bismarckian welfare state, predicted by mainstream economists in the early 1990s, nor the prevailing image of a 'frozen welfare status quo' can be corroborated by the welfare reform experience highlighted above. Over the past two decades, as the above inventory of reforms shows, many European welfare states have – with varying degrees of success – taken measures in order to redirect economic and social restructuring by pushing through adjustments in macroeconomic policy, industrial relations, taxation, social security, labor market policy, employment protection legislation, pensions and social services and welfare financing. The result has been a highly dynamic process of self-transformation of the Bismarckian welfare family (Hemerijck 2002), marked not by half-hearted retrenchment efforts but by more comprehensive trajectories of 'recalibration', ranging from redesigning welfare programs to the elaboration of new principles of social justice (Ferrera, Hemerijck and Rhodes 2000; Ferrera and Hemerijck 2003; Pierson 2001a). It is no exaggeration to say that Continental welfare states are in the midst of a general paradigmatic shift away from systems geared to income and status maintenance towards more universal, but activating and employment-friendly as well as gender-neutral welfare systems. Many reforms were unpopular, but a fair amount occurred with the consent of opposition parties, trade unions, and employer organizations. A core feature, however, is the sequential character of reforms. More far-reaching institutional changes were facilitated by early reforms, initially often of minor character or at the margins of the labor market or the welfare state, but later to be generalized as a consequence of institutional layering (Palier 2005b; Bonoli and Palier 2007).

What stands out in the Bismarckian reform momentum of recent times is the redefinition of the employment problem away from managing unemployment towards the promotion of employment, on the basis of activation, active ageing/avoidance of early retirement, part-time work, lifelong learning, parental leave, gender mainstreaming, flexicurity, balancing flexibility with security, and reconciling work and family life. Moreover, Bismarckian welfare states are in the process of moving away from the breadwinner/caregiver model, under which mothers are expected to stay at home with children, to a model of 'employment for all', under which mothers are expected to enter the labor force. This transition, which Ann Orloff captures in terms of the 'farewell to maternalism', is not merely the product of changing gender values (normative recalibration), it is also part of a more deliberate strategy of policy-makers to attract mothers in the face of population ageing into the work force through activation programs, tax subsidies, part-time employment regulation, and the expansion of family services (Orloff 2006).

Welfare reform in Bismarckian systems remains, as we have exemplified above, extremely difficult, but surely not entirely inconceivable. Path-breaking reforms, such as the Dutch reforms of the 1990s and Hartz reforms in Germany, brought policy reformers to expose the drawbacks of the widely popular welfare status quo, together with the old objectives, purpose and principles standing social policies were based on. By framing reform resistance as problematic, policy reformers offended entrenched policy stakeholders and organized interests in all Bismarckian states. This necessarily implied that reform oriented policy-makers have had to make consistent attempts to legitimize new policies and their underlying (new) normative principles. Communicating will-power to reform, while propagating fair solutions, has proved to be imperative to changing prevailing policy repertoires. In the Bismarckian institutional context, there is an inherent tension here between, on the one hand, exposing stakeholders abuse of their vested interest positions, and, on the other hand, to appeal to stakeholders to rethink reform resistance in order to forge a more productive political and societal consensus. However, structural change in Bismarckian countries also means a recalibration of the relationship between government, employers and trade unions – some of the most important reforms were implemented by the social partners in the government's 'shadow of hierarchy' (Scharpf 1997a) or brought about a structural weakening of social partnership in some countries, e.g. Germany or France, whereas in others such as the Netherlands, Switzerland or Austria, tripartite dialogue was revived and proved capable of adjusting to a new economic and societal environment (See Ebbinghaus, this volume). Moreover, strong and operative social partnership seems to be associated with less severe dualization of labor markets and smoother adjustment.

In recent years, the normative focus of social policy hereby shifts from *ex post* social insurance compensation towards preventive or *ex ante* employability, hinging on the deployment of resources to improve and equalize citizens' individual abilities to compete in the knowledge economy. In order to connect social policy more fully with a more dynamic economy and society, citizens have to be endowed with capabilities, through active policies that intervene early in the life cycle rather than later with more expensive passive and reactive policies (Esping-Andersen et al. 2002). At the heart of the new narrative lies a reorientation in social citizenship, away from freedom from want towards freedom to act, prioritizing high levels of employment for both men and women as the key policy objective, while combining elements of flexibility and security, under the proviso of accommodating work and family life and a guaranteed rich social minimum serving citizens to pursue fuller and more satisfying lives (Diamond 2006). In the shadow of intensified economic internationalization and post-industrial societal change, a relative shift from the social protection function of the welfare state to more of an emphasis on the social promotion function of the welfare state seems imperative. The jury is still undecided whether the Continental welfare systems will intensify the momentum with a greater emphasis on social investments. The differences in the allocation of public resources to either investment policies (such as education and training) or to compensating policies such as social benefits and passive and active labor market policies are most evident in figure 12.9

Figure 12.9   Public social expenditure and spending on education as percentage of GDP, 2005

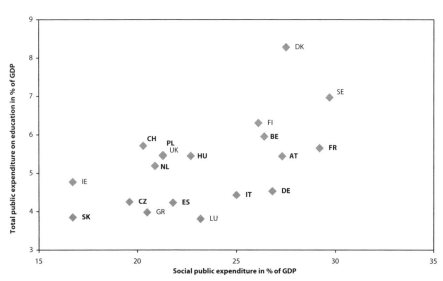

Source: OECD

which shows public spending on education and social expenditure combined in percentage of GPD in 2005. While the overall association between both areas of public spending is positive in the Scandinavian ones, also some Bismarckian countries like Belgium and France now combine above-average spending on social policies with above-average spending on education. Germany and Italy, in contrast, spend a lot on social purposes but are relatively stingy on educational expenditure.

Following several years of sound economic growth and strong employment expansion, European welfare states now face a dramatic economic downturn, for the first time since the launch of the Lisbon strategy in 2000. A major stress test for the Continental welfare state lies ahead. As the financial crisis deepens and spills over into rising unemployment and social duress, the need for resilient employment and social policy is greater than ever. This precarious juncture creates a number of policy temptations. There is the obvious temptation of completely abandoning fiscal discipline to save jobs and maintain, as much as possible, the welfare status quo. Then there is the short-sighted seduction of retrenching current welfare commitments to foster financial and budgetary stability. Equally ineffective is the still alluring strategy to fight unemployment through reducing labor supply through early retirement, for which all Bismarckian welfare systems fell in the 1980s and 1990s. Worse still is the nationalist and protectionist temptation that proved so disastrous in the 1930s. There is a real danger of adopting incoherent policy combinations that may actually deepen the economic downturn, worsening job losses, reducing state revenue, eroding pensions, and widening the gap between rich and poor. Historical mistakes, like deflationary contraction of the 1930s, and Continental labor supply reduction of the 1980s and 1990s, should surely be avoided. In these uncertain times, we must not lose sight of the overall aim of creating employment-friendly, fair and efficient, welfare systems. Short- to medium-term macroeconomic measures are necessary to respond to immediate needs, but such measures should be consistent with the ongoing recalibration efforts to prepare domestic welfare state and EU social policy for the challenges of the 21st century. There are seven policy priorities at stake:

Let Automatic Stabilizers Work
So as to prevent a global economic abyss, it is necessary to let automatic stabilizers work, to protect citizens from the harshest effects of rising unemployment, while at the same time serving to safeguard economic demand. In the longer run, confidence in the economy relies on sound

public finances. Today we can observe, in sharp contrast to the Great Depression, how a fierce anti-deflationary macroeconomic policy response has rapidly come to fruition in the OECD area. There is clear policy consensus that a Keynesian crisis should be met by an expansionary policy of anti-cyclical macroeconomic management across Europe. This kind of European policy coherence was surely lacking in the 1970s and 1980s era of stagflation. Also the stability of the euro should not be underestimated, in that a common currency forestalls any policy of competitive devaluation. The internal market, enhanced in scope and strength by the addition to the EU of ten new member states from Central and Eastern Europe, surely puts a break on excessive protectionism. Last but not least, under the current financial crisis, it should not be forgotten that with social protection outlays averaging 28 percent of GDP in the EU, European social policies already act as important anti-cyclical automatic stabilizers. Rules and regulations in public finances, like the Stability and Growth Pact, define all government expenditures as consumption. Many of the policy proposals listed below concern social investments with a reasonable rate of long-term return for economy and society. We have to find a way to prioritize social investments without undermining the principles of sound public financing. Take social investments out of SGP rules could be a step in the right direction.

Strengthen Long-Term Attachment to the Labor Market

The overriding policy lesson in our advanced economies is that in the face of demographic ageing and in the light of a declining work force, nobody can be left inactive (for long). Impending redundancies should be mitigated by temporary and short-term unemployment benefits, combined with additional training measures. Any kind of job, be it short-term, part-time or subsidized, is better than no job at all to forestall unemployment hysteresis and deskilling. With ageing, labor markets will be tight in the long run. The interaction between economic performance and the welfare state is largely mediated through the labor market. The majority of Europe's Bismarck-type welfare states are confronted with a syndrome of labor market segmentation between 'insiders' and 'outsiders' (Schmid 2008). Relaxed hiring and firing legislation is best combined with generous social protection and active training and labor market policies to maximize employment. The ability to balance careers and family life is also crucial for removing gender biases in the labor market. While there is strong social security on the side of 'guaranteed' breadwinner workers with quasi-tenured jobs, most Bismarckian welfare states continue to provide only inadequate protection for vulnerable groups such as young labor market entrants, women, immigrants and older low-skilled workers. Most likely, labor markets will become ever more flexible. While the boundaries between being 'in' and 'out' of work have been blurred by increases in atypical work, low wages, subsidized jobs, and training programs, one job is no longer enough to keep low-income families out of poverty. Post-industrial job growth is highly biased in favor of high-skill jobs. However, increased labor market flexibility, together with the continuous rise in female employment will, in addition, also encourage the growth of a sizeable amount of low-skill and semi-skilled jobs in the social sector and in personal services. The Bismarckian policy challenge is how to mitigate the emergence of new forms of labor market segmentation through what could be called 'preventive employability', combining increases in flexibility in labor relations by way of relaxing dismissal protection, while generating a higher level of security for employees in flexible jobs. Flexible working conditions are often part and parcel of family-friendly employment policy provisions. There is a clear relation between the ratio of part-time jobs and female employment growth. But the ability of part-time employment to harmonize careers with family depends very much on employment regulation, whether part-time work is recognized as a regular job with basic social insurance participation, and whether it offers possibilities for career mobility.

Active Family Investment Strategy
The revolution in women's roles remains incomplete, raising new welfare problems that need to be addressed. Depressed female participation widens the gender gap and constrains economic growth. Moreover, also fertility hinges on effective gender equality. Generous parental leave, employment security, and, especially, high quality childcare, in turn, positively affect long-term productivity through higher fertility, higher female earnings, more tax revenue and better skills on the part of future generations, thus significantly mitigating the adverse effects of population ageing. The Bismarckian welfare states still have to adjust to the feminization of post-industrial labor markets. As inequalities widen, parents' ability to invest in their children's success is also becoming more unequal. Since life chances are so strongly determined by what happens in childhood, a comprehensive child investment strategy is imperative. Inaccessible childcare will provoke low fertility, low quality care is harmful to children, and low female employment raises child poverty. Increasing opportunities for women to be gainfully employed is a key step. But the concept of early

childhood development needs to *go beyond* the idea that childcare is necessary to allow parents to reconcile work and family life. Early childhood development is imperative to ensure that children will be lifelong learners and meaningful contributors to their societies.

Lifelong Human Capital Investment Push

In the new, knowledge-based economies, there is an urgent need to invest in human capital throughout the life of the individual. Youth with poor skills or inadequate schooling today will become tomorrow's precarious worker. Considering the looming demographic imbalances in Europe, we cannot afford large skill deficits and high school dropout rates, especially in the southern Continental welfare states (above 30 percent in Spain, almost 25 percent in the Netherlands and less than 15 percent in Denmark or Sweden). Strong social inheritance is not affordable in the long run. The architecture of education systems makes a real difference. High inequality and high educational differentiation reinforce cognitive poverty, early stratification, and social segregation. Social and employment policies that are aimed at increasing skills and developing the quality of human resources act as 'productive factors' in our economies. The revitalization of both the Irish and the Finnish economy is in part based on increased investments in education, preventing early departure from formal education and training, and facilitating the transition from school to work, in particular school leavers with low qualifications. Here the majority of Bismarckian welfare states continue to lag behind significantly.

Later and More Flexible Retirement

As life expectancy increases and health indices improve, it will be necessary to keep older workers in the market for longer. Sustainable pensions will be difficult to achieve unless we increase employment rates of older workers and raise the retirement age to at least 67 years. Two trends justify an adjustment in our thinking about retirement: a) the health status of each elderly cohort is better than that of the last; at present a man aged 65 can look forward to a further 10 healthy years. And, b) the gap between old age and education is rapidly narrowing, so that older people in the future will be much better placed than now to adapt in the coming decades with the aid of retraining and lifelong learning. The education gap between the old and the young will begin to disappear when the baby-boomers approach retirement. Beyond the development of multi-pillar, including both PAYG (pay-as-you-go) and funded schemes, in the area of *pension policy*, the challenge lies in how to allocate the additional expenditures that inevitably accompany population ageing (Myles 2002). Of crucial importance remains a general, revenue financed, first tier pension guarantee with a price index guarantee for the next generation of flexible labor market cohorts. Sustainable pensions will be difficult to achieve unless we raise employment rates of older workers and raise the retirement age to at least 67 years. Delaying retirement is both effective and equitable. It is efficient because it operates simultaneously on the nominator and denominator: more revenue intake and less spending at the same time. It is intergenerationally equitable because retirees and workers both sacrifice in equal proportions. We are all getting healthier and more educated with each age cohort. Flexible retirement and the introduction of incentives to postpone retirement could greatly alleviate the pension burden. Although there has been a slight increase of part-time work among the elderly, it has been shown that part-time work and participation rates among older people are positively related; there is still little systematic and comprehensive policy activity to enhance the variable opportunity set for older workers. If older workers remain employed ten years longer than is now typically the norm, household incomes will increase substantially. This means less poverty and need for social assistance as well as greater tax revenue.

Migration and Integration through Participation

Priority should be given to problems of participation and integration of migrant groups, whose rates of unemployment in the EU are, on average, twice that of nationals. Integration and immigration policy should have a central place in our discussion about the future of the Continental welfare state, something we failed to do in the past. In Europe's ethnically and culturally diverse societies, the welfare state faces a major challenge in ensuring that immigrants and their children do not fall behind. Economic exclusion and physical concentration (ghettoization) reinforces educational underperformance, excessive segregation and self-destructive spirals of marginalization.

Minimum Income Support

We cannot assume that the measures described above will remedy current and future welfare deficiencies. Hence, it is impossible to avoid some form of passive minimum income support. An unchecked rise in income inequality would worsen citizens' life chances and opportunities, result in lost productivity and more passive income support costs. It is therefore necessary to have an even more tightly woven safety net below the established welfare state for the truly needy to meet minimum standards of self-reliance. The key lesson of the Great Depression of the 1930s eventually ushered in Keynesian demand-side policies and, after the devastating World War II, firmly established the need for some sort of safety net in every major industrial democracy. This lesson to match social promotion with social protection continues to stand tall.

12.5 Conclusion

Over the last decade, the Bismarckian countries have improved quite significantly in terms of labor market performance. From our point of view, we interpret this not as the cyclical effect of a positive business environment, but as the result of a sequence of reforms leading to a more employment-friendly institutional arrangement. However, with hindsight one can argue that the dynamic economic activity in the EU over the last years has certainly contributed to this positive judgment, having led to increased employment and declining unemployment. The situation will certainly change with the impact of the current global economic crisis on European labor markets. We can expect that some of the increase in employment/population ratios over the last years will be lost and some severe labor market problems may (re)emerge within the next years. So far, core parts of the labor market are still remarkably stable, but flexible jobs such as agency work or fixed-term contracts are more heavily hit so that we see a dualized reaction of labor markets in Bismarckian countries.

However, to the extent that policy-makers in Bismarckian countries do not fall back into policies aiming at reducing labor supply, but follow the lines we defined as elements of a future-oriented policy package combining work and welfare, we can assume that we will not see a structural and persistent employment crisis like that of the late 1970s and the 1980s. Currently, there is some tendency to expand cushioning policies such as short-time work allowances. Emergency action of this kind may help bridge a severe, but short, crisis and help stabilize employment and skilled labor in core sectors of the economy. However, the longer the crisis lasts, the more policy-makers will have to reject the temptation to rely on a social policy approach towards unemployment, such as the withdrawal of activation policies or the reintroduction of implicit or explicit early retirement. Social policies of this kind may appear as an attractive 'soft' solution in the short run, but will eventually result in a reemergence of the 'welfare without work' syndrome, increase financial pressure on the welfare state in a phase of demographic ageing and reduce resources available for future-oriented, investive policies. Hence, it remains to be seen if and to what extent the Bismarckian countries have learned the lessons from the past and, facing an unprecedented crisis, not only refrain from old, but wrong recipes, and take the crisis as a trigger to implement further employment-friendly policies.

13 The Long Conservative Corporatist Road to Welfare Reforms

Bruno Palier

13.1 Introduction

This final chapter provides a cross-cutting reading of the earlier contributions in an attempt to account for the common characteristics of the Bismarckian welfare reform trajectory. It will not concentrate on the detailed contents of each reform[1], or on the differences between them, these having been exhaustively detailed in the national chapters that make up the main part of this volume. Instead, this chapter will focus on the specificities of each phase of the common reform trajectory, with a particular emphasis on the diagnoses, the politics and the consequences of the reforms adopted. The aim is to give a general answer to the question: 'how did Bismarckian welfare systems change'?

Variations across countries and policy fields notwithstanding, it is possible to discern four main stages in this sequential process of change:

1) The first reaction to the crisis consisted mainly of raising social contributions to rebalance the accounts of social insurance schemes, destabilized by increasing unemployment and slow growth. The key focus was to save the economic and social model based on the highly skilled, highly paid, and highly productive sectors and workers. This was done by preserving (and protecting) the jobs and social protection of the most productive male breadwinners, and by removing the least productive workers from the core labor market. Social insurances were highly instrumental in the implementation of this strategy. This first phase happened 'before retrenchment' and involved a 'labor shedding' strategy, an increase in social contributions and some moderate 'consolidation' measures.

2) However, these policies had the consequence of decreasing overall employment rates and increasing labor costs through the continuous

increase in social contributions, as fewer people working had to pay more and more to preserve their social protection and to provide the growing number of inactive people with income. This trend appeared to be in considerable tension with the new economic context of the early 1990s, when the single market was implemented (1992) and preparation for the single currency was underway. Hence a second phase of the reforms trajectory can be identified, with a lot of decisions aimed at stabilizing if not retrenching social expenditure. Aimed at 'saving the welfare system', retrenchment was usually negotiated with the social partners, guaranteeing relatively low costs for current 'insiders' (long phasing in of pension reforms, partial recalibration of unemployment insurance benefits, targeting of activation measures to the outsiders) and introducing a new world of welfare through the development of tax-financed, non-contributory benefits.

3) The political difficulties raised by these attempts at retrenchment – the mid-1990s saw strong political opposition to these measures – as well as their relative failure – social expenditure continued to increase and unemployment to be high – led governments to realize gradually that the institutional setting of the system itself had become a problem. They thus developed more and more 'institutional reforms', aimed at transforming the very basis of the welfare system: changes in the financing mechanisms (towards fewer social contributions and more taxes) as well as in the governance arrangements (weakening of the social partners, privatization or 'étatisation'). These changes undermined the traditional supports of the Bismarckian welfare systems, thus allowing for the more structural changes that occurred from the early 2000s.

4) The last phase consists of paradigmatic changes, since the objectives and instruments of the reforms are quite different from what was the traditional reaction of Bismarckian systems to the social problems. Reforms here include the introduction of funded schemes in the pension system, the activation of the inactive population, including mothers (even lone mothers) and thus defamilializing care, the development of basic safety nets, and the extension of privatization and the introduction of competition in health insurance. These structural changes entail a shift away from the typical answers to the difficulties elaborated within the traditional Bismarckian welfare regime in the 1970s and 1980s, that is, the 'labor shedding strategy' and its associated 'welfare without work' trap. This has also meant a structural transformation

of the Bismarckian welfare systems themselves, at least in respect to their capacity to provide coverage to all, solid income guarantees and comprehensive protection against all social risks. These changes are institutionalizing dualisms both in the labor market and in social protection.

In the next section of this chapter, I detail more fully the main common characteristics of each of these four sequences. The account tries to draw out the main features of the reform trajectory followed by all Bismarckian welfare systems, and is inevitably a generalization that underplays the many differences between the country cases. Its aim is to provide an alternative both to the 'frozen landscape' interpretation of welfare development in Continental Europe, and to the notion that reforms there have simply arisen erratically and unpredictably, in the context of contingent – and perhaps transient – nationally-specific circumstances.[2] The reality is instead that Bismarckian welfare systems have in large measure followed a similar road to reform, partly shaped by their institutional design and by the feedback effects that each sequence of reforms engendered for the following one.

After having shown the common characteristics of the Bismarckian welfare reform trajectory, I will propose a general interpretation of the overall trajectory. I will then assess the main changes in goals and institutions that it entailed for the Bismarckian welfare systems. The chapter concludes by discussing the overall economic and social outcomes of the reforms analyzed in this volume.

13.2 How did Continental European Welfare System Change? The Commonalities of the Typical Bismarckian Reform Trajectory

In what follows, the comparative grid that was developed for the analysis of the national cases is used to draw out common elements of the context, diagnosis, content of policies, types of change and the politics that characterized each sequence in the reform trajectory, as well as the consequences of each sequence for the next one (see tables 13.1 to 13.4).

Before Retrenchment (from the Mid-1970s to the Mid- to Late 1980s)

Table 13.1   Characteristics of the first reactions to the crisis

Context	Diagnosis	Content of the policy
– Economic downturn – Rise in unemployment – Social budget deficits	– Social benefits can help the victims of the crisis	– Increase in social contributions – Changes in the generosity of the benefits – 'Smooth consolidation' – Labor shedding – Welfare without work
Type of change	**Politics of the reforms**	**Consequences**
– First order (mainly changes in the level of social contributions and a few changes in the level of benefits)	– Applying 'good old recipes' – Consensual decisions (between the state and the social partners) – It is easier to raise social contributions than to increase taxes or to cut social benefits	– No big changes of the welfare state, 'frozen landscape' – Increasing inefficiencies of such policies (low rate of employment, high labor cost, rise in unemployment, stagflation)

Context

From the mid-1970s, social protection systems in affluent democracies were exposed to new socio-economic challenges: increasing capital mobility, intensified competition between economies, deindustrialization, mass and structural unemployment, population ageing and rising female labor market participation.[3] This new context translated into relatively different problems in the different welfare regimes, however, since their institutional arrangements acted as filters (Scharpf and Schmidt 2000; Sykes, Palier and Prior 2001).

In Continental Europe, the main problems created by the oil shocks and the ensuing economic slowdown were unemployment and deficits in the social insurance funds. Unemployment has a very direct 'scissor effect' on social insurance budgets, through a reduction in their incomes (based on social contributions levied on wages) and additional spending as more people come to depend on benefits (whether unemployment benefits, invalidity allowances, or early retirement pensions). The financial consequences of an economic downturn for the social insurance schemes are all the more visible given that social insurances budgets are separate from state budgets.

Diagnosis: Social Insurances should Help the Victims of the Crisis

Though neoliberal politicians were about to sweep to power in the UK (1979) and in the US (1981) on a platform of welfare state retrenchment (Pierson 1994), in Continental Europe none of the main political actors criticized welfare systems for being too costly or in some way at the origins of the crisis. On the contrary, social insurance (particularly unemployment benefits, invalidity allowances and early exit pensions) were seen as key instruments to help individuals to cope in these dire times, and to support the main economic strategy initially chosen to face the crisis, namely reflation policies and labor shedding. The deficits in the social insurance funds of course appeared to be a huge problem, but it was a problem that was to be solved either by further increasing social contributions and/or through some limitations in spending in the form of 'consolidation measures'. These measures aimed at guaranteeing the solvency of social insurance funds, in order to preserve them and guarantee their medium-term viability.

For most of the Continental European countries, what was really at stake was to save their (industrial) economic and social system. Deindustrialization particularly hit old industrial countries (or regions) like Germany, France, Belgium, Northern Italy and Austria. Confronted with an increase in international competition, especially in manufacturing, governments in most Continental countries wanted neither to give up on industry in favor of high and low-skill services (the option that, in essence, the UK government adopted), nor to promote and invest in innovation and new industries (as in California or the Nordic countries); instead they decided to defend and preserve as much as possible their traditional industries through productivity increases levered by laying off older and less productive workers, and the outsourcing of many activities (mainly low-skilled services) that had previously provided relatively well paid and protected jobs within industrial firms themselves (Palier and Thelen 2010). In order to support this strategy, unemployment insurances, invalidity allowances and early retirement pensions should be used to provide income to the people 'removed' from the main economic circuits.

Main Policies

Both governments and the social partners agreed upon an apparently contradictory mixture of both expansions and limitations of social benefits. In fact, income maintenance benefits for redundant workers were expanded, while other types of benefits were limited. There were some cuts in health care provision, family benefits, and in assistance benefits. In unemployment insurance, reforms effected a 'reactionary recalibration' (Clegg 2007), increasing benefits for the core workers with long contribution records, and reducing them for the long-term unemployed and those whose contributory record was low or non-existent (young people, the marginally employed, those who had been outside the labor market).

Two contrasting solutions were adopted in the face of deficits in the social insurance funds; either social contributions were increased (and some costs contained) to restore financial balance, or the deficits were simply allowed to build up. As Manow argues in his chapter in this volume, the solution chosen in this respect was highly dependent on the status and policy of the central bank. Where it was independent and thus not accommodating (as in the case of Germany, the Netherlands, Switzerland and to a lesser extent Austria) then consolidation measures were adopted; where it was less autonomous and more accommodating (as in the case of Italy, Belgium, Spain or France before the mid-1990s), social deficits and public debt increased.

The strategies pursued up to the early 1990s were closely linked to the social protection model based on the 'family wage': the man is the source of income for the entire household, from his wages and transfers, and hence it is the income and social protection of this man that should be protected first and foremost. Continental European countries thus favored income guarantees, early retirement and reductions in working hours in order to maintain the salaries and job security of highly skilled, highly productive, permanent (male) workers. Businesses themselves at first privileged a strategy based on high salaries and high quality production, both of which benefited permanent and highly qualified workers at the expense of less qualified or unqualified workers. Workforce reductions were often negotiated on the basis of income guarantees and early retirement, in the hope that the cost of massive retirement could be offset by proportionate gains in productivity (Kohli et al. 1991). These countries sought thus to resolve their employment problem by decreasing the supply of work through the implementation of a 'labor shedding' strategy, which led to what Esping-Andersen (1996a) called a 'welfare without work' syndrome. This strategy was supported by the social protection system, which on the one hand provided significant subsidies for early-retirement arrangements and maintained a high level of unemployment compensation, and on the other started to (re)create a variety of social security benefits designed to guarantee minimal incomes for individuals outside the labor force.

Politics

As is underlined in all country chapters, this first reaction was extremely consensual: all the main actors (among them the social partners, where unions and employers from the manufacturing industry were dominant – see Ebbinghaus and Visser 2000) agreed that the best way to respond to the crisis was to protect the jobs and social protection of the most productive employees, and to remove the least productive ones (who were not well represented anyway in the political and social systems of Continental Europe, see Häusermann 2010b). This strategy of course had a price – numerous and generous allowances had to be financed – but apparently almost everybody was ready to pay this, especially since it was not the state budget and therefore the taxpayers who would have to shoulder this burden, but instead the social insurance schemes and social contributions. Indeed, an often neglected but crucial feature of the Bismarckian welfare reform trajectory is that it was social insurances that had to foot the bill for the labor shedding strategy. 'Loading' the social insurances system in this way was a low-risk political strategy for governments in the short term, as they had neither to impose cuts nor to increase taxes. They could thus claim credit for helping the victims of the crisis, while justifying increases in social contribution rates as necessary to guarantee the viability of highly popular social insurance schemes.

In Continental Europe, therefore, governments long preferred to increase social contributions than to cut social benefits. This is rather counter-intuitive from an Anglo-Saxon (and even a Scandinavian) point of view, where cutting benefits will always be less politically risky than raising taxes. The explanation lies in differences in the type of benefits and in the way that they are financed. In Bismarckian countries, since benefits are mainly contributory, people believe that they have 'bought' their own social benefits through the social contributions they pay or have paid in work. Where Reagan, Thatcher or Major could denounce the excessive weight of taxes and the unwarranted cost of the social benefits delivered to those who 'do nothing', it was much more difficult for Continental European politicians to attack social insurance rights acquired by all the working population through the payment of social contributions. People are simply not ready to accept a reduction in provision for which they have – as they see it – worked and paid. On the contrary, they are ready to pay even more, as long as this guarantees a high level of benefit.

Consequences

These reforms seem at first glance not to have changed anything in the Continental welfare systems (hence the typical 'frozen landscape' assessment). By using the available instruments (social insurance benefits) to confront the crisis, the first reactions to the crisis actually changed the settings of these instruments, thus meaning a first-order change. However, over time, these changes had problematic consequences. Three effects of these policies appeared particularly harmful: low levels of employment, a dualization of the labor market and an explosion of social contribution rates.

Over time, the labor shedding strategy resulted in very low overall levels of employment. While in the 1990s the rate of male labor force participation was comparable to that of the Nordic countries (between 75 percent and 80 percent), the rate for persons between 55 and 64 years of age was far lower: in 1992, only 22.2 percent in Belgium, 36.2 percent in Germany, 29.8 percent in France and 28.7 percent in the Netherlands (Eurostat employment data series). An ever smaller group of people were working and had to pay more and more to support the inactive population.

Moreover, the focus on protecting the most productive core workers and the outsourcing of non-central less productive services, all led to a high degree of labor market polarization between a well integrated segment (skilled males between 25 and 55 years of age) and a marginalized or excluded one (poorly skilled or unskilled workers, youth, women, workers over 55 years of age and migrants) (Esping-Andersen, 1996). More and more, specific new social protection measures appeared necessary for this growing segment of the population. Assistance schemes offering a basic minimum income were either reinvigorated or put in place, and once again it was the shrinking active population that had to pay for them.

Because ever more benefits had to be financed, the volume of social contributions kept increasing. In Austria, Belgium, France, Germany, the Netherlands and Italy, the share of social insurance contributions in GDP went up from 12 percent to above 16 percent between 1970 and 1985 (Manow, this volume). Because fewer people were working and each one thus had to pay higher social contribution rates, during this period the 'non-wage costs' of employment (i.e. employers and employees' social contribution) increased markedly, going beyond half of the total labor cost in many Continental European countries.

At the beginning of the 1990s, this strategy appeared increasingly unsuccessful, and moreover, in contradiction with the main policy orientations being ever more strongly affirmed at the European level. It was in this context that the first negotiated retrenchments started to appear in Continental Europe.

The First Wave of Retrenchment, in the Early 1990s

Table 13.2   Characteristics of the first retrenchments

Context	Diagnosis	Content of the policy
– Persisting debt and unemployment – Single market – Economic recession (early 1990s) – Preparation of the single currency – German unification	– Social insurance schemes are victims of the crisis – The level of social contributions is too high – Social expenditure needs to be limited in order to save the system	– Increase in the contributivity of social insurance benefits – Tax financing of non-contributory benefits

Type of change	Politics of the reforms	Consequences
– Second order (new instruments such as new modes of calculation, new income-tested benefits)	– Mobilization against retrenchment – No reform can be passed without negotiation – Negotiated on the bases of clarification between insurance and assistance/solidarity	– From social to more individual insurance – Seeds of dualization in welfare: social insurances are not universal anymore – Political learning: social partners can prevent profound reforms

Context

After some years of economic recovery in the late 1980s, the new economic downturn of the early 1990s (and the recession of 1992/1993) brought forth the same problems as had been experienced in the late 1970s and early 1980s: rising unemployment, social budget deficits and, for most countries, public indebtedness. This time, however, the problems were aggravated by the effects of the previous path of action, notably the labor shedding strategy. This strategy had the consequence of reducing the overall employment rate and increasing labor cost: once again, the smaller number of people still working had to pay more and more to preserve their social protection and to provide support to the inactive.

These trends were in direct conflict with the new European context of the early 1990s, when the single market was implemented (1992) and the single currency was being prepared (Maastricht criteria adopted in 1993). As Scharpf has demonstrated, European integration seriously limited the policy instruments available to governments. 'The Maastricht criteria for joining the Monetary Union have practically eliminated deficit spending as a policy tool;

and the realization of the Monetary Union has completely removed monetary policy and exchange rate policy from the control of its member states' (Scharpf 2002: 88).

In France, Italy, Spain, Belgium, in accessing countries like Austria and later the Visegrad countries (see respective chapters), these 'European constraints' were crucial in halting the traditional social policy response to economic and social difficulties. Even for countries for whom the Maastricht criteria were not so novel, like Germany and other countries attached to the Deutschmark, the fact that they had previously also increased levels of social contributions (in the name of consolidation and, in the German case, to finance unification) generated problems in the context of globalization and single European market. As all the country chapters underline, what triggered a reversal in the reforms from expanding social benefits to support industrial restructuring and buffer the main consequences of the crisis towards a growing emphasis on cost control was the perception that the level of social contributions was growing to economically unsustainable levels.

Diagnosis: As a Victim of the Crisis, the System should be Rescued

In the early 1990s, the continuing problems of unemployment, slow growth and public deficits resulted in the previous ways of solving problems being increasingly questioned, and many Continental European countries began to perceive themselves as being 'sick' economies. Though the symptoms varied across countries (the 'Dutch disease' of inactivity, soaring deficits and inflation in Italy, huge public debt in Belgium, mass unemployment in many countries...), the diagnosis was everywhere much the same: Continental Europe suffers from excessive labor costs, due to the high level of social contributions (Scharpf and Schmidt 2000; Daly, 2001). As also underlined by Manow in this volume, the 1990s public debate in Continental Europe identified high non-wage labor costs as the most detrimental factor inhibiting employment growth (especially in the low-skilled service sector) and competitiveness.

What is however striking in the discourses justifying most of the reforms of this period is that, even if the level of social contributions was criticized, the system of social insurance as a whole remained unscathed. Indeed, it was most often presented as itself being a victim of the continuing crisis, with unemployment and slow growth increasing deficits and starving the system of resources. When governments presented reform proposals during the 1990s, the announced goal was very often to 'save the system', even if the means to this end was retrenchment.

What changed, though, were the instruments that were used in reforms. This was a result of the delegitimization of previous ways of doing things, such as increasing social contribution levels or debt to avoid retrenchment. A combination of greater awareness of globalization and the advent of Maastricht both undermined these previous alternatives, and policies were reoriented towards retrenchment. In order for the economy to remain competitive, governments thought that they had to limit the increase in social contributions. In order to respect Maastricht criteria, they needed to control public debt. In order to save the social insurance system, that is to avoid their financial bankruptcy, these schemes would have to spend less, or at least the growth in their expenditure would have to be controlled.

Main Policies

These reforms were aimed at reducing levels of social benefits while simultaneously preserving the logic of the system (second-order changes). The Bismarckian logic was in fact at the heart of the reforms, since these generally reinforced the 'equivalence principle' (the contributivity of benefits) and since they also removed from social insurances the 'burden' of having to finance non-contributory benefits.

Whether in old-age pensions, unemployment benefits or invalidity allowances, in all our cases the main technique for reducing social insurances benefits was a strengthening of the link between the amount and duration of contribution and the volume and duration of benefits (through a change in the calculation formula and or stricter entitlement rules). This of course relied on the already existing logic of the schemes (their contributivity, i.e. the right to social benefits derives from paying social contributions), even though these reforms usually meant a shift away from redistributive (horizontal and vertical) towards more actuarial principles. Typically, unemployed (or invalid) people now needed to have contributed during a longer period to be entitled to the full allowance; the number of years for being entitled to a full pension was also increased, and/or deductions for pensions claimed before the standard age of retirement were introduced. Benefits were thus reduced mainly for those who could not have a relatively unbroken and fulltime career, but preserved for the more 'typical' workers. In order to relieve social insurances deficits, decisions were also made to remove the financing of 'non contributory benefits' from the social insurance budget.

Politics

A first noticeable conclusion of the comparison of retrenchment policies in Continental Europe is that partisan politics did not really matter. Both Social Democratic and Conservative governments, as well as coalitions, implemented these same types of policy. Reforms seemed more driven by the EU constraints, and/or the worries about the level of social contributions, than by partisan dynamics. There has of course been political controversy, but comparisons show that different governments have implemented quite similar policies.[4] The real conflicts were more frequently between governments, on the one hand, and trade unions, on the other.

In all our cases, the retrenchment reforms were not presented as a means to dismantling the social insurance system, but rather as a strategy for preserving it. In the political discourses justifying reforms, the message is that if a reform is necessary it is not because the system is dysfunctional, but simply because it suffers from the current situation, where resources are decreasing (because of economic slow down, unemployment) and spending increasing (because of unemployment, aging, new social demands). Since it appears to be no longer possible in the new European context to further increase resources, governments are forced to retrench, a little. Since the benefits to be retrenched are extremely legitimate, these reforms are not enacted in response to criticisms of welfare redistribution, but rather in the name of the crucial necessity to restore its viability.

Despite this cautious rhetoric, that once again contrasts particularly with the accusatory tones in which retrenchment is framed in the Anglo-Saxon world[5], reform projects in the early 1990s often triggered considerable opposition, and had to be negotiated with the social partners to gain acceptance. Since the systems are financed through social contributions levied on wages and not through taxation, and since in many cases they participate in the management of social insurance funds, the representatives of those who contribute to and benefit from the systems (i.e. the wage earners) were among the key players in the political game around social policy reform. Insurance-based transfers are well defended by organized interests and in particular by trade unions of the different branches corresponding to the different professional schemes. They had a say in the process, and the power to block proposals with which they did not agree. Acceptance by the social partners of benefit cuts was thus usually levered as a *quid pro quo* (Bonoli and Palier 1996; Bonoli 1997), linked to adjustments in financing formulas.

As we have seen, during the preceding period, the cost of new social expenditure aimed at buffering the consequences of the crisis, and the cost of labor shedding, was supported by the social insurance schemes, and in Germany social insurances were financing partly the cost of unification. The social partners long complained about this, claiming that much of the new burden weighting on social insurance was not justified (since it was paying benefits without receiving corresponding contribution). According to them, the cost of the non-contributory benefits explained much of the financial difficulties facing the social insurance system. In almost all Continental countries, the social partners asked the state to take on more responsibilities and to finance non-contributory benefits out of taxes. Thus, in Germany the social partners claimed that 'the benefit components not based on contributions out of own earnings (*versicherungsfremde Leistungen*) should not be borne by the community of insured' (Hinrichs, this volume)[6]; in France, the fact that social insurance schemes had to pay benefits for people who exhausted their contributory rights or had paid insufficient contributions was called 'undue charges' ('*charges indues*'), and social partners continuously demanded that the state take over their financing (Palier 2005a and this volume); in Spain, 'the recommendations of the Toledo Pact included the split of financing sources, so that contributory benefits were to be financed out of social contributions and taxes were to be used to finance non-contributory transfers and welfare services' (Guillén, this volume).

Many reforms that passed were those which were accompanied by such a 'clarification of responsibility', with the government offering to take over the financing of non-contributory benefits (flat-rate social minima for the elderly, the handicapped, the long-term unemployed; credit of contribution for period out of work because of unemployment, child rearing...) in return for the acceptance by the social partners of cost containment measures in social insurance benefits.[7] In the eyes of the social partners, such reforms guaranteed the financial viability of social insurances, and secured their future.

Consequences

Though they helped the Continental countries balance their social insurance budgets, and hence to qualify for the EMU in 1998/9, these measures were not able to resolve the problem of unemployment and low employment rates, which were still acute at the end of the 1990s (see Hemerijck and Eichhorst, this volume).

In this phase of reforms, the changes are based on new instruments (changes in calculation rules, creation of new State subsidies...), but are perceived as preserving the very nature of social insurance, and sometimes even as re-enforcing it (the social partners often think that making the state pay for non-contributory benefits helps to 'purify' and thus reinforce social insurance). The reforms do not really challenge the principles of social insurance and can be considered to be second-order changes.

What they did change, however, is the capacity of social insurance schemes to be 'quasi-universal', as they were supposed to be since the 1960s-1970s (see first chapter). By reducing the replacement rates in unemployment benefits or pensions, they no longer ensure 'full income guarantees'. By removing more and more people (with atypical profiles) from social insurance, they no longer cover the whole population. Since one consequence of these reforms is that the coverage of social insurance shrinks (fewer people covered, less generous benefits), more and more space is created for the development of new benefits, on top of compulsory social insurance (voluntary private pensions, for instance), or below it, for those who have lost (or never gained) rights to social insurance (assistance benefits).

As a result of the way they were negotiated, these reforms also sowed further seeds of dualization. In order to 'relieve' social insurance from covering the long-term unemployed and non-standard workers, reforms have institutionalized a new world of welfare for 'atypical' workers, organized around tax-financed, non-contributory, and income-tested benefits. Furthermore, in the negotiations of the retrenchment measures, the trade unions managed to guarantee the position of current 'insiders', through a long phasing-in period for reforms in pension rights (Bonoli and Palier 2007), and a dual recalibration of unemployment insurance benefits, with greater benefits for those who previously worked fulltime and less for those with more broken careers (Clegg 2007).

Moreover, these reforms progressively underscored some structural problems linked with Bismarckian social insurances, but which have never been really 'problematized' all together before: they are unable (and unwilling) to cover those who cannot fully contribute to the system (the socially excluded, precarious workers and those with atypical employment profiles); their main source of financing (social contributions) seems to hinder job creation and competitiveness; and their traditional 'spokesmen' (the social partners, and especially unions) are able to block important reforms. From victim, the welfare systems gradually came to be seen as a major cause of the economic and social difficulties of Continental European countries, ushering in a phase of (incremental) institutional reforms that would set the scene for deeper structural reforms.

Institutional Reforms (Partly Parallel to First Retrenchment, and beyond,
1990s and 2000s)

Table 13.3   Characteristics of the institutional reforms

Context	Diagnosis	Content of the policies
– Past reforms are still unable to solve the unemployment and financial problems; – Institutional and political learning; – Academic literature and international criticism of 'Conservative corporatist' stalemate	– Welfare systems are partly the cause of the crisis: – Contributions damage competitiveness and create unemployment; – Corporatist management rules hinder reform capacities	– New modes of financing, new taxes, lower social contributions – New modes of management (empowerment of the state, new public agencies, or an increasing role for private actors)

Type of change	Politics	Consequences
Institutional change: – Non-Bismarckian institutions are introduced, and traditional ones are incrementally transformed: diminishing of the share of social contributions; new taxes; new decision-making practices and/or new governance arrangements, weakening the traditional 'social partners', new role for the state and/or private actors	– Mostly consensual for shifts in financing, much more conflictual for changes in governance – New provisions and new institutions are implemented at a marginal point in the system – Then they develop so as to change the politics of the system (weakening the unions especially)	– Weakening of traditional social insurance mechanisms and actors – Development of stronger and new state capacities

Context

The first retrenchment initiatives were extremely difficult to implement, triggering widespread discontent and having to be frequently watered down to gain acceptance. The political difficulties they caused and their relative failure in terms of outcomes (social expenditure continued to increase and unemployment remained obstinately high in most countries) taught governments the lesson that the institutional design of the systems had itself become a problem.

Two main institutional characteristics of Bismarckian welfare systems have been of crucial importance in shaping problems and solutions: financing through social contributions and the (formal and/or informal) involvement of the social partners in the governance of the systems. These two institutional traits strongly differentiate Bismarckian social protection systems from statist or market ones. They seem to have generated many of the economic and political problems faced by welfare systems in Continental Europe. The high level of social contributions appeared detrimental from an economic point of view, but also had political consequences, since this mode of financing highlighted the link of Bismarckian social protection to the realm of employment and work and thus to the representatives of this world, who claimed to have a say in the reforms.[8] The social partners, and especially the unions, have often been able to block reforms.

Gradually realizing how much these institutional traits were at the root of their difficulties in carrying through the reforms they sought to implement, governments concentrated more and more on institutional 'meta-policy reforms' (Clegg 2007), aimed at transforming the very bases of these welfare systems. Changes in financing mechanisms (towards fewer social contributions and more taxes) as well as in governance arrangements (weakening of the social partners, privatization or 'étatisation') thus came onto the political agenda.

Diagnosis: From Victim to Cause of the Crisis

Since the early and especially the mid-1990s, welfare systems based on social insurance have increasingly been perceived in their own countries as exacerbating economic and political difficulties. Before retrenchment, social insurance benefits were used as a support for the victims of the crisis (compensation) and as a tool to counter it (reflation policies, labor shedding strategies). In the following period, when continuous increases in social spending appeared to be unsustainable, retrenchments were attempted, but essentially to save a social insurance system perceived as itself a victim of the crisis. Because of continuing difficulties, more and more analyses called for reforms that went further and deeper. In such analyses, the systems themselves had come to be seen as the cause of the crisis.

Social insurance was now accused of being to some extent the cause of a variety of economic and political ills: leading to unbearable social contribution rates, hindering competitiveness[9], preventing job creation (in the low-skilled service sector at least) and weakening the state's capacity to control expenditure and implement reforms by giving undue influence to the social partners. The very characteristics of these systems themselves (contributory benefits, financed by social contribution and managed by the social partners) came to be seen as the causes of difficulties. This being the case, they should not only be retrenched, but also profoundly transformed.

It is, therefore, not only social scientists who acknowledge the impact of institutions on problems, and their role in shaping, and sometimes preventing, change. Through learning processes (and the diffusion of academic analyses), experts and politicians have also come to recognize these effects – and sometimes also to decide to change these institutions. In most of the social insurance based welfare systems, institutional reforms have taken place in order to face these difficulties. Scholars working on welfare state reforms have tended to overlook these changes. As is demonstrated in many chapters in this volume, however, these reforms have been essential in giving governments the capacity to overcome the blockages to change that the typical Bismarckian institutional design had generated. It could be argued that in a second historical reversal, after having initially moved from being seen as 'effects' to being seen as 'causes' (Pierson 1993), welfare institutions have now become objects of reforms, with the aim to render the welfare state more 'movable'.

Main Policies

Some recent reforms have been aimed at modifying these institutional arrangements, especially the predominance of social contributions in the financing of social expenditures and the role played by the social partners in social policy-making (the two often being interrelated). These reforms consisted mainly in trying to reduce the share of social contributions in the financing of welfare systems, and to diminish the role and power of the social partners (mainly the unions) in the national social policy-making process. As they are crucially important for understanding the reform trajectory in Continental Europe, two chapters in this volume are devoted to these institutional traits of Bismarckian welfare systems, and to their progressive transformation (Ebbinghaus on 'Bismarckian corporatism', Manow on financing).

It should be noted that these reforms have sometimes been implemented separately from other types of reforms, and sometimes simultaneously. For the sake of clarity they are treated separately here, but acknowledging that some of them have been part of a package that also included structural reforms (see below). Since we consider changes in the institutional design of Bismarckian welfare systems as 'pre-conditions' for structural reforms, they are dealt with first.

These changes are difficult to categorize as either first-, second- or third-order changes. Visser and Hemerijck (1997) have called changes of this type 'institutional changes', while as mentioned above Clegg refers to 'meta-policy reforms', meaning 'a reconsideration of how to make policy itself' (Clegg 2007: 77; quoting Dror 1968). As various chapters in this volume indicate, these institutional reforms belong to the family of institutional evolutions that have been analyzed by Thelen and Streeck (2005).

CHANGES IN FINANCING

Modifications in financing have usually been rather consensual.[10] They progressively became part of the demands of almost all social protection actors (albeit for different reasons, see Palier 2005b). Since the mid-1990s, many reforms have been triggered by the desire to stop the spiraling of labor costs, often by fixing a ceiling for social contributions.[11] This generated not only the switch towards retrenchment that we have analyzed above, but also the necessity to look for new types or resources, either by moving from contributions to general taxes, or by creating specific new taxes for new expenditures.

Three main mechanisms have driven the movement from contribution to tax financing: firstly, the role of tax financing has been increased in the cases of (negotiated) retrenchment reforms, when governments committed to pay for non-contributory benefits that were financed through social insurances previously[12]; secondly, in the framework of employment policies, many Continental European governments decided to exempt employers from paying some social contribution in order to lower the cost of unskilled labor; in these cases, governments either offered tax subsidies to employers, or compensated the social insurance funds with tax money for the loss of social contributions due to these exemptions, thus again switching the financing of social expenditure from social contribution to taxes[13]; finally, and more rarely, genuine new taxes have been created, either to substitute for social contributions or to finance new types of social expenditure.[14]

CHANGES IN GOVERNANCE

Contrary to changes in financing, the changes in the governance of the system, and especially the attempts to weaken the social partners (primarily the unions) within the social policy-making process, have been hugely controversial. International analysts and commentators have sometimes analyzed the often massive demonstrations organized by trade unions in Continental Europe in response to welfare reforms as mere opposition to retrenchment, when very often it was (also) opposition to the measures that would undermine the unions' power within the system.[15]

Mechanisms that weakened the influence of the social partners have also been varied. One has been removing the social partners as a 'natural' consequence of the changes in financing: when the state finances, it expects to control decision-making, as well[16]; another route has been to simply bypass the social partners, by excluding them informally or formally from consultation/concertation games (see Ebbinghaus, this volume). In many cases this occurred through a shift in power from the social partners to the Parliament, the social partners losing their traditional role in the social policy-making through procedural changes.[17] Administrative reforms have also contributed to weakening the role of the social partners, by changing the governance structure of some important social insurance bodies.[18] Finally, liberalization or privatization (complete or partial) of former funds/agencies held by the social partners has also contributed to reduce their traditional powers.

While it is evident that the state is increasing its decision-making and control capacity over the compulsory social insurance schemes, it should however not be forgotten that, since these compulsory schemes are shrinking, occupational social provision (in pension and health) are expanding (see also below). These are often domains regulated by collective agreements, and in which the social partners are therefore still central actors.[19]

'Meta-policy reforms' have been less important in some countries. In Italy, the main preoccupation was to change the political system itself, and the politics of welfare reforms has remained highly conflictual; in Belgium, 'there have been no changes in social policy-making, only defensive measures. The social partners have sought and largely succeeded to maintain their autonomy from government in the domains of collective bargaining and governance of the social security system' (Hemerijck and Marx, this volume). As we will see in the next section, this partly explains why further structural reforms have been more difficult to implement in these two countries, at least when compared to their neighbors. In the case of the Visegrad countries, trends seem to go rather in the opposite direction, since a greater financing role has been given to social contributions, and policies have tried to reinforce the capacity of civil society through a 'state-led corporatism' that has been instrumental in developing and reforming welfare institutions (Cerami, this volume). This is explained by a quite different point of departure, where the state had a far more central role.

Consequences

While it stabilized or even increased in all other European countries (including the Visegrad countries), the weight of social contributions in Continental European countries has decreased between 1995 and 2006. As a percentage of total taxation, social contributions have declined by -1.5 percentage points in Austria, -2.3 in Belgium, -6.2 in France, -1.8 in Germany, -1.4 in Italy, -3.5 in the Netherlands, and -2.7 in Spain.[20] Even if social contributions still represent the largest share of financial resources for Continental welfare systems, the relative share of other taxes has greatly increased over time.

Changes in financing introduced or increased the role of new instruments, usually linked to a different logic of welfare. It might be logical to assume that a 'hybridization' dynamic is at play, leading to a more mixed type of welfare system. Our analysis on the contrary shows that the changes in financing are contributing to an ever clearer separation between two worlds of welfare, the realm of contributory social insurance financed by social contribution on the one hand, and that of non-contributory benefits on the other, financed by taxes. It is in this second world of welfare that we find the various, basic safety nets. The new sources of finance may also be used to fund new or developing services, more clearly separated from insurance than before, such as health care, services for labor market (job placement, training, etc.) and care policies.

As far as governance is concerned, the trend is also clear. The traditional role of the social partners in compulsory social insurance has been weakened, and governments have progressively gained greater political capacities to impose their reforms, as will be shown in the next section. Again, the conclusion should not necessarily be one of a general weakening of the social partners in labor market and social policies, since employers have been quite influential in shaping the most recent reforms, and collective negotiation may undergo a revival, both in complementary social protection (especially pensions) and within decentralized labor market policies (see Ebbinghaus, this volume).

With these institutional transformations, governments have at a minimum gained more control over the financing and decision-making process in social protection. They have acquired new political capacities to take the tough decisions, and some financing capacities for new types of benefits aimed at either targeting the most needy, and/or covering new social risks. As is shown by our national cases (and by the counter example of Belgium and partly Italy), 'meta-policy reforms' thus appear to be a pre-condition for further changes (see also Clegg 2007: 77). They enabled further retrenchments to be imposed, and paved the way for the deeper structural changes that became visible during the 2000s.

Further Retrenchments, Activation and Structural Reforms: From the Late 1990s/Early 2000s up to the Crisis of 2008

Table 13.4   Characteristics of the structural reforms

Context	Diagnosis	Content of the policies
– Structural economic problems – Greater awareness of socio-demographic changes and new social risks – Spreading of a new social policy paradigm	– Welfare systems need a profound adaptation to the new economic and social contexts	– Multiplication of pillars in pension, active ageing – Selective activation of the unemployed – Competition and more state regulation in health – Timid modernization: – Care policies – Extension of tax-financed basic safety nets
Type of change	**Politics**	**Consequences**
– Third-order, paradigmatic reforms, though not wholesale transformation of the systems	– Divisive reforms – Imposition	– We are all supply-siders now – Bismarckian welfare systems have moved from income maintenance to activation, work incentives, employment-friendly benefits – Recommodification for some, privatization of complementary provision for others, but not liberalization for all – Dualization of the systems (social and private insurances/assistance) – Dualization of society

Context

In the late 1990s, despite a decade of difficult economic and social policy reforms, Continental European countries still faced considerable economic and social problems.

If the level of unemployment was falling everywhere in Europe at the end of the decade, employment rates in Continental Europe were still very low (see Hemerijck and Eirchhorst' figures, starting in 1997, this volume). Though deficits had been contained to meet Maastricht criteria, some countries still had a huge debt (Belgium and Italy especially); and deficits were generally higher in Continental Europe than in many other European countries (some of which even had surpluses in the early 2000s). Apart from a few exceptions (like the Netherlands or Spain), economic growth rates on the continent were lower than in the other European countries (and than in the US or Canada). From outside, 'Old Europe' faced criticism for its poor economic performance, when other models (Anglo-Saxon or Nordic) had demonstrated a capacity to overcome their own difficulties.

In the late 1990s, moreover, the negative impacts of social and demographic changes were becoming more visible. While the inactivity rate of elderly workers was on the increase[21], the 'baby boomers' were nearing retirement age. The demographic dependency ratio (inactive/active) was the most unfavorable in Continental Europe, especially on its southern border. While women wanted to, and did, enter the labor market in most European countries, their difficulties in combining work and family life in most Conservative welfare systems became more evident, and the idea that this could be detrimental to fertility began to be discussed. Finally, although unemployment was fluctuating and in some places declining, long-term unemployment and social exclusion was increasing, especially among low-skilled workers. In the European continent, there was an increasing awareness of the emergence of 'new social risks' (such as precarious employment, long-term unemployment, in-work poverty, single parenthood, or the inability to reconcile work and family life, see Bonoli, 2005), and of the incapacity of the traditional welfare systems to protect people against them.

Confronted with continuous difficulties and the failures of their past attempts to address them, Continental European governments became convinced that to solve their structural difficulties, only structural changes of their welfare systems would suffice, including the adoption of a totally new social policy agenda. For the first time, reforms were explicitly aimed at changing and restructuring the welfare systems.

Diagnosis: The Welfare Systems are Ill-Adapted to the New Economic and Social Context and Need to be Reoriented

In many Continental European countries, there was a sense of an accumulation of failures over the previous two decades, leading some to question the merits of the system itself and push for changing both the instruments and the goals of social policies.[22] A variety of reform failures – inability to solve the deep financial and employment difficulties of European countries (since the late 1970s in many countries), the perception of the detrimental effects of the social insurance structures on the economy (since the late 1980s), the incapacity of the existing social insurances to face the recurrent and emerging social problems (since the late 1990s) – together seemed to suggest that the system itself had failed and needed to be changed. In order for changes to occur, this shared sense of failure is necessary, but it is not sufficient; alternative solutions also need to be available, and credible.

Since the early 1990s, new social policy paradigms and programs, from outside Continental Europe, had been circulating. These new ideas and experiences constituted a credible alternative to the typical Continental answers (i.e. 'passive' income compensation, labor shedding), and seemed adapted to the new economic context (globalization, the single market and increased competition) and the new economic policy orientation that accompanies the Maastricht criteria (a sound public budget, limited debt, low inflation rate). Moreover, these ideas also addressed new social risks, and appeared to have been implemented successfully in some European countries (Nordic countries and, in a different way, UK).

After having contributed to define the new (supply-side) economic or-thodoxy known either as monetarism (Hall 1993) or as the 'Washington consensus' (Williamson 1990), international financial and economic orga-nizations started to define a new (post-Keynesian) orthodoxy concerning labor market and social policies. Flexibility and workfare on the labor market, multi-pillar pensions (including compulsory and voluntary fund-ed schemes), and increased competition and managed care in the health sector were put high on the policy agenda by the OECD and the World Bank.[23] While the first versions were rather crudely neoliberal (and not adoptable as such in 'Old Europe'), by the mid-1990s these ideas had been 'Europeanized' and made more amenable to the European social model. The Dutch and the Nordic reforms of the 1990s (flexicurity, social invest-ment), the British 'Third Way' and the European Employment Strategy and Open Method of Coordination (OMC)[24] all made these new ideas available as an alternative new paradigm to the failed Continental social policy paradigm.

It is not the purpose here to analyze the development and content (and nuances) of this new global social policy paradigm, but simply to underline some of its main trains (at the risk, of course, of caricature). Whereas social expenditure was long conceived as being favorable to eco-nomic growth (under the Keynesian macroeconomic paradigm), one of the main new orientations is now to reduce public social spending and labor costs in order to boost economic activity by restoring and fostering firms' profitability. The reforms should make social protection schemes more conducive to employment by reducing their cost, rather than by increasing social spending. The basic philosophy is to adapt social protection schemes to a supply-side rather than a demand-side macroeconomic policy. According to the new norms being developed, the welfare state should be placed at the service of competition (among businesses, states and individuals).

In this perspective, social programs are supposed to be more employment-friendly by linking benefits to incentives that make it preferable to work rather than to receive social security benefits for doing nothing. Employment and social policies are more and more thought of in terms of incentives rather than in terms of rights (or 'decommodification'). Employment policies are now focused on stimulating labor supply and activation strategies. Increasing female participation in the labor market and therefore facilitating family/work reconciliation is also at the heart of the new social policy paradigm. In pensions, a multi-pillar system which includes both pay-as-you-go and funded schemes (in order to promote investment capacities in the country) is promoted, with an emphasis on the tight link between the level of the pension and the volume of contribution paid. In health care systems, the introduction of managed competition has become the main tool for regulation.

Adopting this new agenda meant, for Continental European countries, a radical reorientation of their main strategies (labor shedding); or as Hinrichs (this volume) puts it, to turn around in what had become perceived to be a dead end. In that sense, it entailed implementing a paradigmatic change in the policies adopted (from labor shedding to activation), but without necessarily implying that the whole system would have to be changed (see below).

Main Policies

Most of the Continental European countries seem to have adopted (even if in somewhat modified form) this new social policy agenda. Since the early 2000s, a new wave of reforms has been developing, that testify a new will to overcome the 'welfare without work' trap. Activation of the unemployed, the limitation of early exit, measures for increasing the participation of women, older workers and unskilled workers are amongst the biggest innovations. Important pension reforms have also been adopted, aimed at further reducing the cost of public pensions and at favoring the development of private fully funded complements. In health care, in the countries with a health insurance system, more regulatory power has been given to the state, and more competition between health insurances is being introduced. Minimum income protection has also been generalized, to protect the weakest from the further retreat of social insurance that has happened through the structural transformation of traditional social insurances (see box 13.1). Finally, reforms (in a more limited number of countries) also include attempts at 'modernizing' Bismarckian welfare systems in order to provide better protection against new social risks through the (more or less timid) development of new social policies.

Box 13.1   The structural reforms in traditional social insurances

• In Germany, the 2001 Riester pension reform planned further restrictions of the level of public pension, but also created the possibility for complementary future pension rights through personal or occupational pension plans. The pension replacement rate was further reduced in 2004, and the postponement of the legal retirement age to 67 is planned; during the early 2000s, the four so-called Hartz reforms deeply transformed German labor market and unemployment insurance, introducing activation and expanding low-cost jobs; between 2003 and 2007, increased healthcare co-payment for patients, increased competition amongst health insurance providers and new tax-financing arrangements were implemented (Hinrichs, this volume).

• In France, the 2001 unemployment reform generalized activation to most of the unemployed, while more and more in-work benefits have been developed (*Prime pour l'emploi, revenu de solidarité active*). The 2003 pension reforms expanded the scope of retrenchment to public sector workers, but also created pension saving plans, both individual and occupational. Throughout the 2000s, co-payments have been increased in the ambulatory health care sector giving private insurance an increasing role in the system, while the 2004 and 2008 health reforms increased the control of national and regional public authorities over the rest of the system (control of patients in general, and over the hospital sector) (Palier, this volume).

• In Austria, the various pension acts of the first half of the 2000s closed early-exit options, harmonized the system by integrating federal civil servants into the general scheme, diminished the level of pay-as-you-go benefits and progressively introduced a supplementary private pillar (financed through the conversion of the previous severance payments). Employment policies have also been characterized by tighter eligibility conditions for unemployment benefits, a stronger reliance on activation policies and increased efforts to create employment opportunities for the unskilled. In health care, due to ever-increasing co-payments, the share of private health expenditure as a percentage of total health expenditure has increased continuously and new funding principles apply (diminishing employers' contributions), while new state agencies have been created to better control the system (Obinger and Tálos, this volume).

• In Belgium, after the reform of unemployment insurance, the focus was more on minimum income protection, some timid activation measures were adopted between 1999 and 2005, and a 'generation pact' aimed at diminishing early retirement was introduced (but without great success); public pensions, as provided through social security, have become so low that average to high earners have come to rely on occupational and private schemes to obtain a pension commensurate with their past earnings. The 2003 Law Vandenbroucke on supplementary pensions aimed to generalize access to such private provision (Hemerijck and Marx, this volume).

• In the Netherlands, activation policies date back to the mid-1990s, with the so-called 'Melkert jobs' for low-skilled workers, women, younger workers, foreign nationals, and the long-term unemployed; activation was pushed further with the introduction in 1997 of cuts in employers' social security contributions for hiring the long-term unemployed and low-paid workers, and with the Jobseekers Employment Act (WIW) in 1998, which imposed an individualized assessment interview on each new unemployment benefit. Competition between health insurance schemes became effective in 2005. Since a majority of pensions were already fully funded, there have not been such big changes in this area as in the other cases, but strong incentives have been created to reduce early exit (Hemerijck and Marx, this volume).

• In Italy, structural pension reforms date back to 1995, the Dini reforms having introduced a public notional defined contribution system, to be implemented through a long transition process that would preserve the unions' core constituencies; in the 2000s, supplementary defined contribution schemes have been highly favored through the automatic conversion of severance payments (Tfr) into pension saving plans; the flexibilization of the Italian labor market as well as active labor market policies (mainly targeted at the most disadvantage groups) were developed in the late 1990s. Blockages could however not be overcome to promote adequate unemployment insurance and a real minimum income safety net (Jessoula and Alti, this volume).

• In Spain, despite the absence of such visible pension reforms as in the German, Italian or French cases, private pensions introduced in the late 1980s have grown steadily. The labor market has also been flexibilized (through the massive use of temporary work contracts), and active labor market policies have also been introduced (Guillén, this volume).

• In Switzerland, fully funded pensions already existed, and private health insurances were already in competition. Changes towards including some 'outsiders' within the scope of insurance schemes have been adopted. The turn to activation is also very visible, starting in 1995 with more access to training, followed in the 2000s with a strengthened commitment to the reintegration of the disabled and changes in family policies to improve the capacity to combine work and family life (Häusermann, this volume).

• In the Visegrad countries, the changes do not go in the same order, since the second half of the 1990s witnessed a lot of liberalization and privatization measures in the pension and health sectors, and these have been reconsidered during the 2000s. Private pillars in pension and health have been recalibrated. However, it is indeed during the 2000s that activation measures have been subsequently taken to overcome employment rates that are among the lowest in Europe (Cerami, this volume).

These structural reforms all entail third order changes: new instruments are implemented (activation, conditional benefits and new services for the unemployed, fully funded pension schemes, new types of financing and management in health care), and one main new goal is put forward: rendering the welfare system employment-friendly by reducing its public part and reorienting benefits from income maintenance towards activity. Of particular importance for the Continental European countries are the attempts at increasing the employment rate of the elderly (meaning a shift away from the early exit strategy) and the attempt to support women's durable entry to the labor market. Since the latter goal cannot be levered only with social insurance, and since other new social risks have emerged, new social policies (marked by both new goals and new instruments) are also emerging: minimum income guarantees, new types of parental leave and care policies. As underlined by Häusermann in this volume, these latter reforms can be described as 'updating recalibration' (Pierson 2001a: 455) or 'modernization' (Bonoli 2005; Häusermann 2006) of the welfare system, 'because they adapt it to specific post-industrial social needs and demands of mostly labor market outsiders and women'.

Confronted with long-term unemployment, more volatility on the labor market, precarious jobs, social exclusion and above all the shrinking coverage of social insurance, all countries but Italy have either created or expanded and generalized minimum income guarantees, either as a general safety net[25], or as specific minimum incomes in different policy fields.[26] Italy launched an experimentation of minimum income, but was unable to overcome institutional and political obstacles to its generalization.

This development of assistance schemes shows that instead of a temporary cyclical change on the labor market, the increasing number of atypical workers, the development of long-term unemployment and the growing numbers of outsiders is now perceived as a durable phenomenon that necessitates a permanent answer. This development (or rediscovery) of assistance schemes was also the result of the politics of retrenchment, which saw social insurance shrink and renounce the responsibility to protect the most 'atypical' profiles. This might be interpreted as a return to Bismarckian origins, when the policy for the worker (*Arbeiterpolitik*) was clearly distinguished from the policies for the poor (*Armenpolitik*, see Leifreid and Tennstedt 1985); but it is also a clear rupture with the post-war compromise, when Bismarckian institutions were supposed to reach Beveridgean goals and cover the whole population. In this context, it appears more as the institutionalization of a new dualism within social protection (see Palier and Thelen 2010).

One should however note that in some countries, while basic safety nets were developed for the poorest, reforms have also tried to reintegrate within social insurances some workers (mainly part-time workers) previously excluded by too strict eligibility criteria. In the Netherlands, better rights to social insurance for part-time workers were decided in 1995 and in 1996, and an agreement on 'Flexibility and Security' was later adopted, paving the way for a new Working Hours (Adjustment) Act in 2000, which gave part-time workers an explicit right to equal treatment in all areas negotiated by the social partners, including wages, basic social security, training and education, subsidized care provision, holiday pay, and second tier pension rights (Hemerijck and Marx, this volume). In Spain, various 'social pacts have resulted in increased protection of non-core labor workers in the late 1990s' (the 'Agreement on Employment and Social Protection of Agrarian Workers' of 1996 enacted in 2000; the 'Interconfederal Agreement for Stability in Employment' of 1997; and a specific agreement on part-time workers reached in 1998). 'Conditions for access to social security were conflated with those of core-workers in terms of the relation between time worked and benefits, and in terms of sickness allowances and maternity benefits' (Guillén, this volume). In Switzerland, the pension rights of non-working women were improved in 1995, the second pillar of occupational pension was extended to more low-income earners, meaning more social rights for part time – mainly female – workers, and unemployment reforms during the 1990s also prolonged the benefit period, thus extending coverage to the long-term unemployed. In France, part-time workers were given some additional pension rights in the 2003 pension reform. In Austria, new professions (quasi-freelancers, self-employed) were included in the unemployment insurance in 2007 and 2008.

Other innovations have also been introduced since the late 1990s to cope with new social risks. In the field of long-term care, Germany expanded its social insurances in 1995 by creating a specific regime to cover this new risk. Apart from the fact that employers were compensated for their social contribution payments to this new scheme (thus breaking the golden German rule of *Parität* in the financing of compulsory social insurances), no significant innovation was introduced with the *Pflegeverischerung*. More innovative were the subsequently adopted tax-financed scheme in Austria (*Pflegegeld*) and the new benefit for the dependent people in France (*Allocation personnalisée d'autonomie*).

What appears really innovative for some Bimarckian systems, however, are the new measures aimed at investing in children's development, conciliating work and family life and promoting gender equality. Some of the most Conservative welfare systems have started to adapt to the demise of the male breadwinner model, providing more formal care facilities for children, reforming their parental leaves so that they no longer inevitably break female careers by encouraging a better share of care work between mothers and fathers, and better protecting single mothers. The changes and other plans in the pipeline – are quite radical in Germany, Spain, Switzerland and the Netherlands, where governments are trying to modernize their welfare systems and render them less Conservative. This 'revolution' is however quite ambiguous, since these policies have been as much about stimulating an expansion in lower paid jobs (for women) in the service sector (Morel 2007) and encouraging higher fertility (Henninger et al. 2008) as they have been about improving conditions for women.

Meanwhile, some other countries – Italy, Austria and most of the Visegrad countries – have remained quite Conservative, mainly as a result of Conservative parties opposing these types of adaptation. France and Belgium are for their part somehow regressing, as some of the traits that traditionally made them distinctive from the typical male breadwinner model are currently being weakened under fiscal constraints. In France, for example, the *écoles maternelles* have recently been closing some classes for the youngest children.

Politics

So far we have seen that partisan politics did not seem to make an enormous difference in the policies implemented, and this remained true for the further retrenchments and structural reforms of traditional social insurances (cf. box 13.1). Here again, whatever the 'color' of the government, similar policies were implemented, and conflicts were again much more between governments and certain unions. Concerning modernization policies, however, a clearer impact of political cleavages is discernible.

Most of the structural reforms implemented in traditional social insurances were conflict-ridden, since projects usually triggered considerable discontent and sometimes – as in Austria (pension reform) and Germany (Hartz IV) – mass strikes and demonstrations. Governments no longer appeared so cautious in their way of presenting the negative impact of social protection structures. Political discourses became explicit: the systems needed to be changed, scaled back, activated and modernized. Not all the unions opposed the reforms, and governments often tried to play on these divisions, giving concessions to the modernizers (such as Ver.di in Germany, or CFDT in France) against more traditional oppositional unions (IG Metall in Germany, FO and CGT in France). These reforms were implemented though social pacts in Spain and in the Netherlands, but this procedure did not necessarily prevent political and social conflicts. Partly because they had gained political capacity as a result of the institutional reforms reviewed above, and partly because of a 'divide-and-rule' strategy, governments were able to impose reforms in spite of opposition and discontent. As we will see, however, concessions were often made to the unions and their core constituencies (long phasing in of pension reforms, strategic targeting of activation measures).

The new social policies were more consensual among the social partners, probably because they did not affect the core social insurances but instead added new layers to the existing social insurance system. The development of assistance-based minimum income benefits was welcomed by most of the social and political actors, because it addressed a manifestly pressing social issue, and furthermore relieved social insurances from an 'undue' burden. Difficulties were not entirely absent though, especially for the policies concerning families and women. Parliament had to bypass the social partners in Switzerland; Schröder's childcare projects were put on hold until the arrival of the grand coalition; the Spanish Catholics strongly opposed Zapatero; and in Italy and Austria, the modernizing projects of the Social Democrats were buried by the Conservatives on their return to office.

These reforms also had a number of significant consequences. These are discussed in detail in two sections below, following our explanation of the Bismarckian welfare reform trajectory as a whole.

13.3   How to Explain the Bismarckian Welfare Reform Trajectory?

The politics of welfare state reform in Continental Europe has been analyzed from a range of theoretical perspectives. As underlined in the first chapter of this volume, most research has used the concept of path dependence, and concluded that Conservative corporatist welfare systems have not changed considerably. As this volume shows, this interpretation will no longer suffice. Among those who identified possibilities for change in Continental European welfare states, some have argued that partisan politics is central. Levy (1999) in particular argued that left-wing parties are in a position to be able to turn 'vice into virtue'. While parts of the story told by the chapters in this volume appear to confirm this argument, it is not able to explain the general and common turn to structural reforms and activation in the 2000s, which have been implemented even under Conservative governments. To understand this shift, we need to take into account the emergence and adoption of a new social policy paradigm. This perspective emphasizes the role of reform learning and policy ideas in the dynamics observed. When comparing the processes traced in this volume with those documented by Peter Hall, however, we see that more explanatory weight needs to be given to mechanisms of institutional evolution, leading us to understand the Bismarckian welfare reform trajectory as a succession of institutional changes nurtured by various reform feedbacks, ultimately leading to the adoption (and 'Conservative corporatist' adaptation) of the dominant orthodox social policy paradigm.

Vice into Virtue?

One possible interpretation for the most recent and significant reforms in Bismarckian welfare systems is that they have been implemented by progressive parties, who have been able to target the 'vices' of these systems in order to render them both more economically efficient and socially just. In his famous article, Levy (1999) suggested that Social Democrats in Continental Europe could profit from the crisis to transform their typical weaknesses into strengths. By attenuating historic inequities, such as 'overtaxation of wage earnings, polarization of benefits, rigid insider-outsider cleavages, and indifference or even hostility to women trying to juggle maternal and career roles' (*Ibid.*: 246), 'progressive reformers have been able to extract resources with which to pursue a variety of "virtuous" objectives: redistributing income towards the poor without increasing public spending; improving the functioning of the economy without reducing benefits to the truly needy; and facilitating (through side-payments) the negotiation of far-reaching, tripartite social pacts to redesign basic parameters of welfare, labor market, and fiscal policy' (*Ibid.*: 240).

Some cases seem to confirm this analysis. Most of the 'modernization' reforms, aimed at improving the condition of part-time workers and especially of women, have been implemented either by Social Democratic governments or by coalitions including parties of the Left. The Italian pension reforms, which depended on the support of the Left, were explicitly aimed at reducing the inherent inequalities of a pension system that paid extremely generous pensions to civil servants and rather poor pensions to the self-employed and farmers. Schröder's 2001 pension reform in Germany created minimum benefits for the elderly and partly improved the pension calculation rules for women. More recently, modernizing changes in social insurances, pushed by the new Left, the Greens and women's organizations, have allowed a better integration of part-time work and an improvement of women's situation in Switzerland, while simultaneously reducing the level of benefits for core insiders. In Spain, the socialist government of Zapatero has greatly contributed to an improvement in the situation of labor market outsiders, and especially women. What is at stake here is whether the new social risks bearers can lever some representation within the parties that are or can be in government (Häusermann 2010b).

However, the implementation of such reforms has not in fact been the monopoly of the center-Left, since in Austria, it was the grand coalition that introduced new measures to cope with poverty and new social risks; in France, the right-wing Fillon government that introduced slightly better calculation rules for part-time work in its pension reform; and in Germany, the grand Coalition that has pushed forward the creation of day care facilities.

Moreover, few clear examples can be found of explicit 'vice-into-virtue' bargains, where those representing insiders make some concession to allow improved protection of the usual losers of Bismarckian systems (atypical workers, labor market outsiders, women, unskilled workers, etc.). We could even underline that, in the recent structural reforms as in earlier ones, material concessions have been made above all to core insiders. Almost all pension reforms have included long phasing in periods, so that the current core constituencies of trade unions will not be immediately hit by the reforms (Bonoli and Palier 2007). Activation has not been imposed on all the unemployed, but mainly targeted on the margins of the labor market. While core workers have continued to benefit from early exit and still relatively generous unemployment benefits, the long-term unemployed and beneficiaries of the new or expanded minimum incomes have progressively been put under activation pressures (Clegg 2007). Care policies have not attempted to alter the gendered division of household labor, and have tended to reproduce the patterns of stratification specific to Bismarckian welfare systems, with lower-income women particularly encouraged to use long, low-paid care schemes that result in their withdrawal from the labor market (Morel 2007).

Many similar reforms have thus been implemented, by right-wing, left-wing and coalition governments. Moreover, the reforms very often reinforce the segmentalist tendencies of Conservative corporatist welfare systems, notably by institutionalizing dualisms (see below, and Palier and Thelen 2010). These reforms cannot therefore be said to have been driven by a 'vice-into-virtue' strategy. This approach can help to explain some of the modernization reforms, but certainly not all of the further retrenchments and the structural reforms of traditional social insurances. As we have suggested, the biggest innovations within the Bismarckian welfare systems, such as the development of minimum income protection schemes, the rise of activation policies and the emergence of private tiers in the pension and health care systems appear instead to be a sort of Bismarckian adaptation of the new orthodox social policy paradigm that has been in circulation since the late 1980s.

However, the turn to this supply-side approach did not happen in exactly the same way as the adoption of the new macroeconomic policy paradigm, as described by Hall (1993). For sure, there are striking similarities in the two processes. The reform of Bismarckian social protection systems featured the three sequences identified by Hall; first, using available instruments: the labor shedding strategy; second, changing the instruments to face the persisting difficulties while trying to save the system: the first retrenchments; third and last, adopting a new social policy paradigm as the only way to overcome the accumulating anomalies that have become a crisis of the system itself. Like Hall, we have also underlined the importance of learning from one reform to the other, and we have seen a shift in the locus of power to allow for the third order change, from a (usually) tripartite social policy-making to a re-enforcement of state capacities and control over welfare reforms. In our cases there have however been more than three steps, and there has been more continuity than Hall observed for macroeconomic policies. Contrary to Hall's case, there was not a complete departure from the past and a general replacement of previous policies by new policies. The adoption of the new paradigm has rather been made possible by the development of past reforms, which served as a basis for implementing new policies.

Because of the 'stickiness' of welfare state institutions (Pierson 2001a), and because of their huge popularity, governments were not able to change the whole system even when they claimed that these systems were failing in dealing with economic and social issues. Structural welfare reforms have rarely been put at the heart of political platforms in Continental Europe. Rather, changes were initially incremental, passing through an intermediary phase based on a relatively 'silent' evolutionary institutional transformation (changes in financing, changes in power relations), that weakened the institutional and political bases of the welfare systems and facilitated structural reforms based on a new social policy paradigm. Even these new social policies have not entirely replaced the former ones, but merely contributed to a conversion of the old system to the new goals.

Hence, our analysis leads us to contest the idea of changes driven by sudden rupture in a long-term equilibrium[27], and instead emphasize evolutionary transformation based on incremental but cumulatively transformative incremental changes (Streeck and Thelen 2005b). The adoption of the new social policy paradigm should not be conceived as a sudden innovation, introduced through a paradigmatic revolution in the 2000s. Even if there was another economic slowdown in the early 2000s, it was no more dramatic than earlier cyclical slowdowns during previous economic cycles occurred, and less so than the commodity price shocks of the 1970s. One cannot therefore explain these changes very well with reference to a critical juncture (Gourevitch 1986) that undermined a pre-existing equilibrium. What led to third order changes was more a progressive transformation through less visible institutional evolution, and this pre-conditioned and enabled the more visible paradigmatic changes.

How did Bismarckian Institutions Evolve?

In Bismarckian social protection systems, structural reform should be understood as the result of an accumulation of previous reforms, which created the conditions for radical transformations to occur. The transformation did not, however, consist in replacing an old welfare system with a new one. Instead, it consisted of a progressive transformation of the whole architecture by the introduction of new 'layers' at the margins, and then the conversion of existing social policies to new goals and orientations. We need therefore to associate Hall's approach with the perspectives developed by Thelen and Streeck to fully understand the process of change. The paradigmatic change was the result of the progressive *exhaustion* of the first responses to the crisis (e.g. labor shedding), and of the shrinkage (a kind of *drift*) of social insurance to allow the implementation of two types of institutional innovations: the *layering* of new social policies, and the implementation of (initially marginal) institutional reforms (new taxes, new governance procedures,). Finally, despite the explicit rupture with the past in many reforms of the early 2000s, much happened through the *conversion* of existing policies (activation of assistance policies, residualization of compulsory social insurances), and through new interactions and *drifts* between the various segments of the social protection system.

The first mechanism documented in our cases is the implementation and then progressive *exhaustion* of the first type of reaction to the crisis, typically driven by the Bismarckian framework of social policy, i.e. the labor shedding strategy as well as increases in social contribution rates. These first policies were partly exhausted by their endogenous disequilibrium: asking the ever fewer people in work to be ever more productive, and to pay for ever more social expenditure. The more deeply this strategy was implemented, the fewer human and fiscal resources there were to sustain it.

Despite the endogeneity of such mechanisms, however, there was an exogenous element that pushed actors to reassess their strategy, and that provided arguments (if not real constraints) for a first reorientation. In most of the cases, this exogenous element came from the implementation of the single market and the preparation of the European single currency (with unification being more important in the German case). This new context was crucial for revealing the failure of the initially adopted strategy. Governments then turned to second order changes, the content of which were also tightly bound to the existing welfare institutions: retrenchments 'à la Bismarckian'.

These retrenchments were implemented through stricter calculation rules to access social insurances (typically, longer contribution periods are necessary to acquire rights to the same benefits). Not only does this not change the basic elements of the system, it on the contrary reinforces them: the contributivity of the benefits is increased and the 'equivalence' principle reaffirmed.

These retrenchments however led to a first kind of *drift* in the system, in this case shrinkage in the coverage of social insurances that has been compensated by new types of social provisions. As discussed in the first chapter, the characteristics of Bismarckian welfare systems as they were (in the late 1970s) included the aim to (directly or indirectly) cover the whole population for all the risks they were exposed to, by guaranteeing the maintenance of living standards of the insured and their family. The retreat of social insurances has diminished the coverage capacity of social insurances: fewer people are covered, replacement rates are lower, while certain risks – new social risks – are not covered. Social insurance has retracted such that in many countries it has been reduced to mainly covering core workers exposed to traditional risks; and covering the latter less well than in the past.

This shrinkage is another endogenous mechanism that led to the *layering* of innovative politics, at the margins of the system, which themselves contributed to make the paradigmatic changes of the early 2000s possible. New gaps in coverage had to be compensated or plugged in some way, and they have been by new types of policies. In order to compensate for the reduced coverage of people, a new *layer* of assistance policies (tax-financed targeted minimum income benefits) has been either expanded or created for those not contributing enough or at all to social insurances. This has been done not to replace the social insurances but instead to 'purify' them, with social insurance henceforth financing only contributory benefits, and social assistance delivering 'non-contributory' benefits. The expansion of the latter was initially symmetrical to the retreat of social insurance (the fewer people are covered by insurance, the more of them fall under assistance schemes).

In order to compensate for the lower replacement rates guaranteed by traditional social insurances, new *layers* of private pension funds and private health insurance provisions have expanded on top of the system. The development of these private pillars within systems that were originally meant to be sufficient to guarantee the maintenance of standard of living has also been incremental. It was initially through individuals' own initiatives to save more for their pension as they anticipated the consequences of the first retrenchments that private pensions have grown (Bonoli and Palier 2007); it was only progressively that private health insurances have grown to complement the compulsory system (Hassenteufel and Palier 2007). In both cases, we can speak of a *creeping privatization*.

The dynamics unleashed by the first retrenchments have thus allowed the development of new policies at the two ends of the system. The multiplication of new layers has led to a more heterogeneous system of social protection, which combines different types of entitlement rules, of benefits and of financing modes and which was much more complex to control, run and manage. Confronted with this increasing complexity, as well as with the increasing conflict around the decisions to be taken, governments (and on occasion social partners) learned from the failures of past reforms and decided to 'clarify' things by defining more clearly who finances what, and who decides on what. What we have called in-stitutional reforms (changes in financing and in policy-making proce-dures) were supposed to solve these problems of complexity by using taxes to finance the increasing amount of non-contributory benefits, and enhancing the state's power to push through decisions perceived as necessary.

As has been shown, the turn to structural reforms occurred as the re-sult of an adoption of new social policy goals (activation, modernization), and implementation of innovative social policy instruments. They were however made possible only by the institutional reforms and by the previ-ous development of the new layers just mentioned.

The development of private pensions relied on existing trends and tools. It consisted merely in encouraging an already existing tendency to increasing saving, either by creating new instruments (such as the Riester funds in Germany, and the PERP and PERCO in France) or by converting already existing measures such as the redundancy payment systems in Italy and Austria.

In many cases, other important *conversions* of existing policies and in-struments towards the new social policy goals are visible.

Firstly, activation has mainly been implemented in Continental Europe through the activation of social assistance schemes, and limited to labor market outsiders. Instead of the entire unemployment benefit system be-ing turned into a system of conditional benefits for all, new conditions (and sometimes services) have been grafted onto income- or means-tested benefits, thereby *converting* assistance schemes into in-work benefits (the Hartz IV reforms in Germany and the creation of the RSA in France are the clearest examples).

Secondly, replacement rates in pensions were further reduced in the early 2000s, thereby *converting* old-age insurance goals from income maintenance to the provision of a basic pension guarantee. Through in-creases in the retirement age and in the number of contribution years nec-essary to receive a full pension, actuarial neutrality has been put forward as the new principle for calibrating pensions. In some cases, the replace-ment rate has been lowered so much that adequate income replacement is no longer guaranteed, but instead a (relatively generous) minimum in-come (like in Belgium, Germany or Austria). People are encouraged to rely on funded complementary schemes to replace their past income in the future. This residualization of pensions has been facilitated by the development of the private complements, as governments could explain that the future role of private complements is to ensure income replacement while the role of the public pension schemes is to guarantee basic pensions.

The analysis here largely confirms Thelen and Streeck's hypothesis that complex institutional systems change fundamentally through an interaction between existing institutions and various layers that have been introduced initially at the margins as merely adaptive adjustments. Their notion of policy *drifts*, through which the relative importance of different policy segments changes so much as to ultimately transform the whole institutional architecture, is also relevant. Table 13.5 tries to classify the various types of change seen in Bismarckian social protection systems according to whether they are changing the goals and/or the instruments of social policies and with reference to Thelen and Streeck's typology of institutional changes.

Before asking whether this new architecture means a real welfare regime change for Continental Europe, it should be reiterated that the trajectory sketched out should be read only as the 'typical' trajectory, and that 'real' countries have always followed their own route, with their own idiosyncrasies. Even a focus on these differences, however, very much confirms our basic hypothesis, namely that welfare institutions matter very much in shaping welfare reform trajectories, but do not prevent important consequential change.

Accounting for Differences: Welfare Institutions Matter!

As any scrupulous reader of the country chapters in this book will have noticed, the exact same reform trajectory has not been followed everywhere. The Netherlands started structural reforms much sooner, Belgium has not really witnessed a turn to activation, and Italy and Austria did not modernize their social policies. The politics of reform has also been different; reforms have been very conflictual in some countries and negotiated through social pacts in others, Europe mattered more in some cases – such as Italy, Spain, Belgium and France – than in others, and so on...

Some chapters discuss the reasons for these variations (see especially the chapters on Belgium/the Netherlands, on Spain and on Switzerland). The stated intention of this chapter is not to explain variation, but instead to underline the similarities. Relying on the chapters mentioned, we can nonetheless highlight some variables that appear to help us understand the 'variations on the common theme'.

Table 13.5   The various types of changes implemented in Bismarckian welfare systems

Goals, principles	Welfare institutions	
	Same	**New**
Same	STATUS QUO Towards EXHAUSTION? Belgium unable to close its early exit route (data, if not policies, show similar trends in many other countries), Italian incapacity to reform its labor market, and to implement a minimum income Italian and Austrian conservatism on family policy *Frozen Landscape*	RECALIBRATION DUALIZATION THROUGH LAYERING AND DRIFT 'Reactionary recalibration': long phasing in of public pension reforms for current insiders – supplementary private pensions accessible mainly to the well off – Increase in or maintenance of unemployment allowances for insiders, decrease for outsiders (plus more conditionality), – Increasing role of assistance schemes – Care policies: From labor shedding to cheapening labor, the fallacies of free choice *Neo-Conservative/neo-corporatist welfare system*
New	CONVERSION From income maintenance to minimum income guarantees: – Belgian unemployment insurance – Old-age public pensions in Germany, Belgium, Austria, Italy Activation of assistance schemes Targeted activation *A 'Liberal' dynamic in Bismarckian welfare system*	INNOVATIONS Through LAYERING and DRIFTS Progressive universalization of health care Development of childcare facilities *Post-Bismarckian reforms*

When Politics Matter

As already mentioned, if partisan politics does not appear to matter much for the retrenchments and structural reforms of Continental European welfare systems, it is more significant for their modernization. It is when parties (usually, but not always, of the center-Left) are able to build new coalitions including new social risk bearers that modernization policies are implemented (see Häusermann 2010b). Inversely, it is largely when there is a clear Conservative majority in government that they are not.

In general, the rhythm of the reform trajectory is also highly dependent on partisan politics, very often a change in sequence being triggered by the arrival in power of a new majority or coalition. The political color of this new government does not however seem to determine much the content of the new phase (cf. the striking similarities in the policies implemented by Schröder in Germany and right-wing governments in France).

Macropolitical institutions such as the structure of the state, the electoral system and the degree of fragmentation in the industrial relations system are also of crucial importance in accounting for variations, especially in timing and intensity (if not the content) of reforms. This is very well illustrated by the Dutch-Belgian comparison: 'the two countries are distinct in terms of the institutional frameworks of the political system within which their welfare states and industrial-relations systems are embedded, suggesting possible explanatory variables for *divergent* policy outcomes. Compared to the Netherlands, Belgian federalism and linguistic regionalism have decisively constrained the scope of government intervention not only in wage bargaining but also in a host of other social and economic policy areas. Also social partnership is more fragmented, making it difficult to establish and enact broad corporatist social pacts' (Hemerijck and Marx, this volume). Further comparisons would certainly demonstrate that macropolitical institutions can help explain differences in timing, political mechanisms (negotiation, blockage or imposition) and in the depth of reforms between countries.

Welfare Institutions Matter

What seems, however, to be the main explanandum for whether countries have followed the same trajectory or not is related to the initial *institutional configuration of their welfare systems*. In this book, the main divergences are explained by differences in the point of departure. This is obvious for health care in the case of Italy and Spain. As the Spanish chapter makes clear, it is because the health insurance system was not based on a diversity of autonomous funds that it could be universalized.[28] In general, as Guillén (this volume) puts it, in Spain 'some of the corporatist institutional arrangements were missing, especially those related to the existence of independent professional funds and those concerned with the management and administration of the system and the role played by the social partners (...) it is precisely this lack of intense corporatist traits that eased the way for the paradigmatic reforms of the 1980s and the recalibration of the 1990s. Conversely, the "Conservative familialist" character of the Spanish welfare state has proved more difficult to overcome.' In the same vein, the initial structure of pensions and health care in the Netherlands or in Switzerland account for much of their specific reform trajectories. The same could be said to explain the Belgium exceptionalism as far as unemployment is concerned[29], or some reverse tendencies in the Visegrad countries.

As Hemerijck and Marx point out (this volume), 'national social policy legacies and political institutional particularities shape both the options available to state and non-state policy actors to reconfigure Continental welfare arrangements'. To put it in a nutshell, the more the point of departure diverged from the Bismarckian norm, the more 'deviant' the reform trajectory has also been.

Otherwise, it should also be acknowledged that similar trends (and even trajectories) to the ones described in this volume can also be seen outside Continental Europe. To a large extent, this again confirms our basic hypothesis, for generally these similarities are to be found in social policy fields where at least parts of the welfare institutions are similar to the ones to be found in Continental Europe (especially entitlements based on work record and a predominance of contributory benefits). Remaining differences are again explained by variations in the institutional architecture of welfare systems, especially in terms of financing and governance. An exhaustive account of welfare state changes in the world is obviously beyond the scope of the present chapter, but a few can be mentioned. Most countries adopted explicit or implicit early exit policies as a first response to the crisis in the mid-1970s, but many did not persist with these, largely because the financing of this strategy was not as heavily based on social contributions as in Continental Europe. The politics of pension reform in the US shows some similarities with the trends analyzed in our cases, and this should be attributed to the fact that the American *Social Security* is a strongly contributory system. Finally, the turn to activation often follows a similar route to the one we have analyzed, and dualization can also occur elsewhere, including in Scandinavia (Davidsson 2009). What should be remembered here is that in most countries unemployment protection is organized as a social insurance, and hence follows a relatively similar route. However, the importance of dualization in Nordic countries should be scrutinized closely, and compared to the size of the phenomenon in Continental Europe (Martin and Thelen 2007).

It is now possible to turn to the general assessment of the impact of the welfare reform trajectories in Continental Europe, starting with the effect of reforms on the systems themselves (outputs), and then turning to their economic and social consequences (outcomes).

13.4 What have the Bismarckian Welfare Systems Become?

We have seen that in recent decades many reforms have introduced new principles and new instruments in Continental European social protection systems, thus implementing third order changes. Does that entail a wholesale change in the welfare systems of these countries? All national chapters assess the transformation of their own welfare system, and many differences are visible. There are however similar evolutions that merit being underscored. Referring to the general goals, principles and institutions of Bismarckian welfare systems as they were stated in the first chapter of this volume, it is possible to measure the general changes that have occurred, starting with changes in the goals and principles, and then looking at changes in the social policy instruments. Taken together, all the reforms have contributed to a reorganization of the entire welfare systems: they have lost their encompassing capacities, partly turned to activation and employment-friendliness, and weakened the strongest elements of their male breadwinner bias. Instead of the emergence of new hybrid welfare systems, we conclude that Continental Europe witnessed the development of dual welfare systems that differentiate between the protection of the core workers and the activation of the 'atypical' (low-skilled) ones.

A Long Goodbye to Encompassing Social Insurances

A first key change is that the compulsory social insurances are no longer able to guarantee income maintenance, to cover the whole population, and to protect against all the main social risks.

As seen in the first chapter, the main goal of social protection in Bismarckian systems was initially to provide income security to workers and their families. This goal was broadened in the late 1960s, and social insurances were then supposed to cover the whole population, all social risks and guarantee near-total income maintenance. Even if they did not in reality cover the whole population in the past, at least in the late 1960s and the 1970s (and sooner for Germany, see the 1957 pension reform), covering the whole population – directly through social insurance for male workers or indirectly for their spouse and children through the 'family wage' (Esping-Andersen 1996a) – was clearly the objective. The explicit goal was to include the whole population in the social insurance schemes and for social assistance to be consigned to history.

As we have seen, the various waves of retrenchments have increased the 'contributivity' of benefits and the 'equivalence' principle, leading coverage and replacement rates to decline. In most of the cases, fewer people are covered than before and a lower proportion of past wages are replaced in both old-age insurance and unemployment insurance. Though some recent reforms have endeavored to include part-time workers within the systems (in the Netherlands, Switzerland, Spain and partly Austria, France and Germany), social insurance can no longer be considered as 'quasi-universal' (Leisering 2009).

The goal of securing the previously achieved standards of living has also vanished. In most of the cases, replacement rates have been lowered in pensions, so that people need a private complement to maintain their standard of living during old age. In some cases the equivalence principle has itself disappeared (in Belgian unemployment insurance, where it did not really exist for long, but more importantly, in German, Austrian, Belgian and Italian compulsory old-age insurance), to be replaced by a relatively generous minimal pension guarantee. Income maintenance does not seem to be an achievable goal for Bismarckian welfare systems anymore, and is being progressively replaced by *minimum income maintenance*.

More and more assistance schemes have been developed to cover the uninsured and to guarantee a basic safety net, thus adding a new goal to the system: *preventing poverty*. What Bleses and Seeleib-Kaiser (2004: 92) observe for Germany can be applied to all Continental European countries; 'the principle of *publicly* guaranteeing the achieved living standard is on the retreat, while the principle of publicly securing a minimum of existence is increasingly gaining importance'.

As demonstrated by Armingeon and Bonoli (2006) as well as in the chapters in this volume, traditional Bismarckian welfare systems were also not easily able to cope with new social risks, and needed to add new social policies to address them. Hence it can also be said that the typical Bismarckian institutions are no longer able to cover all social risks, and needed other types of policies (new services and targeted benefits).

If the Bismarckian welfare systems are less fragmented in various social insurances funds than before (there have been mergers, concentration and reduction of the number of schemes and funds in many countries), they are now simultaneously more fragmented into a greater diversity of social policies, the core of social insurance no longer being able to suffice.

Farewell to Maternalism?

As shown in the various papers, the Bismarckian welfare systems have also tried to adapt to changes in society, notably the demise of the male breadwinner model. It certainly cannot be said that in Continental Europe social policies have driven the entry of women into the labor market, but they have belatedly tried to adjust to this trend by offering more scope for women to combine work and family life. This however has been done in quite a 'Conservative' way, since in the name of 'free choice' low-skilled women are still given incentives to stay at home to take care of the children, while more skilled women are offered more (but still very expensive) possibilities to have their children cared for (Morel 2007).

Towards Employment-Friendliness

Progressively, at least in the reforms, the former goal of supposedly 'passive' income maintenance has been replaced by a new one, *activation*, in all fields: unemployment, active ageing, and supporting women's participation in the labor market. As Hinrichs (this volume) puts it: 'Instead of income support, the focus is now on a maximum integration of the (long-term) unemployed, older workers and mothers into paid employment.' As will be seen below, this activation has been relatively successful in terms of employment rates, but not in terms of job quality and associated social protection.

All the common trends are very well summed up by Hinrichs in this volume: 'Reduced levels of income security through wage earner schemes, accompanied by demands for self-responsibility and more private provision, stronger reliance on means-tested benefits, and stricter activation measures.'

Next to these new goals and principles, there has also been a modification in the policy instruments deployed.

Dual Welfare Systems

The multiplication of policies and the diversification of goals and principles might lead us to conclude that the Continental European welfare systems have become more hybrid, where traits of the two other 'worlds of welfare' can today be found. Instead of a blurred and incoherent mix of policies, however, we would instead argue that the new welfare systems of Continental Europe are in fact characterized by a dualized structure, comprised of (less and less) social insurance on the one hand (for the 'insiders') and more developed targeted assistance and activation schemes (for the 'outsiders').

Access to Benefits

In most of the countries studied, *entitlements* to old-age pension, unemployment insurance, invalidity and work accident insurance are still based on work records and status. However, as a result of retrenchment policies, the amount of contribution paid is more central to the calculation of the benefits than before, thus increasing the 'actuarial' principles in the eligibility criteria.

Next to the traditional social insurances, access to other benefits is now based on different criteria: citizenship is more and more a defining entitlement to health care, family benefits and access to services such as childcare. Poverty and citizenship conditions are often combined into what some authors call a 'selective universalism' (Ferrera 2006) that defines access to minimum income assistance schemes.

Types of Benefits

There has been a clear diversification of the *types of benefits* in recent decades. Though contributory cash benefits still play the most important role, they are now less proportional to former wages than calibrated on 'real' amounts and durations of contributions paid. One can even see a certain residualization of benefits in some cases (old-age pension in Germany, Austria, Italy and Belgium; unemployment benefit in Belgium), where formerly proportional earnings-related benefits are becoming more and more like minimum income guarantees.

For those who can no longer access contributory benefits, income and sometimes means-tested benefits have been either expanded or created in all countries. In-work benefits have been added to assistance ones (cf. the '1 euro jobs' in Germany, or the RSA in France).

Bismarckian welfare systems still lack social services, despite plans to increase child and elderly care. In many cases, instead of these new services being directly provided, cash benefits (often income-tested) are used to pay for these services whose growth in the market sphere is being encouraged either by subsidies or by social contribution exemptions.

Next to public welfare, private protection is also playing an increasing role, especially in pensions and health care. Complementary private pension funds are voluntary, and can take two main forms, either collective (thus being funded jointly by employees and employers, with state subsidies), or individual (with the state subsidizing individuals or households).

Financing

As shown in the various chapters and as analyzed by Manow (this volume), the modes of *financing* have also changed, drifting from social contributions to taxes in order to make the welfare system's financing more 'employment-friendly'. After a sharp increase in social contributions up to the mid-1990s, a reversal has subsequently been implemented, and the share of social contributions has been decreasing since the mid-1990s (from 17 percent to less than 15 percent of GDP on average in Manow's Bismarckian cluster, including Austria, Belgium, France, Germany, the Netherlands and Italy). Social contributions are far less than before the main means of financing social benefits in Continental Europe, even though they still play the biggest role (see the precise figures in the various country chapters, but on average, they got closer to 60 percent of all resources, compared to the earlier average of 70 percent). Once again, this is not so much suggestive of a blurring of the system, since in many countries reforms have strictly distinguished between the uses of social contributions (to pay for contributory benefits in social insurance), and the use of other forms of taxation, to be allocated to non-contributory (either universal or targeted) benefits.

Governance

Due to other institutional reforms, *social policy-making* has also greatly changed in Continental Europe. In most countries, the social partners can no longer be considered as veto players, at least for compulsory social insurances. Because of *étatisation* or privatization, and sometimes both together, they have increasingly been bypassed in reform events. Even if the status of social insurance funds has rarely been changed (with the notable exception of health insurance in the Netherlands, Germany and France), those who decide on and manage them are closer to the state (national or local public authorities) than it was the case before. Moreover, private companies play a much more important role, whether in employment policies and job placement, pensions (new facultative funded pension plans) or health care (*mutuelles complémentaires* in France, health insurances for glasses and dental care in Germany).

We are all Supply-Siders Now!

The interpretation of these shifts is not easy (see table 13.5), and varies within this volume. For Hinrichs (this volume), these changes suggest a turn to the Liberal model. For Häusermann (this volume), by contrast, 'abandoning the income maintenance of the breadwinner is likely to be accompanied by the introduction of innovative goals (poverty prevention), principles (selective universalism) and policy instruments (minimum insertion income, means-tested family benefits, development of social services) that, if fully institutionalized, might have helped to bridge the traditional insiders/outsiders gap.'

With reference to the above discussion of the welfare reform trajectory, we can in fact consider that these new goals and new instruments reflect the adoption of the new orthodoxy in social policy: we are all supply-siders now! This adoption does not however mean a total absorption and radical transformation of Continental welfare systems. As much as Hall (1989) detected different variants of Keynesianism, we see here the emergence of a Continental European *variant* of supply-side social policies. The new supply-side orientations have been adapted to Bismarckian ways of thinking and doing. Though one can see some Liberal dynamics in the residualization of public pensions, the increasing role of private ones, and the development of assistance schemes (see the bottom-left cell in table 13.5), one should notice that many private pensions are based on collective agreements, and thus keep a corporatist flavor. Furthermore, when assistance schemes were activated, these targeted only the outsiders, while shielding most of the former insiders. What is most striking is the dualization of welfare, which makes most of the Continental European countries switch to what can be called a neo-Conservative, neo-corporatist welfare system (top-right in table 13.5). Only few 'post-Bismarckian' social policy fields have emerged: universal health care in some countries, development of childcare facilities (bottom-right in table 13.5). This dualization of welfare both reflects and contributes to the dualization of Continental European labor markets and societies.

13.5 What are the Main Economic and Social Consequences of the Welfare Reform Trajectory?

The Economic and Social Consequences of the Reforms

By adopting but also adapting the new 'orthodox' social policy agenda, Bismarckian systems may have found their own specific 'way out' of their economic and social difficulties. As Häusermann puts it in this volume: 'We may be witnessing the start of a genuinely Continental "way out" of the post-industrial challenges: the inegalitarian and insurance-related aspects are reinforced with the reduction of replacement rates, the lengthening of contribution periods and the inclusion of [some] former outsiders in the insurance schemes. At the same time, however, a basic minimum protection allows for this reform strategy by easing the most pressing poverty risks, and by providing the reforms with the necessary political legitimacy.'

How successful has this strategy been in overcoming the specific problems that have haunted Continental Europe for decades: mass unemployment, low employment rates, slow growth rates and high labor costs? According to Hemerijck and Eichhorst (this volume), these countries have recorded impressive successes on the employment front (before the 2008 crisis), but modernization remains limited and further efforts are needed. However, the welfare reforms have also contributed to increase dualisms both in labor markets and in societies more generally.

Away from the Labor Shedding Strategy

The data analyzed by Hemerijck and Eichhorst are striking. After two decades of slow 'jobless growth', Bismarckian welfare systems seem to have been able to overcome the 'welfare without work' trap. Between 1997 and 2007, all key economic indicators seem to switch in a positive direction: lower levels of unemployment, higher employment rates for women and for older workers (Germany and the Netherlands being even able to reach the EU targets of 50 percent of activity for the 55-64) and for the low-skilled. This can arguably be attributed to structural reforms (activation) and to changes in financing. Bismarckian welfare systems have been able to address their main regime-specific challenges, as first outlined by Esping-Andersen (1996a) and Scharpf and Schmidt (2000): the cost of (unskilled) labor has been reduced, 'passive' income maintenance has been transformed into targeted activation and in-work benefits. What remains to be seen is whether the increase in unemployment and the huge level of public debts and deficits associated with the 2008/2009 crisis will be addressed in the same ways as in the 2000s or if different approaches will be used, whether older recipes or the kind of social investment strategy proposed by Hemerijck and Eichhorst, as well as Esping-Andersen, in this volume.

From Labor Shedding to Labor Cheapening and Flexibilization: Increased Dualism on the Labor Market

Though relatively good results have been obtained on the employment front from a quantitative point of view, the quality of many of the jobs created is in fact low. During the 1990s, and in parallel to the first wave of retrenchment, Continental European countries introduced more flexibility on the margin of their labor markets, leading to the development of a growing secondary sphere of temporary and part-time jobs generally attached to limited levels of protection (Palier and Thelen 2010). In the 2000s, the activation turn, the development of subsidized jobs through social contribution exemption (such as mini and midi jobs in Germany, *emplois aidés* in France) and the development of in-work benefits have all driven the further expansion of this secondary labor market. Even if their number is increasing fast, these new jobs are often called 'atypical' in Continental Europe, with the term itself implying that different norms and rules apply in this segment of the labor market. To the extent that such employment is considered 'exceptional', even as it grows, it is also not allowed to compete with the core sector (i.e. not putting so much pressure on it so as to compromise the wages and security of insiders) (Palier and Thelen 2010).

Like for the welfare systems, labor market transformation is progressive and does not attack the core frontally: the core labor market remains highly protected, though fewer and fewer 'typical' jobs are created, while more and more of the 'atypical' jobs are created instead. Since in most of the cases 'atypical' jobs do not benefit from typical social protection (with the notable exception of the Netherlands, and some part-time workers in various countries), it can hardly be concluded that, in Continental Europe, the outsiders benefited unambiguously from the labor market and welfare reforms.

As comparative and general data on labor markets (such as OECD employment protection legislation indicators) does not capture these real trends well – on average, employment protection legislation is still 'rigid' in Continental Europe –, we can refer to some of the national chapters in this volume to illustrate this growing dualization of Continental labor markets[30] (see box 13.2).

Box 13.2   The increased dualism in Continental labor markets

In Germany, in 2006, 14.3 percent of fulltime and 23.4 percent of (covered) part-time workers earned an hourly wage of less than two-thirds of the median (Bosch et al. 2008). The spreading of the working poor is only one aspect of increasing labor market flexibility. Furthermore, fewer employment careers corresponding to the *Standard Employment Relationship* model result from more frequent spells of (long-term) unemployment, (marginal) part-time work or periods of uncovered self-employment. Very often, workers in low-paid or precarious jobs lack the funds to additionally save for a *Riester-Rente* that becomes indispensable to ensure a modest standard of living after retirement (Hinrichs, this volume).

In France, the number of 'atypical' working contracts and jobs has expanded massively since the 1970s. In 1970, atypical jobs (fixed term, part-time and agency jobs) represented 3 percent of all employment, but this figure had jumped to more than 25 percent by 2007. Most strikingly, perhaps, 70 percent of the new job contracts are currently 'atypical' (Castel 2009: 165). As for other countries, this trend started in the 1990s, and has increased during the 2000s. 'Between 1990 and 2000, people employed with a short-term contract grew by 60 percent, those who benefited from a training period or special contract with public financing by 65 percent, and temporary workers by 130 percent. During the same period, employment in "regular" jobs increased by only 2 percent. In France, the victims of the kind of flexibility represented by new forms of work are mainly found among youth, women, and groups with lower skill populations.' (Lallement 2006: 57). The number of subsidized fixed-term, low-paid jobs for low-skilled workers peaked in 2005 at around 500,000. In 2004, 7.3 billion euros was spent on these jobs, to which one should add the social contribution exemption of 17 billion euros for the low-paid 'normal' jobs (Palier and Thelen 2010).

In Austria, between 2000 and 2006, the number of quasi-freelancers and persons holding a marginal job increased by some 20 percent. In addition, the ratio of part-time workers went up from 14.7 percent in 1997 to 21.1 percent in 2006 (Obinger and Tálos, this volume).

In Italy, though a high level of job protection (and stability) has been maintained for the 'insiders' – due to the strong resistance by the major unions on this issue – the pattern of employment based on fulltime permanent contracts has been overcome, at least for the new entrants in the labor market, and flexibilization has rapidly increased. In Italy, the share of 'atypical workers' on total employment has gone from 9.3 percent in 1993 to 16.2 percent in 2003. The spread of flexible contracts amongst the new entrants the labor market indicated that at least for the younger generations the traditional pattern of job security had been abandoned (Jessoula and Alti, this volume).

In Spain, since the mid-1980s, labor market liberalization took place. This move had a decisive influence on the configuration of the Spanish labor market. Temporary contracts facilitated the adaptation of staffing to cyclical conditions and stimulated the creation of employment. Still, fixed-term contracts quickly reached 30 percent of all salaried workers (the highest rate in the EU up to the present), produced a dualization of the labor market structure and were not able to drastically reduce unemployment (15 percent at the end of the 1980s) (...) The deep fragmentation of the Spanish labor market, the still soaring proportion of fixed-term jobs, and the fact that it is young people and women who are the losers is hardly a reason for rejoicing (Guillén, this volume).

In Switzerland, by 2000, the proportion of part-time employees in the Swiss labor market had reached 30 percent, almost 80 percent of which being female. About 5 percent of the workforce holds employment contracts of less than two years duration and self-employment has increased over the 1990s from about 15 to almost 20 percent (Häusermann, this volume.)

This increasing dualism on the labor market and in social protection has reinforced and nurtured dualism in European societies.

The Institutionalization of Dualisms in Society

The reforms of the last decades that we have analyzed have resulted in multiple dualizations: the development of two worlds of welfare within the public system; the addition of a private component to the public system; and the division of the population between insured insiders and assisted and/or activated outsiders. The shrinking of social insurance has left space both above (for private voluntary components, i.e. private pension funds and private health insurances) and underneath (for covering the poorest with minimum incomes) the public system. As we have seen, beside the remaining – but more individualized and partly privatized – social insurance schemes, a secondary world of work and welfare is developing for outsiders, made up of secondary 'atypical' jobs, activation policies and income-tested targeted benefits. This is a new architecture for the Bismarckian welfare systems, with social insurance still central but no longer hegemonic. This new architecture has created new forms of vertical dualism in society and will probably generate more social inequalities.

The population itself seems to be increasingly divided into, on the one hand, those who can rely on rather generous social insurance programs and continue to have access – thanks to their employers or their own wealth – to private complements, and on the other hand, those who have fallen out of that system and are dependent on minimum benefits. To the latter group, one should probably add those being activated into 'atypical' contracts under which they benefit from second rank jobs and social protection (Clegg 2007). Social protection reforms have thus contributed to increase inequalities and divide society between insiders and outsiders.

In many countries (especially Italy, Belgium, Germany and Austria), public pensions provided through social security have become so low that average to high earners will have to rely on occupational and private schemes to obtain a pension commensurate with their past earnings. A duality has emerged between people with access to such schemes and those without (Jessoula, this volume). Even if some governments (like the German one) have planned a progressive state subsidy (taking the income and number of children into account), the development of complementary pension funds will induce broader inequalities among pensioners, again entrenching divides between insiders (having good income and being employed in large firms, where they enjoy good collectively bargained benefits) and outsiders, whose employers are too small to afford pension plans, and who themselves do not have the means to put extra money aside.

In countries where private complementary health insurances are playing a growing role (France, but also Germany, the Netherlands or Switzerland, in their own fashion), the same trends can also be observed in the health care sector (Hassenteufel and Palier 2007).

What is also striking is the social impact of the dualization of welfare itself. The creation of a secondary world of welfare, made of assistance schemes (and subsidized cheap jobs), for those who cannot afford 'normal' social insurances is in itself institutionalizing dualism in society.

It may be in Germany that the trend towards dualization is most visible and consequential. With the Hartz IV reforms, 'the unemployed with no prior or insufficient *ALG I* entitlements are dependent on the flat-rate benefit from the very start. *ALG II* is not merely a basic security scheme for the registered unemployed: rather, it is designed to serve all needy people of working age. As with social assistance before, *ALG II* may be paid if income from employment is too low to meet the needs of the household' (Hinrichs, this volume). Increasing poverty in Germany can be traced to the implementation of this dualizing reform. Hinrichs (this volume) underlines the increased number of poor children in Germany. 'Unemployment of their parents and single parenthood are the primary reasons. In January 2008, three years after the implementation of the *Hartz IV* act, about 1.9 million children below the age of 15 lived in households of *ALG II* recipients (*Bedarfsgemeinschaften*), i.e. every sixth child received means-tested benefits.'

In France, the number of RMI recipients has continuously increased over the 1990s, reaching 1.2 million in 2007, about 3.5 percent of the population (family members of the recipients are included). About 10 percent of the population depends on a minimum income, and more and more of the poorest are 'activated' into bad jobs. As Gazier and Petit (2007: 1051) point out: 'the composition of poverty [has] changed dramatically. The poor (defined as households living with less than 50 percent of the median household income) at the beginning of the 1980s were mainly out of the labor force; during the 1990s, poor households with at least one member belonging to the labor force became the majority. (...) In order to fight exclusion, the French policies largely contributed to create a new segment of disadvantaged workers: the working poor often combining low pay and transfer payments.'

In Austria, 'the strengthening of the equivalence principle makes clear that the losers of past welfare state reforms are employees whose employment record deviates from the standard employment relationship. These groups consist mainly of women, immigrants and low-skilled workers. As a consequence of the dualization between insiders (the fulltime employed labor force) and the new social risk groups, a higher share of the population will be doomed to rely on means-tested benefits. For example, the number of recipients of social assistance benefits increased by 105 percent between 1996 and 2008' (Obinger and Tálos, this volume).

If the dual route to welfare and labor market reform is the typical 'Conservative-corporatist' way of adapting to the new economic and social environment, this segmented pathway will be quite robust and will shape the future of Continental Europe. Even if the situation was already fragmented and inegalitarian before, certainly in Germany, France, Italy and Austria, but also partly so in most of the rest of Continental Europe, recent trends will deepen divisions and lead to the consolidation of an increasingly cleaved world: dual labor markets, dual welfare systems and a society divided between insiders and outsiders.

13.6 The Crisis and Beyond

Since 2008, the world has entered a period of intense crisis, which has led to economic recession and a sharp increase in unemployment. It is of course impossible to predict precisely what the consequences of this crisis will be on the welfare reform trajectory of Bismarckian welfare systems. Before the crisis, welfare systems seemed to have adapted to new circumstances, but often at the price of an increasing number of jobs of bad quality and the institutionalization of a 'second division' in society, living off assistance schemes and subsidized precarious jobs. Only some countries have started to positively modernize their welfare systems.

As argued by Esping-Andersen in this volume's prologue and by Hemerijck and Eichhorst in their chapter, what is at stake is the capacity to improve economic growth and the social situation of people, by investing in knowledge-based economic activities, and thus in human capital formation, childcare, education and lifelong learning, and – as long advocated by the feminist scholars who first directed attention to care work – by paying more attention to the situation of women (Orloff 1993 and for a review, see Orloff 2009). These are the conditions for a positive adaptation of Continental Europe to the new world of the 21st century.

Will this crisis provide the opportunity for further changes in such a direction? Or will its consequences (and especially its fiscal consequences) on the contrary lead to the implementation of further reactionary dualizing retrenchments? The explosion of public deficits and debts in 2009 may well augur ill for the future, if governments continue to rely on their existing instruments and strategies. As we have seen in this volume, the first reactions to deep crises are not normally dramatic changes in the instruments and goals of the policies, but rather the continued use of the previous existing policy instruments and recipes.

One likely scenario for the years to come is thus an acceleration of some of the trends we have analyzed, pushed by the new economic circumstances. The main reaction of governments in 2008 and 2009 has been to 'let automatic stabilizers play' through unemployment insurance and job subsidies, all leading to enormous increases in public deficits and debts. Confronted with this, governments may in the near future feel forced to implement a third wave of retrenchments, to further residualize public social insurances and to force people to rely ever more heavily on private insurance for their income maintenance. Governments will also be tempted to add stricter conditions to assistance schemes, to implement further activation programs and to support the multiplication of low-paying, poorly protected low-skilled jobs in the service sector. This would not overcome but reinforce the most negative effects of the typical Bismarckian welfare reform trajectory, especially dualism and inequality, but also sluggish growth.

Adopting the policies advocated by Esping-Andersen, Hemerijck and Eichhorst and others would require a very different path of reforms. If important changes are to come, however, it will probably be more incrementally than through a social policy revolution. Against the idea that paradigm change is inevitably a result of a rupture in the past equilibrium, we have seen amply in this volume that they have also (and more often) come through an accumulation of incremental but cumulatively transformative reforms. We can conclude this volume by summing up what the main conditions for such structural changes in deeply institutionalized social protection systems appear to be:

- a shared sense of failure of past reforms;
- changes in the European context;
- layering of new social policies, at the margin of the existing system;
- meta-policy reforms to circumvent institutional and political obstacles to further moves;
  the availability of a new social policy paradigm, and
- for modernizing policies, a renewed political coalition involving new social risks bearers.

For the proposed 'social investment' strategy[31] to be fully implemented in Continental Europe, the following conditions should be met:
- a shared sense that past reforms have increased dualisms, and do not provide tools for economic sustainable growth and social progress;
- an explicit endorsement of the social investment strategy for the post-Lisbon agenda. The Lisbon strategy ambiguously adopted some of the traits of the social investment approach in 2000, but they were downplayed in 2005. It remains unclear what will come after 2010;
- an expansion and stabilization of the few new policies already implemented in some Continental European countries, such as 'continuous minimum income support', 'active family investment strategy', focusing on childcare, parental leave, and further investments in employment policies that 'strengthen long-term attachment to the labor market, promote lifelong human capital investment, and push later and flexible retirement'. New policies towards migration, aimed at 'integration through participation', should also be developed (Hemerijck and Eichhorst, this volume);
- meta-policy reforms to circumvent institutional and political obstacles to further moves: renewed attempts to develop social pacts, transformation of fragmented social insurances into more inclusive systems, creation of new taxes to replace some social contributions and pay for new policies;
- the diffusion and adoption in Continental Europe of the social investment perspective as the new social policy paradigm;
- the emergence of new political coalitions favoring further modernizing policies, involving both insiders and new social risks bearers.

If these conditions could be brought together, there would really be an opportunity to say goodbye to the most negative aspects of the Bismarckian welfare tradition.

Notes

Prologue

1   The following draws on G. Esping-Andersen (2009). *The Incomplete Revolution*. Cambridge: Polity Press.

Chapter 1

1   I wish to thank Daniel Clegg for his careful reading of this text, and for his support and friendship.

2   The present book is one of the products of a broader project, which also involved comparative analyses of 'sectoral reforms'. These studies have been published in a special issue of *Social Policy and Administration* (2007, vol. 41, no. 6), and as a book: Palier B. and Martin, C. (Eds.) (2008) *Reforming Bismarckian welfare systems*, Oxford, Blackwell. In our project, sectoral reforms in old age insurance (Bonoli and Palier 2007), sickness insurance (Hassenteufel and Palier 2007), unemployment insurance (Clegg 2007) and child and elderly care policies (Morel 2007) were compared.

3   Esping-Andersen (1996b); Ferrera and Rhodes (2000); Scharpf and Schmidt (2000); Ebbinghaus and Manow (2001); Huber and Stephens (2001); Leibfried (2001); Pierson (2001b); Sykes, Palier and Prior (2001); Swank (2002); Wilensky (2002).

4   See for instance Pierson (1994); Orloff, O'Connor and Shaver (1999); Kautto et al. (2001); Hvinden (2007).

5   For example on the Netherlands (Visser and Hemerijck 1997), Italy (Ferrera and Gualmini 2004), France (Palier 2005a) or Germany (Bleses and Seeleib-Kaiser 2004)

6   I would like to thank Karen Anderson for having pointed this out to me. For a good illustration of how pension program structures do influence politics, see Anderson and Meyer (2003).

7   Castles (2007) has shown that from an analysis of expenditure data not so

much appears to have changed in the worlds of welfare states over the last 30 years, especially compared to developments in other policy fields.

8   For an illustration of this method, see the tables 3.2 to 3.4 on France, 4.2 to 4.5 on Austria and 8.2 to 8.5 on Switzerland, where institutional changes at the beginning and the end of the period studied are summarized and compared.

9   Jelle Visser and Anton Hemerijck (1997) have similarly underlined the importance of 'institutional changes' in the Dutch case, especially concerning the role of the social partners within the system.

10   An increasing number of scholars have adopted this framework of analysis to understand social policy reforms, especially in Bismarckian countries (see for instance Visser and Hemerijck 1997; Palier 1999; Hinrichs 2000, among others).

11   Myles and Quadagno (1997) illustrate this. Within pension systems, a transition from a defined benefit to a defined contribution scheme involves a change in the mode of pension benefit from deferred wages to savings, for instance.

12   Thelen and Streeck identify five main mechanisms of this type: layering, conversion, drift, exhaustion and displacement.

13   For example, under a Keynesian interpretation, unemployment is perceived as a consequence of weak demand, and calls essentially for reflation policies. Under a neo-classical interpretation, by contrast, unemployment is conceived of as a problem of supply, and calls for very different policies such as lowering labor costs, flexibilization of labor markets and increasing the incentives for unemployed people to look for and accept jobs. The same problem can thus lead to diametrically opposed policy recommendations, with more or less social spending depending on the diagnosis adopted.

14   Traditionally, no social policy reforms could be passed in Continental Europe without (at least implicit) agreement of (at least a majority of) the social partners. On the notion of 'veto players' more generally, see Tsebelis (2000).

15   This section is partly based on Palier (2010).

16   In opposition to so-called new social risks, especially badly covered by Bismarckian social insurances, such as long-term unemployment, lack of education and skills, lone parenthood, difficulties to combine work and family life, old age dependency. On new social risks, see Bonoli (2005).

17   See for instance the German replacement rates in the early 1980s: 'No income losses occured to workers whose sickness lasts less than six weeks and, after the employer's wage continuation ends, sick pay regularly amounted to 90 percent of net earnings in 1980. That year, the target replacement rate (net) for a "standard pensioner" – which assumed an insurance career of 45 years and always having earned the average wage – stood at 70.3 percent.

Unemployment insurance benefits, paid up to a maximum of 12 months, amounted to 68 percent of former net earnings until 1984.' Hinrichs (this volume).

Chapter 2

1   Traditionally, the term 'welfare state' has had a negative connotation in Germany – meaning excessive state interventions, suppressed self-responsibility and weak economic incentives. It is still not widely used in public discourses. More common is the term '*Sozialstaat*'. In the constitution (Basic Law) it is defined in a normative way as an objective of the state (cf. Kaufmann 1997: 21-6). Because a direct translation ('social state') would be somewhat awkward I will use the term 'welfare state' (but not 'welfare system') throughout this article.

2   In tying social policy development to the SER concept, Germany was very much similar to other 'conservative' welfare states (Lewis 1992).

3   The *Ersatzkassen*, sickness funds which until the 1990s were only accessible to white-collar workers and certain blue-collar occupations, have always been an exception. Here the employers are not represented.

4   Some side-payments made to states led by a SPD/CDU government bribed them to vote in favor of that part of the reform package requiring a majority in the Bundesrat.

5   At present, 25 years of always earning the average wage is required to obtain a public pension as high as the basic security level when retiring at standard age (proportionally more years at a lower covered wage). In 2030, for a single worker about 30 years will be required to avoid becoming dependent on means-tested benefits (Sachverständigenrat 2007: 192-5).

Chapter 3

1   I would like to thank George Ross, Daniel Clegg, Silja Häusermann and Chantal Barry for inspired comments on this chapter.

2   For example, a minimum pension benefit was created in 1956 for people with insufficient contribution records in old age insurance pension, but it was partly financed through social contributions. The social partners denounced this as an 'undue charge' weighing on social insurance (Valat 2001).

3   Though this representation of *acquis sociaux* is widespread in France, historical work shows that, as in other Bismarckian countries, the power resource

approach is not the best theory to explain the development of the French welfare system (Hatzfeld 1989).

4   AGIRC (*Association générale des institutions de retraite des cadres*) and ARCCO (*Association des régimes de retraites complémentaires*).

5   One can find a presentation of the content of all these plans in Palier, 2005a, appendix 1.

6   In 1980, 76.5 percent of the health expenditure paid by the insured person was reimbursed by the basic social insurance funds, 74 percent in 1990 and 73.9 percent in 1995.

7   Source: Statistics from the Ministry of Social Affairs: SESI (various years). *Comptes de la protection sociale.*

8   Father Wresinski is the founder of the association *Aide à toute détresse quart monde.*

9   15 years of successive shift work or production line service, more than 200 nights shifts a year over 15 years, or disability.

10   UNCAM – *Union Nationale des Caisses d'Assurance Maladie.*

11   *Agence régionale de santé.*

12   The remaining ones are to be found among low income groups. 10 percent of workers and employees of small companies do not have complementary health insurance and 22 percent of the poorest do not have such insurance, whereas the rate is at 7.7 percent for the whole population. *Observatoire des inégalités.*

Chapter 4

1   We thank Frank Castles and Bruno Palier for their valuable comments.

2   Differences between blue- and white-collar workers in health insurance have leveled out over time.

3   Post-war Austria maintained one of the largest public enterprise sectors in the Western world.

4   Health care is along with social assistance the program where the impact of federalism is most pronounced.

5   Recall that the Social Democrats attempted to rollback tax breaks in the 1970s.

6   In cases of financial hardship, however, caregivers can apply for a special grant.

Chapter 6

1   Opinions expressed in this article are those of the authors and do not reflect an official position of the related institution.

2   Especially in the field of old-age protection, however, fragmentation was high due to the proliferation of numerous independent (i.e. non-public, self-administered) funds for those categories not included in *Inps* (public transportation and maritime workers, and others).

3   See Ferrera and Gualmini (2004) for a comprehensive presentation in English.

4   After 1966, individual firing was restricted by law to cases of motivated dismissal and, above all, with the adoption of the Worker's Chart (*Statuto dei Lavoratori*) in 1970 a crucial provision (article 18) stated that (in firms that employed more than 15 workers) employers were obliged to reintegrate fired workers if the Court did not accept the motivations for dismissal.

5   Due to this change, in the following we will not analyze the developments of the health care sector in Italy. See Maino (2001) for a full illustration.

6   A report by the Treasury Ministry forecast an increase of pension expenditure to 11.7 percent of GDP in 1985 and 18-19 percent in 2000 (Ministero del Tesoro 1981).

7   Also plans for more comprehensive pension reforms were proposed by almost every government during the 1980s, but these plans were never adopted. For a detailed illustration of the Italian pension policy over the last three decades see Cazzola (1995), Franco (2002), Ferrera and Jessoula (2005, 2007), Jessoula (2009).

8   The *Tfr* (*Trattamento di fine rapporto*) is a compulsory severance pay for private employees, financed through social contributions (ca. 7 percent of gross yearly wage) and managed by employers. See Jessoula (2008).

9   Only a few, minor interventions were included in the 1995 budget law.

10 Cfr. Bonoli and Palier (2007).

11 According to this mechanism, workers would have six months – from January 2008 – to decide if they want to keep the Tfr or transfer it to supplementary pension funds. In the default option ('silence'), the Tfr would be automatically paid into occupational pension funds. See Jessoula (2008, 2009).

Chapter 7

1   With the exception of two autonomous regions, namely the Basque Country and Galicia.

2   The Spanish Constitution defines the state as a-confessional. The Catholic Church is the only one mentioned explicitly in the Constitution but its pressure power has decreased steadily. Abortion, gay marriage and adoption by gay couples are allowed in Spain.

3   http://ec.europa.eu/economy_finance/indicators/general_government_data/government_data_en.htm.

4   http://ec.europa.eu/economy_finance/indicators/general_government_data/government_data_en.htm.

5   See, for example, Rodríguez Cabrero (1989), Moreno and Sarasa (1993).

6   http://ec.europa.eu/economy_finance/indicators/general_government_data/government_data_en.htm.

7   For example, a worker's kin was covered until they became of age (18), then until they reached their 21st birthday and finally for their whole lives provided, of course, that they were not working themselves.

8   This has been due to the opposition of the unions to change the eligibility principle, although, as noted it has not impeded to reach universal coverage.

9   http://ec.europa.eu/economy_finance/indicators/general_government_data/government_data_en.htm.

10 El Mundo, 1 March 2007, p. 45.

11 On Europeanization of the Spanish welfare state, see Guillén and Álvarez (2004). On the influence of the OECD on Spanish social and economic policy (see Álvarez and Guillén 2004).

Chapter 8

1   The transfer of the authority from the cantonal to the national level even requires a 'double majority', meaning that it has to be approved by both a majority of the voters and a majority of the cantons. This excess majority-rule introduces an additional break to the development of national welfare policies.

2   This does not imply, however, that inequality is much higher in Switzerland than in other countries, because of the rather egalitarian distribution of incomes. Hence, the Gini-coefficient in Switzerland before taxes and transfers is roughly equal to the Gini-coefficient in France after taxes and transfers (Künzi and Schärrer 2004: 106).

3   Sources for figures 8.1 to 8.3: Comparative political dataset (http://www.ipw.unibe.ch/content/team/klaus_armingeon/comparative_political_data_sets/index_ger.html); Welfare state data set (http://www.lisproject.org/publications/welfaredata/welfareaccess.htm); www.oecd.org; Eurostat;

4   Most of the rise in social assistance costs must be attributed to the exclusion of long-term unemployed from unemployment insurance benefits after 1.5 to 2 years of unsuccessful job search.

5   Excluding health care costs, which are paid for mainly by individual premiums.

6   It was so far the most clear and 'purest' attempt at retrenchment. Moreover, it was subjected to the popular vote simultaneously with a tax reform alleviating taxes for higher income classes, so that the voting campaign gave rise to a strong left-right class cleavage (Engeli 2004).

7   Swiss supplementary pension benefits are means- and not only income-tested, since they also take into account assets, estates (including those that the elderly have previously transferred to their children as an advancement of heritage). However, they do not take into account the own income and assets of the children.

8   In addition, several left-wing propositions to make contributions earnings-related were declined in popular referenda. The last one in March 2007, when a popular initiative by the Socialist party for a single public insurance provider and incomes-related contributions was rejected by more than 75 percent of the voters.

9   However, unlike in many other Bismarckian countries, there was no strategy to introduce 'mini jobs' in Switzerland, i.e. low-skilled low-paid jobs exempt from social contributions. This difference may be due to the relatively flexible labor market in Switzerland, employment-protection being comparatively weak (The OECD employment protection legislation index for Switzerland is about 1.5, whereas the other Bismarckian countries have values ranging between 2 and 3).

10   Social assistance is not reported here, because these benefits are regulated at the sub-state level and – apart from a limited harmonization of benefit levels – were not significantly changed. There is also no minimum income in Switzerland.

Chapter 9

1   This study has been made possible thanks to a post-doctoral scholarship received by the author from the Centre d'Études Européennes of Sciences Po in Paris. During the writing of this chapter, I have, directly and indirectly, benefited from several discussions, comments and critiques. I must give particular mention to F. Bafoil, B. Ebbinghaus, D. Clegg, M. Dauderstädt, H. Ganßmann, A. Hemerijck, K. Hinrichs, P. Manow, J. O'Connor, G. Ross, V.

Schmidt, B. Tomka and J. Zeitlin. Special thanks should, however, be given to the editor of this volume, Bruno Palier, whose patience and tolerance have, in innumerable occasions, been tested. It goes without saying that whatever faults remain are entirely my own responsibility.

2   In February 1991, representatives of Czechoslovakia, Hungary and Poland met in the city of Visegrad (Hungary) and agreed on a 'Declaration of Co-operation on the Road to European Integration', which represented the first attempt to establish a common platform in order to discuss their future in Europe.

3   This was probably a reaction of the communist government to the Prague Spring. While after the demonstrations in Hungary in 1956 the government responded by making liberal concessions to the populations in exchange for social peace, in Czechoslovakia the response was primarily concerned with re-establishing the communist orthodoxy.

4   Please note that it would be impossible to analyze social security expenditures in CEE without considering other 'indirect social policies' such as job security, price subsidies, subvention to firms, for housing, education, etc.

5   By monetization the process of converting benefits and rights into practical monetary means is meant. During communism money had only a virtual value, since it did not respond to the law of demand and offer.

6   The most emblematic example is provided by the so-called 'opposition contract' between the ODS and the Czech Social Democratic Party (ČSSD) in the Czech Republic. The pact between the two main leaders, as Vodička (2005: 145-46) explains, was: Miloš Zeman would have renounced his position as Secretary of the ČSSD in order to be elected as candidate *super partes* to the next presidential elections of 2003, while Václav Klaus would have received, in exchange for his support, the position of Prime Minister in the ODS minority-led government. When Zeman appointed Vladímir Špidla as his successor, it was implicit that tolerance for Klaus' economic preferences would have been due. Unexpectedly, Špidla, instead of supporting the already existent 'opposition contract', decided on campaigning against the ODS, but he was then subjected to a coup d' état conducted by the members of his own party.

7   For Lamping and Rüb (2004), the German welfare system is in transition from the classical Bismarckian type to an 'uncertain something else' that the authors cautiously call a 'conservative universalism'. Please note that the term recombinant property has first been used by Stark (1996) to describe the evolution of Central and Eastern European markets. For the term recombinant governance, see Crouch (2005).

Chapter 11

1   Comments by Robert Boyer, Eric Seils, Wolfgang Streeck, Kathy Thelen, Bruno Palier and Robert Franzese to previous (and quite different) versions of this chapter are very gratefully acknowledged. I am also grateful to Thomas Plümper for extended discussions and much help in data analysis, although only very little of our common work shows up in this version of the argument.

2   This correlates with the welfare state's performance/output side: does it emphasize transfers or the public provision of welfare services, including prominently active labor market policies (Huber and Stephens 2000; 2001)?

3   Welfare state spending (the fiscal structure of the welfare state) has been primarily studied as a dependent variable, but not as an independent variable that itself may explain different patterns of welfare retrenchment or public debt growth. Central Bank Independence (CBI) has been primarily studied in connection with national systems of wage bargaining (see the work of Scharpf 1987; Franzese 1999; Hall and Franzese 1998; Iversen 1998a; 1998b; 1999; Way 2000, among many others), but not in connection with welfare state/ public spending.

4   Given that in some countries welfare state revenue from social insurance contributions amount to more than 40 percent of total government revenue, it seems necessary that the literature on 'fiscal constitutionalism' (cf. Hallerberg 2004) starts to take the welfare state budget process into account more systematically.

5   While it is often claimed that in economic terms there is not much of a difference between taxes and social insurance contributions, in fact there are some profound differences: social insurance contributions are usually levied from a much smaller proportion of the population than taxes, usually only from those 'dependently employed', and they are usually deducted only from wages, not from other sources of income. Often they are also much more regressive, because they start at much lower levels of income than taxes, often at the first euro earned (no tax exemptions), and they are regularly only levied up to an upper limit, sparing higher incomes from 'social insurance taxation'.

6   This case study draws heavily on Palier and Coron (2002) and Palier (2005a). I am grateful that Bruno Palier allowed me to refer extensively to his work.

7   See Eurostat 1995: table 3.35, p. 164.

8   Rapport du Comité des Sages des états généraux de la Sécurité sociale 1987: 62.

Chapter 12

1   As with the other figures, the Bismarckian countries are shaded dark grey.

Chapter 13

1   These themes have partly been developed in my previous publications on the content of the Bismarckian welfare reform trajectory; see Palier (2006) and Palier and Martin (2007a). For the main sequences in the turn from 'labor shedding' to employment-friendly reforms, also refer to the summary in chapter 12 of this volume, section 12.3.

2   For a similar argument, see Clegg 2007.

3   The comparative welfare state literature published at the turn of the 21st century (see note 3 in chapter 1) has been extensively discussing and documenting these trends, so that we do not need to develop these analyses here again.

4   The most striking case is probably Germany, where the intense political conflicts about retrenchment between the Social Democrats and the Christian Democrats between 1996-1998 now appear more strategic than ideological, given the policies later implemented by the Schröder government.

5   But also with the terms of the political debate in the Nordic countries in the early 1990s, where 'rationalization', bringing the systems back to their traditional 'workline', and emphasizing social investment towards children, education and women were on the agenda (Palme et al. 2002).

6   'In Germany, in 2005, the scientific council of the Ministry of Economics estimated that the volume of all "undue charges" not covered by tax-based transfers out of the public budget but financed by insurance contributions amounted to 65 billion euros.' For further developments on this, see Manow, this volume.

7   See for instance the 1993 'Balladur' pension reform in France, where the government agreed to pay for the non-contributory minimum income for the elderly, or the shift in financing in the 'Hartz' reforms in the mid-2000s in Germany, where the federal government agreed to fully cover the expenditure on ALG II cash benefits and social insurance contributions on behalf of the recipients.

8   This was not all talk, as shown by the widespread opposition that unions have been able to mobilize against reforms they disagreed with, even in countries where they lost their role in the management of the welfare system. The massive demonstrations in Italy against Silvio Berlusconi's planned pension reforms in 1995 offer a case in point.

9   As Scharpf and Schmidt noted however: 'Contrary to widespread assumptions about international competitiveness, there is practically no statistical

association between the overall tax burden and employment in the exposed sectors' (Sharpf, Schmidt, 2000, p. 76). Huber and Stephens also note that, if any, the problem of labor cost is less important in the export sector than in the private service sector (Huber, Stephens, 2001).

10 Unless they meant a total change in the nature of the system (like in the health sector in France and in Germany, both of them triggered or are triggering heated debates, Hassenteufel and Palier 2007).

11 In the Netherlands, the Purple coalition wanted to fix pension premiums at their 1997 level of 18.25 percent; the 2001 Riester pension reform in Germany was clearly aimed at capping old age social contribution at the level of 22 percent, and in general, all the Schröder reforms and those of the following grand coalition aimed at keeping social contributions under the level of 40 percent of gross wages; the Austrian reforms in the 1990s also started with the explicit aim of capping the level of social contributions.

12 For France, see the 1984 unemployment reform, when new tax financed assistance benefits were created for those without enough sufficient contribution records or for the long-term unemployed (Clegg 2007), or the 1993 Balladur reform with the creation of *Fonds de solidarité vieillesse*, (Palier, chapter 3 in this volume); for Spain, see the recommendations of the Toledo Pact already mentioned, which included the splitting of financing sources so that contributory benefits would be financed out of social contributions and taxes would be used to finance non-contributory transfers and welfare services (Guillén, this volume). For Germany, see the Hartz IV reform after which the federal government fully covers the expenditure on *ALG II* cash benefits and social insurance contributions on behalf of their recipients, or the 2003 health reform which 'also included tax revenues from an increased tobacco tax that were funneled into SHI and meant to cover spending items "alien" to this scheme (like maternity benefits)' (Hinrichs, this volume).

13 For France, see the massive exemption of social contribution on the lowest wages within the *plan quiquennal pour l'emploi* implemented in 1993 (Palier, chapter 3 in this volume); for Spain, see inter alia the 1993-1994 reforms that included promoting job creation through new tax and social contribution exemptions for employers contracting young people, the long-term unemployed, people aged 45 and over, and the disabled (Guillén, this volume); for Belgium, see the measures adopted in the late 1990s to boost demand for unskilled labor, when the government planned a sizeable reductions in employers' social security contributions. To compensate for lost social security contributions some alternative financing was introduced, mainly in the form of earmarked VAT levies; for the Netherlands, see the introduction in 1997 of cuts in employers' social security contributions for hiring the long-term

unemployed and low-paid workers (Hemerijck and Marx, this volume); Germany, Switzerland, Austria have also decided to cap the level of social contributions and to add on more tax finance to compensate.

14 Like the *Contribution sociale généralisée* in France and the *Ökosteuer* in Germany (see Manow, this volume).

15 Otherwise, one could not understand why certain retrenchments were accepted (like the 1993 Balladur pension reform in France), and others were not (like the Juppé pension plan in 1995). The main difference between the two reforms was that the unions found the former in line with their organizational interests, and the latter not (Bonoli, 1997).

16 The progressive *étatisation* of the French health care system offers the clearest example.

17 In Germany, during the 1990s, government 'no longer left the initiative to reform and compromise-building to corporatist bodies, but rather, took the lead and partly ignored the social partners' (Hinrichs, this volume); also in Germany, '"Government by commission" was another feature of social policy-making after the year 2000 and also meant to take agenda-setting out of the hands of (remaining) "old politics" actors' (ibid.) ; in France, in 1996 the Constitution was amended so that the Parliament would vote every year the budget of social insurances *(loi de financement de la sécurité sociale)* (Palier, chapter 3 in this volume) ; in Austria, 'consociational democracy and corporatism virtually came to an end at the turn of the new millennium' because 'the center-right government launched institutional reforms in order to bypass the informal veto powers held by the unions within the system of social partnership' by using majority rules in the Parliament (Obinger and Tálos, this volume); in the Netherlands, in 1993 a very important parliamentary report 'revealed that social security was being "misused" by the social partners for the purpose of industrial restructuring and advocated a fundamental recasting of bipartite governance in Dutch social security administration' (Hemerijck and Marx, this volume); In Switzerland, 'in virtually all the important reforms of the 1990s – the pension reforms of 1995 and 2003, the unemployment reform of 1995 and the current disability insurance reform – it was only in Parliament that the modernizing elements of reform were added' (Häusermann, this volume).

18 See the reduced role of the social partners in the Federal Labor Agency (FLA) in Germany after the Hartz reforms; the disappearance of the social partners' administrative boards in health insurance Funds in France after 2004; and the creation of the Centers for Work and Income (CWIs) in the Netherlands with the new 'Work and Income (Implementation Structure) Act,' which came into force on 1 January 2002, reducing the role of the social partners in this area (Hemerijck and Marx, this volume).

19 As pointed to us by Karen Anderson; see also Ebbinghaus (this volume).

20 Eurostat, *Taxation trends in the European Union*, Table A.3_T p.255.

21 Effective (pre)retirement age was well under 60 in most Continental European countries in the late 1990s – Hemerijck and Eirchhorst, this volume.

22 We can draw some parallel here with the 'third order' of changes observed by Peter Hall (1993), even though the process – which passed through more incremental channels – can be less clearly traced than in the case of macroeconomic policy, and despite the fact that the changes were ultimately less radical.

23 On the OECD, see for instance Armingeon and Beyerler (2004), and on the World Bank, see World Bank (1994) and Holzmann and Jorgensen (2000).

24 With the OMC, European bodies have created a new form of intervention which is less aimed at institutional harmonization or legislation than at harmonizing ideas, knowledge and norms of action, in order to have policy goals converging towards 'a common political vision'. The aim is 'to organize a learning process about how to cope with the common challenges of the global economy in a coordinated way while also respecting national diversity.' (Note from the Portuguese presidency 'The on-going experience of the Open Method of Coordination', 13 June 2000). On the OMC and its impact on welfare states, see Zeitlin and Pochet (2005); Heidenreich and Zeitlin (2009).

25 Like the Belgian *minimex*, the French RMI (subsequently renamed RSA), the Spanish regional assistance benefits or the basic safety nets implemented in the Visegrad countries.

26 Such as the assistance income for the long-term unemployed (ALG II) or the minimum income for the elderly created in Germany, the many minimum protection schemes developed in Switzerland in various fields (supplementary means-tested pension benefits, subsidies for low-income earners), and similar measures in Austria and the Netherlands.

27 On policy changes as punctuated equilibrium, see Baumgarnter and Jones (2002).

28 'The creation of a national health service was eased in Spain because of the existence of several institutional features, namely the fact that the health care system was not split in independent funds right from its creation and was managed and administered by a centralized institution. It also helped greatly that doctors were salaried employees from the beginning and doorkeepers of the system.' (Guillén, this volume).

29 'The fact that the equivalence principle was historically not as strongly entrenched probably also accounts for this peculiarity of the Belgian trajectory' (Hemerijck and Marx, this volume).

30 As said, the Netherlands appears as an exception – only very partially copied by other countries such as Spain or Switzerland – where 'atypical' jobs are also

created but are at the same time given more social rights, thus implementing the flexicurity model. As for Belgium, it seems that strong resistance from the social partners, as well as the 'universal' flat-rate unemployment insurance, has prevented an increase in new types of more flexible jobs, at the price of a high unemployment and low employment rate.

31 On the social investment strategy, see Esping-Andersen et al. (2002), Jenson and Saint Martin (2006), Jenson (2009) and Morel, Palier and Palme (2009).

Bibliography

Aarts, L.J.M., and de Jong, P.R. (1996). 'Evaluating the 1987 and 1993 Social Welfare Reforms: From Disappointment to Potential Success'. In L.J.M. Aarts, R.V. Burkhauser and P.R. de Jong (Eds.), *Curing the Dutch Disease: An International Perspective on Disability Policy Reform*. Aldershot: Avebury.

Abelshauser, W. (2004). *Deutsche Wirtschaftsgeschichte seit 1945*. München: C.H. Beck.

Abrahamson, P. (1999). 'The Welfare Modelling Business'. *Social Policy and Administration*, 33 (4), 394-415.

Aguilar, M. et al. (1994). 'Las rentas mínimas de inserción de las Comunidades Autónomas'. *Documentación Social*, 96, 201-23.

Alonso, J.A. (2005). 'Comercio exterior'. In J.L. García Delgado and R. Myro (Eds.), *Lecciones de economía española*. Navarra: Aranzadi/Thomson, Civitas.

Alti, T. (2003). 'Politiche anti-povertà: una questione europea'. In S. Fabbrini (Eds.), *L'Unione Europea. Le istituzioni e gli attori*. Roma: Laterza.

Álvarez, S., and Guillén, A. (2004). 'The OECD and the Reformulation of Spanish Social Policy: a combined search for expansion and rationalization'. In K. Armingeon and M. Beyeler (Eds.), *The OECD and European Welfare States*. Cheltenham: Edward Elgar.

Anderson, K. (2007). 'The Netherlands: Political Competition in a Proportional System'. In E. Immergut, K. Anderson and I. Schulze (Eds.), *The Handbook of West European Pension Politics*. Oxford: Oxford University Press.

Anderson, K., and Meyer T. (2003). 'Social Democracy, Unions, and Pension Politics in Germany and Sweden'. *Journal of Public Policy*, 23 (1), 23-55.

Andries, M. (1996). 'The Politics of Targeting: the Belgian Case'. *Journal of European Social Policy*, 6 (3), 209-33.

Annesley, C. (2007). 'Lisbon and Social Europe: Towards a European "Adult Worker Model" Welfare System'. *Journal of European Social Policy*, 17 (3), 195-205.

Armingeon, K. (2001). 'Institutionalising the Swiss Welfare State'. *West European Politics*, 24 (2), 145-68.

Armingeon, K., and Beyerler, M. (Eds.) (2004). *The OECD and European Welfare States*. Cheltenham: Edward Elgar.

Armingeon, K., and Bonoli, G. (Eds.) (2006). *The Politics of Post-Industrial Welfare States: Adapting Post-War Social Policies to New Social Risks*. London: Routledge.

Arriba, A. (2001). 'Procesos de implantación de políticas de rentas mínimas de inserción en España'. In L. Moreno (Ed.), *Pobreza y exclusión: la 'malla de seguridad'*. Madrid: CSIC.

Arriba, A., and Moreno, L. (2005). 'Spain: poverty, social exclusion and "safety nets"'. In M. Ferrera (Ed.), *Fighting poverty and social exclusion in Southern Europe. Dilemmas of organization and implementation*. London: Routledge.

Arts, W., and Gelissen, J. (2002). 'Three Worlds of Welfare Capitalism or More? A state-of-the-art report'. *Journal of European Social Policy*, 12 (2), 137-58.

Bach, H.-U., Gaggermeier, C., and Klinger, S. (2005). 'Sozialversicherungspflichtige Beschäftigung: Woher kommt die Talfahrt?' *IAB-Kurzbericht*, Nr. 26 (v. 28.12.2005). Nürnberg: Institut für Arbeitsmarkt- und Berufsforschung.

Badelt, C., and Österle, A. (1998). *Grundzüge der Sozialpolitik. Spezieller Teil: Sozialpolitik in Österreich*. Wien: Manz-Verlag.

Bakken, G. (2008). *Social Protection Systems in Central and Eastern Europe: A New World of Welfare?* Unpublished Master's thesis. Madison, WI: University of Wisconsin-Madison.

Ball, L. (1993). 'What Determines the Sacrifice Ratio?' *NBER Working Paper* 4306. Cambridge, Massachusetts: National Bureau of Economic Research.

Barucci, P. (1995). *L'isola italiana del tesoro*. Milano: Rizzoli.

Bauer, T., Strub, S., and Stutz, H. (2004). *Familien, Geld und Politik*. Zürich: Rüegger.

Baumgartner, F. R., and Jones, B. D. (Eds.) (2002). *Policy Dynamics*. Chicago: University of Chicago Press.

Béland, D. (2001). 'Does Labor Matter? Institutions, Labor Unions and Pension Reform in France and the United States'. *Journal of Public Policy*, 21 (2), 153-72.

Berclaz, J., and Füglister, K. (2003). *The Contentious Politics of Unemployment in Europe. National Template for Switzerland*. Geneva: University of Geneva. http://www.eurpolcom.eu/unempol/reports.cfm.

Berger, S. (2002). 'Germany in Historical Perspective: The Gap between Theory and Practice'. In S. Berger and H. Compston (Eds.), *Policy Concertation and Social Partnership in Western Europe: Lessons for the 21st Century.* New York: Berghahn Books.

Berger, S., and H. Compston (Eds.) (2002). *Policy Concertation and Social Partnership in Western Europe: Lessons for the 21st Century.* New York: Berghahn Books.

Bichot, J. (1997). *Les politiques sociales en France au 20ème siècle.* Paris: Armand Colin.

Bispinck, R., and Schulten, T. (2000). 'Alliance for Jobs – is Germany following the path of "competitive corporatism"?' In G. Fajertag and P. Pochet (Eds.), *Social Pacts in Europe: New Dynamics.* Brussels: ETUI.

Bleses, P., and Seeleib-Kaiser, M. (2004). *The Dual Transformation of the German Welfare State.* Houndmills, Basingstoke: Palgrave Macmillan.

BMAS – Bundesministerium für Arbeit und Soziales (2008a). *Statistisches Taschenbuch 2008,* Referat Information, Publikation, Redaktion. Bonn: BMAS.

BMAS – Bundesministerium für Arbeit und Soziales (2008b). *Sozialbudget 2007. Tabellenauszug,* Berlin: BMAS.

BMFSFJ – Bundesministerium für Familie, Senioren, Frauen und Jugend (2008). *Dossier: Armutsrisiken von Kindern und Jugendlichen in Deutschland.* Berlin: Kompetenzzentrum für familienbezogene Leistungen im BMFSFJ.

BMGS – Bundesministerium für Gesundheit und Soziale Sicherung (2005). *Sozialbericht 2005.* Berlin: Bundesministerium für Gesundheit und Soziale Sicherung.

BMSK – Bundesministerium für Soziales und Konsumentenschutz (2007). *Bericht über die Soziale Lage 2003-2004* (http://www.bmsk.gv.at/cms/site/liste.html?channel=CH0338, 26 July 2007).

BMUJF – Bundesministerium für Umwelt, Jugend und Familie (1999). *Zur Situation von Familie und Familienpolitik in Österreich* (4. Österreichischer Familienbericht). Vienna: Bundesministerium für Umwelt, Jugend und Familie. 2 vols.

Boix, C. (1998). *Political Parties, Growth, and Equality: Conservative and Social Democratic Economic Strategies in the World Economy.* New York: Cambridge University Press.

Bohle, D., and Greskovits, B. (2007). 'Neoliberalism, Embedded Neoliberalism, and Neocorporatism: Paths Towards Transnational Capitalism in Central-Eastern Europe'. *West European Politics,* 30 (3), 443-66.

Bönker, F. (2005). 'Changing Ideas on Pensions: Accounting for Differences in the Spread of the Multipillar Paradigm in Five EU Social Insurance Countries.' In P. Taylor-Gooby (Ed.), *Ideas and Welfare State Reform in Western Europe*. Houndmills, Basingstoke: Palgrave Macmillan.

Bonoli, G. (1997), "Pension Politics in France: Patterns of co-operation and conflict in two recent reforms." *West European Politics*, 20 (4), 111-24.

Bonoli, G. (1999). 'La 10e révision de l'AVS: une politique consensuelle de retranchement?' In A. Mach (Ed.), *Globalisation, néo-libéralisme et politiques publiques dans la Suisse des années 1990*. Zurich: Seismo.

Bonoli, G. (2000). 'Public Attitudes to Social Protection and Political Economy Traditions in Western Europe'. *European Societies*, 2 (4), 431-52.

Bonoli, G. (2001). 'Political Institutions, Veto Points, and the Process of Welfare State Adaptation'. In P. Pierson (Ed.), *The New Politics of the Welfare State*. Oxford: Oxford University Press.

Bonoli, G. (2005). 'The Politics of New Social Policies. Providing coverage against new social risks in mature welfare states'. *Policy and Politics*, 33 (3), 431-49.

Bonoli, G. (2006). 'Les politiques sociales'. In U. Klöti, P. Knoepfel, H. Kriesi, Wolf Linder and Y. Papadopoulos (Eds.), *Manuel de la politique suisse* (2nd edition). Zürich: NZZ Verlag.

Bonoli, G. (2007). 'Time Matters, Postindustrialisation, New Social Risks, and Welfare State Adaptation in Advanced Industrial Democracies'. *Comparative Political Studies*, 40 (5), 495-520.

Bonoli, G., Bertozzi, F., and Gay-des-Combes, B. (2005). *La réforme de l'Etat social en Suisse*. Lausanne: Presses Polytechniques et Universitaires Romandes.

Bonoli, G. and Palier, B. (1996). 'Reclaiming Welfare. The Politics of Social Protection Reform in France'. *Southern European Society and Politics*, 1 (3), 240-59.

Bonoli, G., and Palier, B. (1998). 'Changing the Politics of Social Programmes: Innovative Change in British and French Welfare Reforms'. *Journal of European Social Policy* 8 (4), 317-30.

Bonoli, G., and Palier, B. (2000). 'How Do Welfare States Change? Institutions and their Impact on the Politics of Welfare State Reform'. *European Review*, 8 (2), 333-52.

Bonoli, G., and Palier, B. (2007). 'When Past Reforms Open New Opportunities: Comparing Old Age Insurance Reforms in Bismarckian Welfare Systems'. *Social Policy and Administration*, 41 (6), 555-73.

Bosch, G., Kalina, T., and Weinkopf, C. (2008). 'Niedriglohnbeschäftigte auf der Verliererseite'. *WSI-Mitteilungen*, 61 (8), 423-30.

Brooks, C., and Manza, J. (2007). *Why Welfare States Persist. The Importance of Public Opinion in Democracies*. Chicago: University of Chicago Press.

Brugiavini, A., Ebbinghaus, B., Freeman, R., Garibaldi, P., Holmund, B., Schludi, M., and Verdier, T. (2001). 'Part II: What Do Unions Do to the Welfare States?' In T. Boeri, A. Brugiavini and L. Calmfors (Eds.) *The Role of Unions in the Twenty-First Century: A Report to the Fondazione Rodolfo Debenedetti*. Oxford: Oxford University Press.

BSV – Bundesamt für Sozialversicherungen (1995). *Bericht des eidgenössischen Departementes des Innern zur heutigen Ausgestaltung und Weiterentwicklung der schweizerischen 3-Säulen-Konzeption der Alters-, Hinterlassenen- und Invalidenvorsorge*. Bern: Beiträge zur sozialen Sicherheit.

BSV – Bundesamt für Sozialversicherungen (2003). *Schweizerische Sozialversicherungsstatistik. Div. Jahrgänge*. Bern.

Bundesagentur für Arbeit (2008). *Analyse der Grundsicherung für Arbeitsuchende. Mai 2008*, Analytikreport der Statistik, Nürnberg: Bundesagentur für Arbeit.

Bundesrechnungshof (2007). 'Bemerkungen des Bundesrechnungshofes 2007 zur Haushalts- und Wirtschaftsführung des Bundes'. *Deutscher Bundestag, Drucksache* 16/7100 (21.11.2007), Berlin.

Bundesregierung (2006). 'Siebter Familienbericht. Familie zwischen Flexibilität und Verlässlichkeit'. *Deutscher Bundestag, Drucksache* 16/1360 (26.04.2006), Berlin.

Cabiedes, L. (2004). 'Reformas sanitarias recientes'. In *Informe anual del Sistema Nacional de Salud*. Madrid: Observatorio del SNS, Ministerio de Sanidad y Consumo.

Cabiedes, L., and Guillén, A. (2001). 'Adopting and Adapting Managed Competition: health care reform in Southern Europe'. *Social Science & Medicine*, 52, 1205-17.

Cantillon, B., Van Mechelen, N., Marx, I., and Van den Bosch, K. (2004). 'L'Evolution de la protection minimale dans les Etats-Providence au cours des années 90: 15 Pays Européens'. *Revue Belge de Sécurité Sociale*, 2004/3, 513-49.

Casey, B.H. (2004). 'The OECD Jobs Strategy and the European Employment Strategy: Two Views of the Labour Market and the Welfare State'. *European Journal of Industrial Relations*, 10 (3), 329-52.

Castel, R. (1995). *Les métamorphoses de la question sociale*. Paris: Fayard.

Castel, R. (2009). *La montée des incertitudes: travail, protection, statut des individus*. Paris: Le Seuil.

Castellino, O. (1988). *L'abito di Arlecchino*. In G. Vialetti (Eds.), *Le pensioni degli italiani*. Venezia: Marsilio.

Castles, F. G. (2003). 'The World Turned Upside Down: below replacement fertility, changing preferences and family-friendly public policy in 21 OECD Countries'. *Journal of European Social Policy*, 13 (3), 209-27.

Castles, F. G. (Ed.) (2007). *The Disappearing State? Retrenchment Realities in an Age of Globalisation*. Cheltenham: Edward Elgar.

Castles, F. G, and Obinger, H. (2007). 'Social Expenditure and the Politics of Redistribution'. *Journal of European Social Policy*, 17 (3), 206-22.

Catrice-Lorey, A. (1995). 'La sécurité sociale et la démocratie sociale: impasse ou refondation?' *Prévenir*, no 29, 2ème semester, 61-79.

Cazzola, G. (1995). *Le nuove pensioni degli italiani*. Bologna: Il Mulino.

Cerami, A. (2006). *Social Policy in Central and Eastern Europe. The Emergence of a New European Welfare Regime*. Berlin: LIT Verlag.

Cerami, A. (2008). 'Europeanization and Social Policy in Central and Eastern Europe'. In F. Bafoil and T. Beichelt (Eds.) *Européanisation. D'Ouest en Est*. Paris: L'Harmattan, coll. Logiques Politiques.

CES – Consejo Económico y social (1993 to 2006, annual publication). *España 1992-2005. Economía, trabajo y sociedad. Memoria sobre la situación socioeconómica y laboral*. Madrid: CES.

CES – Consejo Económico y Social (2003). *La situación de las personas con discapacidad en España*. Madrid: CES.

Chulià, E. (2006). 'Spain: Incremental changes in the public pension system and reinforcement of supplementary private pensions'. In K.M. Anderson, E. Immergut and I. Schulze (Eds.), *Oxford Handbook of West European Pension Policies*. Oxford: Oxford University Press.

Clasen, J. (2005). *Reforming European Welfare States: Germany and the United Kingdom Compared*. Oxford: Oxford University Press.

Clasen, J. and Siegel, N. (2007). *Investigating Welfare State Change, The 'Dependent Variable Problem' in Comparative Analysis*. Cheltenham: Edward Elgar.

Clegg, D. (2007). 'Continental Drift: On Unemployment Policy Shift in Bismarckian Welfare Systems'. *Social Policy and Administration*, 41 (6), 597-617.

Conceição-Heldt, E.D. (2007). 'France: The Importance of the Electoral Cycle'. In E. Immergut, K. Anderson and I. Schulze (Eds.), *The Handbook of West European Pension Politics*. Oxford: Oxford University Press.

Connor, W. (1997). 'Social Policy Under Communism'. In E.B. Kapstein and M. Mandelbaum (Eds.), *Sustaining the Transition: The Social Safety Net in Post-Communist Europe*. New York: Council on Foreign Relations.

Consensus Programme II (1999). 'Country Report: Czech Republic' In *Monitoring the Development of Social Protection Reform in the CEECs*. (Part 1-4). Brussels: Consensus Programme II.

CONSOC Recherche (2003). *Situation économique des rentiers. Analyse introductive et générale dans la perspective d'une 13ème rente AVS*. Rapport réalisé par Valérie Legrand-Germanier et Stéphane Rossini. Berne: USS.

Cour des Comptes (various years*). Rapports sur la certification des comptes de la Sécurité Sociale*. Paris: La documentation française.

Cox, R.H. (1993). *The Development of the Dutch Welfare State: From Workers' Insurance to Universal Entitlement*. Pittsburgh: University of Pittsburgh Press.

Cox, R.H. (2001). 'The Social Construction of an Imperative: Why Welfare Reform Happened in Denmark and the Netherlands but Not in Germany'. *World Politics*, 53 (3), 463-98.

Crouch, C. (1986). 'Sharing Public Space: States and Organized Interests in Western Europe'. In J.A. Hall (Ed.), *States in History*. Oxford: B. Blackwell.

Crouch, C. (1993). *Industrial Relations and European State Traditions*. Oxford: Clarendon Press.

Crouch, C. (2001). 'Welfare State Regimes and Industrial Relations Systems: The Questionable Role of Path Dependency Theory'. In B. Ebbinghaus and P. Manow (Eds.), *Comparing Welfare Capitalism: Social Policy and Political Economy in Europe, Japan and the USA*. London: Routledge.

Crouch, C. (2005). *Capitalist Diversity and Change. Recombinant Governance and Institutional Entrepreneurs*. Oxford: Oxford University Press.

CRPS – Commissione per la Riforma della Previdenza Sociale (1948). *Relazione sui lavori della Commissione*. Roma: Ministero del Lavoro e della Previdenza Sociale.

Cruz Roche, I. (1994). 'La protección por desempleo'/'La dinámica y estructura de la universalización de las pensiones'. In *V Informe sociológico sobre la situación social en Españ*a. Madrid: Fundación FOESSA.

Czada, R. (2004). 'Die neue deutsche Wohlfahrtswelt – Sozialpolitik und Arbeitsmarkt im Wandel'. In S. Lütz and R. Czada (Eds.), *Wohlfahrtsstaat – Transformation und Perspektiven*. Wiesbaden: VS Verlag für Sozialwissenschaften.

Dafflon, B. (2003). *La politique familiale en Suisse: enjeux et défis*. Lausanne: Réalités sociales.

Daly, M. (2001). 'Globalization and the Bismarckian Welfare States'. In R. Sykes, B. Palier and P. Prior (Eds.), *Globalization and the European Welfare States: Challenges and Change*. London: Macmillan Press.

Daly, M. (2004). 'Changing Conceptions of Family and Gender Relations in European Welfare States and the Third Way'. In J. Lewis and R. Surender (Eds.), *Welfare State Change. Towards a Third Way?* Oxford: Oxford University Press.

Daniel, C. and Tuchszirer, C. (1999). *L'État face aux chômeurs, l'indemnisation du chômage de 1884 à nos jours*. Paris: Flammarion.

Davidsson, J. B. (2009). 'The Politics of Employment Policy in Europe: Two Patterns of Reform'. Paper presented at the ECPR conference in Lisbon, 14-19 April 2009.

DARES (1996). *40 ans de politiques d'emploi*. Paris: La documentation française.

Deacon, B. (1992). *The New Eastern Europe: Social Policy, Past, Present and Future*. London: SAGE.

Deacon, B. (2000). 'Eastern European Welfare States: The Impact of the Politics of Globalization'. *Journal of European Social Policy*, 10 (2), 146-62.

Deacon, B. (2007). *Global Social Policy & Governance*. London: SAGE Publications.

Deacon, B., Hulse, M., and Stubbs, P. (1997). *Global Social Policy. International Organizations and the Future of Welfare*. London: SAGE Publications.

De Lathouwer, L. (1997). 'Twintig jaar beleidsontwikkelingen in de Belgische Werkloosheidsverzekering'. *Belgisch Tijdschrift voor Sociale Zekerheid*, 39 (3-4), 817-79.

Deleeck, H. (2001). *De architectuur van de welvaartsstaat*. Leuven: Acco.

Deutscher Bundestag (1997a). 'Entwurf eines Gesetzes zur Reform der gesetzlichen Rentenversicherung (Rentenreformgesetz 1999 – RRG 1999)'. *Drucksache* 13/8011 (24.06.97), Bonn.

Deutscher Bundestag (1997b). *Plenarprotokoll 13/185* (27.06.1997), Bonn.

Diamond, P. (2006). 'Social Justice Reinterpreted: New Frontiers for the European Welfare State'. In A. Giddens, P. Diamond and R. Liddle (Eds.), *Global Europe, Social Europe*. Cambridge: Polity Press.

Dimmel, N. (2003). 'Armut trotz Sozialhilfe'. In E. Tálos (Ed.), *Bedarfsorientierte Grundsicherung*. Vienna: Mandelbaum Verlag.

DREES (2007). 'L'épargne retraite en 2005'. *Etudes et résultats*, no. 585, July 2007.

DREES (various years). 'Les bénéficiaires du RMI'. *Etudes et Résultats*.

Dror, Y. (1968). *Public Policy-Making Re-examined*. San Francisco: Chandler.

Duclos, L. and Mériaux, O. (1997). 'Pour une économie du paritarisme'. *La revue de l'IRES*, no. 24, printemps-été, 43-60.

Dupuis, J.-M. (1989). 'La réforme du financement de la protection sociale. Inventaire bilan'. *LERE, rapport pour la Mire*. convention no. 310/88.

Ebbinghaus, B. (2001). 'Reforming the Welfare State Through "Old" or "New" Social Partnerships?' In C. Kjaergaard and S.-Å. Westphalen (Eds.), *From Collective Bargaining to Social Partnerships: New Roles of the Social Partners in Europe*. Copenhagen: The Copenhagen Centre.

Ebbinghaus, B. (2005). 'Can Path Dependence Explain Institutional Change? Two Approaches Applied to Welfare State Reform'. *MPIfG Discussion Paper 05/2*. Cologne: Max-Planck-Institut für Gesellschaftsforschung.

Ebbinghaus, B. (2006a). *Reforming Early Retirement in Europe, Japan and the USA*. Oxford: Oxford University Press.

Ebbinghaus, B. (2006b). 'Trade Union movements in post-industrial welfare states. Opening up to new social interests?' In K. Armingeon and G. Bonoli (Eds.), *The Politics of Post-Industrial Welfare States. Adapting post-war social policies to new social risks*. London: Routledge.

Ebbinghaus, B., and Eichhorst, W. (2007). 'Distribution of Responsibility for Social Security and Labour Market Policy – Country report: Germany'. *AIAS working paper 2007-52*. Amsterdam: AIAS, University of Amsterdam.

Ebbinghaus, B., and Hassel, A. (2000). 'Striking Deals: Concertation in the Reform of Continental European Welfare States'. *Journal of European Public Policy*, 7 (1), 44-62.

Ebbinghaus, B., and Manow, P. (2001). *Comparing Welfare Capitalism, Social Policy and Political Economy in Europe, Japan and the USA*. London: Routledge.

Ebbinghaus, B., and Visser, J. (2000). *Trade Unions in Western Europe since 1945 (Handbook and CD-ROM)*. London: Palgrave Macmillan.

Eichhorst, W., and Hemerijck, A. (2008). 'Welfare and Employment: A European Dilemma'. *IZA Discussion Paper 3870*.

Eichhorst, W., and Konle-Seidl, R. (2008). 'Does Activation Work?' In W. Eichhorst, O. Kaufmann and R. Konle-Seidl (Eds.), *Bringing the Jobless into Work?* Berlin: Springer.

Eichhorst, W., and Sesselmeier, W. (2007). *Die Akzeptanz von Arbeits-marktreformen am Beispiel von Hartz IV*. Bonn: Friedrich-Ebert-Stiftung, Abteilung Wirtschafts- und Sozialpolitik.

Eijffinger, S.C.W., and de Haan, J. (1996). 'The Political Economy of Central Bank Independence'. *Special Papers in International Economics*, No. 19. Princeton: Princeton University, Department of Economics.

Engeli, I. (2004). 'Analyse des votations fédérales du 16 mai 2004'. *VOX*, no. 83. Genève: Université de Genève.

Esping-Andersen, G. (1990). *The Three Worlds of Welfare Capitalism*. Cambridge: Polity Press.

Esping-Andersen, G. (1996a). 'Welfare States without Work: The Impasse of Labour Shedding and Familialism in Continental European Social Policy'. In G. Esping-Andersen (Ed.), *Welfare States in Transition: National Adaptations in Global Economies*. London: Sage.

Esping-Andersen, G. (Ed.) (1996b). *Welfare States in Transition. National Adaptions in Global Economies*. London: Sage.

Esping-Andersen, G. (1999). *Social Foundations of Postindustrial Economies*. Oxford: Oxford University Press.

Esping-Andersen, G. (2009). *The Incomplete Revolution*. Cambridge: Polity Press.

Esping-Andersen, G., Gallie, D., Hemerijck, A., and Myles, J. (2002). *Why We Need a New Welfare State*. Oxford: Oxford University Press.

Esping-Andersen, G., and Korpi, W. (1984). 'Social Policy as Class Politics in Post-War Capitalism: Scandinavia, Austria and Germany'. In J.H. Goldthorpe (Ed.), *Order and Conflict in Contemporary Capitalism*. Oxford: Clarendon Press.

Estevez-Abe, M., Iversen, T., and Soskice, D. (2001). 'Social Protection and the Formation of Skills: A Reinterpretation of the Welfare State'. In P.A. Hall and D. Soskice (Eds.), *Varieties of Capitalism: The Institutional Foundations of Comparative Advantage*. Oxford: Oxford University Press.

EU Commission (2006). 'Implementation and Update Reports on 2003-2005 Naps/Inclusion and Update Reports on 2004/2006 Naps/Inclusion'. Commission staff working document. 23 March 2006. Brussels: EU Commission.

European Observatory on Health Care Systems (2000). *Health Care Systems in Transition. Switzerland*. AMS 5012667 (SWI), Target 19.

Eurostat (1995). *Basic statistics of the European Communities 1994*. Brussels: Eurostat.

Eurostat (2005). *Structures of the Taxation Systems in the European Union 1995-2003*. Brussels: Eurostat.

Ewald, F. (1986). *L'Etat-providence*. Paris: Le Seuil.

Falkner, G., Treib. O., Hartlapp, M., and Leiber, S. (Eds.) (2005). *Complying with Europe: EU harmonization and soft law in the Member States*. Cambridge: Cambridge University Press.

Fenger, H. J. M. (2007). 'Welfare Regimes in Central and Eastern Europe: Incorporating Post-Communist Countries in a Welfare Regime Typology'. *Contemporary Issues and Ideas in Social Sciences*, 3 (2), 1-30.

Ferge, Zs. (2001). 'European Integration and the Reform of Social Security in the Accession Countries'. *Journal of European Social Quality*, 3 (1-2), 9-25.

Ferrera, M. (1984). *Il welfare state in Italia*. Bologna: Il Mulino.

Ferrera, M. (1987). 'Il mercato politico-assistenziale'. In U. Ascoli and R. Catanzaro (Eds.), *La società italiana degli anni ottanta*. Bari: Laterza.

Ferrera, M. (1993). *Modelli di solidarietà*. Bologna: Il Mulino.

Ferrera, M. (1996). 'The "Southern Model" of Welfare in Social Europe'. *Journal of European Social Policy*, 6 (1), 17-37.

Ferrera, M. (1997). 'Introduction Générale'. In MIRE (Ed.) *Comparer les systèmes de protection sociale en Europe – Volume 3: Rencontres de Florence. France – Europe du Sud*. Paris: Ministère du Travail et des Affaires Sociales.

Ferrera, M. (1998). 'The Four "Social Europes": between Universalism and Selectivity'. In Y. Mény and M. Rhodes (Eds.), *The Future of Welfare in Europe. A New Social Contract?* New York: St Martin's Press.

Ferrera, M. (2005). *The Boundaries of Welfare: European Integration and the New Spatial Politics of Social Protection*. Oxford: Oxford University Press.

Ferrera, M. (2006). *Le politiche sociali. L'Italia in prospettiva comparata*. Bologna: Il Mulino.

Ferrera, M., and Gualmini, E. (2000). 'Italy: Rescue from Without?' In F.W. Scharpf and V. Schmidt (Eds.), *Welfare and Work in the Open Economy. Volume II*. Oxford: Oxford University Press.

Ferrera, M. and Gualmini, E. (2004). *Rescued by Europe? Social and Labour Market Reforms from Maastricht to Berlusconi*. Amsterdam: Amsterdam University Press.

Ferrera, M and A. Hemerijck (2003). 'Recalibrating European Welfare Regimes'. In J. Zeitlin and D. Trubek (Eds.), *Governing Work and Welfare in a New Economy: European and American Experiments.* Oxford: Oxford University Press.

Ferrera, M., Hemerijck, A. and Rhodes, M. (2000). *The Future of Social Europe: Recasting Work and Welfare in the New Economy.* Oeiras: Celta Editora.

Ferrera, M. and Jessoula, M. (2005). 'Reconfiguring Italian pensions: from policy stalemate to comprehensive reforms'. In G. Bonoli and T. Shinkawa (Eds), *Ageing and Pension Reforms Around the World.* Cheltenham: Edward Elgar.

Ferrera, M. and Jessoula, M. (2007). 'Italy: a narrow gate for path-shift'. In E. Immergut, K. Anderson and I. Schulze (Eds.), *Handbook of West European Pension Politics.* Oxford: Oxford University Press.

Ferrera, M., and Rhodes, M. (Eds.) (2000). 'Recasting European Welfare States'. *West European Politics*, 23 (2), special issue.

Fink, M., and Tálos, E. (2004). 'Welfare State Retrenchment in Austria: Ignoring the Logic of Blame Avoidance?' *Journal of Societal & Social Policy*, 3, 1-21.

Flaquer, L. (2000). *Las políticas familiares en una perspectiva comparada.* Barcelona: Fundación 'la Caixa'.

Flora, P., and Alber, J. (1981). 'Modernization, democratization, and the development of welfare states in Western Europe'. In P. Flora and A.J. Heidenheimer (Eds.), *The Development of Welfare States in Europe and America.* New Brunswick: Transaction Books.

Flora, P., and Heidenheimer, A.J. (1981). 'The Historical Core and Changing Boundaries of the Welfare State'. In P. Flora and A.J. Heidenheimer (Eds.), *The Development of Welfare States in Europe and America.* New Brunswick: Transaction Books.

Franco, D. (2002). 'Italy: a Never-Ending Pension Reform'. In M. Feldstein and H. Siebert (Eds.), *Social Security Pension Reform in Europe.* Chicago: The University of Chicago Press.

Franzese, R.J. Jr. (1999). 'Partially Independent Central Banks, Politically Reponsive Governments, and Inflation'. *American Journal of Political Science*, 43 (3), 681-706.

Franzese, R.J. Jr. (2002). *Macroeconomic Policies of Developed Democracies.* New York: Cambridge University Press.

Freire, J.M. (2004). 'La atención primaria de salud y los hospitales en el Sistema Nacional de Salud'. In V. Navarro (Ed.), *El Estado del Bienestar en España.* Madrid: Tecnos.

Fuchs, S., and Offe, C. (2008). 'Welfare State Formation in the Enlarged European Union Patterns of Reform in the Post-Communist New

Member States'. *Hertie School of Governance working paper, no. 14.* Berlin: Hertie School of Governance.

Fultz, E. (Ed.) (2002). *Pension Reform in Central and Eastern Europe. Restructuring of Public Pension Schemes: Case studies of Czech Republic and Slovenia* – Volume 2. Budapest: ILO Subregional Office for Central and Eastern Europe.

Fundación BBVA – Fundación Bilbao Vizcaya Argentaria (2005). *Estadísticas históricas de España.* Bilbao: Fundación BBVA.

Fundación FOESSA (1983). *Informe sociológico sobre el cambio social en España 1975-1982.* Madrid: Euramérica.

Gál, R., Mogyorósy, Zs., Szende, Á., and Szivós, P. (2003). 'Hungary Country Study'. In GVG e.V. (Ed.), *Study on the Social Protection Systems in the 13 Applicant Countries.* Brussels: European Commission – DG Employment and Social Affairs.

Garrett, G. (1998). *Partisan Politics in the Global Economy.* New York: Cambridge University Press.

Gans-Morse, J., and Orenstein, M.A. (2006). 'Postcommunist Welfare States: The Emergence of a Continental-Liberal World'. Paper presented at the 38th National Convention of the American Association for the Advancement of Slavic Studies, November 2006, Washington D.C., USA.

Gazier, B., and Petit, H. (2007). 'French Labour Market Segmentation and French Labour Market Policies since the Seventies: Connecting Changes'. *Socio-Économie du travail, Économies et Sociétés AB,* no. 28, 1027-55.

Gerlinger, T. (2003). 'Rot-grüne Gesundheitspolitik 1998-2003'. *Aus Politik und Zeitgeschichte,* 53 (33-34), 6-13.

Geroldi, G. (2005). 'Il sistema degli ammortizzatori sociali in Italia: aspetti critici e ipotesi di riforma'. In P. Onofri and S. Giannini (Eds.), *Per lo sviluppo. Fisco e welfare.* Bologna: Il Mulino.

Goebel, J., and Richter, M. (2007). 'Nach der Einführung von Arbeitslosengeld II: Deutlich mehr Verlierer als Gewinner unter den Hilfeempfängern'. *DIW-Wochenbericht,* 74 (50), 753-61.

Götting, U., Haug, K., and Hinrichs, K. (1994). 'The Long Road to Long-Term Care Insurance in Germany: A Case Study in Welfare State Expansion'. *Journal of Public Policy,* 14 (3), 285-309.

Gourevitch, P. A. (1986). *Politics in Hard Times: Comparative Responses to International Crises.* Ithaca: Cornell University Press.

Government Program (2000). *Zukunft im Herzen Europas. Österreich neu Regieren.* Vienna.

Grabka, M.M., and Frick, J.R. (2008). 'Schrumpfende Mittelschicht – Anzeichen einer dauerhaften Polarisierung der verfügbaren Einkommen?' *DIW-Wochenbericht*, 75 (10), 101-8.

Graziano, P. (2004). *L'Europeizzazione delle politiche pubbliche italiane. Coesione e lavoro a confronto.* Bologna: Il Mulino.

Graziano, P. (2007). 'Adapting to the European Empoloyment Strategy? Recent Developments in Italian Employment Policy'. *International Journal of Labour Law and Industrial Relations*, 23 (4), 543-65.

Gualmini, E. (1998). *La politica del lavoro.* Bologna: Il Mulino.

Guillén, A. (1996). 'Citizenship and Social Policy in Democratic Spain: The Reformulation of the Francoist Welfare State'. *South European Society and Politics*, 1 (2), 253-271.

Guillén, A. (1999). 'Pension Reform in Spain (1975-1997). The role of organized labour'. *European University Institute Working Papers*, no. 99/6.

Guillén, A. (2002). 'The Politics of Universalization: Establishing National Health Services in Southern Europe'. *West European Politics*, 25 (4), 49-68.

Guillén, A., and Álvarez, S. (2004). 'The EU's Impact on the Spanish Welfare State: the role of cognitive Europeanization'. *Journal of European Social Policy*, 14 (3), 285-300.

Guillén, A., and Palier, B. (2004). 'Introduction: Does Europe Matter? Accession to EU and Social Policy Developments in Recent and New Member States'. *Journal of European Social Policy*, 14 (3), 203-9.

Gutiérrez, R., and Guillén, A. (2000). 'Protecting the Long-Term Unemployed. The Impact of Targeting Policies in Spain'. *European Societies*, 2 (2), 195-216.

Haddock, B. (2002). 'Italy in the 1990s: Policy Concertation Resurgent'. In S. Berger and H. Compston (Eds.), *Policy Concertation and Social Partnership in Western Europe: Lessons for the 21st Century*. New York: Berghahn Books.

Hagen, J. von (2006). 'Political Economy of Fiscal Institutions'. In B. R. Weingast and D. Wittman (Eds.), *The Oxford Handbook of Political Economy*. Oxford: Oxford University Press.

Haggard, S. and Kaufman, R. (2008). *Development, Democracy, and Welfare States*. Princeton: Princeton University Press.

Hall, P.A. (1986). *Governing the Economy: the politics of state intervention in Britain and France.* New York: Oxford University Press.

Hall, P.A. (Ed.) (1989). *The Political Power of Economic Ideas*. Princeton: Princeton University Press.

Hall, P.A. (1993). 'Policy Paradigms, Social Learning, and the State: The Case of Economic Policymaking in Britain'. *Comparative Politics*, 25 (3), 275-96.

Hall, P.A. (1997). 'The Role of Interests, Institutions, and Ideas in the Comparative Political Economy of the Industrialized Nations'. In M. Lichbach and A. Zuckerman (Eds.), *Comparative Politics. Rationality, Culture, and Structure*. Cambridge: Cambridge University Press.

Hall, P.A., and Franzese, R.J. Jr. (1998). 'Mixed Signals: Central Bank Independence, Coordinated Wage Bargaining, and European Monetary Union'. *International Organization*, 52 (3), 505-35.

Hall, P.A., and Soskice, D. (Eds.) (2001). *Varieties of Capitalism: The Institutional Foundations of Comparative Advantage*. Oxford: Oxford University Press.

Hall, P.A., and Taylor, R. (1996). 'Political Science and the Three New Institutionalisms'. *Political Studies*, 44 (5), 936-57.

Hallerberg, M. (2004). *Domestic Budgets in a United Europe*. Ithaca: Cornell University Press.

Hallerberg, M., and Hagen, J. von (1999). 'Electoral Institutions, Cabinet Negotiations, and Budget Deficits in the European Union'. In by J. M. Poterba and J. von Hagen (Eds.), *Fiscal Institutions and Fiscal Performance*. Chicago: University of Chicago Press.

Hallerberg, M., Strauch, R. and Hagen, J. von. (2001). 'The Use and Effectiveness of Budgetary Rules and Norms in EU Member States'. Report Prepared for the Dutch Ministry of Finance by the Institute of European Integration Studies.

Hartog, J. (1999). *Country Employment Policy Review: The Netherlands*. Report for symposium on 'Social Dialogue and Employment Success'. Geneva: International Labour Office.

Hassel, A., and Trampusch, C. (2006). 'Verbände und Parteien: Die Dynamik von Parteikonflikten und die Erosion des Korporatismus'. In J. Beckert, B. Ebbinghaus, A. Hassel, and P. Manow (Eds.), *Transformation des Kapitalismus*. Frankfurt/New York: Campus.

Hassenteufel, P. and Palier, B. (2007). 'Comparing Health Insurance Reforms in Bismarckian Countries: Towards Neo-Bismarckian Health Care States?' *Social Policy and Administration*, 41(6), 574-96.

Hatzfeld, H. (1989). *Du paupérisme à la Sécurité sociale. Essai sur les origines de la Sécurité sociale* (2nd edition). Presses Universitaires de Nancy.

Häusermann, S. (2002). *Flexibilisation des relations d'emploi et sécurité sociale. La réforme de la loi suisse sur la prévoyance professionnelle*. Unpublished manuscript. Lausanne: Idheap.

Häusermann, S. (2006). 'Changing Coalitions in Social Policy Reforms: the politics of new social needs and demands'. *Journal of European Social Policy*, 16 (1), 5-21.

Häusermann, S. (2010a). 'Solidarity With Whom? Why Organized Labor is Losing Ground in Continental Pension Politics', *European Journal of Political Research*, 49 (2), 223-56.

Häusermann, S. (2010b). *The Politics of Welfare State Reform in Continental Europe: Modernization in Hard Times*. Cambridge: Cambridge University Press.

Häusermann, S., Mach, A., and Papadopoulos, Y. (2004). 'From Corporatism to Partisan Politics. Social Policy Making under Strain in Switzerland'. *Swiss Political Science Review*, 10 (2), 33-59.

Heclo, H. (1974). *Modern Social Politics in Britain and Sweden*. New Haven: Yale University Press.

Heidenreich, M., and Zeitlin, J. (Eds.) (2009). *Changing European Employment and Welfare Regimes. The Influence of the Open Method of Coordination on National Reforms.* London: Routledge.

Hemerijck, A. (2002). 'The Self-Transformation of the European Social Model(s)'. In G. Esping-Andersen, D. Gallie, A. Hemerijck and J. Myles (2002), *Why We Need a New Welfare State*. Oxford: Oxford University Press.

Hemerijck, A. (2003). 'A Paradoxical Miracle: the politics of coalition government and social concertation in Dutch welfare reform'. In S. Jochem and N.A. Siegel (Eds.), *Konzertierung, Verhandlungsdemokratie und Reformpolitik im Wohlfahrtstaat – Das Modell Deutschland im Vergleich*. Opladen: Leske und Budrich.

Hemerijck, A. (2008). 'Welfare Recalibration as Social Learning'. Paper presented at the ESPAnet Doctoral Researcher Workshop *The Politics of Recalibration: Welfare Reforms in the Wider Europe*, 5-7 June 2008, University of Bologna, Bologna, Italy.

Hemerijck, A., and Manow, P. (2001). 'The Experience of Negotiated Reforms in the Dutch and German Welfare States'. In B. Ebbinghaus and P. Manow (Eds.), *Comparing Welfare Capitalism: Social Policy and Political Economy in Europe, Japan and the USA*. London: Routledge.

Hemerijck, A., Unger, B., and Visser, J. (2000). 'How Small Countries Negotiate Change: Twenty-Five Years of Policy Adjustment in Austria, the Netherlands, and Belgium'. In F.W. Scharpf and V. Schmidt (Eds.), *Welfare and Work in the Open Economy – Diverse Responses to Common Challenges*. Oxford: Oxford University Press.

Hemerijck, A., van der Meer, M., and Visser, J. (2000). 'Innovation Through Co-ordination – Two Decades of Social Pacts in the Netherlands'. In G. Fajertag and P. Pochet (Eds.), *Social Pacts in Europe: New Dynamics*. Brussels: ETUI.

Hemerijck, A., van Kersbergen, K., and Manow, P. (2000). 'Welfare Without Work? Divergent experiences of reform in Germany and the Netherlands'. In S. Kuhnle (Ed.), *Survival of the European Welfare State*. London: Routledge.

Henninger, A., Wimbauer, C., and Dombrowski, R. (2008). 'Demography as a Push toward Gender Equality? Current Reforms of German Family Policy'. *Social Politics*, 15 (3), 287-314.

Hibbs, D.A. Jr., and Madsen, H.J. (1981). 'Public Reactions to the Growth of Taxation and Government Expenditure'. *World Politics*, 33 (3), 413-35.

Hinrichs, K. (1991). 'Irregular Employment Patterns and the Loose Net of Social Security: Some Findings on the West German Development'. In M. Adler et al. (Eds.), *The Sociology of Social Security*. Edinburgh: Edinburgh University Press.

Hinrichs, K. (1996). 'Das Normalarbeitsverhältnis und der männliche Familienernährer als Leitbilder der Sozialpolitik'. *Sozialer Fortschritt*, 45 (4), 102-7.

Hinrichs, K. (2000). 'Elephants on the Move: Patterns of Public Pension Reform in OECD Countries'. *European Review*, 8 (3), 353-78.

Hinrichs, K. (2002). 'What Can Be Learned from Whom? Germany's Employment Problem in Comparative Perspective'. *Innovation: The European Journal of Social Science Research*, 15 (2), 77-97.

Hinrichs, K. (2005). 'New Century – New Paradigm: Pension Reforms in Germany'. In G. Bonoli and T. Shinkawa (Eds.), *Ageing and Pension Reform Around the World: Evidence from Eleven Countries*. Cheltenham: Edward Elgar.

Hinrichs, K. (2007). 'Reforming Labour Market Policy in Germany'. *Benefits: The Journal of Poverty and Social Justice*, 15 (3), 221-31.

Hinrichs, K. (2008). 'Kehrt die Altersarmut zurück? Atypische Beschäftigung als Problem der Rentenpolitik'. In G. Bonoli and F. Bertozzi (Eds.), *Neue Herausforderungen für den Sozialstaat*. Bern: Haupt.

Hinrichs, K., and Kangas, O. (2003). 'When Is a Change Big Enough to Be a System Shift? Small System-Shifting Changes in German and Finnish Pension Policies'. *Social Policy & Administration*, 37 (6), 573-91.

Höcker, H. (1998). 'The Organisation of Labour Market Policy Delivery in the European Union'. In P. Auer (Ed.), *Employment Policies in Focus: Labour Markets and Labour Market Policy in Europe and Beyond – International Experiences.* Berlin: IAS/MISEP: 191-214.

Hofmarcher, M. (2006). 'Gesundheitspolitik seit 2000: Konsolidierung gelungen – Umbau tot?' In E. Tálos (Ed.), *Schwarz-Blau. Eine Bilanz des 'Neu-Regierens'.* Vienna: LIT Verlag.

Hofmeister, H. (1981). 'Ein Jahrhundert Sozialversicherung in Österreich'. In P.A. Köhler and H.F. Zacher (Eds.), *Ein Jahrhundert Sozialversicherung.* Berlin: Duncker & Humblot.

Holzmann, R., and Jorgensen, S. (2000). 'Social Risk Management: A New Conceptual Framework for Social Protection and Beyond'. *World Bank Discussion Paper*, no. 0006. Washington: The World Bank.

Huber, E., and Stephens, J.D. (2000). 'Partisan Governance, Women's Employment, and the Social Democratic Welfare State'. *American Sociological Review*, 65 (2), 323-42.

Huber, E., and Stephens, J.D. (2001). *Development and Crisis of the Welfare State. Parties and Policies in Global Markets.* Chicago: University of Chicago Press.

Hvinden, B. (Ed.) (2007). *Citizenship in Nordic Welfare States.* London: Routledge Taylor & Francis.

IDA FiSo I (1996). Interdepartementale Arbeitsgruppe 'Finanzierungsperspektiven der Sozialversicherungen': *Bericht über die Finanzierungsperspektiven der Sozialversicherungen unter besonderer Berücksichtigung der demographischen Entwicklung.* Bern: BSV.

IDA FiSo II (1997). Interdepartementale Arbeitsgruppe 'Finanzierungsperspektiven der Sozialversicherungen': *Analyse der Leistungen der Sozialversicherungen; Konkretisierung möglicher Veränderungen für drei Finanzierungsperspektiven.* Bern: BSV.

ILO/MZES (2001). *CD-ROM: Cost of Social Security. Database of Financial Transactions of Social Protection Schemes in 23 Countries.* Geneva: ILO/MZES.

IMF (various years). *Government Finance Statistics Yearbook* [GFSY]. Washington, D.C: International Monetary Fund.

Immergut, E.M. (1991). 'Institutions, Veto Points, and Policy Results: A Comparative Analysis of Health Care'. *Journal of Public Policy*, 10 (4), 391-416.

Immergut, E.M. (1992). *Health Politics. Interests and Institutions in Western Europe.* New York: Cambridge University Press.

Immergut, E., and Anderson, K. (2007). 'Editors' Introduction: The Dynamics of Pension Politics'. In E. Immergut, K. Anderson and I. Schulze (Eds.), *The Handbook of West European Pension Politics*. Oxford: Oxford University Press.

Inglot, T. (2003). 'Historical Legacies, Institutions, and the Politics of Social Policy in Hungary and Poland, 1989-1999'. In G. Ekiert and S.E. Hanson (Eds.), *Capitalism and Democracy in Central and Eastern Europe. Assessing the Legacy of Communist Rule*. Cambridge: Cambridge University Press.

Inglot, T. (2008). *Welfare States in East Central Europe, 1919-2004*. Cambridge: Cambridge University Press.

INPS (1993). *Le Pensioni Domani: Primo Rapporto sulla Previdenza in Italia*. Bologna: Il Mulino.

IRDES (2008). 'L'Enquête Santé Protection Sociale 2006'. *Questions d'économie de la santé*, no. 131.

IRES (1983). 'La protection sociale'. *Les dossiers de l'IRES*, no. 1, November 1983.

Iversen, T. (1998a). 'Wage Bargaining, Central Bank Independence and the Real Effects of Money'. *International Organization*, 52 (3), 469-505.

Iversen, T. (1998b). 'Wage Bargaining, Hard Money and Economic Performance: Theory and Evidence for Organized Market Economics'. *British Journal of Political Science*, 28 (1), 31-61.

Iversen, T. (1999). *Contested Economic Institutions: The Politics of Macroeconomics and Wage Bargaining in Advanced Democracies*. New York: Cambridge University Press.

Iversen, T., and Wren, Anne (1998). 'Equality, Employment, and Budgetary Restraint: The Trilemma of the Service Economy'. *World Politics*, 50 (4), 507-46.

Jenson, J., and Saint Martin, D. (2006). 'Building Blocks for a New Social Architecture: the LEGOTM paradigm of an active society'. *Policy & Politics*, 34 (3), 429–51.

Jenson, J. (2009). 'Lost in Translation: The Social Investment Perspective and Gender Equality'. *Social Politics*.

Jessoula, M. (2009). *La politica pensionistica*. Bologna: Il Mulino.

Jessoula, M. (2010). 'Italy: From Bismarckian Pensions to Multi-pillarization under Adverse Conditions'. In Ebbinghaus, B. (Ed.), *Varieties of Pension Governance: Pension Privatization in Europe*. Oxford: Oxford University Press (forthcoming).

Jobert, B. (1991). 'Democracy and Social Policies: The example of France'. In J. Ambler (Ed.), *The French Welfare State*. New York: New York University Press.

Jordan, T.J. (1997). 'Disinflation Costs'. *Weltwirtschaftliches Archiv*, 133 (1), 1-21.

Karlhofer, F. (1999). 'Verbände: Organisation, Mitgliederintegration, Regierbarkeit'. In F. Karlhofer and E. Tálos (Eds.), *Zukunft der Sozialpartnerschaft*. Vienna: Signum Verlag.

Karlhofer, F., and Tálos, E. (2006). 'Sozialpartnerschaft am Abstieg'. In E. Tálos (Ed.), *Schwarz-Blau. Eine Bilanz des 'Neu-Regierens'*. Vienna: LIT Verlag.

Katzenstein, P.J. (1985). *Small States in World Markets. Industrial Policy in Europe*. Ithaca: Cornell University.

Kaufmann, F.-X. (1997). *Herausforderungen des Sozialstaates*. Frankfurt am Main: Suhrkamp.

Kautto, M., Fritzell, J., Hvinden, B., Kvist, J., and Uusitalo, H. (Eds.) (2001). *Nordic Welfare States in the European Context*. London: Routledge.

Kersbergen, K. van (1995). *Social Capitalism: A Study of Christian Democracy and the Welfare State*. London: Routledge.

Kersbergen, K. van, and Manow, P. (2009). *Religion, Class Coalitions, and the Welfare States*. Cambridge: Cambridge University Press.

Khol, A. (2001). *Die Wende ist geglückt. Der schwarz-blaue Marsch durch die Wüste Gobi*. Vienna: Molden.

Kitschelt, H. (1999). 'European Social Democracy between Political Economy and Political Competition'. In H. Kitschelt, P. Lange, G. Marks and J.D. Stephens (Eds.), *Continuity and Change in Contemporary Capitalism*. New York: Cambridge University Press.

Klammer, U. (1997). *Alterssicherung in Italien: Eine institutionelle, theoretische und empirische Analyse*. Berlin: Duncker & Humblot.

Kohli, M., Rein, M., Guillemard, A.-M., and Gunsteren H. Van (1991), *Time for Retirement*, Cambridge, Cambridge University Press.

Kommission 'Moderne Dienstleistungen am Arbeitsmarkt' (2002). *Vorschläge der Kommission zum Abbau der Arbeitslosigkeit und zur Umstrukturierung der Bundesanstalt für Arbeit*. Berlin: Bundesministerium für Arbeit und Sozialordnung.

Kommission 'Nachhaltigkeit in der Finanzierung der Sozialen Sicherungssysteme' (2003). *Bericht der Kommission*. Berlin: Bundesministerium für Gesundheit und Soziale Sicherung.

Konle-Seidl, R., Eichhorst, W., and Grienberger-Zingerle, M. (2007). 'Activation Policies in Germany: From Status Protection to Basic Income

Support'. *IAB-Discussion Paper*, no. 6/2007, Nürnberg: Institut für Arbeitsmarkt- und Berufsforschung.

Kornai, J. (2001). 'The Borderline between the Spheres of Authority of the Citizens and the State: Recommendations for the Hungarian Health Reform'. In J. Kornai, S. Haggard and R.F. Kaufman (Eds.), *Reforming the State. Fiscal and Welfare Reform in Post-Socialist Countries.* Cambridge: Cambridge University Press.

Korpi, W. (1983). *The Democratic Class Struggle.* London: Routledge & Kegan Paul.

Korpi, W. (2001). 'Contentious Institutions: An Augmented Rational-Action Analysis of the Origins and Path Dependency of Welfare State Institutions in Western Countries'. *Rationality and Society*, 13 (2), 235-83.

Korpi, W., and Palme, J. (2003). 'New Politics and Class Politics in the Context of Austerity and Globalization. Welfare State Regress in 18 Countries. 1975-1995'. *American Political Science Review*, 97 (3), 425-46.

Kriesi, H. (1980). *Entscheidungsstrukturen und Entscheidungsprozesse in der Schweizer Politik.* Frankfurt: Campus Verlag.

Krömmelbein, S., Bieräugel, R., Nüchter, O., Glatzer, W., and Schmid, A. (2007). *Einstellungen zum Sozialstaat.* Opladen and Farmington Hills: Verlag Barbara Budrich.

Kuhnle, S. (Ed.) (2001). *The Survival of the European Welfare State.* London: Routledge.

Kuipers, S. (2006). *The Crisis Imperative. Crisis Rhetoric and Welfare State Reform in Belgium and the Netherlands in the Early 1990s.* Amsterdam: Amsterdam University Press.

Künzi, K., and Schärrer, M. (2004). *Wer zahlt für die Soziale Sicherheit und wer profitiert davon? Eine Analyse der Sozialtransfers in der Schweiz.* Zürich: Rüegger.

Ladó, M. (2003). 'Hungary: Why Develop Sectoral Social Dialogue?' In Y. Ghellab and D. Vaughan-Whitehead (Eds.), *Sectoral Social Dialogue in Future EU Member States: The Weakest Link.* Budapest: International Labour Office – European Commission.

Lallemand, M. (2006). 'New Patterns of Industrial Relations and Political Action since the 1980s'. In P. Culpepper, P. Hall, and B. Palier (Eds.), *Changing France. The Politics That Markets Make.* London: Palgrave.

Lamping, W., and Rüb, F.W. (2004). 'From the Conservative Welfare State to an "Uncertain Else": German Pension Politics in Comparative Perspective'. *Policy & Politics*, 32 (2), 169-92.

Lauber, V., and Pesendorfer, D. (2006). 'Wirtschafts- und Finanzpolitik'. In H. Dachs et. al. (Eds.), *Politik in Österreich. Das Handbuch*. Vienna: Manz Verlag.

Lehmann, H., Ludwig, U., and Ragnitz, J. (2005). 'Originäre Wirtschafts-kraft der neuen Länder noch schwächer als bislang angenommen'. *Wirtschaft im Wandel*, 11, 134-45.

Lehmbruch, G. (1999). 'Verhandlungsdemokratie, Entscheidungsblock-aden und Arenenverflechtung'. In W. Merkel and A. Busch (Eds). *Demokratie in Ost und West. Für Klaus von Beyme*. Frankfurt: Suhrkamp.

Leibfried, S. (Ed.) (2001). *The Future of The Welfare State*. Cambridge: Cambridge University Press.

Leibfried, S., and Pierson, P. (2000). 'Social Policy: left to courts and markets?' In H. Wallace and W. Wallace (Eds.), *Policy-making in the European Union*. Oxford: Oxford University Press (4th edition).

Leibfried, S. and Tennstedt, F. (1985), « Armenpolitik un Arbeiterpolitik », in Leibfried, S. and Tennstedt, F. (eds.) *Politik der Armut und die Spaltung des Sozialstaats*, Frankfurt: Suhrkamp 1985, pp. 64-93.

Leisering, L. (1995). 'Grenzen des Sozialversicherungsstaats? Sozialer Wandel als Herausforderung staatlicher Einkommenssicherung'. *Zeitschrift für Sozialreform*, 41 (11/12), 860-80.

Leisering, L. (2009). 'Germany: A Centrist Welfare State at the Crossroads'. In P. Alcock and G. Craig (Eds.), *International Social Policy. Welfare Regimes in the Developed World*. Basingstoke: Palgrave (2nd edition).

Leitner, S. (2005). 'Conservative Familialism Reconsidered: the Case of Belgium'. *Acta Politica*, 40, 419-39.

Lendvai, N. (2004). 'Review Essay: The Weakest Link? EU Accession and Enlargement: Dialoguing EU and Post-Communist Social Policy'. *Journal of European Social Policy*, 14 (3), 319-33.

L'état de la France, (2000-2001). Paris: La Découverte.

Levy, J. (1999). 'Vice into Virtue? Progressive Politics and Welfare Reform in Continental Europe'. *Politics & Society*, 27 (2), 239-73.

Levy, J. (2005). 'Redeploying the State: Liberalization and Social Policy in France'. In K. Thelen, W. Streeck (Eds.), *Beyond Continuity, Institutional Change in Advanced Political Economies*. Oxford: Oxford University Press.

Lewis, J. (1992). 'Gender and the Development of Welfare Regimes'. *Journal of European Social Policy*, 2 (2), 159-73.

Lister, R. (2004). 'The Third Way's Social Investment State'. In J. Lewis and R. Surender (Eds.), *Welfare State Change. Towards a Third Way?* Oxford: Oxford University Press.

Mabbett, D., and Bolderson, H. (1999). 'Devolved Social Security Systems: Principal-Agent Versus Multi-level Governance'. *Journal of Public Policy*, 18 (2), 177-200.

Maino, F. (2001). *La politica sanitaria*. Bologna: Il Mulino.

Malo, M.A., Toharia, L., and Gautié, J. (2000). 'France: The Deregulation that Never Existed'. in G. Esping-Andersen and M. Regini (Eds.), *Why Deregulate Labour Markets?* Oxford: Oxford University Press.

Manow, P. (1997). 'Social Insurance and the German Political Economy'. *MPIfG Disscussion Paper 2/97*. Cologne: Max-Planck Institute for the Study of Societies.

Manow, P., and Seils, E. (2000). 'Adjusting Badly: The German Welfare State, Structural Change, and the Open Economy'. In F.W. Scharpf and V.A. Schmidt (Eds.), *Welfare and Work in the Open Economy. Vol. II: Diverse Responses to Common Challenges*. Oxford: Oxford University Press.

Maravall, J.M. (1995). *Los resultados de la democracia*. Madrid: Alianza.

Mares, I. (2003). *The Politics of Social Risk. Business and Welfare State Development*. New York: Cambridge University Press.

Marshall, T.H. (1950). *Citizenship and Social Class. The Marshall Lectures*. Cambridge: Cambridge University Press.

Martin, C. J., and Thelen, K. (2007). 'The State and Coordinated Capitalism: Contributions of the Public Sector to Social Solidarity in Post-Industrial Societies'. *World Politics*, 60 (1), 1-36.

Marx, I. (2007a). *A New Social Question? On Minimum Income Protection in the Postindustrial Era*. Amsterdam: Amsterdam University Press.

Marx, I. (2007b). 'The Dutch Miracle Revisited: The Impact of Employment Growth on Poverty'. *Journal of Social Policy*, 36 (3), 383-97.

Marx, I., and Verbist, G. (2008). 'When Famialism Fails: the nature and causes of in-work poverty in Belgium'. In H.J. Andreß and H. Lohmann (Eds.), *The Working Poor in Europe; Employment, Poverty and Globalization*. Cheltenham: Edward Elgar.

Masciandaro, D., and Tabellini, G. (1988). 'Monetary Regimes and Fiscal Deficits: A Comparative Analysis'. In H.-S. Cheng (Ed.), *Monetary Policies in Pacific Basin Countries*. Boston/Dordrecht: Kluwer.

Mayhew, D.R. (1974). *Congress: The Electoral Connection*. New Haven: Yale University Press.

McBride, S., and Williams, R.A. (2001). 'Globalization, the Restructuring of Labour Markets and Policy Convergence: The OECD "Jobs Strategy"'. *Global Social Policy*, 1 (3), 282-309.

Merrien, F.-X. (1990). 'État et politiques sociales: contribution à une théorie "néo-institutionnaliste"'. *Sociologie du Travail*, 32 (3), 267-94.

Milanovic, B. (1998). *Income, Inequality and Poverty during the Transition from Planned to Market Economy*. Washington D.C.: World Bank.

Ministerio de Asuntos Sociales (1993). *Indicadores de protección social. Servicios sociales y programas de igualdad durante el periodo 1982-1992*. Madrid: Ministerio de Asuntos Sociales.

Ministerio de Trabajo y Asuntos Sociales (1996). *Anuario de Estadísticas Laborales y de Asuntos Sociales 1995*. Madrid: Ministerio de Trabajo y Asuntos Sociales.

Ministero del Tesoro (1981). *La Spesa Previdenziale e i Suoi Effetti sulla Finanza Pubblica*. Roma: Istituto Poligrafico e Zecca dello Stato.

Ministero del Welfare (2001). *Libro Bianco sul Mercato del Lavoro in Italia*. Rome: Ministero del Welfare, October 2001.

Ministero del Welfare (2002). 'Report on National Strategies for Future Pension Systems'. Retrieved from: http://www.europa.eu.int/comm/employment_social/soc_protection/pensions_en.htm.

Ministero del Welfare (2003). *Libro bianco sul welfare*. Roma: Ministero del Welfare.

MISSOC (2008). *Social Protection in the Member States of the European Union, of the European Economic Area and in Switzerland*. Brussels: European Commission – DG Employment and Social Affairs.

Morel, N. (2007). 'From Subsidiarity to "Free Choice": Child- and Elder-care Policy Reforms in France, Belgium, Germany and the Netherlands'. *Social Policy and Administration*, 41 (6), 618-37.

Morel, N., Palme, J., and Palier, B. (2009). *What Future for Social Investment?* Stockholm: Institute for Future Studies.

Moreno, L., and Sarasa, S. (1993). 'Génesis y desarrollo del estado del bienestar en España'. *Revista Internacional de Sociología*, 6, 27-69.

Mosley, H., Keller, T. and Speckesser, S. (1998). 'The Role of the Social Partners in the Design and Implementation of Active Measures'. *ILO Employment and Training Papers*, 27.

Mückenberger, U. (1985). 'Die Krise des Normalarbeitsverhältnisses – Hat das Arbeitsrecht noch Zukunft?' *Zeitschrift für Sozialreform*, 31, 415-34, 457-75.

Müller, K. (2004). 'The Political Economy of Pension Reform in Central and Eastern Europe'. In OECD (Ed.), *Reforming Public Pensions. Sharing the Experiences of Transition and OECD Countries*. Paris: OECD.

Myles, J. (1989). *Old Age in the Welfare State: The Political Economy of Public Pensions*. Lawrence: University Press of Kansas (2nd edition).

Myles, J. (2002). 'A New Social Contract for the Elderly'. In G. Esping-Andersen, D. Gallie, A. Hemerijck and J. Myles (2002), *Why we Need a New Welfare State*. Oxford: Oxford University Press.

Myles, J., and Pierson, P. (2001). 'The Comparative Political Economy of Pension Reform'. In P. Pierson (Ed.), *The New Politics of the Welfare State*. Oxford: Oxford University Press.

Myles, J., and Quadagno, J. (1997). 'Recent Trends in Public Pension Reform: a comparative view'. In K. Banting and R. Broadway (Eds.), *Reform of Retirement Income Policy. International and Canadian perspectives*. Kingston: Queen's University, School of Policy Studies.

Natali, D., and Rhodes, M. (2004). 'The "new politics" of the Bismarckian Welfare State: Pension Reforms in Continental Europe'. *European University Institute Working Papers SPS*, no. 2004/10.

Natali, D., and Rhodes, M. (2005). 'La riforma previdenziale del governo Berlusconi e l'emergere di un 'doppio cleavage' nelle politiche distributive'. In C. Guarnieri and J.L. Newell (Eds.), *Politica in Italia/Italian Politics*. Bologna: Il Mulino.

Naumann, I. (2005). 'Child Care and Feminism in West Germany and Sweden in the 1960s and 1970s'. *Journal of European Social Policy*, 15 (1), 47-63.

Nelson, J.M. (2001). 'The Politics of Pension and Health-Care Reforms in Hungary and Poland'. In J. Kornai, S. Haggard and R.F. Kaufman (Eds.), *Reforming the State. Fiscal and Welfare Reform in Post-Socialist Countries*. Cambridge: Cambridge University Press.

Nova, C., and Häusermann, S. (2005). *Endlich existenzsichernde Renten. Erste Säule stärken – 3000 Franken Rente für alle*. Bern: Schweizerischer Gewerkschaftsbund: Dossier 34.

Nullmeier, F., and Rüb, F.W. (1994). 'Erschöpfung des Sozialversicherungsprinzips? Gesetzliche Rentenversicherung und sozialstaatlicher Republikanismus'. In B. Riedmüller and T. Olk (Eds.), *Grenzen des Sozialversicherungsstaates*. Opladen: Westdeutscher Verlag.

Oates, W.E. (1991). 'On the Nature and Measurement of Fiscal Illusion: A Survey'. In W.E. Oates. *Studies in Fiscal Federalism*. Vermont: Edward Elgar.

Obinger, H. (1998). *Politische Institutionen und Sozialpolitik in der Schweiz*. Frankfurt am Main: Peter Lang.

Obinger, H. (2009). 'Sozialpolitische Bilanz der Großen Koalition in Österreich'. In H. Obinger and E. Rieger (Eds.), *Wohlfahrtsstaatliche Politik in entwickelten Demokratien*. Frankfurt/New York: Campus.

Obinger, H., and Tálos, E. (2006). *Sozialstaat Österreich zwischen Kontinuität und Umbau. Eine Bilanz der ÖVP/FPÖ/BZÖ-Koalition*. Wiesbaden: Verlag für Sozialwissenschaften.

OECD (1991). *Employment outlook*. Paris: OECD.

OECD (2007). *Pensions at a Glance*. Paris: OECD.

Offe, C. (1991). 'Smooth Consolidation in the West German Welfare State: Structural Change, Fiscal Policies, and Populist Politics'. In F. Fox Piven (Ed.), *Labor Parties in Postindustrial Societies*. Cambridge: Polity Press.

Orenstein, M.A. (2008). *Privatizing Pensions. The Transnational Campaign for Social Security Reforms*. Princeton: Princeton University Press.

Orenstein, M.A., Bloom, S., and Lindstrom, N. (Eds.) (2008). *Transnational Actors in Central and Eastern European Transitions*. Pittsburgh: University of Pittsburgh Press.

Orloff, A. (1993). 'Gender and the social rights of citizenship'. *American Sociological Review*, 58(3), 303-28.

Orloff, A.S. (2006). 'Farewell to Maternalism'. In J.D. Levy (Ed.), *The State After Statism*. Cambridge: Harvard University Press.

Orloff, A. (2009). 'Gendering the Comparative Analysis of Welfare States: An Unfinished Agenda'. *Sociological Theory*, 27 (3), 317-43.

Orloff, A., O'Connor, J., and Shaver, S. (1999). *States, Markets, Families: Gender, Liberalism and Social Policy in Australia, Canada, Great Britain, and the United States*. Cambridge: Cambridge University Press.

Oschmiansky, F., Mauer, A., and Schulze Buschoff, K. (2007). 'Arbeitsmarktreformen in Deutschland – Zwischen Pfadabhängigkeit und Paradigmenwechsel'. *WSI-Mitteilungen*, 60 (6), 291-97.

Ostner, I. (2006). 'Paradigmenwechsel in der (west)deutschen Familienpolitik'. In P.A. Berger and H. Kahlert (Eds.), *Der demographische Wandel. Chancen für die Neuorientierung der Geschlechterverhältnisse*. Frankfurt/New York: Campus.

Palier, B. (1999). 'Réformer la Sécurité sociale, les interventions gouvernementales en matière de Sécurité sociale depuis 1945, la France en perspective comparative'. PhD thesis. Paris: Sciences Po.

Palier, B. (2005a). *Gouverner la sécurité sociale: Les réformes du système français de protection sociale depuis 1945*. Paris: PUF (2nd edition).

Palier, B. (2005b). 'Ambiguous Agreement, Cumulative Change: French Social Policy in the 1990s'. In K. Thelen and W. Streeck (Eds.), *Beyond*

Continuity, Institutional Change in Advanced Political Economies. Oxford: Oxford University Press.

Palier, B. (2006). 'The Politics of Reforms in Bismarckian Welfare Systems'. *Revue Française des Affaires Sociales*, 1/2006, 47-72.

Palier, B. (2010). 'Continental Western Europe – the "Bismarckian" welfare systems'. In S. Leibfried et al. (Eds), *The Oxford Handbook of Comparative Welfare States*. Oxford: Oxford University Press, 601-15.

Palier, B., and Bonoli, G. (1995). 'Entre Bismarck et Beveridge: "Crises" de la Sécurité Sociale et Politique(s)'. *Revue française de science politique*, 45 (4), 668-99.

Palier, B., and Coron, G. (2002). 'Changes in the Means of Financing Social Expenditure in France since 1945'. In C. de la Porte and P. Pochet (Eds.), *Building Social Europe through the Open Method of Co-ordination*. Bruxelles: Peter Lange.

Palier, B., and Manning, N. (2003). 'Globalisation, Europeanization and the Welfare State'. *Global Social Policy*, 3 (2), special issue.

Palier, B., and Martin, C. (2007a). 'From "a Frozen Landscape" to Structural Reforms: The Sequential Transformation of Bismarckian Welfare Systems'. *Social Policy and Administration*, 41 (6), 535-54.

Palier, B., and Martin, C. (Eds.) (2007b). 'Reforming the Bismarckian Welfare Systems'. *Social Policy and Administration*, 41 (6), special issue.

Palier B. and Martin, C. (Eds.) (2008). *Reforming Bismarckian Welfare Systems*. Oxford: Blackwell.

Palier, B., and Thelen, K. (2010). 'Institutionalizing Dualism, Complementarities and Changes in France and Germany'. *Politics and Society*, 38 (1), 119–48.

Palme, J., Bergmark, Å., Bäckman, O., Estrada, F., Fritzell, J., Lundberg, O., Sjöberg, O., and Szebehely, M. (2002). 'Welfare Trends in Sweden: balancing the books for the 1990s'. *Journal of European Social Policy*, 12 (4), 329-46.

Parties and Elections in Europe (2008). *Parliamentary Electoral Results: Czech Republic, Hungary, Poland and Slovakia 1989-2008.* (http://www.parties-and-elections.de/).

Paugam, S. (1993). *La société française et ses pauvres*. Paris: PUF.

Peeters, H., and Larmuseau, H. (2005). 'De solidariteit van de gelijkgestelde periodes – een exploratie naar de aard, het belang en de zin van de gelijkgestelde periodes in de totale pensioenopbouw bij werknemers'. *Belgisch Tijdschrift voor Sociale Zekerheid*, 2005/1, 97-125.

Pfeil, W. (2000). *Österreichisches Sozialhilferecht*. Vienna: ÖGB Verlag.

Pierson, P. (1993). 'When Effects Become Cause: Policy Feedback and Political Change'. *World Politics* 45 (4), 595-628.

Pierson, P. (1994). *Dismantling the Welfare State? Reagan, Thatcher, and the Politics of Retrenchment.* Cambridge: Cambridge University Press.

Pierson, P. (1996). 'The New Politics of the Welfare State'. *World Politics*, 48 (2), 143-79.

Pierson, P. (1997). 'The Politics of Pension Reform'. In K.G. Banting and R. Boadway (Eds.), *Reform of Retirement Income Policy: international and Canadian perspectives.* Kingston: Queen's University, School of Social Policy Studies.

Pierson, P. (1998). 'Irresistible Forces, Immovable Objects: Post-industrial Welfare States confront Permanent Austerity'. *Journal of European Public Policy*, 5 (4), 539-60.

Pierson, P. (2001a). 'Coping with Permanent Austerity: Welfare State Restructuring in Affluent Democracies'. In P. Pierson (Ed.), *The New Politics of the Welfare State.* Oxford: Oxford University Press, 410-55.

Pierson, P. (Ed.) (2001b). *The New Politics of the Welfare State.* Oxford: Oxford University Press.

Pierson, P. (2004). *Politics in Time. History, Institutions, and Social Analysis.* Princeton: Princeton University Press.

Pratscher, K. (2008). 'Sozialhilfe, Behindertenhilfe und Pflegegeld der Bundesländer im Jahr 2006 und in der Entwicklung seit 1996'. In *Statistische Nachrichten 2008.* Vienna: Statistik Austria.

Radaelli, C. (2002). 'The Italian State and the Euro: institutions, discourse and policy regimes'. In K. Dyson (Ed.), *European states and the Euro.* Oxford: Oxford University Press.

Ramos-Díaz, J. (2004). 'Empleo precario en España: una asignatura pendiente'. In V. Navarro (Ed.), *El Estado del Bienestar en España.* Madrid: Tecnos.

Rechsteiner, R. (2002). *Flexibilität und soziale Sicherung in der Schweiz unter besonderer Berücksichtigung der Alterssicherung.* Basel.

Regini, M., and Regalia, I. (1997). 'Employers, Unions and the State: The Resurgence of Concertation in Italy?' *West European Politics*, 20 (1), 210-30.

Rein, M., and Wadensjö, E. (Eds.) (1997). *Enterprise and the Welfare State.* Cheltenham: Edward Elgar.

Reynaud, E. (Ed.) (2000). *Social Dialogue and Pension Reform: United Kingdom, United States, Germany, Japan, Sweden, Italy, Spain.* Geneva: International Labour Office.

Rico, A. (1997). 'Regional Decentralization and Health Care Reform in Spain (1976-1996)'. In M. Rhodes (Ed.), *Southern European Welfare States. Between Crisis and Reform*. London: Frank Cass.

Riel, B. van, Hemerijck, A., and Visser, J. (2003). 'Is There a Dutch Way to Pension Reform?' In G. Clark and N. Whiteside (Eds.), *Pensions in the 21st Century: Re-drawing the Public-Private Divide*. Oxford: Oxford University Press.

Rodríguez Cabrero, G. (1989). 'Orígenes y evolución del Estado del Bienestar español en su perspectiva histórica. Una visión general'. *Política y sociedad*, Winter, 79-87.

Rodríguez Cabrero, G. (1994). 'La política social en España: 1980-92'. *Documentación Social*, 96, 175-201.

Ross, F. (2000). 'Interests and Choice in the "Not Quite so New" Politics of Welfare'. *West European Politics*, 23 (2), 11-34.

Rothschild, K.W. (1985). 'Felix Austria? Zur Evaluierung der Ökonomie und Politik in der Wirtschaftskrise'. *Österreichische Zeitschrift für Politikwissenschaft*, 1985/3, 261-74.

Sabatier, P. (1998). 'An Advocacy Coalition Framework of Policy Change and the Role of Policy-Oriented Learning Therein'. *Policy Sciences*, 21 (2-3), 129-68.

Sachverständigenrat zur Begutachtung der gesamtwirtschaftlichen Entwicklung (2006). *Widerstreitende Interessen – Ungenutzte Chancen. Jahresgutachten 2006/07*. Wiesbaden.

Sachverständigenrat zur Begutachtung der gesamtwirtschaftlichen Entwicklung (2007). *Das Erreichte nicht verspielen. Jahresgutachten 2007/08*. Wiesbaden.

Sartori, G. (1966). 'European Political Parties; the case of polarized pluralism'. In J. LaPalombara and M. Weiner (Eds.), *Political Parties and Political Development*. Princeton: Princeton University Press.

Scarbrough, E. (2000). 'West European Welfare States: The Old Politics of Retrenchment'. *European Journal of Political Research*, 38 (2), 225-59.

Scharpf, F.W. (1987). *Sozialdemokratische Krisenpolitik in Europa*. Frankfurt am Main/New York: Campus.

Scharpf, F.W. (1997a). *Games Real Actors Play. Actor centered institutionalism in policy research*. Boulder: Westview Press.

Scharpf, F.W. (1997b). 'Employment and the Welfare State: A Continental Dilemma'. *MPIfG Working Paper* 97/7. Cologne: Max-Planck Institute for the Study of Societies.

Scharpf, F.W. (1999). *Governing in Europe: Effective and Democratic?* Oxford: Oxford University Press.

Scharpf, F.W. (2000). 'The Viability of Advanced Welfare States in the International Economy: Vulnerabilities and Options'. *Journal of European Public Policy*, 7 (2), 190-228.

Scharpf, F.W. (2002). 'Globalization and the Welfare State. Constraints, Challenge, and Vulnerabilities'. In Sigg, R. and Behrendt, C. *Social Security in the Global Village*. New Brunswick, Transaction Publisher, 85-116.

Scharpf, F.W., and Schmidt, V.A. (Eds.) (2000). *Welfare and Work in the Open Economy*. 2 Volumes. Oxford: Oxford University Press.

Schludi, M. (2005). *The Reform of Bismarckian Pension Systems. A Comparison of Pension Politics in Austria, France, Germany, Italy and Sweden*. Amsterdam: Amsterdam University Press.

Schmähl, W. (2007). 'Dismantling an Earnings-Related Social Pension Scheme: Germany's New Pension Policy'. *Journal of Social Policy*, 36 (2), 319-40.

Schmid, G. (2008). *Full Employment in Europe: Managing Labour Market Transitions and Risks*. Cheltenham: Edward Elgar.

Schmidt, V.A. (2002). *The Futures of European Capitalism*. Oxford: Oxford University Press.

Schmidt, V.A. (2006). 'Bringing the State Back into the Varieties of Capitalism and Discourse back into the Explanation of Change'. Paper prepared for presentation at the Annual Meeting of the American Political Science Association, 31 August – 3 September, Philadelphia, USA.

Schmidt, V.A. (2008). 'Discursive Institutionalism: The Explanatory Power of Ideas and Discourse'. *Annual Review of Political Science*, 11, 303-26.

Schulze, I., and Jochem, S. (2007). 'Germany – Beyond Policy Gridlock'. In In E. Immergut, K. Anderson and I. Schulze (Eds.), *Handbook of West European Pension Politics*. Oxford: Oxford University Press.

Sciarini, P. (1999). 'La formulation de la decision'. In U. Klöti et al. (Eds.), *Handbuch der Schweizer Politik*. Zürich: NZZ Verlag.

Sirovátka, T., and Saxonberg, S. (2008). 'Neo-liberalism by Decay? The Evolution of the Czech Welfare State'. Paper presented at the Annual ESPAnet Conference, 18-20 September 2005, Helsinki, Finland.

Sozialbeirat (1998). 'Gutachten des Sozialbeirats zum Rentenversicherungsbericht 1998'. In Bundesregierung, *Rentenversicherungsbericht 1998*. Deutscher Bundestag, Drucksache 13/11290 (17 July 1998), Bonn.

Spies, H., and Berkel, R. van (2000). 'Workfare in the Netherlands – Young Unemployed People and the Jobseeker's Employment Act'. In I.

Lødemel and H. Trickey (Eds.), *'An Offer You Can't Refuse': Workfare in International Perspective*. Bristol: Policy Press.

Standing, G. (1996). 'Social Protection and Eastern Europe: a Tale of Slipping Anchors and Torn Safety Nets'. In G. Esping-Andersen (Ed.), *Welfare States in Transition: National Adaptations in Global Economics*. London: Sage.

Stark, D. (1996). 'Recombinant Property in East European Capitalism'. *American Journal of Sociology*, 101 (4), 993-1027.

Starke, P. (2007). *Radical Welfare State Retrenchment: A Comparative Perspective*. Basingstoke: Palgrave Macmillan.

Stiefel, D. (2006). 'Die österreichische Wirtschaft seit 1950'. In H. Dachs et.al. (Eds.), *Politik in Österreich. Das Handbuch*. Vienna: Manz Verlag.

Streeck, W. (1999). *Korporatismus in Deutschland. Zwischen Nationalstaat und Europäischer Union*. Frankfurt: Campus.

Streeck, W., and Thelen, K. (2005a). 'Introduction: Instiutional Change in Advanced Political Economies'. In W. Streeck and K. Thelen (Eds.), *Beyond Continuity. Institutional Change in Advanced Political Economies*. Oxford: Oxford University Press.

Streeck, W., and Thelen, K. (Eds.) (2005b). *Beyond Continuity. Institutional Change in Advanced Political Economies*. Oxford: Oxford University Press.

Stummvoll, G. (1977). 'Der Sozialstaat am Scheideweg'. *Die Industrie*, 1977/24.

SVR [Sachverständigenrat zur Begutachtung der gesamtwirtschaftlichen Entwicklung] (2005). *Die Chance nutzen – Reformen mutig voranbringen. Jahresgutachten 2005*, Wiesbaden.

Swank, D. (2002). *Global Capital, Political Institutions and Policy Change in Developed Welfare States*. Cambridge: Cambridge University Press.

Swenson, P. (2002). *Capitalists Against Markets: The Making of Labor Markets and Welfare States in the United States and Sweden*. New York: Oxford University Press.

Sykes, R., Palier, B., and Prior, P. (2001). *Globalization and European Welfare states: challenges and changes*. London: Palgrave.

Szalai, E. (2005). *Socialism. An Analysis of its Past and Future*. Budapest/New York: CEU Press.

Szalai, J. (2005). 'Poverty and the Traps of Post-communist Welfare Reforms in Hungary: A Fourth World of Welfare Capitalism on the Rise'. Paper presented at the Annual Conference of RC19, ISA *Retheorizing Welfare States: Restructuring States, Restructuring Analysis*, 8-10 September 2005, Northwestern University, Chicago, USA.

Szikra, D. (2004). 'The Thorny Path to Implementation: Bismarckian Social Insurance in Hungary in the Late 19th Century'. *European Journal of Social Security*, 6 (3), 255-72.

Tálos, E. (1982). *Staatliche Sozialpolitik in Österreich: Rekonstruktion und Analyse*. Vienna: Verlag für Gesellschaftskritik.

Tálos, E. (1986). 'Sozialpolitik in Österreich seit 1970'. In E. Fröschl and H. Zoitl (Eds.), *Der österreichische Weg 1970-1985*. Vienna: Europa Verlag.

Tálos, E. (1987). 'Arbeitslosigkeit und beschäftigungspolitische Steuerung'. In E. Tálos (Ed.), *Arbeitslosigkeit*. Vienna: Verlag für Gesellschaftskritik.

Tálos, E. (2004). 'Umbau des Sozialstaates? Österreich und Deutschland im Vergleich'. *Politische Vierteljahresschrift*, 45 (2), 213-36.

Tálos, E. (2005a). *Vom Siegeszug zum Rückzug. Sozialstaat Österreich 1945-2005*. Innsbruck: Studienverlag.

Tálos, E. (2005b). 'Vom Vorzeige- zum Auslaufmodell? Österreichs Sozialpartnerschaft 1945 bis 2005'. In F. Karlhofer and E. Tálos (Eds.), *Sozialpartnerschaft. Österreichische und Europäische Perspektiven*. Vienna: LIT-Verlag.

Tálos, E. (2008). *Sozialpartnerschaft. Ein zentraler politischer Gestaltungsfaktor in der Zweiten Republik*. Innsbruck: Studienverlag.

Tálos, E., and Wörister, K. (1998). 'Soziale Sicherung in Österreich'. In E. Tálos (Ed.), *Soziale Sicherung im Wandel*. Vienna/Cologne/Weimar: Böhlau.

Taylor-Gooby, P. (Ed.) (2001). *Welfare States Under Pressure*. London: Sage.

Titmuss, R. (1974). *Social Policy: an introduction*. London: Allen and Unwin.

Toharia, L. (1997). 'El sistema español de protección por desempleo'. *Papeles de Economía Española*, 72, 192-213.

Tomeš, I. (2003). 'Pensions'. In GVG e.V. (Ed.), *Study on the Social Protection Systems in the 13 Applicant Countries: Czech Republic*. Brussels: European Commission – DG Employment and Social Affairs.

Tomka, B. (2004a). 'Wohlfahrtsstaatliche Entwicklung in Ostmitteleuropa und das europäische Sozialmodell, 1945-1990'. In H. Kaelble and G. Schmid (Eds.), *WZB Jahrbuch 2004. Das europäische Sozialmodell. Auf dem Weg zum transnationalen Staat*. Berlin: Edition Sigma.

Tomka, B. (2004b). *Welfare in East and West. Hungarian Social Security in an International Comparison 1918-1990*. Berlin: Akademie Verlag.

Trampusch, C. (2003). 'Ein Bündnis für die nachhaltige Finanzierung der Sozialversicherungssysteme: Interessenvermittlung in der bundes-deutschen Arbeitsmarkt- und Rentenpolitik'. *MPIfG Discussion Paper* 03/1. Cologne: Max-Planck Institute for the Study of Societies.

Trampusch, C. (2005). 'From Interest Groups to Parties: The Change in the Career Patterns of the Legislative Elite in German Social Policy'. *German Politics*, 14 (1), 14-32.

Trampusch, C. (2006). 'Sequenzorientierte Policy-Analyse: Warum die Rentenreform von Walter Riester nicht an Reformblockaden scheiterte'. *Berliner Journal für Soziologie*, 16 (1), 55-76.

Tsebelis, G. (2000). 'Veto Players and Institutional Analysis'. *Governance*, 13 (4), 441-74.

Unger, B. (2001). 'Österreichische Beschäftigungs- und Sozialpolitik von 1970 bis 2000'. *Zeitschrift für Sozialreform*, 47, 340-61.

Unger, B., and Heitzmann, K. (2003). 'The Adjustment Path of the Austrian Welfare State: Back to Bismarck?' *Journal of European Social Policy*, 13 (4), 371-87.

Vail, M.I. (1999). 'The Better Part of Valour: The Politics of French Welfare Reform'. *Journal of European Social Policy*, 9 (4), 311-29.

Valat, B. (2001). *Histoire de la Sécurité sociale (1945-1967)*. Paris: Economica.

Valiente, C. (1995). 'Rejecting the Past: Central government and family policies in post-authoritarian Spain'. In J. Brannen and M. O'Brien (Eds.), *Childhood and Parenthood*. University of London: Institute of Education.

Vandenbroucke, F. (2001). 'The Active Welfare State: a social-democratic ambition for Europe'. *Policy Network Journal*, 2001/1.

Vanhuysse, P. (2006). *Divide and Pacify. Strategic Social Policies and Political Protests in Post-Communist Democracies*. Budapest: CEU Press.

Veen, R. van der, and Trommel, W. (1999). 'Managed Liberalization of the Dutch Welfare State'. *Governance*, 12 (3), 289-310.

Velarde Fuertes, J. (1990). *El tercer viraje de la Seguridad Social*. Madrid: Instituto de Estudios Económicos.

Visser, J. (2001). 'Industrial Relations and Social Dialogue'. In P. Auer (Ed.). *Changing Labour Markets in Europe. The Role of Institutions and Politics*. Geneva: International Labour Organisation.

Visser, J., and Hemerijck, A. (1997). *'A Dutch Miracle': Job Growth, Welfare Reform, and Corporatism in the Netherlands*. Amsterdam: Amsterdam University Press.

Vodička, K. (2005). *Das politische System Tschechiens*. Wiesbaden: VS Verlag für Sozialwissenschaften.

Wagener, H-J. (2002). 'The Welfare State in Transition Economies and Accession to the EU'. *West European Politics*, 25 (2), 152-74.

Wanner, P., and Ferrari, A. (2001). *La participation des femmes au marché du travail. Rapport intermédiaire effectué dans le cadre du mandat accordé par l'Office fédéral des assurances sociales.* Neuchâtel: Forum suisse pour l'étude des migrations.

Way, C. (2000). 'Central Banks, Partisan Politics, and Macroeconomic Outcomes'. *Comparative Political Studies*, 33 (2), 196-224.

Weaver, R.K. (1986). 'The Politics of Blame Avoidance'. *Journal of Public Policy*, 6 (4), 371-98.

Weaver, R.K. (1988). *Automatic Government. The Politics of Indexation.* Washington D.C.: The Brookings Institution.

Weaver, R.K., and Pierson, P. (1993). 'Imposing Losses in Pension Policy'. In B. Rockman and K. Weaver (Eds.), *Do Institutions Matter? Government capabilities in the United States and abroad.* Washington DC: Brookings Institution.

Widmaier, U., and Blancke, S. (1997). 'Germany'. In H. Compston (Ed.), *The New Politics of Unemployment: Radical Policy Initiatives in Western Europe.* London: Routledge.

Wilensky, H.L. (1975). *The Welfare State and Equality. Structural and Ideological Roots of Public Expenditures.* Berkeley: University of California Press.

Wilensky, H. (2002). *Rich Democracies: Political Economy, Public Policy, and Performance.* Berkeley/Los Angeles, California: University of California Press.

Williamson, J. (1990). 'What Washington Means by Policy Reform'. In J. Williamson (Ed.), *Latin American Adjustment: How Much Has Happened?* Washington: Institute for International Economics.

Wilthagen, T. (1998). 'Flexicurity: A New Paradigm for Labor Market Policy Reform?' *WZB Discussion Papers*, FS I, 98-202.

Winckler, G. (1988). 'Der Austrokeynesianismus und sein Ende'. *Österreichische Zeitschrift für Politikwissenschaft*, 1988/3, 221-230.

World Bank (1994). *Averting the Old Age Crisis: Policies to Protect the Old and Promote Growth.* Washington/ New York: The World Bank and Oxford University Press.

World Bank OED (2004). *Economies in Transition. An OED Evaluation of World Bank Assistance.* Washington D.C.: World Bank.

WRR – Wetenschappelijke Raad voor het Regeringsbeleid (1990), *Een Werkend Perspectief. Arbeidsparticipatie in de Jaren '90.* Reports to the Government 38, The Hague, SDU.

Zeitlin, J. (2005). 'The Open Method of Coordination in Action: Theoretical Promise, Empirical Realities, Reform Strategy'. In J. Zeitlin and P. Pochet (Eds.), *The Open Method of Co-ordination in Action. The European Employment and Social Inclusion Strategies.* Brussels: SALTSA, P.I.E.-Peter Lang.

Zeitlin, J., and Pochet, P. (Eds.) (2005). *The Open Method of Co-ordination in Action. The European Employment and Social Inclusion Strategies.* Brussels: SALTSA, P.I.E.-Peter Lang.

About the Contributors

Tiziana Alti has worked for various governmental bodies in Italy. She is an expert in the fields of social assistance policies and non profit organisations.

Alfio Cerami is Research Associate at the Centre d'Études Européennes at Sciences Po, Paris. His research concentrates on social protection reforms and the process of democratization. In 2009, he co-edited with P. Vanhuysse *Post-Communist Welfare Pathways. Theorizing Social Policy Transformations in Central and Eastern Europe* (Palgrave Macmillan).

Bernhard Ebbinghaus is Professor of Sociology and Director of Mannheim Centre for European Social Research (MZES) at the University of Mannheim. His Research interests include European labour relations and organized interests, European social policy and welfare-state regimes. In 2006, he published *Early Retirement in Europe, Japan, and the USA* (Oxford University Press).

Werner Eichhorst is Deputy Director of Labor Policy at the Institute for the Study of Labor (IZA) in Bonn, Germany. His main research area is the comparative analysis of labor market institutions and performance as well as the political economy of labor market reform strategies.

Gøsta Esping-Andersen is Professor of Sociology at the Universitat Pompeu Fabra. His work centres on life course dynamics, social stratification and comparative social policy. In 2009, he published *The Incomplete Revolution: Adapting to Women's new Roles.* (Polity)

Ana M. Guillén is Professor of Sociology at the University of Oviedo, Spain. She has written extensively on comparative social policy. In 2009, she co-edited with S.-A. Dahl *Quality of Work in the EU. Concept, data and Debates from a Transnational Perspective* (Peter Lang).

Silja Häusermann is Assistant Professor (Oberassistentin) at the University of Zurich, Switzerland. Her interests are in comparative political economy and comparative politics. Her current research focuses on welfare state reforms and party system change. In 2010, she published *The Politics of Welfare Reform in Continental Europe. Modernization in Hard Times* (Cambridge University Press).

Anton Hemerijck is Dean of the Faculty of Social Sciences of the Free University of Amsterdam.
He was the director of the Netherlands' Scientific Council for the Government Policy from 2001 to 2009. In 2010, Oxford University Press will publish his latest monograph, *In Search of a New Welfare State*.

Karl Hinrichs is Senior Researcher at the Centre for Social Policy Research at the University of Bremen and professor of political science at Humboldt university in Berlin. His main research focus is on comparative welfare state analysis, the development of social policy in Germany, and the study of old-age security policies and politics in ageing societies.

Matteo Jessoula is Assistant Professor at the Faculty of Political Sciences, University of Milan. His main research field is the comparative analysis of welfare states, policy developments and political dynamics in pensions, employment and social assistance sectors. In 2009, he published a volume on pension policy (La politica pensionistica, in Italian, Il mulino).

Philip Manow is Professor for Political Science at Heidelberg University. His research interests include comparative political economy, comparative welfare state research, German political system, European integration. In 2009, together with Kees Van Kersbergen he co-edited the volume *Religion, Class Coalitions and the Welfare State* (Cambridge University Press).

Ive Marx is a Senior Researcher at the Centre for Social Policy, University of Antwerp. His work is on poverty and minimum protection, especially in relation to labour market change and migration.

Herbert Obinger is a Professor of Comparative Public and Social Policy at the Center for Social Policy Research of the University of Bremen. He is co-editor of the Oxford Handbook of the Welfare State (Oxford University Press 2010).

Bruno Palier is CNRS Researcher at Sciences Po, Centre d'Etudes Euro-péennes, Paris. He has published numerous articles on welfare reforms in France and in Europe, and various books, including *Reforming Bismarck-ian welfare systems* (ed. with Claude Martin) in 2008 with Blackwell.

Emmerich Tálos is Professor Emeritus of Political Science at the University of Vienna. He has published numerous books and articles on the welfare state, Austrian corporatism and the Austrian political system in the 20th century.

Index

23-24, 39-41, 49, 66, 74, 93-94, 96, 102, 119, 124, 126, 130, 132, 146, 159, 161, 172, 178, 180, 188, 190-193, 199-200, 204-206, 211, 213, 220, 225-228, 231, 234, 237, 243-246, 251, 301, 316-319, 322-323, 341, 346, 375, 377-379, 394, 396

Vandenbroucke, F. 144
varieties of capitalism 43
Veil, S. 269
veto players 27, 33, 178, 180, 260-261, 378
Visegrad countries (CEE, Central and Eastern European) 40, 233-235, 244-245, 301, 310, 322, 342, 351-352, 358, 361, 373
Visser, J. 30, 350, 390
Vranitzky, F. 108

welfare institutions 21, 23-27, 38, 43, 165, 233-234, 237-238, 246, 250, 259, 349, 351, 367, 370, 373

welfare regime 19, 22-23, 26, 28-29, 38, 74, 82, 101, 145, 188, 214, 234, 251, 258, 282, 301-303, 305, 334, 370
women (female) 12, 14-16, 20, 23, 39, 41 42, 44, 48, 63 64, 110, 116-117, 120, 124, 126-127, 135-136, 147 148, 150, 152, 159, 170, 175, 187-188, 198-199, 205-206, 209, 214-215, 218, 220, 222-223, 225-226, 228-230, 256, 267, 302, 306, 308-309, 311-312, 325, 328, 336, 340, 354, 356, 358-364, 376, 380, 382-383, 385-386, 398
work accident 36, 39-40, 377
World Bank 248-249, 251-252, 355

young (youth) 12, 14, 16, 42, 63, 83-85, 117, 159, 195, 206, 228, 256, 275, 315, 328-329, 338, 340, 382-383, 399

Zapatero, J. 362, 364

CHANGING WELFARE STATES

PREVIOUSLY PUBLISHED

Jelle Visser and Anton Hemerijck, *A Dutch Miracle. Job Growth, Welfare Reform and Corporatism in the Netherlands*, 1997
ISBN 978 90 5356 271 0

Christoffer Green-Pedersen, *The Politics of Justification. Party Competition and Welfare-State Retrenchment in Denmark and the Netherlands from 1982 to 1998*, 2002
ISBN 978 90 5356 590 2

Jan Høgelund, *In Search of Effective Disability Policy. Comparing the Developments and Outcomes of the Dutch and Danish Disability Policies*, 2003
ISBN 978 90 5356 644 2

Maurizio Ferrera and Elisabetta Gualmini, *Rescued by Europe? Social and Labour Market Reforms from Maastricht to Berlusconi*, 2004
ISBN 978 90 5356 651 0

Martin Schludi, *The Reform of Bismarckian Pension Systems. A Comparison of Pension Politics in Austria, France, Germany, Italy and Sweden*, 2005
ISBN 978 90 5356 740 1

Uwe Becker and Herman Schwartz (eds.), *Employment 'Miracles'. A Critical Comparison of the Dutch, Scandinavian, Swiss, Australian and Irish Cases Versus Germany and the US*, 2005
ISBN 978 90 5356 755 5

Sanneke Kuipers, *The Crisis Imperative. Crisis Rhetoric and Welfare State Reform in Belgium and the Netherlands in the Early 1990s*, 2006
ISBN 978 90 5356 808 8

Anke Hassel, *Wage Setting, Social Pacts and the Euro. A New Role for the State*, 2006
ISBN 978 90 5356 919 1

Ive Marx, *A New Social Question? On Minimum Income Protection in the Postindustrial Era*, 2007
ISBN 978 90 5356 925 2

Monique Kremer, *How Welfare States Care. Culture, Gender and Parenting in Europe*, 2007
ISBN 978 90 5356 975 7

Sabina Stiller, *Ideational Leadership in German Welfare State Reform. How Politicians and Policy Ideas Transform Resilient Institutions*, 2010
ISBN 978 90 8964 186 1

Barbara Vis, *Politics of Risk-taking. Welfare State Reform in Advanced Democracies*, 2010
ISBN 978 90 8964 227 1